THIS ... OR SOMETHING BETTER

...

Finding My Way Home

By Linda Jones Hope Jenkins

LUCKY DOG PRESS

THIS ... OR SOMETHING BETTER

Copyright © 2023 by Linda Jones Hope Jenkins

ISBN: 978-1-0082-1039-0
Printed in the United States of America

Published in the United States of America by
Lucky Dog Press in Hull, Georgia.
www.LuckyDogPress.com

LUCKY DOG PRESS

COVER PHOTO: JILL FINEBERG | COVER AND INTERIOR DESIGN: TRACY N. COLEY
EDITING: TRACY N. COLEY | PROOFREADING: LEE SHORT

For my children Tony, Ellen, and Clif,
my grandchildren Eric and Caroline,
my great-grandchildren Eli and Andrew,
and to all those who follow.

DEDICATION

I dedicate this autobiography to my brother, Robert (Bobby) Franklin Jones, who has always been my mentor, my champion, and my greatest inspiration. This is what he said about memoir that motivated me to capture the stories of my life.

. . .

The great thing about writing memoirs is that it allows you to live life twice . . . in the actual moment . . . and later, when you recall it and write about it. Now, so many phantoms on parade in the darkening sky . . . I am grateful for the gift of memory, yet how sad, too, that, the repository of memory does not survive the body – the loss of one means the loss of the other . . . except there is the pen. The pen in mightier than the vulnerable memory. A wasting memory is not only a destroyer – it can deny one's very existence.

A day unremembered is like a soul unborn, worse than if it had never been. What indeed was that summer hoeing weeds in the corn field of Little Mill Road if it is not recalled? . . . That journey to the Penny Arcade in Ocean City? . . . That act of love when Aunt Bessie had cookies waiting for two mule-bartered boys? . . . To whom did it happen if it has left you with nothing? So, any bits of warm life preserved by the pen are trophies snatched from the dark . . . are branches of leaves fished out of the flood . . . are tiny arrests of mortality saved from the great Tide of Life.

I no longer speculate about longevity, siding with a great thinker (Montaigne) that "it is not in the number of your years that you will have lived enough." It is rather what makes up the content of the years you live through. I have had an unimaginably good life and reach this milestone with no major regrets. My dearest hope is that well before I get dragged away to a nursing home, I may be allowed to board the "boat" that drifts down the silent river to that mysterious land from which, so far, none have ever returned. Until then, may I keep on scribbling . . . or snatching trophies from the dark.

CONTENTS

LINDA JONES FAMILY TREE

Jones Side

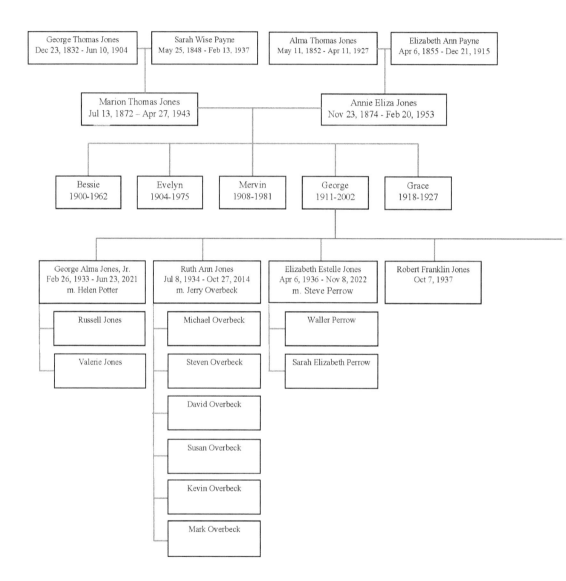

McGee Side

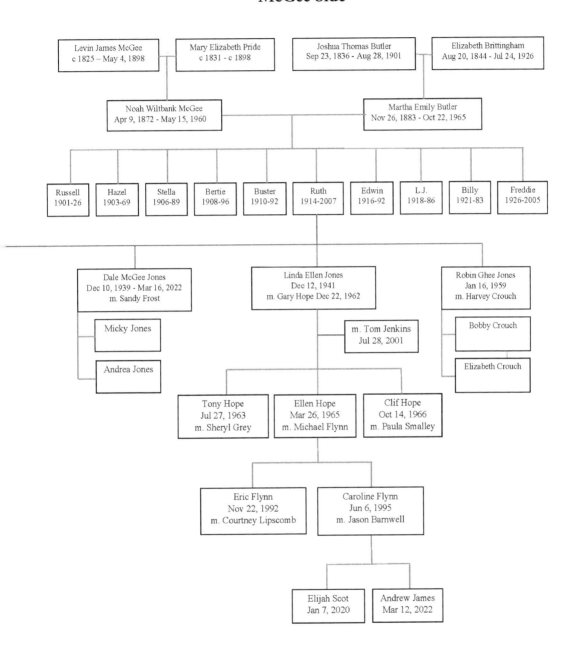

PREFACE

THIS ... OR SOMETHING BETTER

A year or two after I retired in 2014, I decided to tackle those boxes of family photographs I had gathered and stored in a closet. My husband scanned my photo albums while I sorted through the thousand slides taken when my children were young. On visits to see my brother Bobby and my mother, we scanned their photo albums too. I spent the next couple of years editing and labeling this treasured collection, then organized them chronologically in files on my computer. If there is an easier way to create an electronic album, don't tell me now. It was a labor of love. Whenever my siblings and I got together, we lived our lives again as we sat together in the living room and watched our lives unfold on the television screen. We could go back to any point in our history and see the proof of our lives. Each picture would call forth a memory, and as we told each other our stories, I thought they would make a good book.

In the summer of 2019, I told my dear friend Kia Woods about the pleasure my family derived from my slide shows, and we both expressed – not for the first time – our desire to leave a written legacy, a memoir, for our children and grandchildren. I told her that I had recently read that if you have six or seven stories to tell, you can weave them together, and those narratives can become your book. Confident that we could harvest at least that many stories, we made a promise to support each other in writing a memoir.

Having settled on my goal and with a clear vision, the memoir took on a life of its own. Within a week or two of declaring my intention, I learned that a memoir writing group was meeting once a month less than five miles from my home. I immediately joined. Members came together each month to read memories they wrote from their lives. Inspired by my fellow memoirists, I created a new story each month and began keeping a list of the events in my life I wanted to share. Apart from my writing group, Kia and I became writing partners, and each week we read our stories to each other, offering encouragement and praise.

By March of 2020, with the COVID-19 pandemic in full swing, my memoir writing group began meeting on Zoom. Forced to stay home, I asked two other friends, Beverly Joyce and Jonyl Adams, to also be my writing partners. While they wrote poetry, I scribed events from my life. Overflowing with inspiration and creativity, we met every day for a month ... until we came to our senses and reduced it to five days, and then to one day a week. My list exploded beyond six or seven stories; 43 chapters of my book blossomed before me. As soon as I began thinking about how to publish it, Tracy Coley joined my memoir writing group. When I learned she was an editor, I asked her to help me take my memoir over the finish line.

Thanks to a promise to a friend and to myself to leave a written legacy for my family, and thanks to the pandemic that gave me the isolation and time to devote to such an endeavor, here I am, at the end of three years, having written the story of my life. I could not have written this memoir without the help and support of my husband Tom, my brother Bobby, the members of my memoir writing group, and writing partners Kia, Beverly, and Jonyl. Their love and support are written on every page. I have included one of Jonyl's poems on the opposite page; one of Beverly's is at the end of the book.

SEEDS

I found a small tin box of seeds
While clearing out my head
I put them there for future needs
They all looked dry and dead

Saved from gardens of my youth
Their names could not be found
The only way to find the truth
Was to plant them in the ground

I covered them in fertile soil
And watered every day
And tended them with daily toil
It is the gardener's way

I remember mother saying
You reap what you sow
And no amount of praying
Will make an unplanted garden grow

Nurtured memories come alive
And grow like summer corn
Watered seed will grow and thrive
No matter what you've borne

The seed of love lives in me
It's up to me to tend it
No matter what the rift may be
Only I can mend it

A garden grows, then seems to die
When winter's chill arrives
Forgotten seeds in limbo lie
Til the warmth of spring arrives

Memories and seeds when stored are dry
With no hint of what's in store
When watered by a teary eye
They spring to life once more

© Jonyl Adams, June 11, 2021

PART ONE

MY FAMILY AND CHILDHOOD
(1931-62)

Jones children: (back) Bobby, Betty, Ruth Ann, (front) Dale, Sonny, Linda, 1942.

HOMES FOR
LINDA JONES AND FAMILY
(1933-63)

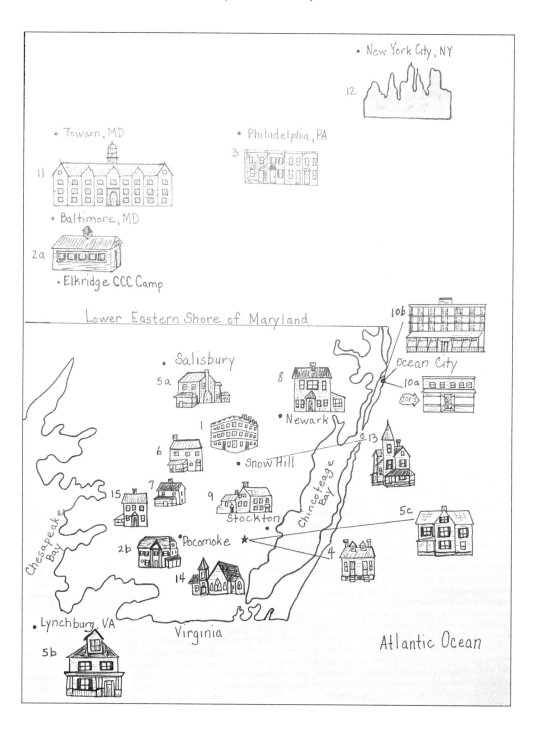

LEGEND

1. Purnell Hotel, Snow Hill and unidentified apartment on Collins Street
   George and Ruth's first and second homes (1932-33).
2. George and Ruth lived separately due to Depression (1933-34).
   a. CCC Camp, Elkridge, Md.
   George managed kitchen at Patapsco State Park camp #3.
   b. Covington House, Brantley Road, Pocomoke, Md.
   Ruth, Sonny, and Ruth Ann alternated staying with parents and Jones
   in-laws on Little Mill Road* (see 5c).
3. Row house, Philadelphia, Pa.
   George, Ruth, Sonny, Ruth Ann, Betty (1935-37).
4. Old House, Little Mill Road*, Stockton, Md.
   George, Ruth, Sonny, Ruth Ann, Betty, Bobby, Dale (1937-41).
5. Family fragmented with move to Salisbury.
   a. Ranier Farm, Mount Hermon Road, Salisbury, Md.
   George, Ruth, Sonny, Ruth Ann, Dale, Linda (1941-42).
   b. Lynchburg, Va.
   Betty goes to stay with Aunt Stella and Uncle Hubert.
   c. Big House, Little Mill Road, Stockton, Md.
   Bobby stays with Jones Grandparents.
6. Log Cabin on Corkers Creek, Pocomoke Road, 4 miles west of Snow Hill
   (1942-46).
7. Chicken Coop, Dividing Creek Road, Pocomoke, Md. (for 6 months in 1946).
8. Tyndall Farm, Newark, Md. (1947).
9. Rowley Farm, Stockton, Md. (1948-59). Parents stayed until 1961.
10. Summers in Ocean City
    a. Lived on Talbot Street; worked at Joe's Restaurant on the boardwalk at the
    pier (1957 and 1958).
    b. Lived and worked at Beach Plaza Hotel, 13th Street & Boardwalk
    (1959 and 1960).
11. Towson State Teachers College, York Avenue, Towson, Md. (1959-1960).
12. 452 Fort Washington Ave, NY, NY – lived with Betty and Robin (1960-61).
13. 211 W. Federal Street, Snow Hill, Md. – lived with George, Ruth, Bobby,
    Robin (1961-63).
14. Remson Church, 4249 Sheephouse Road, Pocomoke, Md. – family church.
15. McGee Grandparents, Dividing Creek Road, Pocomoke, Md.

1 | The First Ten Years (1931-41)

In the Beginning (1931)

My father George Jones grew up on the Jones Homestead, a 100-acre farm on Little Mill Road, 2 miles from the little town of Stockton, on the lower Eastern Shore of Maryland. His first job away from the farm was as a clerk in Tom Wharton's grocery store in town while still in high school. In the summers, he got a job working in the Tom Purnell restaurant in Public Landing, a nearby bay-side resort. When he finished high school in 1931, he was promoted to run the restaurant in the Purnell Hotel in Snow Hill, 12 miles from the farm.

In the spring of 1932, at the height of the Great Depression, Dad was at work in the hotel restaurant when he first spotted my mother, Ruth McGee, an 18-year-old girl, sitting atop the

George Jones and Ruth McGee, Public Landing, Snow Hill, Md., 1932.

cab of a truck on a hayride with several other teenagers. They had stopped for refreshments, and after one look, he told everyone who would listen, "I got one glimpse of this black-haired beauty, sit.ting up there, swinging her beautiful legs back and forth, and I turned to my friend, telling him, 'I'm going to marry that girl.'"

While he prepared Cokes for her and her friends, he told the server to tell my mother that he had already paid for hers. He soon went out to talk to her and asked her for a date, which she accepted. However, when he showed up at her house a few days later to take her to the movies, he was disappointed to find that she was out with friends. Not one to waste an opportunity, young George spent the evening making friends with her mother, which helped his suit. My grandmother later chastised my mother for not keeping her word with the nice young man. Dad subsequently pursued the woman of his dreams, supported by his future mother-in-law, and his black-haired beauty finally succumbed to his charms. My parents married before the end of the summer – in August.

Dad continued working as a cook while managing the restaurant at the hotel in Snow Hill after my parent's marriage in 1932. The owner, Mr. Purnell provided the young couple a room in the hotel for several months until they moved to an apartment on nearby Collins Street. My dad prepared all their meals during that time, and when they had their own home, he taught his new bride how to cook. It always surprised me that she didn't know how to cook, having grown up in a family with 10 children. Perhaps her job had been taking care of the younger ones, and her older sisters took care of the kitchen duties. My mother told me that Dad's mother told her, shortly after they were married, that she shouldn't worry about cooking for him. "No matter what you fix, George will want something that isn't on the table."

I remember that both my parents were excellent cooks, but Dad was always stingy with his compliments. When they were visiting my house in later years, I said to him one evening after dinner, "Dad, I spend a lot of time preparing our meals, and I'm not sure you like what I'm fixing. I would like for you to let me know when you like something I have served." His answer? "I'd tell you if I didn't like it." I inferred that silence would be my only compliment.

Shortly after they moved out of the hotel, their first child, George Jr., was born on February 26, 1933, at the Salisbury hospital, 20 miles away. Sonny, as he was nicknamed, turned out to be Mother's largest baby, weighing 10 pounds and two ounces. After 40 hours of labor, an emergency cesarean was performed. Her sister Bertie, 24, who was a nurse in Philadelphia and not yet married, took the train home to be with the new mother, just barely 19. Mother had to spend six weeks in the hospital, and, according to accepted medical practice at the time, was ordered to complete bed rest. That advice was so detrimental that she suffered inflammation and thrombosis of the femoral vein and would be plagued with varicose veins and thrombosis for the rest of her life.

As the Depression wore on, the hotel's business was negatively impacted, causing a reduction in staff and cuts in wages. When Dad was given notice that his wages would be cut in half, he was motivated to leave the hotel and take a job with the Civilian Conservation Corps. His new position with the CCC, running the kitchen and dining hall at their camp in Elkridge, Maryland, paid a higher salary, but it required him to be in the Baltimore area, hours away, on the other side of the Chesapeake Bay. So, Mother took her baby boy home to live with her parents, where daughter Ruth Ann followed in July 1934, also born in the Salisbury hospital but with no complications this time. My mother and her two children alternated staying with the two sets of grandparents during the time Dad worked 5-6 hours away, coming home whenever he could.

THE MOVE TO PHILADELPHIA (1935)

My parents had married in 1932 when the Depression was getting tiresome. Three years into their marriage, with two babies, long separations, and no home to call their own, they grew weary of trying to piece together life as a married couple with children. Hartley Jones, Dad's uncle who lived in Philadelphia, told my father about the General Baking Company, a bread company hiring country-fresh farm boys to drive their horse-drawn, home-delivery wagons on their bread routes. Their rationale was that farm boys would know the ways of horses and wagons better than city boys. Dad accepted the job selling Bond Bread in 1935 and soon moved his young family to Philadelphia.

Mom and Dad rented a row house in an Italian neighborhood where they forged a lifelong friendship with the Berger family who lived next door. Teenager Emma Berger, not much younger than my mother, had just finished high school and enjoyed nothing more than dressing up the two little Jones children and parading them around the neighborhood. Her babysitting services were as free as the air and were put to more use a year later, on April 6, 1936, when my sister Betty was born. A trip to Stockton was soon made to show off the new baby.

Dad related that one snowy day, he showed up at work well before dawn, with Philly under a good foot of snow that concealed all the customers' house numbers. How would he know where to deliver his bread? He soon discovered the horses knew every stop. Just as he knew the ways of horses and wagons, the horses knew the ways of snow and the city. Running a bread route with a team of horses was hard work with long hours, and it was very difficult in the Depression to get customers to keep their accounts paid up. By 1937, Dad was likely buying bread for a fourth of his customers – and there were three children at home to feed.

Grandmom Jones holding Betty, Sonny, Grandpop Jones holding Ruth Ann, 1936.

BACK ON THE FARM (1937)

"George, if you can find no better work in Philadelphia, come home. We can fix up the old tenant house, and you can help me on the farm." Marion, Dad's father, must have used words very similar to these in the spring of 1937. Mom and Dad gratefully accepted Grandpop's offer to return to the farm in Stockton, Maryland,

Mr. Berger (left) and George in front of the Old House after the family's move from Philadelphia, 1937.

with their family. At least there would be a vegetable garden, as well as eggs, butter, and milk, and, according to the season, fried chicken or cured pork, with a turkey on the table for Christmas and Thanksgiving.

Back on Little Mill Road, Grandpop fixed up the old 1820's homestead where my father had been born in 1911. When my grandparents built a new farmhouse in 1913, one large section of the original house, consisting of two rooms downstairs and two rooms with dormers upstairs, had been moved across the county road to be used as a tenant house. To accommodate Dad's growing family, Grandpop added a kitchen with an interior hand-pump for water in the back of the house. No vacuum cleaner and no washing machine – only a broom made of straw to sweep the floors and a metal tub and a washboard to wash the clothes. Cooking and heating were done with wood; lighting provided by kerosene lamps. Electricity wasn't available on Little Mill Road until 1947, and telephone service did not arrive until 1952.

This century-old house would be their ever-so-humble home for four years in the pre-war years. My parents were living in the old Jones homestead – literally "homesteading" it! They had given up the city life and all the comforts they had grown used to in Philadelphia and moved back to the country with their three children – and, yes, another on the way. In the summer of 1937, Sonny was four, Ruth Ann was three, and Betty was just a year old. Four months after their move on October 7, a second son, my brother Bobby, was born in the Salisbury hospital.

While the Great Depression touched all lives in the 1930s, lucky were the unemployed ones who had parents with a family farm with chickens, pigs, and cows. With no money coming in, at least there was food for hungry mouths. Lucky too were those with parents who had a little tenant house for a family of six. It was a hard-scrabble life

Back: Ruth Ann, mother Ruth, father George; front: Betty, Bobby, Sonny, 1937.

for Mother, doing all her clothes-washing (and wringing out) by hand, cooking on a woodstove, and keeping children warm, fed, clothed, and diapered with noses wiped and hair, ears, and fingernails clean. Our cousin, Frances Taylor Hickman, who was 13 in 1937, insists that she saw a very happy life in our family with lots of love and laughter. She was a frequent visitor, often coming to help her favorite aunt with her four children and the myriad of chores. Though ten years separated aunt and niece, they forged a close friendship that lasted throughout their lives. Frances recalls Dad, in the kitchen, filling a glass gallon jar with milk, ice cream, and chocolate syrup, then shaking it vigorously, to the children's delight. He poured out foaming, delicious "chocolate milkshakes" in seven glasses, many filled twice.

One of brother Bobby's earliest memories, was the path the children wore down, across the field, going back and forth between the "Old House" and the "Big House," where my grandparents lived with Bessie, their eldest daughter, who never married or left home. Their son, Mervin, a confirmed bachelor had also returned home – another victim of the Depression. Bobby's observation: "Soon, we children felt as if we belonged in the big house just as we did in the 'Old House,' the name we ever after called the tenant house. We ate and slept as easily in one as in the other."

Both Dad and Uncle Mervin helped on the farm for about three years. They all came to realize that the farm was not big enough to support parents and Aunt Bessie, plus two adult sons, one with a family of four and again, one more on the way. My brother Dale, arriving on December 10, 1939, would be the only child born in the Old House, the same house where our father was born 28 years previously. Mervin soon found a job delivering ice, and Dad landed a door-to-door route with the Bond Bread Company in Salisbury. Although Dad's bread

Grandpop Jones leading cows out to pasture, assisted by his son George, 1938.

route was in the Stockton area, he decided to move his family to a little farm on Mount Hermon Road on the outskirts of Salisbury to be closer to the bread plant and his delivery truck.

By this time, my mother was pregnant with me, her sixth and final child, with five little ones under the age of 8. My dad rented a brown-shingled house on the Ranier farm; this time we would have electricity, running water, and a bathroom. Before we moved, my four-year-old sister, Betty, went to Lynchburg, Virginia, to stay with my mother's sister, Aunt Stella, and her husband, Uncle Hubert. Three-year-old Bobby was left in the care of our grandparents at the big house on Little Mill Road.

Perhaps both situations started as a temporary arrangement but ended up permanent. My grandmother cried and put up such a fuss every time my dad went to take Bobby to his new home, that he finally agreed to allow his son to stay there until Grandmom died. Aunt Stella and Uncle Hubert were childless and could offer Betty a life that my parents were unable to provide. Our family would be fractured: one child in Lynchburg with an aunt and uncle; one child on the Stockton farm with his grandmother and grandfather; and the rest of us in a small farmhouse near Salisbury, where brother Sonny and sister Ruth Ann attended the nearby one-room Mount Hermon schoolhouse, perhaps the last one to close in Wicomico County. While Dad was delivering bread, Dale stayed at home with Mother, awaiting my arrival.

LINDA ARRIVES (1941)

On a snowy day, December 12, 1941, I came into the world, with Grandmother McGee attending. When my mother went into labor after a lunch of fresh sausage, my father went to a neighbor's house to call the doctor and fetch the midwife. Not waiting for help to arrive, I entered the world by squirming into my grandmother's arms where she held me until the midwife arrived to cut the cord. Dad came later with the doctor and the birth certificate.

The name, Linda, was always such a boring name to me. Why couldn't I be Belinda or Glenda or Gretchen? And, Ellen, as a middle name? Who wants to be named after an old maid aunt who was always yelling at us when we were children, "Ott, ott, don't you go near that barn…or chicken house…or woods!" When I went away to college, I changed my name to Lynne, not legally, but introduced myself as Lynne and everyone at school called me Lynne.

Linda, 1943.

When I was a little girl, I remember my mother singing the song, "Linda," to me, and assumed I was named Linda because she liked the song so much. Having forgotten the words and with the advent of the internet, a couple of years ago, I went to Wikipedia and learned the song was written for Linda McCartney, future wife of Paul McCartney of Beatles fame. She was born three months before me. However, as I dug deeper, I learned that her father, a lawyer to songwriter, Jack Lawrence, asked him to write a song for his daughter for her second birthday, or maybe her fourth, depending on which source you use. The song was first recorded by Buddy Clark in 1947, and went to #1 on the charts when Linda and I were six. So much for being named for a song.

My father told me once that he wanted to name me Portia and I have always been glad that didn't get any traction. So, the doctor arrived with my birth certificate – not a blank one, mind you, but one with the name Tyrone Paul Jones already filled in. No explanation was ever passed on to me so I have made up a story that the doctor must have just come from delivering a baby boy, whose parents decided to change his name from Tyrone Paul Jones as soon as they saw it written on the birth certificate. Changed to what, I'll never know, but the doctor must have had only two birth certificates. He gave them a new one with the baby's new name, and when he was called to attend to my birth, he had only the slightly used one. My official birth certificate now bears the crossed-out name of Tyrone Paul and then, my name, Linda Ellen. It's either that story, or perhaps when my father announced, "We'll name her Portia," and when the doctor put pen to paper, my mother, in my defense, snatched the certificate from his hands and wrote "Tyrone Paul Jones" on it. "There! We'll name her Tyrone." Horrified at such a travesty, my father relented and quickly agreed to Linda Ellen Jones, and the doctor hurriedly scratched out "Tyrone Paul" and wrote my given name.

My five older brothers and sisters used to tease me about my middle name, Ellen, saying I was named for an overbearing and strict great-aunt, Aunt Ellie. My mother said she just liked the name Ellen. As for Linda, she said she liked the name from Linda Darnell, an actress from 1939-49. I finally grew to love both my names and even gave my daughter, Ellen, my middle name. The Jones part came from my father and although I am half Jones and half McGee, I have always identified more with the Jones family. Even though we visited both families weekly when I was young, I spent more time on the Jones family farm because Bobby was there.

Our house, in Mount Hermon, was adjoining the future Salisbury Airport. Across the field, there were gigantic excavating and grading machines, three or four times bigger than any tractor we had ever seen. The massive equipment was already creating an airport runway, and my family had a front-row seat, without a clue as to what a "runway" was.

George and Ruth at the Boston Farm, 1932 (left) and on a date in Ocean City, 1932.

Above, from left: Baby #1 George Jr. (Sonny), held by Ruth, born Feb. 26, 1933; Baby #2 Ruth Ann, held by Ruth, born July 8 1934; Baby #3 Betty, held by Grandmom Jones, born Apr. 6, 1936. Below, from left: Baby #4 Robert (Bobby), born Oct. 7, 1937; Baby #5 Dale, born Dec. 10, 1939; Baby #6 Linda, born Dec. 12, 1941.

(Front row from left) Betty, Bobby Grandmom Jones holding Dale, Ruth Ann, Sonny; (back row from left) Ruth, Aunt Bessie, Grandpop Jones, George, 1940.

Left: Dale, 4 months, held by Sonny (7) with Ruth Ann (6) and Bobby (2) on left and Betty (4) on right, 1940. Right: (from left) Bobby, Betty, Ruth Ann, Sonny, 1941.

By 1943, Bobby, (left with Grandpop), was living on the farm with our Jones Grandparents. Betty (right, with Uncle Hubert) was living in Lynchburg, Va., with Aunt Stella and Uncle Hubert. The remaining nucleus family (center) stayed together, (from left) Sonny, Ruth, Ruth Ann with Dale and Linda in front). George taking picture.

The young Jones family reunited at the McGee homestead on Dividing Creek Road, Pocomoke, Md., (from left) Ruth with Dale, Linda in front of Betty and George, and Bobby in front of Ruth Ann and Sonny, 1945.

2 | FROM PILLAR TO POST (1942-47)

THE LOG CABIN (1942-46)

My parents married in August 1932, and by the end of 1941, when I was born, they had moved six times and brought six little ones into the world. In 1942, when I was six months old, Dad left his job with the Bond Bread Company in Salisbury when he was offered the job as a forest warden with the Maryland Forestry Department. The pay was better, a beautiful log cabin was provided for housing, and the family would be much closer to both sets of grandparents. The Log Cabin, situated on Corker's Creek at the edge of the Pocomoke Forest, was our home from 1942-46. The house was on the Snow Hill-Pocomoke Road, about 4 miles west of Snow Hill.

By the time we moved to the Log Cabin, Bobby (4½) had been living with our Jones Grandparents on their farm for a year, and sister Betty (6) had been in Lynchburg, Virginia for a year. Even though they didn't live with us, I always knew they were my brother and sister – they just lived with relatives, somewhere else. We got to see Bobby more often since he was only 5 miles away, while Betty was only with us for holidays and summers. It seemed normal to me.

We felt like Abe Lincoln, living in our very own charming log cabin that stood in a grove of tall pine trees on the banks of Corker's Creek, a tributary of the Pocomoke River. The upstairs of the house had three bedrooms across the front, and a fourth bedroom and a bath at the rear. A large knotty-pine living room, the kitchen and pantry, plus an office with an outside entrance, comprised the downstairs. Electricity was provided by a generator, with a wood and coal burning furnace heating the house. We had an icebox and a wood stove in the kitchen, and although we had running water, Mom still used a wash tub and scrub board for laundry. The house had been built by the state in the

1930s, possibly a project of the CCC for housing the local forest warden, a position my father held during World War II. Sadly, the house was torn down in the 1970s, likely due to irreparable termite damage or creosote issues.

When we moved to the Log Cabin, Dale was a toddler and I still a baby. Since Ruth Ann and Sonny were in school, Dale was my only playmate. My mother has often told the story of watching Dale sit by my crib, pat me to sleep, and then slowly and gently remove the bottle from my hands so he could finish off the rest of the milk.

Mother soon got a job in a shirt factory in Pocomoke, 5 miles away, and left us in the care of Mandy, who lived down the

Dale and Linda in front of the log cabin, 1944.

road in a makeshift apartment above a chicken house. Sister Ruth Ann told me that once she walked with Mandy to her house because she wanted to show her family the cute little baby who was in her care. When my 8-year-old sister saw Mandy hold me in one arm, balanced on her hip, using the other arm to steady us up a ladder, the only access to her home, Ruth Ann was terrified that Mandy would drop me.

My first memory around the age of three or four is playing with a snapping turtle that my dad had caught and put in an old metal tub in the back yard. While Dale and I waited for him to take it down to the creek to release, we poked sticks at it, laughing when it snapped at our intrusions. We also had fun making frog houses by digging our bare feet into a muddy area after a rain. When our feet were in the muck as far as they would go, we'd cover the tops with an inch or two of mud. After patting it down, we moved our feet around ever so slightly, and then carefully pulled our feet out, leaving a "frog house." In no time, we could build an entire community for our little hop-along amphibian friends who never showed up to occupy their houses.

We had a dog when we lived in the log cabin, but I don't remember its name, although I have a picture of Ruth Ann holding the dog. I once heard the story that my brother Sonny rolled over on a puppy during the night and accidentally smothered him, but I was never able to corroborate that story. I also heard that Sonny buried a dead dog (maybe it was the puppy?) with his head sticking out of the ground so he could still breathe. My parents made him go back and do it again.

Dad kept a vegetable garden in a cleared area behind the house near the woods. While he tended the garden, I would enter the land of the fairies and search for lady slippers on the forest floor. They were silky and soft to the touch, and I always left them there for the forest creatures.

When my parents lived in Philadelphia in the 30s, they formed a lifetime friendship with their next-door neighbor, Emma Berger. Having just finished high school, she often helped Mom with her three small children and became like a sister to my mother and a favorite aunt to us children. When my parents left the city to move back to the family farm, Emma came every year to spend her one-week vacation with us. She came to visit us several summers at the log cabin, and I can remember her letting me sit on the kitchen counter while she prepared sandwiches for lunch. When I asked her what kind of sandwich she was making, she told me she was making booger sandwiches. Upon hearing an adult say, "a booger sandwich," I laughed hilariously, as only a three-year-old can. Emma was always so much fun.

Dale told me a story about Dad's work while we lived at the log cabin. During the war, POWs from Germany were housed in neighboring Somerset County. They were brought to the log cabin, which served as a staging area for their work, clearing roads and making fire lines throughout the Pocomoke Forest. As the forest warden, Dad supervised this work as the prisoners used mules to pull trees and brush out of the way. The mules were kept in a fenced area in the forest nearby, where there were other small buildings for supplies and equipment. Dale said Dad would let him ride the mules when the POWs needed them to clear vegetation and to work on the roads. He recalled that Dad told him that since the mules did not understand German, Dale's job was to interpret the prisoners' commands that they gave to the mules. He also remembered that when their work was done, the prisoners would swim in the creek during hot spells.

We were a family who loved to sing, and both my parents had lovely voices. Whenever we were going somewhere in the car, Dad would start us off singing *In the Evening by the Moonlight*, followed by *Carolina Moon* and *Oh Them Girls, Girls, Girls*, all of us joining in. As we were nearing our destination, Mom would end with a solo of *Mona Lisa*. It was a smart way to keep us entertained and relatively quiet. At least we were singing the same songs, usually in key.

We also loved listening to the radio and singing along. One day, Dale told me that there were tiny people who lived inside the radio – little people who talked and sang and played on miniature instruments. He further told me that if we took the radio apart, we would be able to hold these mini-musicians in our hands and play with them. And I believed him. As he collected the tools to begin dismantling the radio, I remember sitting on the floor, watching and eagerly waiting to welcome all those little people. I could barely contain my enthusiasm at the prospect of soon holding a handful of miniature singers. My father, hearing my excitement, came into the room to see what we were up to. Before Dale got too far along in the disassembly process, Dad put a stop to our antics.

THE CHICKEN COOP (1946)

In the spring of 1946, after four years in the Log Cabin, Dad was hired as a deputy game warden with the state, requiring us to leave our picturesque setting on Corker's Creek. Dad moved us into a tiny tenant house on Dividing Creek Road, intended for use by the farm hands on the Duncan Farm, although it would have better served the little storytellers and vocalists that Dale and I were unable to free from the inside of our radio.

The move put us even closer to my mother's parents, just a couple of miles down the road from us. We dubbed the house the Chicken Coop because it was so tiny, consisting of a kitchen, living room, and a bedroom downstairs with one large attic room upstairs. My dad strung a rope down the middle of the attic room and hung a sheet on it, separating the boys' side from the girls'. My mother was still cooking on a wood stove, and we got our water from the pitcher pump in the kitchen. With no electricity, I remember sitting with my older siblings at the kitchen table while they did their homework by kerosene lantern light. After three years of modern conveniences and indoor plumbing, yes, we were reduced to using an outhouse again. Luckily, we stayed there for only six months.

Emma visited us the summer we lived in the Chicken Coop, bringing her nephew who was my age. While it's true that her job as an elevator operator in a Philadelphia department store had to be boring, it's still hard to understand that she would choose to spend her yearly vacation visiting a family of six noisy children living in houses that sometimes lacked any modern conveniences. She was beloved by us all, so I'm sure that made up for any amenities we lacked. One day while Emma's nephew was there, Dale lured me to the back yard under a hornet's nest hanging from a tree. Showing off, he began throwing stones at the nest to send the hornets down on my head, but fortunately, I saw his intent and scampered into the house, probably to tattle-tell on him.

Dale finished first grade while we still lived in the log cabin and started second grade when we moved to the Chicken Coop, joining our siblings at the kitchen table doing homework by lamplight. He only went through the first half of the second grade because we moved again during Christmas vacation. During that fall/winter, he must have been out of school as much as in because he had whooping cough. Even as a three-and-a-half-year old, I cringed at the horrible rasping sound, and I was aware that my parents were really worried about him. The only childhood illness I remember getting was measles when I was in elementary school. I never got mumps, and I didn't get chicken pox until I was in my early 20s.

One day, Dale and I were playing cowboys in our parent's bedroom, and my cowboy brother came into my general store, looking to buy a gun. I saw the pistol Dad carried as a game warden on top of the bureau and reached up to get it. I offered the gun to Dale and encouraged him to test it out. He took the gun, turning it over in his hands, feeling its weight and smoothness, examining the barrel and the sights. Holding the pistol in his right hand, with his finger on the trigger, he aimed it out the window and squeezed the trigger, just like we had seen Roy Rogers and Gene Autry do in the movies. He pulled as hard as he could but was unable to activate the trigger. Requiring a better strategy, the little cowboy grabbed the gun handle with both hands, with both forefingers on the trigger. Once again, he aimed it out the window and pulled the trigger, but still was unable to fire the gun. Deciding he needed even more leverage, again holding it in both hands and with both forefingers on the trigger, this time he aimed the gun toward the floor. Pulling as hard as he could, with that added control, he finally had sufficient strength to pull the trigger.

The sound was deafening ... and terrifying. I immediately leapt onto the bed and started screaming and jumping up and down. My mother came running into the room, grabbed me – since I was the one making all the noise – and started exploring my body to see where I had been shot. When she found no blood, no hole, nothing, we both turned to look at Dale, the gun hanging loosely from his hand. He was white-faced, standing in a pool of blood. Mom dropped me on the bed and rushed to Dale to see what damage he had done. She took the gun from him, and seeing the blood coming from his foot, Mom wrapped it in a towel, and rushed him to the doctor. Luckily, the bullet had not hit any bone, having gone through the side of his big toe, leaving a bullet-sized hole. I remember asking to look at his foot every day, fascinated by the process of watching the hole close over a little more every day, and the skin and flesh eventually filling the hole. Dad was always extra vigilant on getting home from work to remove the bullets from his gun and put it in a safe place. On this day, he had failed to follow his own safety protocol and had left it on the bureau. We were fortunate to have escaped permanent damage – or even reducing the size of the family.

NEWARK (1947)

I am convinced that my mother was the force behind our next move, although Bobby thinks Dad's job as game warden required someone to live in the northern section of Worcester County. I'm sure Mom's complaints about the lack of modern-day conveniences and her unwillingness to go through one more winter in "that" tenant house drove my dad to find another residence. He found a big, brown-shingled farmhouse on the Tyndall Farm on Five Mile Branch Road, about one mile west of Newark, Maryland. Once again, we had running water and electricity, a bathroom, and even a wringer washing machine. We still hung clothes on the line to dry, but no longer had to wash and wring them out by hand.

Linda standing on the fender of the family's 1939 Chevrolet in back of the Tyndall farmhouse near Newark, Md., 1947.

Toward the end of summer 1947, before I started first grade, Dale sat with me under the claw-footed dining room table and told me that I had to learn to tie my shoes before I could go to school. There would be no one there, including Dale, who would tie the shoes of a first-grader, he said. He was very patient and encouraging while he showed me over and over how to make a single knot, and then make the first loop, holding it between my left thumb and forefinger.

"Use your right hand to wrap the other lace around the loop and the thumb and forefinger holding the loop, and then using your right thumb or forefinger, poke the lace through the loophole to form the second loop," he told me. "With your left hand grab the loop that you pushed into the small hole and pull both loops tight so the tied laces won't come undone."

It was very complicated for a five-year-old, but I practiced and practiced until I had it down because I knew he didn't want to tie my shoes at school. With all those detailed instructions, he should have been a writer for a military procedures manual.

The first day of school, shoes tightly tied, I walked down the lane with my brothers and sister to meet the bus. Just as it was stopping to pick us up, in my

Clockwise from left: Dale and Linda on her first day of school in Newark, Md., 1947; Dale and Linda dressed for play on the Tyndall Farm, Newark, Md., 1947; Linda and Dale with Emma, 1947.

excitement, I dropped my pencil box, and all of my new school supplies fell out onto the dirt. The door opened and the bus driver patiently waited while my older siblings helped gather everything to put back in my box. Head down, burning with shame for being so clumsy, I climbed on the bus. I thought I would never be able to hold my head up again.

The Newark Elementary School that Dale and I attended was a two-room schoolhouse with grades 1-3 in one room, 4-6 in another. The only memory I have of my first-grade classroom was the day I had worn Jodhpurs to school. When I committed some offense against the rules of classroom order, the teacher left the front of the room and walked briskly down the aisle to swat my bottom. Instead, she swatted the material that billowed out on my pants – I always loved those pants. I was afraid Dale would tell Mom the teacher had paddled me, but I don't recall that he did. Another day, during recess, when a bully threatened me on the playground, Dale came to my rescue, driving the tormentor away. Dale claims it was he, himself, who got two black eyes from that encounter – the first when he drove the bully away, and the second when he went back to even the score.

After living in the Chicken Coop, our new farmhouse was so huge that there was one room downstairs and two bedrooms upstairs that we didn't even use. Mr. Tyndall, our landlord, stored furniture and other items in those rooms, which we were forbidden to enter. We used the back stairs off the living room to access our own bedrooms. Before going to bed each night, Dale and I performed a nightly ritual, standing on "our stage," the second step of the back stairway, and sang:

Good night Mother
Good night Father
Good night Everyone
We're going to leave you now.

It was always a big hit, especially when we had company. I'm sure if Dale and I were teenagers now, we would already have auditioned for *American Idol*.

Fire was always a danger in the old wooden farmhouses we occupied, and the brown-shingled house was no exception. One evening, someone reported seeing sparks coming out of the chimney, and my dad called the fire department. Dale and I, with a reprieve from the usual bedtime ritual, sat in a chair together and listened for the fire engine sirens. Bored with waiting, we start making the siren sounds ourselves, until we were told to knock it off. I have no memory of the arrival of fire trucks or the outcome of that adventure, but I was left with a fear of future houses catching fire.

During the summer of 2021, I was visiting Bobby in Stockton where he now lives, when we happened to be in the Newark area. We drove out in the country and found our old house, the only house I lived in as a child that is still standing. We drove up the lane just to get a closer look and found a beautifully restored white house. We saw a woman standing outside by her

Restored Tyndall farmhouse in Newark, Md. 2021

car looking a little perplexed to have visitors. When we told her that we used to live in her house, she graciously invited us inside to see our childhood home. I could envision where the table stood under the window where Dale taught me to tie my shoes. I took my place on the second step of the back stairway, Dale's and my stage, and was encouraged to sing our Goodnight song. As I reached the second floor, I was unable to call forth one memory. I couldn't have said which room I shared with my sister, Ruth Ann, or which room was Mom and Dad's.

By this time, Emma was an integral part of our lives and the highlight of our summers. Dale and I were sure she came from the city just to play with us. She was always fun to be around, playing games with us, and never talking down to us. We thought of her as our friend as much as Mom's friend. We could always count on a trip to Ocean City when Emma visited. One summer, we spent a weekend in the houseboat that my uncles rented on the bay side back in the day before high rise buildings. In the mid-60s, the land where the houseboat sat was developed into the Jolly Roger amusement park. Later, in the 70s, when my siblings and I vacationed in Ocean City, we would frequently drop off our kids at Jolly Roger for an afternoon of fun for them and a little down time for us. Our children were playing on the same land where my family and I slept on a houseboat and swam in the bay back in the 1940s.

It must have been when we were living in Newark, when I was four or five, that I went with Dad to visit his parents and Bobby in Stockton. On the way home, about a mile before reaching Snow Hill, our car ran out of gas. My dad got out and soon flagged down the first car that came along. When the door opened, all I could see was a dilapidated car, overflowing with brown-skinned people – migrant workers, all laughing and talking. I'm sure I expected my father to insist they proceed on their way and flag down a car that would have room for both of us. Instead, from the front seat of our 1939 Chevrolet, I observed horror-struck, as he squeezed onto someone's lap in the crowded back seat. He called to me over his shoulder, "There's no room for you in here. I'll be back in a few minutes with gas."

With a sense of abject betrayal, I watched as the jalopy drove away and disappeared from sight. He abandoned me, and I was alone on the side of the road. Terrified, I started screaming and crying and jumping up and down on the front seat of the car, but no one could hear me. I don't know how long I continued crying or how long it took him to come back, but I still have that adverse image of abandonment in my memory, but not the positive one where he returned and soothed my hurt feeling and eased my fears, which surely he did.

Finally, in the winter of 1947, the family moved to Stockton to our final rental – into the "Rowley House," a large farmhouse owned by Walter and Nell Hancock; and Nell became one of my mother's lifelong friends. After having 10 different addresses our first 15 years, my family stayed put for the next 14.

Summer at the houseboat in Ocean City, Md., 1947. Left: George flanked by Ruth Ann (left) and Betty, with Dale and Linda standing. Center: Dale and Linda playing in the Assawoman Bay. Right: Agnes McGee (Ruth's cousin), George, Emma, Linda.

3 | Living in Stockton (1948-61)

The Rowley Farm (1948-61)

During the Christmas holidays of 1947 and two weeks after my sixth birthday, my family moved back to the little town of Stockton, population 300. Our farmhouse, purported to be the oldest in Stockton – likely built about 1800 – boasted its own Rowley family burial site in the middle of the field and a basement with a dirt floor. There was a crawl

The Joneses lived for 14 years in the Rowley House, built c. 1800.

space off the basement that looked like a dungeon. As kids, when we finally got the nerve to crawl through the opening, we expected to find skeletons still chained to the foundation of the house. It would be considered a fixer-upper today – no indoor plumbing, no central heat, an icebox on the porch, and a wood stove in the kitchen, and then there was the outhouse – again after having had indoor plumbing for a year. My parents paid $20 a month for rent, which, to our landlord's credit, never increased during the 14 years we lived there.

The large farmhouse started its life as a four-room house – a kitchen and living room downstairs and two bedrooms up. A future addition made it a two-story shotgun house with four bedrooms upstairs, and downstairs were two living rooms, a breakfast room, and kitchen. A screened-in porch at the side of the house went the length of the kitchen and breakfast room. The wood stove, the icebox, and the outhouse wouldn't be replaced with modern conveniences until the early 50s. The downstairs was heated by a kerosene space heater in the living room and a little wood stove in the breakfast room. We did have electricity, and there was running water in the kitchen. The two living rooms were separated by French doors, and in the winter, the front room was closed off to conserve heat. The upstairs was unheated, and a glass of water left on the nightstand would freeze overnight in the winter. It was the fifth house we had lived in, during my short life, and it was where I stayed until I graduated from high school in 1959. My parents would linger in their empty nest for another two years when they bought the Federal Street House in Snow Hill.

The Rowley House (background) overlooks the farmyard as Linda watches over her chickens, a 4-H Club project, 1954.

Our house was on the first farm at the edge of town just across the county road from the elementary school. Stockton was a crossroad town 3 miles north of the Virginia line, 2 miles west of the Chincoteague Bay, 10 miles east of Pocomoke, and 9 miles south of Snow Hill. We had sidewalks leading from the elementary school to Stockton's "downtown," where Dalt's Grocery store stood on the corner next to the post office. The other three corners sported Shay's beer joint and pool hall, Mason's hardware store, and a teen hangout. Down the street toward Pocomoke was Merv Burgage's grocery store, Cutright's car repair shop, Jim Pruitt's woodworking shop, an ice house, a chicken plant, and a bank building that had closed its doors as a result of the Depression. During the 40s and 50s Stockton still had a small, declining seafood industry on the bay at the end of George Island Landing Road. We also had an operating sawmill at the edge of town on the Snow Hill Road.

The town was made up of beautiful Victorian houses with front porches and small grassy yards. Today, the population has dwindled to about 80 souls due to the now defunct seafood industry in that area and the closing of the Chincoteague Naval Air Base in 1959. Many of the houses have been unoccupied for years and are in gross states of disrepair. The only business remaining in Stockton is a bar at the edge of town, requiring residents to do all their shopping at the Wal-Mart in Pocomoke.

My immediate playground included the barn, two chicken houses, a smokehouse, and a corn crib. Our generous yard had the best climbing trees a tomboy could wish for. Down the lane and across the county road, the school playground was soon incorporated into my area of play, as well as the sidewalk in front of the school, which I used for roller skating. As I got older, I rode my bike to my grandparents' farm, just 2 miles away on the other side of town. There, I could bridle my brother's horse, jump on her back, and explore the entire countryside and woods by horseback. We were frequently accompanied by my sidekick,

Trixie, a little rat terrier that my dad brought home for me shortly after we moved.

STOCKTON ELEMENTARY SCHOOL

I had started my educational pursuits in a two-room schoolhouse in Newark, a miniature version of the three-room Stockton Elementary School. When we moved in the middle of my first grade year, I transferred to the same schoolhouse that my father and his siblings had attended and graduated from 30 years earlier. My brother Bobby was in the fifth grade when Dale and I started school. The school had a cafeteria and six classrooms, all of which were in use when my father graduated from there – two grades, 1-12, in each classroom. Since it was an elementary school when I was a student, only three classrooms were used, still with two grades in each room. Each teacher used an adjoining activity room where painting, inside games, and other projects could take place without disturbing the other students. The rooms surrounded a central auditorium, which had a stage.

My first and second-grade teacher, Miss Mae Jones, was my father's first cousin, which didn't earn me any special favors. My report cards throughout elementary school usually included a paragraph about how I spent too much time visiting with my "neighbors" during class time, instead of attending to my lessons. Miss Jones always added that I loved to read.

One of the first days I was in Miss Jones' class, she asked me to get supplies from another teacher down the hall. I wasn't given a written note but was asked to remember the message and repeat it. "Go tell Miss Shockley I need some more colored paper, some pencils, and crayons." From past experience in my family, I already knew that I couldn't be trusted to remember what I was supposed to be looking for. When asked by my mother to go upstairs to get something, I was easily sidetracked by my own agenda and frequently went back and told my mother, "I couldn't find it," having no idea what I had been sent to fetch.

So, I started on my first-grade mission, and wanting to get it right, I repeated over and over to myself, as I walked through the auditorium to Miss Shockley's room, "Pencils, paper, and crayons. Pencils, paper, and crayons." If I'm honest, it's not that much different now, seven decades later, when I walk down the hall from my bedroom to the kitchen, "Take meat out of freezer. Take meat out of freezer."

My first boyfriend in the first and second grades was Billy Baylis. One of Miss Jones' activities for her students was to have us lie down on large sheets of white paper so she could outline our bodies with black crayons. Then, we would cut along the lines she had drawn. The resulting silhouette labeled with our names were hung on the walls of the activity room.

Linda's first grade portrait, 1948.

Billy and I had ours done at the same time, and seeing our silhouettes hanging side by side, I just knew he was my boyfriend. It didn't take much back then.

Toward the end of second grade, my boyfriend Billy was riding his bike from the country store less than half a mile from his home when he was hit by a truck and died instantly. His little friends were in shock when we heard the news. Aside from animals dying, it was my first experience of death. Miss Jones selected me as the class representative to accompany her to his parents' home to pay our respects as he lay in his little casket in their living room. I was aware of his younger sister Judy, and it dawned on me how lonely she would be for the rest of her life after the loss of her big brother. The entire class went to the funeral a few days later. It was a sad, sad day.

The school auditorium was the setting for my first kiss. When I was in the sixth grade, we children were called to an assembly to find out our roles in the upcoming Christmas pageant. My classmate seated next to me would play Joseph, and I would play Mary. We were both so excited about our rise to celebrity status by the announcement that we spontaneously hugged and kissed.

I had already tried unsuccessfully to contrive a way to get a kiss from Micky Ward, Dale's best friend two years older than me. Television being new to the scene, my fourth-grade classmates and I were given an assignment of putting together a TV show. Using a washing machine-sized box for our console TV, we cut out a square hole for the screen and drew knobs on the front and used a bent coat hanger for rabbit ears on top. We set about writing a TV show about a family where I would be the mother. Needing an older student to play the father, I wrote Micky into the scene, which would require an obligatory kiss with his wife in a scene we would do together. When my teacher got wind of my intentions, she nixed the plan and Mickey was written out of the script. So, my first kiss would be unintentional and unexpected, and my planned kiss unconsummated.

Throughout school, I was a mediocre student. We were graded "O" for Outstanding, "S" for Satisfactory, and "N" for Needs Improvement. My elementary report cards were populated with an army of Ss, standing as humped-back sentinels to my unexceptional performance. I was more interested in friendships and playground activities than learning my lessons. It would be in a real estate course in the late 70`s when I finally understood the relationship between fractions, decimals, and percentages. This lack of understanding about basic math plagued me throughout my education. Maybe if they had taught that there was a relationship, I would have understood it earlier.

I envied my classmates who had good handwriting, could draw, and seemed to easily understand what was going on in the classroom. I am convinced now that my love of reading enabled me to have some measure of accomplishment in school. By the time I was through elementary school, I had read every book in the library. And I always looked forward to going to Pocomoke on Saturdays where the public library would be my first stop. Library card in hand, I would climb the steps to the library in search of horse books, Nancy Drew, the Bobbsey Twins, and, later, Trixie Beldon mysteries and Cherry Ames Student Nurse books.

My best friend was Barbara Wessels, but after the fifth grade, I wasn't allowed to play with her anymore. She was a spunky little girl being raised by her grandparents on a farm on the other side of town. The attribute I most admired as a 10-year-old was her ability to sing and yodel. She tried to teach me to yodel, but I'm pretty sure that aptitude is genetic. We bonded over our love of horses, and even more enviable than singing and yodeling, she could whinny and sounded just like a horse. I never could get that down either. I suspect whinnying is in the same genetic category as yodeling. During recess, we could be seen galloping around the playground on our imaginary horses.

The other thing I admired her for resulted in our undoing – she claimed that she had a "boyfriend." She was definitely more advanced than I was, and after telling me some of the questionable activities she and her boyfriend were involved in, I told her I needed some proof. One day she came to school with a letter that he had written to me, but, she instructed, I couldn't read it until I was alone. Excited to have a letter, and especially from a boy, I quickly excused myself to go to the girls' room and settled myself in a lavatory stall. I unfolded the letter, ignoring that the handwriting looked very similar to Barbara's. I began to read:

Dear Linda,
Barbara and I go to the barn and buck.

That was as far as I got when the door flung open. Standing before me was my teacher, Principal Catherine Etchison, extending her arm and snatching the letter from my hands. As she read it, I stood with my head down, using the time to develop my story. It was easy to see that she was furious, and I thought to myself, "What could be wrong with playing horses and bucking?" Further, it sounded reasonable to me that a cursive f and b were difficult to differentiate at my age, so I decided that would be my story. It looked like "buck" to me … and that was as far as I read.

After school, my teacher drove me home with the troublesome letter in her purse and met with my parents. I told them what I knew of the letter's contents, feigning innocence and maintaining the integrity of my story. After Miss Etchison's departure, my parents and I got in our car and drove to Barbara's grandparents' house, where I was to remain in the car while they went in the house. I looked around hoping to see Barbara's boyfriend, her horse, or Barbara, all to no avail. I don't remember any discussion on the ride home or any repercussion from my parents. Soon thereafter, Barbara left our school to complete her primary education at Pocomoke Elementary. I never saw her again and have always wondered what goodies the rest of that letter contained.

THE CIRCUS

Each year in the final days of my childhood summers, just before school started, I held a one-ring circus of sorts. I invited friends and neighbors and charged a dime for admission. I don't remember crowds larger than five or six attendees, but it was a fairly big undertaking for a 10- or 11-year-old girl. Inspired by the "daring young man on the flying trapeze" I saw at a circus that set up tents in a nearby town, I talked my father into installing a trapeze on a tree in the front yard. My aerial acts included standing up on the trapeze while flying through the air with the greatest of ease, and, while swinging, I could drop to a sitting position and then drop to hanging by my knees. Also featured were Trixie the Wonder Dog, who could do a few simple tricks (if she was in the mood), but was mostly available for belly rubs. Sometimes there also would be kittens or puppies for attendees to hold. Casper and Jasper, the Friendly Pigeons was the act that drew the most oohs and aahs. When I called out their names, our pet pigeons Casper and Jasper would come swooping down from their perch in the barn loft, fly across the yard, and land on my shoulders, one on the left and one on the right. Pony rides were the biggest hit.

The summer before sixth grade, I was practicing a new circus act that required standing upright on the seat of my bicycle with both my arms held out to the side, very much like the scene in Titanic. One hot August day, as my bicycle sped along the macadam country road in front of my grandparents' farm, I pumped as hard and fast as I could to attain the velocity I had calculated I would need to perform this daring feat. Moving quickly but carefully, I moved my feet from the pedals to the seat, and as soon as I felt balanced, I smoothly and slowly removed my hands from the handlebars and started to stand up. Almost immediately, but too late, in a blinding glimpse of the obvious, I realized I hadn't accounted for the several scenarios that were now materializing in rapid succession: how quickly the bicycle's speed would diminish, the unevenness of the macadam road, the body-wobble factor, or the certain betrayal of the front wheel. Before I even began to straighten my knees, the front wheel did a 180, while I did a free-fall down to the road. I ended up a few hours later in Dr. Cohen's office with a cast on my broken right arm. There would be no bicycle act in my circus in the summer of 1952.

The polio epidemic that year was the worst outbreak in U.S. history. Of the 57,628 cases reported that year, 3,145 people died and 21,269 were left with mild to disabling paralysis. One of my fifth-grade classmates, Bobby Bunn, was one of those unfortunate children stricken with polio, and he was kept out of school for a year. He came back to school in September for the sixth grade with a brace on his leg and was no longer able to run on the playground.

During the first recess that September, Bobby Bunn and I got together and assessed our handicaps as they applied to playground activities. In Red Rover, Red Rover, Bobby Bunn held our place in line while I ran to break through our opponent's line. He was much better at holding, though, than I was at breaking through. Even with dogged intention and running like the wind, my small stature usually kept me from breaking through, unless I could spot a weak link. Our greatest partnership, however, was on the softball field. He was no longer able to run with a brace on his leg, and I couldn't swing a bat with a cast on my arm. So, that fall we offered ourselves as a team. He hit the balls, and I ran the bases. When teams were chosen, we were usually first to be chosen because the team captain was getting two players for the price of one, and we were both good at what we did.

MOVIES IN POCOMOKE

The highlight of my life as a young girl in the late 40s and early 50s was going to the movies. Westerns and Tarzan movies were my favorites. Comedies, like *Francis the Talking Mule* and whatever antics Dean Martin and Jerry Lewis were up to, were also a big hit. Roy Rogers and especially his Palomino horse, Trigger, were at the top on my heroes list. I didn't see that Dale Evans added anything to the saga, except, of course, for her buckskin horse Buttercup. On the second tier of the movie ratings of a 10-year-old  girl was the Lone Ranger, but mostly because of his fiery white horse with the speed of light, a cloud of dust, and a hearty "Hi-Ho Silver!" Gene Autry, the Singing Cowboy, and his sorrel horse Champion also held a place on the second level. Ranking third, in no particular order, were Hop-Along Cassidy with his horse Topper; Lash LaRue with Black Diamond; The Cisco Kid with Diablo; and Zorro with Tornado. In truth, the horses were the stars who held top billing in my world.

Every Saturday afternoon after our chores were finished, my family would pile in the car and head to Pocomoke, 10 miles away. After getting books from the library, Mom and Dad dropped us kids off at the MarVa (Maryland/Virginia) movie theater for the Saturday matinee, while they did the grocery shopping at the Acme Super Market. With a bag of popcorn in my lap, I settled into my seat, eagerly anticipating the dimming of the sconces on the wall, and then that lovely rustling sound as the heavy red curtains slowly swept open to reveal a new fantastical world every week. There was always a cartoon at the beginning, and then a serial that resumed the story of what had played the week before. Superman and Batman never failed to delight with a dazzling cliffhanger at the end to keep us coming back for more. And finally, the introduction to the feature film by the roaring lion. Oh, it was my two hours of heaven every week.

BROTHERS RUN AWAY

On a particular Saturday in July when I was about 9, my teenage sister Ruth Ann and I were dressed and ready to leave for Pocomoke. The phone rang. My Aunt Bessie informed us that when Uncle Mervin went back to the cornfield after lunch to continue weeding with Bobby and Dale, he realized the boys were nowhere to be seen nor heard. All Mervin saw were two lone hoes, lying in the furrow between the rows of weed-ridden corn.

Now, there was a lot I envied about my brothers: They were both older than me, close to the same age, and it seemed to me they engaged in more fun and dangerous pursuits than a mere girl was allowed to do. However, I did not envy the work they had to do on the farm. I was glad that I was never called on to get the cows from the far end of the pasture and bring them back to the barn to be fed and milked. I never had to get the bales of hay out of the barn loft to spread out to feed the animals. I was never told to go slop the hogs, chop wood for the wood box, or hoe the weeds in the cornfield. Oh, I may have helped with those chores when I was visiting, but it seemed to me that Dale and Bobby were used as slaves.

I've shared the story many times about how my brothers were traded to a neighbor in exchange for two mules. Uncle Mervin needed his neighbor's mules and plow for a certain job on his farm, and unbeknownst to Dale and Bobby, Mervin had promised a day's work from them in exchange. They were invited to ride in the pickup with Mervin, presumably to help harness the mules, which they set about doing with great pride. They went to the barn, put the bridles on before getting the mules out of their stalls, and then arranged the collars and set all the harnesses, straps, and fasteners in place, and even double checked that everything was secured.

As they were bringing the mules out of the barn, they had begun imagining they would be allowed to ride them back to Mervin's farm. When Uncle Mervin took the reins and got up on the seat, that's when he gave them the bad news. They would be staying at the neighbor's, giving "a good day's work" weeding his corn, which they did, begrudgingly. It didn't take them long to realize they were being traded for two mules.

Later in the day, Uncle Mervin, having completed his chore, came back to return the mules and to pick up his nephews. As the neighbor was telling Uncle Mervin what a good job they had done and how hard they had worked, Dale and Bobby could hear him jingling coins in his pocket. Immediately they began to imagine how much he might give them to make their labor in the field worthwhile to them. He turned to the exhausted but hopeful boys and asked, "How much do I owe you?" Before they could formulate an answer, Uncle Mervin laughed and said, "Oh, you don't owe them nothing. That's what neighbors are for." And the neighbor's hand came out of his pocket – empty.

After years of such treatment, Dale and Bobby commenced working on a scheme to run away. Usually, they conspired when they were in bed after a hard day's work. In the event they had to flee separately, they chose a bobwhite's call as their signal. They pre-selected a stump in the woods nearest the cornfield, where the first-to-flee would leave a certain arrangement of sticks, indicating his departure. From there, a tree had been designated for the first runaway to climb and wait for his brother. And, finally, from the cover of foliage at the top of the tree, the bobwhite whistle would announce their arrival from a distance. It was the perfect plan.

They bided their time, until one particular Saturday, after returning to the field from lunch, Bobby selected a row that had a lot of weeds that caused him to lag behind Dale and Uncle Mervin. When they were 50 or so feet ahead, Bobby saw his chance, dropped his hoe, and fled to the woods. After arranging his sticks on the designated stump, he headed straight to the look-out tree, climbing high enough to be hidden from sight at ground level. Periodically, he whistled his bobwhite call and wondered how long he would have to wait for Dale.

But wait! This isn't the story of their running away. It's the story of my ruined day. We had to go help look for them. As we rode along the county road in the back of Dad's car, calling out their names, Ruth Ann and I got madder and madder. How dare those two asinine brothers ruin our precious Saturday afternoon – Movie Day.

I imagine that with darkness falling, the adults began to really worry. I remember gathering at the kitchen table at the farm with everyone around. There may have been talk of calling the police and reporting them as missing. But just then, the cat came casually strolling into the kitchen from the front hallway, a wide-eyed look alerting her humans that something is amiss. Uncle Mervin took one look at her and rose from the table and quickly walked through the front hall, where he found Dale and Bobby half in and half out of the parlor window. We could hear Uncle Mervin, "Hah! I caught you. The cat gave you away."

The boys had been hearing us call for them off and on all afternoon. As dusk turned to darkness, they began to fear they might be in real trouble. They quickly developed a foolproof strategy. They decided if they could get back in the house through the parlor window on the front porch and then creep up the stairs with no one seeing them, they could undress, put on their pajamas, get in bed, and pretend they had been there asleep all afternoon, worn out from all that weeding. I guess they hadn't considered the cat's detection talents in their plan.

BROTHERS PLAYING TRICKS

Often, I would join Dale when he went to the farm, where we usually had more fun with Bobby than staying home. We would always help with chores so there was more time for play. I will now tell you about what I had to put up with as the youngest child and a *girl*, if that girl wants to play with two older brothers who were not too keen on playing with their little sister. This is one of both brothers' favorite stories. They don't tell it the same way I do because they never focus on what, to me, was the most important consequence in the tale, but that's fairly common, isn't it? We were the last three children in a litter of six, with only nine years separating the first-born and me, the youngest. According to whom you talk, I was spoiled rotten (the oldest three), or I was an easy target and a pain in the ass (my two brothers closest in age). If you talked to me, I would say that early on, in order to survive in my world, I learned unique navigational skills that would enable me to plot a course through seven giants of varying size and disposition.

I loved playing with Dale (two years older) and Bobby (four years older), and I frequently begged to be included in their games since they were the only playmates close to my age. To my credit, I was

Left: Linda and Dale, 1948. Right: Bobby and Linda, 1950.

somewhat of a tomboy, but they generally turned me down because they liked playing rough, as boys normally do. Unless they allowed me to play with them, or more likely, were forced to do so, I was relegated to the house playing with my dolls. I don't know why I sought them out because typically I was the brunt of some trick or tomfoolery. I honestly think it was because I was an optimistic child and hoped they eventually would see what a desirable playmate I could be.

One summer day, when I was about 8, my brothers decided they would invite me to play with them in a broad-jumping contest, an activity that Bobby had learned at school. They said they would call me as soon as they prepared the course, located behind the old dairy. They cleared an area, roughly 14 feet long by 4 feet wide, to allow for a running approach and the jump. They turned the earth to make the dirt loose so it would provide a super-soft landing, and then raked the course smooth. After experimenting with several run and jumps, they forecasted the likely distance a mere girl could jump. About two feet from the end, my brothers dug a hole to neatly accommodate the feet and legs, up to the knees, of their 8-year-old sister.

I don't know how much planning went into perfecting their scheme, but, having settled on the location and depth of the pit, they made several trips down to the barn to add the finishing touches to their engineering feat. They filled buckets with fresh cow manure and water and one by one, they lugged them back to the broad jump area and stirred the mixture until they were delighted with its gooey consistency. Back and forth they went, lugging, mixing, and emptying their concoction into the pit until the slurry was almost level with the top. After covering the top of the hole with 3 or 4 layers of old newspapers, pulled taut over the pit, they spread a very thin layer of fresh dirt to conceal the newspapers and any uneven surfaces, then raked it until it looked like a Zen Garden – not a lump or a seam could be detected.

Satisfied that it was ready for "the mark," they made their way into the house to rescue me from helping Aunt Bessie make clothes for my doll. After cheerfully telling me the course was ready for a broad-jumping competition, we made our way outside to the "Zen Garden." When I saw the course, I could see they had spent time preparing it, and I was impressed. They identified the designated starting place, explaining there was enough space to get a running start to launch ourselves into the broad jump, and, in this way, we could see which of us could jump the farthest. Because I was the youngest, I could go first, they said. Usually, I was last, so I should have been more suspicious at that point, plus they "wanted" me to play with them. Why didn't I know something was amiss? For once, I didn't have to beg.

According to both my brothers, they watched as I took my stance at the starting line, bent over slightly to get a good push-off. I took a few deep breaths, charting out my strategy, and with little arms pumping and legs looking like wheels you see on cartoon characters, I ran a few power steps in the space provided, gathering steam, and with all my might, launched myself into the air to triumph with my broadest jump possible. As their engineering calculations bore fruit, I came down exactly in the cow-pie pit they had prepared. They say I jumped out almost as quickly as I had jumped in, all in one movement. To the music of their gleeful laughter and the sound of congratulatory back slapping, I ran off to the barn to wash off my smelly, chocolate-covered, knee-high socks at the cow watering-trough, cursing as only an 8-year-old girl can.

Over the years, I have heard this story at most family gatherings – amid lots of laughter when either Bobby or Dale trots out the story. Since we are a big family, we have had a lot of family gatherings. The broad-jumping tale is the highlight of any reunion, especially if there has been a wedding bringing new members into the fold. In later years, I insisted on telling my version of the end of the story. However, at the age of 75, I finally decided that their narrative was much better than mine. Their version gets more laughs, and my trying to set things straight didn't add one interesting or funny tidbit. So, I decided to stop telling my story after they told theirs. I will not altogether keep quiet though. In fact, I will tell a story that they are not likely to tell. And I may tell this one every time they talk about the infamous broad jump.

Dale and Bobby, knowing that I loved horses, decided to take advantage of my eagerness to play any game that included a horse, especially if I got to be the horse. Usually, when we played cowboys and Indians, they always gave me the role of Indian – never the beau role back in those days, to be sure. To this day, I think that by being cast in the role of the underdog throughout my childhood is why I now have such a strong connection with our Native-American brothers and sisters.

One rainy day, my dear brothers called me into the front parlor, inviting me to play a new cowboy game they had contrived, and this time I could be the horse. I saw they had built a stable by turning chairs on their side and covering them with blankets. They explained, "Because you are a wild horse that we just caught, we don't want you to run away, so we have constructed a special stable for you." I could see that they had also arranged a blanket over an opening for the stable door. While I bucked and reared and whinnied, as horses do, one of them grabbed me while the other opened the stable door, and, as soon as I was pushed inside, they quickly secured the blanket door behind me so that I couldn't get out. It was only at that moment, and in semi-darkness, that I realized the smell that surrounded me was worse than the horse stall in the barn. You see, they had prepared my stable beforehand by going inside themselves, and farting – as much, and as many times, and as long as they could before making it air-tight, and only then invited me to join their cowboy game. No, they don't tell THAT story!

You say you want to hear my version of the broad jump? What actually happened? It's not so different from their story, and this really will be the last time I'll tell it from my perspective. Do you remember when I said, "I should have been more suspicious," after seeing their fancy broad jumping course? Well, I was. So suspicious, in fact, that I said to them, "I don't trust you. You're up to no good. I'm going to walk the course first to make sure you haven't laid a trap for me."

I surmise that they thought it didn't matter so much if I jumped in or walked in, so they didn't object when I started my walk-about on the course. And now you can guess the rest. When I came to that section, two feet from the end, my right foot slid neatly into the slurry cow pie pit, and I hopped out with one chocolate-covered leg (not two) and ran off to the barn to wash it off. As I fought to control my temper, and the cursing that normally would accompany it, I remember thinking as I ran, "Boys will be boys." For me, it was the first time I remember controlling my temper when my two older brothers played a mean trick on me.

See what I mean? Their story is much better.

4 | CAST OF CHARACTERS WHO INFLUENCED MY LIFE

BIG CITY MISS RUTH ANN

My big sister Ruth Ann was a significant influence throughout my life. From the moment I was born, when she was 7½, she became my "little mommy." She was my babysitter and caregiver during her teen years until she left home, my mentor when we had children, and my best friend as we grew older. For the last two years of her life, she lived near me, and we saw each other often and Skyped every evening.

My sister was born in 1934, the first daughter and second child to George and Ruth Jones. I always thought of Ruth Ann as my second mom. She was 7½ years older than me, and I was often left in her care. She told me once that when I was born, she thought of me as her own living baby doll. She fed me, changed my diapers, dressed me, and rocked me to sleep. I asked her once to tell me what she remembered about my growing up, and she said she just remembered me as her baby. Of course, the age difference could account for her scant memories of my childhood. When she graduated from high school and left home in 1952, I was only 11. It's also true that I don't remember much about her during her teenage years, except for a couple of memories.

During my elementary school years, Mother worked the night shift at the Bird's Eye Chicken Plant in Pocomoke while Dad's job as a game warden often required him to work at night, catching illegal deer hunters. Ruth Ann was left in charge of Dale and me, and we started calling her "long-neck nanny" – behind her back, of course, because she always seemed to be sticking her nose (and long neck) in our business. When we were adults, she told me she thought we called her that because she had a long and

Left: Ruth Ann's first steps on Little Mill Road, 1935.
Right: Ruth Ann holding Linda, 1942.

beautiful neck. We hated telling her the truth. But, by then, the song *Big City Miss Ruth Ann* was popular, and I started calling her "Big City."

One evening when she was in charge, I was mad with her because she wouldn't let me stay up late. When she told me I had to go to bed, I flopped myself down in a chair and announced that I was going to stay up until Mom got home (usually about 3 a.m.). Ruth Ann was always wise about choosing her battles and said that was fine with her. Promptly saying, "Good night," she went upstairs to bed – leaving me alone downstairs with all the ghosts and creaking of a 150-year-old house. It wasn't long before I caved in and scampered upstairs, jumped in bed and covered my head where I thought I would be safer.

One battle she did choose to wage was with our older brother Sonny. Mom and Dad were going to a wedding one Saturday and left teenagers Sonny and Ruth Ann with a list of chores to complete. Ruth Ann was to clean the house, while Sonny was charged with weeding the vegetable garden. As the sun made its way across the sky and shadows began to lengthen, Ruth Ann was pursuing her own interests upstairs in her bedroom, her work having been finished hours beforehand. Sonny, just returning home after being gone all day, made his way upstairs, demanding that Ruth Ann help him weed the garden so it would be finished before Mom and Dad came home. When she politely refused, he adamantly told her that she would help him, whereupon he picked her up and headed down the stairs with her over his shoulder. In an attempt to stand her ground, she grabbed one of the spindles on the staircase with both hands. Sonny pulled her so hard, and she held on so tightly, that the spindle broke. Undeterred, he continued down the stairs, whereupon she grabbed a second spindle which also broke. At that point, he put her down, knowing he'd be in more trouble for the broken spindles than for not weeding the garden.

Ruth Ann took a bold and daring step for 1952 when she was a senior in high school and a representative from the FBI came to the school on career day. She was immediately captivated with the idea of working for the FBI, and especially moving away from the Eastern Shore to Washington, D.C. She didn't tell Mom and Dad she had applied for a job, thinking it would probably come to nothing. But, after a thorough FBI background check, she was called for an interview that resulted in a job offer. It just about broke both my parents' hearts when she told them of her new plans, but they didn't stand in her way. After graduation at the age of 18, Ruth Ann set off for the western side of the Chesapeake Bay, headed for our nation's capital to pursue her future. She loved working as a file clerk for the FBI and living in D.C. She shared an apartment with a co-worker, and within a year she met Jerry Overbeck, a soldier from Galveston, Texas. She had found a new gene pool. She always said her intention was to improve the family gene pool by marrying someone not from the Shore.

Ruth Ann's wedding day, with Linda, 1954.

Jerry, too, had a dream – that of being a pharmacist. They married in 1954, and when he left the service three years later, they moved back to Texas with their two little boys, Mike and Steve. They made their home in Austin, where she worked at Brackenridge Hospital to support him in pharmacy school while also taking care of her children. Over the next eight years, Jerry would receive his college degree, get a job as a pharmacist, and four more children would join their family. I saw it as it happened, and I still don't know how they did it.

Aside from her letters home and an occasional summer visit, Ruth Ann and I were not in close contact for about 10 years. However, after I graduated from high school, went to college for a year, and then lived in New York for another year, I decided to pay her a visit in Houston, where they had moved after Jerry's graduation. I was in Key West, Florida, visiting my best high school friend, Kathy Black. I don't remember all the arranging that must have happened. We didn't have cell phones, and we didn't make many long-distance phone calls. It's a marvel now how we ever got to any destination with people waiting for us at the right time. I got on a Greyhound bus in Key West, and arrived in Houston two days later, with Ruth Ann and her family waiting for me at the bus station. I was nearly 20, and she was 27. It was during that visit that we became best friends for the rest of our lives. She would become my role model for parenting, not only because of her mothering me when I was a child, but also because she had her sixth child two days after I had my first one, so she taught me everything she had learned. Ruth Ann was a great mother – always patient, kind, affectionate, and ready for a hearty laugh.

Nearly every summer after my visit, Ruth Ann packed up and loaded the children in the family station wagon, and she and Jerry made the two-day trip from Houston to our parents' house in Snow Hill. Wherever I was living – Pittsburgh, Indianapolis, Baltimore – I always packed up my children and coordinated my visit with hers. We always slept in the same bed on our first night together so we could talk through the night about all the things that had happened in the last year, and about our fears and hopes and dreams for the future. There were times, thinking we had said all our words and as we were drifting off to sleep, one of us would remember something we'd forgotten to share, and we'd be off again.

Maybe it was because she had six children to keep up with and care for, but I always marveled at how she always had whatever someone needed, and not just an extra pair of socks or an aspirin. Once, when we were driving home after picking up a bushel of oysters at the bay, I said to her, "Boy, if I had an oyster knife, I'd stop right here and open a few oysters for our lunch." I saw her digging in her purse, and thought, "No way," and was amazed when she pulled out an oyster knife – nothing to do but pull over at the next picnic area and have raw oysters for lunch. I'm pretty sure if I had said I wanted an oyster stew, she would have pulled out a pint of milk and some oyster crackers, along with the oyster knife.

Ruth Ann's visits were also the highlight of our mother's life. She had depended on Ruth Ann so much while she lived at home and missed her terribly when she left. Over the years, Mother complained that all her daughters had moved away and told us of a "Mrs. So-and-So" whose daughters married locally, lived nearby, and how lucky she was. This lamentation ended in June 1971 when dyed-in-the-wool Texan Jerry Overbeck agreed to accept a job at Welsh Pharmacy in Ocean City, less than an hour from Snow Hill. They moved their six children into a three-bedroom trailer off 22nd Street, then later to a three-bedroom condo on 42nd Street. In March 1972, the Overbecks bought a house at 212 Walston Avenue in Salisbury, just 17 miles from Snow Hill. Jerry purchased Bambridge Drugs in Cambridge, and then Salisbury Drugs in 1975.

From then on, nearly every

Overbeck Family in 1965, from left: Mike, Mark, David, Jerry, Kevin, Ruth Ann, Steve, Susan.

Ruth Ann (left) and Ruth, Ocean City, Md., 1971.

weekend in the summers, I packed up my children after work on a Friday to drive from Baltimore to the Shore. By noon on Saturday, Mom had fried chicken, potato salad, cake, and a thermos of lemonade ready for a picnic on Assateague Island. Off we went with Ruth Ann's six children, my three, and sometimes with Dale and Sandy and their two, and Betty and her two

Jones grandchildren, from left: Susan O., Clif H., Mike O., El-len H., Tony H., Mark O., Kevin O., Robin J., Steve O., David O., c. 1970.

if they were on the Shore. After an afternoon of playing in the surf and sand, and a picnic supper on the beach, the children put together plays and performed for us until dusk called an end to the day. And we were ready to do it all over again the next weekend. If it was a rainy weekend, I stopped in Salisbury to spend Friday night with Ruth Ann and her family. One or more of my children would frequently stay on at her house while I went to Snow Hill the next morning, taking one or two of hers with me.

As our children got older, we began spending a week in Ocean City each summer. One year we each rented apartments on the second floor of a building with a balcony connecting the apartments. I awoke one morning to discover my children gone and immediately ran down to Ruth Ann's apartment where I found everyone sitting around the kitchen table laughing and talking – and eating chocolate cake. "Cake!" I shrieked, "Cake, for breakfast?" And my dear sister said, "Give them something sweet in the morning, and they will stay sweet all day." My children loved their Aunt Ruth Ann. One year at the beach, Ruth Ann and I decided to tackle our dad's clam chowder recipe. We got tired of dicing the potatoes as small as the recipe called for, and we ended up with a soup that we forever-after called "big-potato clam chowder." It was still just as good.

Their stay in Maryland lasted for nearly eight years before they headed back to Texas in 1979, nearly breaking our mother's heart yet again. We had been able to celebrate the weddings of three of Ruth Ann's children during that time, as well as Mom and Dad's 40th wedding anniversary, which Ruth Ann hosted. We got together for family picnics and reunions, many birthdays, and Christmas and Thanksgiving dinners. After their return to Houston, we continued our week at the beach in the summers and gathering whenever and wherever we could for family events. It was during these years that Ruth Ann, Betty, Bobby, and I began to steal away for a week of laughing and bridge. Sometimes we would laugh so hard that we would have to go in different rooms to gain control of ourselves. I remember, once, crawling out of a room because I was laughing so uncontrollably, I couldn't stand up or catch my breath. "I thought I would die laughing" took on new meaning because we thought it really would be possible to die laughing. But wouldn't it have made a good family story? "Yeah, back in the day, I remember the time your Aunt Linda died from laughing."

As our parents aged, Bobby was the first to step up to the plate and invited them to live with him and his partner, Jacques Denier in Cookeville, Tennessee. Bobby met Jacques while he was pursuing post-graduate studies at the Sorbonne in Paris, 1966-68. When Jacques came to visit after Bobby's return to the States, the family met him and welcomed him into the fold as another brother. Jacques was wonderful to our parents and treated them just like his own.

During Mom and Dad's six-year stay in Tennessee, Ruth Ann visited with them for a week or two several times a year to give Bobby and Jacques a chance to get away for a few days for a well-deserved respite from parental oversight. Frequently, I timed my weekend trips there to overlap with Ruth Ann's just to get in a visit albeit a short one. When Bobby was ready to retire, dear Ruth Ann, living north of Houston in the Woodlands, stepped up and offered to take on the responsibility of Mom and Dad. She made arrangements with The Forum, an assisted living facility where they could live near her and Jerry. Ruth Ann visited them daily, did their laundry, took over their finances, and took them to doctor's appointments and shopping. She also included them in family dinners that included three of Ruth Ann's children and six grandchildren who lived nearby.

Every year I went to Texas for a week to oversee mom's care so Ruth Ann and Jerry could take a vacation from care giving. After Dad died in 2002, Mother continued living on her own at the Forum until it became necessary to place her in a higher level of care. That's when Tom and I decided to bring her to Athens to live out her days in our home. Ruth Ann flew with her to Athens and stayed for a week to help her get adjusted. Within a year or so of that time, Ruth Ann had a stroke, so it was perfect timing that Mom came to us when she did. Ruth Ann always felt bad that she couldn't come to relieve me as I had done for her. I did get help from other family members.

When Mother died in 2007, the family gathered on the Shore for her memorial service. Ruth Ann, Betty, and I found a beautiful house to rent on the Chincoteague Bay near Dale and Bobby. Each spring and fall, for the next six years, we spent a week or two on the bay where the family could gather to eat crabs, look at family pictures, tell our stories, and laugh. We decided during our

Ruth Ann, Bobby, Linda, Betty at Captain's Cove on the Chincoteague Bay, Va., 2010.

last visit in 2014 that the next year, after my retirement, we would take a full month to enjoy being together on the bay. Sadly, Ruth Ann died before that could happen.

Ruth Ann was the favorite of everyone in the family, and each of us was her favorite. She would have loved this memoir I've written. I wish I had written it while she was still alive. She was the best of all of us. She always made life easy and fun. Once when she was visiting me in the Big House in Catonsville, Maryland, we decided to paint the kitchen yellow. We bought the paint, came home, and painted the kitchen in one morning. After it dried, we stood back and looked at our job, looked at each other, and said, "It's too YELLOW." After lunch, we went back to the store, bought a more toned-down mellow yellow, came home, and painted the kitchen again that same afternoon. Like I said, she made life easy and fun. I was blessed to have her as my little mommy, my big sister, my role model, my mentor, and my best friend.

Memories with Betty

Before I was born, my sister Betty went to Lynchburg, to live with our mother's sister Aunt Stella and her husband Uncle Hubert. Aunt Stella was 34, Uncle Hubert was 64 and Betty was 4 years old. Aunt Stella went to nurses training in Lynchburg and met her handsome and wealthy husband when she was a nurse and he was on the board of directors of the hospital. They had been married four years when Betty was added to their family. There can only be supposition about their marriage contract negotiations, especially since there was a 30-year age difference. They had dated for several years, and we know that he waited to marry her until his mother, who lived with him, died. Did Stella secure a promise to buy a farm and build a house for her parents? Did she ask him to agree to adopt a child if they were unable to have children? We can't know those things now. There is no one to ask. However, we do know that they married in 1937, and two years later her parents moved into their new house on a farm near Pocomoke paid for by Uncle Hubert. Three years later, in 1940, 4-year-old Betty was living in their home. As a child, I was told, or I assumed, she went there to visit when I was born, as a way of helping my mother. My parents moved six months before I was born, and it is my theory that Aunt Stella was visiting from

Left: Betty in Lynchburg, Va., 1942. Right: Betty (left) with Aunt Stella and Uncle Hubert, 1953.

Lynchburg and offered to take Betty home with her so mother would have one less child to deal with. And then the temporary arrangement became permanent.

While Betty was in Lynchburg, Aunt Stella showered her with beautiful clothes and toys, even a tricycle, and I was told would not let her bring them with her when she came home for visits. I also remember being told that Betty missed her "things" so much that she chose to go back to Lynchburg instead of staying with her family, which she has vehemently refuted. She claimed she would much rather have stayed with her parents and siblings, even when we had no indoor plumbing or central heat and no electricity, than go back to her life of comfort and privilege in Lynchburg.

Betty came home every year for spring break, Christmas, and summer vacations. One year, when Aunt Stella went to a sanitarium for treatment for severe menopausal symptoms, Betty came home for a whole year, her ninth grade of high school. She still claims, even now, that she didn't mind the outhouse or the unheated bedrooms in the winter. I always thought of my sister Betty as a princess, because back in Lynchburg, she lived in a beautiful house with her own sunken bedroom with beautiful matching furniture, an adjoining sitting room with a wall full of books, and a cushioned window seat just perfect for reading. She came home with lovely cashmere sweaters with matching skirts, saddle shoes, and beautiful coats, nightgowns, and fancy underwear, the likes of which I had never seen.

I considered her the chosen one to have been given such an easy and privileged life. In 2017 when I was visiting her in the assisted living facility where she had been dragged kicking and screaming following a stroke five years earlier, we were talking about her life in Lynchburg and my life on the farm. Her puzzled 10-year-old grandson, who was present, asked, "Why didn't Mam live with her family on the farm?" and Betty quickly quipped, "Because I was the throw-away child." Seeing his heartbroken expression, I quickly explained that poor farm families, as we were in the 40s, frequently sent children to live with relatives who were able to offer them a better life. I told him that we always thought that she was the favored one, the one who was given opportunities and a comfortable life. That seemed to satisfy him, but it left me feeling sad about how my sister viewed her life.

Betty was always a fanciful child, which stayed with her as an adult, and we learned that her perceptions didn't always line up with actual facts. If pressed, she might have said they were alternative facts. She told us odd stories that we suspect couldn't possibly be true, but it was never easy to challenge her "memories." For example, not long before she died in 2022, she told me that at the age of 6 Aunt Stella put her on the train in Lynchburg to go to Stockton to visit her family. That meant she traveled alone, on the train, to Norfolk – a five-hour trip. When she got to Norfolk, she claimed she walked the six blocks to the bus station carrying her suitcase to catch the bus to Pocomoke – another four hours that included crossing the Chesapeake Bay on a ferry. If you knew my mother and Aunt Stella, you would know that didn't happen, couldn't happen. They would never let a 16-year-old girl, let alone a six-year-old child, attempt such a journey on her own. Betty's dabbling in fantasy, however, gave her an advantage as a great storyteller, and she could keep her three younger siblings entertained for hours. She was always very loving, easy-going, and good natured. She loved to read and would rather spend time with her nose in a book than going outside to play. And she was beautiful – the prettiest child in the family.

Perhaps preferring my "chosen one" version over her "throw-away" version, she later gave me a new account of how she came to be sent to Lynchburg. She recalled Uncle Hubert telling her that when he was visiting my grandparents, he was reading a newspaper with four-year-old Betty on his lap, reading along with him. Telling my mother how smart she was, he convinced her to let Betty come live with him and Aunt Stella where she would have an opportunity for a better life than if she stayed with her birth family. I'm fairly certain that is not how it happened, but if that version made her happy, I'm ok with it. I do know that Uncle Hubert loved Betty dearly, and his love was returned as long as he lived.

I remember when I was about 9 and she was 14, Betty wove a fantastic story for me about the horses in Australia, and when we grew up, she promised, she would take me there. We spent that summer elaborating about all we would do "down under," the house we would have, and the horses I could have. The funny thing is that she actually won a trip to Australia about 25 years ago, but no mention was ever made of taking me with her, instead of her husband. Alas, she didn't remember our dream. In 1987, I spent a month touring Australia, but not one horse did I see. So, we both got there, just not together.

In 1957, when I was 15 with a newly minted learners permit, Betty was home from college for summer vacation. We got a call from Aunt Stella that Uncle Hubert was sick, and Betty was needed in Lynchburg to help care for him. We talked it over with our parents, and we agreed that Betty and I would drive my dad's 1953 Plymouth the 300 miles to Lynchburg, which involved an hour-long ferry ride from Kiptopeek to Norfolk. We started off early in the morning and were so excited to be free of parental supervision – and on an actual road trip. About 30 miles from home, Betty looked in the rear-view mirror and reported that Dad was following us in mother's car. We decided to act like we hadn't seen him and continued on our way, hoping he would give up his mission and turn around. Eventually, he pulled closer to us, honked his horn, and waved for us to pull over to the shoulder of the road. He informed us that Mom had become so fretful, worrying about us as soon as we drove down the lane that his only option was to come after us and bring us back home. So, around we turned to drive the half hour back to Stockton. Some road trip! The next day, Dad drove us to Pocomoke where we caught a bus to Washington, D.C., and then took a train to Lynchburg. It was my first train ride.

Betty and I have had many wonderful times together over the years. We worked and lived together in Ocean City in the 50s, and spent a year living together in New York City in the 60s. She ended up living in Lynchburg where she married Steve Perrow, and had two children, Waller and Sarah Elizabeth. We took many family vacations together with our parents, Ruth Ann, Bobby, and Dale and their families throughout our lives. Even though Betty wasn't raised in our household, to me, it was as if she had been.

Memories of My Brother Bobby

Even though I can tell stories on my brothers that might put them in a bad light, we can all laugh about them now. The memories and experiences we had as children cemented our relationships. I wrote the following letter, A Snapshot of Memories, to Bobby on the occasion of his 80th birthday in 2017.

. . .

Dear Bobby,

My first memory of you is riding the bus home with you from grade school after we moved to Stockton. I was in first grade and you were in the fifth. I never asked anyone why you lived with Grandmom, Aunt Bessie and Uncle Mervin on the family farm on Little Mill Road, and not with us in town. It's just the way it

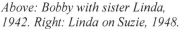
Above: Bobby with sister Linda, 1942. Right: Linda on Suzie, 1948.

was. Walking in the farmhouse kitchen, I can still see Aunt Bessie, standing at the ironing board near the kitchen window, using a flat iron, while listening to Stella Dallas on the radio. After cookies and milk, you and I go upstairs, to find old clothes for me to wear in the barnyard so I won't get my school clothes dirty. You roll up the pant legs of your outgrown trousers, and, when we can't find a belt that will fit me, you thread hay bale twine through the remaining belt loops to hold up my pants. It wasn't a fashion show; I was playing with my big brother.

I don't have a memory of your teaching me to ride a horse, but I'm certain it was you who hoisted me up on your pony, Suzie, for the first time. I'm also sure it was you, who later showed me how to lead Suzie beside a stump that I could climb on so I could swing my leg over her wide back to gain a straddle. As we got older, and you traded Suzie for a bigger horse, I had to ride our neighbor Joyce Ann's little Shetland pony, while you sat astride Sea Star. One evening, as darkness was falling, we had ridden farther afield than we intended which required us to make fast tracks to get home before dark. Galloping along the country roads, I can still hear the hoof beats ringing in the air while I feel myself bouncing up and down with each short pony stride, while you glided across the land.

I can picture us sleeping on the upstairs portico, me in the hammock and you on blankets on the floor, listening to the Whippoorwills and Bobwhites, and whistling back their calls in the dark. At the woodpile the next day, I held out my arms for you to load wood, chunk by chunk, higher than I could see over, and I proudly carried each load onto the porch and dumped it into the wood box, armful by armful until it was full. One day, when I was about ten, you went to the closet and brought down Aunt Bessie's nurses training book and showed me pictures of a woman's reproductive system and told me about menses, and how babies are made. You said that I would soon become a woman and reassured me that I needed to know these things. I remember your playing the piano for me while I belted out a Kay Starr hit, Wheel of Fortune, for a talent show at the elementary school. What I wouldn't give for a recording, or even a picture of that performance. I remember that we practiced a lot. When I was in 6th grade, you told me you had met the boy that I would marry when I grew up. And, I married that boy, Gary Hope, the cousin of your best friend, John Boyer.

When you went away to finish your last two years of high school in Lynchburg, Va., you bequeathed me your horse, Sea Star, and I rode her every chance I got, and I loved her as much as you did. I looked forward to receiving your letters, and even then, I appreciated your correcting my grammar and sending back my letters with the corrections. You taught me to say, "I don't want any potatoes," instead of, "I don't want no potatoes." You'd ask, "Do you want "yes potatoes?" to help me remember. Each time you wrote, you gave me three or four new vocabulary words that you expected me to use in sentences in my next letter to you. I always knew you were doing it to make me a better person, and didn't resent it. When you were home from

Bobby and Linda in Snow Hill, Md., 1968.

college and we were on a double-date, you were the one who taught me to drive a car on Nassawango Road. You also made it conceivable for Mom and Dad to let me work at the beach in Ocean City when I was 15. You told Mom you would look out for me, but I don't remember seeing you for the rest of the summer.

As we got older, we got together many times for a weekend with our sisters and played bridge. We laughed so hard that one of us would have to leave the room so we could catch our breaths in order to finish a sentence...or someone else would finish it for us and that would be even funnier. I remember crawling out of the room once because I was laughing too hard to stand up, and I knew if I didn't leave, I would die laughing. One year, Gary and I visited you in Tennessee on our way home after a vacation in Texas. When we arrived, you had a hot bath waiting for me and insisted dinner would wait until I had soaked away my travels.

After you and Jacques moved to Little Mill Road, you organized a family reunion in 2001. When Tom and I saw the guest list of 50 relatives, we asked

Little Mill Road

Before and After

if we could use your venue for our wedding ceremony. We got married under the maple tree that our dad had planted when he was ten years old and where we had played together when we were children. The entire family salutes you for turning the working family farm into the showplace it is today. You have always been "home" for me even though we grew up in different households. I always felt loved and accepted by you. I treasure our relationship and our lifetime of memories.

Love,
Linda

SNAPSHOT MEMORIES OF DALE AND LINDA

As the sibling closest in age to me, Dale is an integral character in my coming-of-age story. We were best friends and playmates in our early years, and as sometimes happens, became more antagonistic in our teens. I confess to being mostly responsible for that because, truth to tell, I was a tattletale. It took a long time for me to learn that tattling never added any points to my brother's score card. What I remember most about my brother Dale:

Moving from house to house – Chicken Coop, Log Cabin, dusty old farmhouses. Sunday dinners with cousins, aunts, and uncles. Grandmom's chicken and dumplings and Grandpop's apple cider. Side-by-side, we stood on the stairs, singing *Good Night Everyone.*

"Before you start to school," you said, "you have to learn to tie your shoes." We sat under the dining room table, and practiced over and over, until I got it right. "Make a loop and hold it, wrap the lace and push it through. Pull both loops tight," you instructed.

Staying awake all night, singing every song we knew. Reading comic books and listening to the radio, *The Lone Ranger*, *Sky King*, *The Shadow*. Who knows what evil lurks in the hearts of man? The Shadow knew. Saturday night movies in Pocomoke to see our heroes – Batman and Robin, Tarzan, Roy Rogers, and Gene Autry, and then acting out the scenes when we got home.

We built a Bat Cave in the barn. We played Tarzan and Jane, swinging from vines in the woods. We played cowboys and Indians, fighting for survival and dominance. We watched as Spot and Trixie dug for rats under the corn crib. We tamed two pigeons, Casper and Jasper, who flew to our bedroom windowsills and flew to sit on our shoulders when we called them. We climbed to the top of the barn roof when no one was home to see.

Staying at the houseboat in Ocean City. Watching out for the monster in the sea. A trip to the boardwalk. Our favorites – Thrasher's French fries, Dumser's ice cream, and Dolle's popcorn. We rode the Ferris wheel, tilt-a-whirl, merry-go-round. I remember meeting at the Fun House before the long journey home. Singing in the car, everywhere we went.

Ladies Aid picnics at Public Landing with Aunt Bessie. Crabbing and swimming in the bay. Riding the bus to high school. Singing in the church choir and going to revival meetings. Going to the farm with Bobby, and playing in the barn loft. Hanging from the hay fork, holding tight all the way to the rafters. Letting go and falling to the soft pile of hay below. Throwing calves and riding cows and pigs and mules.

Climbing trees. Playing tag. *You're it. You can't catch me. Let's play hide and seek. Count to 100*

Above: Linda (left) and Dale on Log Cabin pond, 1945. Below: Linda and Dale at the Little Mill Road farm, 2000.

Dale's and Linda's children with Robin in Indian costumes. Back: Micky, Robin, Tony; front: Ellen, Clif, Hansel, Andrea, c. 1970.

backwards while I hide. Racing to the house when darkness fell. *Last one in is a rotten egg. Olly, olly, in free.*

We were happy with oranges, apples, and nuts in our Christmas stockings, along with a comic book and a candy bar. Ice skating in our shoes on Big Mill Pond. Our first taste of pizza. I thought it would be a pie. Riding on a sled in the snow, pulled behind a pickup truck because there were no hills.

Checking off our chores listed on the kitchen wall so we could get our allowance. Washing and drying dishes. Raising chickens and rabbits and pigs. 4-H Club meetings and fairs. Selling vegetables from the garden so we could go somewhere. Working at the Tastee-Freez. Then to Ocean City to work at Joe's. Leaving home when our time came. Having families of our own. Our children becoming friends who still love each other. They learned what we had known.

MY DAD

One night in 2001, as I was lying in bed waiting for sleep to transport me to the dream world, I began thinking of my father, his approaching 90th birthday, and our 60 years together. I decided I was going to recount everything I could remember about him – from my very earliest memory. I closed my eyes and allowed my mind to go back in time in search of the first picture I had of my dad.

It was a cold and snowy day in December, shortly after hog killing time, when I decided to make my grand entrance into the Jones clan. I was the youngest of six. Mom, Dad, and Grandmom McGee were enjoying fresh sausage for lunch, and Sonny and Ruth Ann were in school when I announced my impending arrival. Dad went to a neighbor's house to call the doctor and then to fetch the midwife.

George and Linda at the Log Cabin, 1943.

While he was gone, the three generations of women – Butler, McGee, and Jones – did what women have done since the beginning of time. Grandmom attended my birth and held me in her arms, cord intact, until Dad returned with the midwife; the doctor arrived later.

I'm certain that as soon as he could, Dad gently took me in his arms while the ladies buzzed about their birthing baby chores. I am also certain that he gazed lovingly into my face and that I looked intently back, connecting with his eyes, as only a tiny baby can. I'm sure, in that moment, our souls met beyond our shimmering eyes, assuring each other that we were bonded for life and that we would love, protect, and honor each other, a promise stronger than any marriage vow ever spoken – father and daughter.

...

Every year, my father planted a garden that provided vegetables for our family throughout the summer. I remember both sets of grandparents canning every fall, but our garden was emptied, leaving nothing for canning. One of the reasons we didn't have vegetables to can was because Dad enlisted us kids to help him sell vegetables off the back of a pickup truck. He would wake us up early, and we'd all head to the garden to pick baskets of sweet corn, tomatoes, and beans, then load them on the truck. We then headed to Snow Hill to Harrison's Peach Orchard to buy baskets of peaches, then on to a farm near Salisbury to buy cantaloupes and watermelons. Then we'd drive to Pocomoke to set up shop at Corny Wilkerson's gas station.

I loved helping Dad when I was little, but when I got to be 11 and 12, it was humiliating to be so poor that you had to sell produce to get money. When a customer said, "Oh, you're selling some of your vegetables, huh?" And my dad answered with a grin, "Yeah, just trying to get a little money to go 'sommers'," I would hang my head in shame. My little girl eyes and heart could not see that he was a man ahead of his time – with his own organic farmer's market. Seventy years later, I can say with certainty that I have never tasted any vegetables or fruit that were as good as the ones my dad grew or bought. He claimed it was the sand in the soil that make the cantaloupe and watermelon so tasty, and the rich, black loamy soil that was perfect for corn and tomatoes.

Left: George, Linda, Ruth at Public Landing, 1946. Center: George and Linda with 40th wedding anniversary present, a china cabinet, 1972. Right: Linda and George in Cookeville, Tenn., 1992.

My dad was famous in our family for never being able to pass up a good bargain. I will never forget the cases of canned vegetables he purchased at Willie's Fair, a discount store in Salisbury. The boxes were filled with cans of assorted vegetables – lima beans, peas, green beans, and spinach. The reason they were so cheap was because they didn't have labels on them. Dad stacked the cases upstairs in the little room that opened to the attic stairs. Whenever I was sent to get a can of vegetables for dinner, I prayed on my way upstairs, while making my selection, and back down to the kitchen, "Please don't let this be spinach." Although all the choices were bad, spinach was the worst. One year while shopping at Willie's Fair, Dad

Linda, Betty, Ruth Ann try out new red bathing suits in Stockton, 1949.

discovered they were having a close-out sale on bathing suits. My sisters and I were delighted when he showed us the three red bathing suits he bought for us. We put them on right away and ran outside to turn the hose on ourselves to try them out. It didn't take us long to run back inside and take them off because they were so scratchy. We never wore them again.

My father's job as game warden afforded him the use of a small motorboat, which we sometimes used to go crabbing. While my dad went to the chicken plant where my mother worked to get chicken necks to use for bait, Dale and I uncoiled the two 150-foot trotlines. Once Dad returned, we attached a chicken neck every 4-5 feet, using slip knots, then re-coiled the lines in a bushel basket. The Scarborough Landing boat ramp, between Stockton and Girdletree where we launched the boat, was only 10 minutes from home. Within an hour we could be in the boat with our crab net and basket of trotlines baited with chicken necks. After much yelling by my mercurial dad, the boat would finally be unloaded from the trailer and lowered in the water. After we were all aboard, he would then motor the boat to stobs visible above the waterline. We'd string a trotline between two stobs, about 100 feet apart, then repeat this procedure nearby for the second trotline.

After giving the crabs sufficient time to be drawn to the chicken necks, Dad lined the boat up with the first trotline, and trolling slowly along, my job was to gently pick up the line while Dale, using the crab net, scooped under the crab, feasting on the neck. If it was a male crab, and if it was large enough to keep, he would dump it in the basket; the little ones and the female crabs were tossed back in the water to grow and to go forth and multiply. Back and forth we went

Above: George poses in his game warden uniform, c. 1950. Right: George digs for clams, c. 1963.

until our bushel basket was full of crabs for dinner. After the work was done, Dad always gave us time to swim and play in the bay while he went clamming.

One might assume that I would have learned how to swim because of the amount of time I spent in the water. They would be wrong. The one and only time anyone came close to trying to teach me to swim was on a day after crabbing when I continued to play in the water after being told to get in the boat. After Dad's last unheeded warning, he started the motor, saying he was going to shore to load the boat on the trailer, and I could walk back to the landing. The water was only chest deep in the bay, and it was less than 50-yards to the dock, so I was enjoying the extra time in the water. Especially, I was glad that I wouldn't have to listen to my dad yell instructions about getting the boat out of the water and back onto the trailer. I don't think it ever occurred to him that he could complete that task without yelling.

Since I had always been in the boat between where we crabbed and clammed and the landing, I was oblivious to the fact that there was a deep channel ahead. As I cheerfully walked through the water nearing the boat ramp, I suddenly stepped off the muddy bottom of the bay, into the channel, discovering the water was well over my head. As I began thrashing around and screaming for help, Dale and Dad cheered me on from the shoreline, encouraging me to swim to them. I finally got control of my lizard mind, and eventually used a modified dog paddle and was able to get across the channel to land. I was furious with Dad and Dale. I never learned to swim properly, or even improve on that dog paddle.

During the summer months when we were out of school, Dad would sometimes take Dale and me with him to work. One time, we met a local chicken farmer at a fox den in the forest. The farmer, tired of the foxes killing his chickens, had called my father, the game warden, to take care of the varmints. I watched from the car as Dad gassed the den, killing the mother and her cubs.

Since I now love foxes, I always feel sad that I watched that scene without feeling remorse or sadness for a life not lived. I was a tough little farm girl, and having raised chickens, knew that chickens gotta live.

On a lighter note, another time, we set out wild turkeys and their baby chicks to increase the turkey population in the Pocomoke Forest. Now when I'm on the Shore, it is common to see a flock of turkeys foraging at the edge of the woods, and I like to think I helped make that happen. Another one of my favorite outings with Dad was planting loblolly pine trees in straight rows. It was always fun, in future years, to drive down that stretch of road and see how the trees were growing. As they got bigger, the rows became more obvious, and it felt rewarding to know I had a hand in planting them.

MY MOM

I wrote the following tribute and letter to my mom on the occasion of her 90th birthday in 1995. Each of her seven children and 15 grandchildren wrote memories of her, and we made the words of praise into a booklet. I include my letter here to offer a picture of her many virtues.

· · ·

By the time Mom got to me – the sixth child – she had already changed upwards of 50,000 diapers. Not just changed them, but washed them on a scrub board, rinsed and wrung them out by hand, and hung them outside on a clothesline to dry. Sometimes in the winter, when she took the diapers off the line, they would be frozen, stiff as boards. She brought them in and folded and stacked them. If she changed that many diapers, I started wondering how many bottles she sterilized, how many nights she was awakened by a child's cry, how many days and nights had she tended a sick child with whooping cough, measles, mumps, chickenpox, scarlet fever? How many spoonsful of baby food did she lovingly put in our mouths? How many times did she say, "God is good. God is great. Now I lay me down to sleep?"

My Tribute to Mother is a montage of memories, snapshots collected through the years, and woven into the fabric of who I am. I didn't know until I was a grown woman, and pregnant with my firstborn, that I had been born at home, delivered by Grandmom McGee – just after they finished a lunch of sausage – from a freshly butchered pig, I was told. I was preparing to deliver my firstborn by "natural" childbirth, thinking I was doing something on the leading edge, when she told me that's how she had birthed her last two children – Dale and me.

As a child, I remember standing next to my mom, leaning against her, while she was talking with someone. She would absently gather my hair in her fingers, and smooth it behind my ear, over and over. Even after her repetitious stroke be-

came annoying to me, I didn't stop her because I loved her touch so much. She still has the most beautiful and tender hands. I remember her sitting in the front seat of the car with Dad, getting all of us to sing along with them. It not only kept us all focused and quiet, it also engendered teamwork and harmony. I always loved her finale solo, Mona Lisa. *On Sat-*

Ruth holding Linda, with Bobby (left) and Dale, 1942.

urday nights, Mom and Dad took us kids to the movies in Pocomoke while they shopped for the weekly groceries. When they finished, Mom would be sure Dad parked the car in front of the theater so I could run out to the lobby to make sure I hadn't been left behind. It didn't matter to me that I could see that my brothers and sisters were still in the theater. I wanted to make sure Mom was there.

Of course, I always loved our family trips to the Ocean City boardwalk. While the kids scattered to the four directions, Mom and Dad would situate themselves on a bench in front of the fun house, so we would know where to find them. I'm sure I made several trips back and forth, between the merry-go-round and the ferris wheel, to make sure my touchstone was still there. I never considered, until now, how many times she must have heard the repetitive cackle of the fun house Laughing Woman, "Sal," as she leaned to and fro, "Ah, ha, ha, ha, ha, ha, ha, ha" over and over. When we were finished for the day, Mom would be sure to have a box of Dolle's caramel popcorn or Thrasher's French fries for us to share on the long ride home.

One Christmas Eve, when I was about eight years old and Dad was in the hospital, Mom and I went to stay overnight at Grandmom McGee's. It was the year Santa Claus brought my dollhouse, constructed of painted sheet metal – fully furnished with plastic furniture, a fireplace and curtains painted on the walls, rugs painted on the floor, and it even had a bathroom. To me, it was a four-room "mansion," home to the hard rubber family that came with it. I also got a Betsy Wetsy doll that year – one that had a bottle and "wetted." I thank you, Mom, for working all those years, and sacrificing so much, in order to give us more than the essentials, symbolizing your love and caring.

I loved going to Grandmom McGee's with Mom. It was there I learned to play Canasta, and said my first "bad word" in front of both of them when Grandmom "went out," leaving me with a hand full of points. Neither Mom nor Grandmom fussed, and I could tell they had a hard time concealing their laugh-

ter. After Grandmom's first stroke, she came to stay with us for a couple of months to recuperate. Dad rigged up a pulley next to Grandmom's place at the kitchen table so she could exercise her arm. I remember Mom encouraging her to hold the handle on the pulley with her bad arm, and they would get to laughing about Grandmom's cradling her arm "like

Ruth and Grandmom Martha McGee on Dividing Creek Road, Pocomoke, Md., 1955.

a baby," certainly finding humor in a bad situation.

I remember when Mom and Dad had friends over for an evening of card playing. After going upstairs to bed, I could still hear them all laughing and having a good time. I loved being with Mom when she was with her friends – especially Jean McFord and Mabel Burbage – because they always laughed so much. Jean worked with us at the Tastee-Freez, and she and Mom would laugh so hard that they could hardly wait on customers, and the customers and I would laugh right along with them. When I was getting ready to go away to college, Mom wanted to make sure I would make a good presentation at school. She and I took all my skirts and dresses to Mabel's house and spent the day, measuring and shortening hemlines. I remember feeling so grown up, that I was one of "them" – working, talking and laughing with Mom and her friend.

I learned many valuable lessons from my mom; the most memorable was "Don't waste time complaining about a task – use that time to get your work done." In the summertime, I heeded that advice for I knew that as soon as my assigned chores were finished, I could take off the rest of the day, exploring the countryside and woods on my horse. Mom always gave me the freedom to exercise my independence and trusted me to use good judgement. Given that Mom enjoyed her life, she also advised her children, "Always find the humor in a situation. No matter how bad something might seem, there's always something to laugh about."

I lived at home the first six months of my pregnancy with Tony while Gary was finishing college. Mother made maternity dresses for me – one a beautiful, elegant blue brocade outfit that I wore to Gary's graduation. After Ellen was born, she also made dresses for her. Whenever someone complemented Ellen's clothes, I always felt proud to say, "My Mom made that." Mom potty trained all three of my children. I always said that I would never bribe my children, but she certainly changed my mind after she trained each of them in three days by

Linda's blue brocade maternity outfit, 1963.

bribing them with M&Ms. This was after I had spent weeks or probably months.

Mom, I not only appreciate all the ways you showed that you loved and cared for me, but also all the wonderful memories you helped to build for my children. Whenever we went to your house, you always welcomed us with open arms and a bountiful spread of our favorite foods. While Dad initiated sweet corn, crabs, oysters, and clams, you were the one who introduced the children to dumplings, cornbread, and homemade ice cream. My children always loved being at Mom Mom's and I always felt they were in the best of hands there. When we lived in Baltimore, we went to Snow Hill almost every weekend in the summertime. Mom, you were always ready with hampers of fried chicken, hamburgers to cook on the grill, potato salad, iced tea, and after lunch, off we would go to Assateague Island with all the kids – whoever was there – for an afternoon at the beach and a picnic supper. What wonderful memories!

Mom, you always prepared the most lavish holiday dinners – for casts of dozens. Both the dining and kitchen tables were extended to their limit to accommodate all of us. Everything was hot and ready to go on the tables at the same time, and there were always leftovers to be enjoyed the following day. It was the norm to have three meat dishes (turkey, ham, and crab imperial), 3-4 vegetable dishes (always turnip greens, a favorite), rolls and sweet potato biscuits, and two kinds of dressing (sage, especially for Ruth Ann and oyster). You always made the best cakes and pies in the world, and it seemed an unending supply. No matter what time my family arrived for a visit, it seemed there was always fried chicken, or leftover crab cakes, and turnip greens in the refrigerator for us to eat after our long journey. And, Mom, it always seemed to me that you did all this with the greatest of ease, good humor, and enjoyment. I always said that you could work circles around me – even into your 70s.

I love you, Mom, and thank you from the bottom of my heart for being my mom – for loving me and for always wanting the best for me. Thank you for loving my children and for sharing your love, your wisdom, and your humor with them. Thank you for helping us build all these wonderful memories – of a warm and vibrant household filled with love and laughter.

Love,
Linda

MEMORIES OF GRANDMOM AND GRANDPOP MCGEE ON DIVIDING CREEK

In the spring of 2018, while purging and organizing my file cabinet, I came across a 100th Wedding Anniversary Salute to my maternal grandparents, Noah and Martha McGee. Bobby, our family historian, had put it together in November of 2000, having invited the 25 grandchildren to share their memories of our grandparents. I discovered that my memories were missing; I must have been traveling at the time the tribute was assembled. I decided then and there to capture every memory I had, especially of my grandmother, as a way of honoring my relationship with her. The following account, written February 11, 2019, turned out to be the beginning of my memoir and served as the inspiration to write my autobiography. Eighteen years makes a difference in one's perspective. We realize that if we don't record our memories today, they will die when we do. How I would love to read my mother's and grandmother's memories of their grandparents.

In 1900, when my grandmother, Martha Butler, was 16 years old, she married my grandfather, Noah McGee, 12 years her senior. Over the next 26 years, they had 10 children – six sons and four daughters – and during that time, they moved 10 times with the help of Old Dan, their mule. My grandfather was a tenant farmer, and when a better situation presented itself, he packed up the family's meager possessions and moved to the next house that was provided.

The oldest of their children, my Uncle Russell, died at the early age of 25

Left: Grandparents Noah and Martha McGee, North Wales, Pa., 1957. Right: McGee Family from left: (front) Buster, Ruth, Bertie; (middle) Grandpop Noah holding Edwin, Grandmom Martha holding L.J.; (back) Hazel, Russell, Stella, c. 1920.

when the car he was driving was struck by a train. On July 3, 1926, he had driven into town, accompanied by two young cousins, ages 13 and 7, to buy supplies for the July 4th celebration planned for the following day. My mother, age 12, begged to go too, but my grandmother kept her home to help with preparations for the party. July 4th, thereafter, was never celebrated with any degree of joy in the family. It was only a bitter memory of a tragic family loss, along with quiet gratitude that my mother was not with them when the accident happened. In 1926, Martha not only lost her oldest son, Russell, but her beloved mother died too – all this while she was nursing her 10th and final baby. It was an unbearable year for my grandmother, yet she bore it all.

Two of Grandmom's daughters, Stella and Bertie, left home after high school for nurses training and both married well – Bertie, a dentist, and Stella, a businessman. By 1939, Stella was situated well enough to buy a small farm outside of Pocomoke on Dividing Creek Road where she built a house for my grandparents to live in until they crossed the River Jordan – Grandpop in 1960 and Grandmom in 1965. The house had all the modern conveniences of running water, indoor plumbing, central heat, and best of all, they never had to move again. Seven of their children set up their own homes in the same area; three (eventually five) lived within a short walk down the lane and across the county road from my grandparents' house. Since I was born in 1941, this was the only house I knew them to occupy. I am aware, from a child's perspective, that I thought those years were a lifetime, but it was only 25 years – such a short time span now.

Even though I was the 11th grandchild, I like to think my grandmother and I formed a special, unbreakable bond in those first moments of my life when she held me in her arms awaiting the arrival of the midwife. However, the connection started long before my birth. I was amazed when I learned in later years that my grandmother had carried part of me inside her womb when she was pregnant with my mother. Since a female fetus is born with all the eggs she will ever have in her lifetime, I was a tiny egg in my mother's ovaries when she was in Grandmom's womb.

I grew up in Stockton about 10 miles from my grandparent's house, and typically my family paid a

Grandmom and Grandpop McGee's house on Dividing Creek Road, built by daughter Stella, 1965.

visit on Sunday afternoons when various aunts, uncles, and cousins assembled. I had 19 cousins of varying ages and five brothers and sisters, so there was always an assortment of youngsters to play with. We children played outside while the adults had dinner, after which we were called in to eat. Neither of my grandparents were disciplinarians, in part because Grandpop's sister, Aunt Ella, who lived with them, sat on the porch, watching us children like a hawk. When any of us strayed out of her approved territory and began moving toward the chicken house or barn, she raised her cane over her head, shaking it at us, and yelling, "Ott, ott, ott" as a reminder to remember where we were not supposed to be.

When Aunt Bertie brought her daughters Peggy Ann and Bobby Lynn from North Wales, Pennsylvania, to visit our grandparents, I usually was invited to spend a night or two with Bobby Lynn, since we were just a year apart in age. She was the only girl in the family close to my age. I recall our stealing a cigarette on one of those sleepovers, probably from one of our mothers. Sneaking it upstairs to the room we slept in, we opened the window for the smoke to escape, because surely no one would be able to smell cigarette smoke with the window open. Since I don't recall any repercussions from that escapade, I conclude that we got away with it.

My grandfather, an avid reader of Zane Gray and other Western writers, could always be found

Above: From left, cousins Peggy Ann and Bobby Lynn with Dale, Linda, Ruth Ann, 1944. Below: Maternal grandparents Noah and Martha McGee, 1955.

with his face buried in a book, one leg draped over the arm of his chair. Bobby Lynn tells the story that one day when she and Grandpop were reading in the living room, he called to Grandmom in the kitchen to come close the window because it was getting chilly. Bobby Lynn thought that was the height of laziness, but my grandmother catered to his request. In fact, my grandmother shaved my grandfather every week of his life. With a towel draped around his neck, he situated himself on a chair in front of the kitchen sink, watching while she sharpened the straight razor on a strap and prepared the brush and soap. We grandkids always gathered around to watch the shaving process. I always thought that it was an unusual sight but was fascinated, nevertheless. I never heard them argue, and I never heard them speak ill of anyone. According to family lore, I don't think anyone else ever did either.

I remember going to the chicken house with my grandfather to help him feed and water the chickens. Because of the smell, I only liked helping when the chickens were babies and the wood shavings new and fresh. There was a long wooden trolley attached to a track on the ceiling that could be pulled from one end of the chicken house to the other. Feed sacks and water (and sometimes me) were loaded onto the trolley and pulled down the length of the house, to distribute feed and water to the biddies. I helped collect the water jars, fill them, and set them out again while Grandpop poured feed into the bins. In the fall, he kept a wooden cask filled with apple cider in the feed room, and a small cup was my reward for helping.

Early on, my grandparents cleared two paths to Dividing Creek that ran along the edge of their property. One path led through the open field behind the barn and into the woods to the creek. The other was behind the chicken house. Benches were constructed at each bank so the fishermen could sit. When Grandmom announced it was time to go fishing, I helped her dig worms that we found under old pieces of wood and rocks. We put the worms in a can and when we had a sufficient number, she and I walked down to the creek to do some fishing. Sitting on the bench on Dividing Creek with my grandmother catching perch and sunfish was always a highlight of my visits. I don't recall that we kept them to eat because they were fairly small. Once when I was about 8 and

McGee grandparents' Dividing Creek farm, Pocomoke, Md.

fishing with Grandpop, I asked him how deep he thought the water was. When he answered, "It's up past your pretty little thing," I was shocked into silence. I was humiliated that he would mention my "thing," such a "no-no." Sad to say, it's the only "conversation" I remember having with him.

One Christmas, when I was 8, when my dad was in the hospital with tick fever or to have a cancerous finger removed, my mother and I went to stay with Grandmom and Grandpop. When I came downstairs Christmas morning I found the most beautiful doll house, complete with plastic molded furniture and a little rubber family – parents and a baby for the crib. I also got a Betsy Wetsy "drink and wet" doll who had a tube running from her slightly opened mouth to her lower plumbing. Whenever I gave her a bottle of water, I had to change the diaper after the water ran through. I'm sure my doll housekeeping and diaper changing chores kept me busy and out of the way for several days when I stayed with Grandmom while Mom visited Dad in the hospital.

My grandmother loved to play cards – mostly Canasta and Rook. She taught all her 25 grandchildren how to play and was always eager to get out the card table. One particular evening when I was playing Canasta with my mom and grandmom, I was strategically saving up my melds so that I could "go out" in a blaze of glory to win the game. Suddenly, Grandmom laid down all her cards and "went out." I was so shocked and utterly dismayed that she beat me to it that the word, "Shit!" slipped out before I realized it. It took all of us by such surprise. I sat, embarrassed, as I watched both my mom and grandmom erupt in laughter. I was afraid I would get a tongue lashing, but it was all brushed aside, as was my displeasure at being beaten, again, by my grandmother.

One of my favorite places at Grandmom's house was her side porch. I loved to sit on the porch swing and read. It was also there that I helped Grandmom shell black-eyed peas and butter beans – sitting, rocking, and shelling. That was pure heaven. One of my chores when I visited was helping with the dishes. My job was to dry while Grandmom washed. On one occasion, I picked up a wet dish and saw that it was not thoroughly clean. When I handed it back to my grandmother, pointing out that it wasn't clean, she said with a chuckle, "It's a common dish dryer that can't clean a dish." I wish I could remember more of our conversations. They have all been reduced to two or three pitiful sentences. I always felt loved by my grandmother and tolerated by my grandfather.

My grandmother had a stroke when I was living in New York 1960-61. When I came home to visit her in the hospital, she was amazed that I was there. "You've come all that distance just to see me." When she had a second stroke a couple of years later, losing the use of her right arm, she came to stay with my parents in Snow Hill for her recuperation. I had left New York by then and was living at home, working in Salisbury at GMAC. Dad rigged a pulley next to her place at the kitchen table so that she could attach a strap to her right hand and use her left to pull the lame arm up and down, exercising it. When she was finished, she would cradle her right arm against her body, holding it with her left hand, and she and mother, laughingly, started calling it her "baby."

In December of 1962 I married Gary Hope. When I was looking for something old and something borrowed, Grandmom offered to lend me her wedding ring to satisfy both re-

Four Generations, from left: Grandmother Ruth Mc-Gee Jones, Great-Grandmother Martha McGee holding Tony, and Mother Linda, 1963.

quirements. When I returned the ring to her, I thanked her for allowing it to be a part of my wedding ceremony. A few years later, the ring was given to my cousin, Mary Beth. As a baby, Mary Beth had been taken to Philadelphia by her mother when she divorced Uncle Billy. I was 10 at the time and never saw Mary Beth again. I heard that she came to visit her father before her own wedding, and Uncle Billy gave her Grandmother's ring. As far as I know, she didn't come to visit the family again. I have spent some time on the internet searching for her, but have been unable to find a thread to pull.

The next winter when I came home to visit, I brought my first-born Tony to meet his Great Grandmother McGee. When I put him in her arms, I thought about her being present at my birth and holding me. And it was a good opportunity to have a picture taken with four generations. Even with 25 grandchildren and 18 great-grandchildren, it was easy to see the love she showered on the new little ones when she took them in her arms. Tony is the only one of my children who got to meet his great-grandmother.

My memories of my time with my grandparents are few, but I treasure each one of them. I am fortunate my brother is the family historian. He kept every letter he received and even made copies of the ones he wrote. From time to time, he will bring out one to share, giving us all a glimpse through the window of our childhood. He found a trove of 20 letters that Grandmom McGee wrote to her daughter Stella in the 1950's. Bobby is publishing them in the *McGee Chronicles*, an accounting of the life of Grandmom and Grandpop McGee and their 10 children.

MEMORIES OF GRANDMOM AND GRANDPOP JONES ON LITTLE MILL ROAD

My paternal grandfather Marion Thomas Jones died before I was 2 years old, so I have no memories of him. My grandmother Annie died when I was in sixth grade, and my memories of her are few. She was sick and in bed often, and her daughter Aunt Bessie was more like a grandmother to me. I remember Grandmom telling me that when Grandpop first held me and saw that I was holding my tiny hands

Grandparents Marion and Annie Jones, c. 1933.

into tight little fists, he predicted that I would be tightfisted with my money. The stories my brother Bobby told me are the only way I truly know my grandfather.

In 2008-09, Bobby sailed around the world for six months on a container ship, the *Singapore*. With plenty of free time for his mind to wander, he started thinking about our grandfather who died in 1943 when Bobby was 5½ years old. My brother had been living with our grandparents for two years when Grandpop died, and Marion was more like a father than his grandfather. Bobby mused that since his memories would disappear when he passed from this world, he should get busy harvesting every memory he had so Grandpop wouldn't be forgotten. He didn't want to lose a single memory, and every day, as he made the rounds of the *Singapore* deck, he called up every fragmented memory archived in his mind.

His best memory of Grandpop, he said, is of their skipping together. For a long time, Bobby was not able to pronounce words with two consonants together. For example, instead of saying "skip," he would say "sip." In another domain, he was slow mastering the art of skipping. He could skip with one foot but not with both. Bobby was told much later that he used to say, "Grandpop, look at me, I can sip on one soot." Grandpop, by then 70, would skip right along with his young grandson, both laughing and skipping together. "It was a total transcendent joy."

As a man is sometimes clumsy when he tries to put a tie on someone else, so was Grandpop when he helped Bobby get dressed. As his grandson faced him, Grandpop would hold Bobby's underwear up as if he, himself, were going to step in, and, of course, it ended up backwards on the child. This amused both of them a great deal, and Bobby would laugh because Grandpop was laughing. Grandpop frequently took Bobby with him when he was working in the field. Bobby always considered it a privilege to be allowed to ride on Kate the mule's back as Grandpop plowed the fields. What friends they all were! Grandpop, Bobby, and Kate too.

Bobby on Kate the mule, 1941.

The only time Bobby could remember Grandpop's anger was the spring, perhaps 1942, when Bobby decided to have his own sweet potato patch. Grandpop was setting out sprouts in the field behind the barn while his grandson prepared his own garden right next to the barn. He doesn't know why he didn't ask for some sweet potato slips, but after the day's work was done and Grandpop was safely in the house, Bobby went into the sweet potato field and pulled up a slip here and a slip there, probably not more than 20. "He will not notice," he thought to himself.

Whether the misdeed was discovered the next day because of the missing spots in his freshly laid out rows, or whether he found the new garden spot, we don't know, but Grandpop yelled out from the scene of the crime loud enough for his voice to reach Bobby playing in the house. He doesn't remember being punished – Grandpop didn't even come to the house to scold him, but the hollering hurt as much as a good thrashing would have done.

One day Bobby went with Grandpop to Pocomoke, where he was to get a haircut while Grandpop ran errands. Bobby was aware that he would be left alone in the barbershop, so he made a special effort to pay close attention to where the car was parked so he could find his way back. As they walked to the barbershop about two blocks away, he noticed that it involved two turns. Once inside, Grandpop told his grandson to wait in the barbershop after his haircut for him to return.

While waiting, Bobby remembered watching for Grandpop's arrival through the screen door. Becoming bored with waiting, he decided to surprise his grandfather and wait for him in the car. Trusting his memory, he proceeded toward the car, making the two turns, only to find a strange car in its place. Or, maybe he failed to remember correctly? Bobby started down the street studying each car with negative results, and suddenly overtaken with panic, he began to cry. He was soon rescued by a woman of Amazonian proportions who scooped him up and held him close to her bosom as my brother cried. By the time they returned to the barbershop, Grandpop was arriving, and Bobby was one happy little boy. He doesn't remember being scolded, but he learned a good lesson, "DO AS YOU ARE TOLD."

Oyster shells were an important commodity for road building in the early days. In certain counties of New Jersey, oyster-shell roads were in use soon after the Civil War. A 1907 local newspaper article stated: "Once in good condition, shell roads are undoubtedly more satisfactory to travel over for horse, man, or automobile than the majority of roads. They are almost noiseless and seem to possess a resiliency unequaled by any other material that can be considered by a rural district."

Until 1876, since Stockton was built on top of a sand hill, its name was "Sandy Hill." When cart loads of oysters wended their way up George Island Landing Road from the bay to Stockton's train station, the drivers dreaded the incline at the intersection. The sand was so bad that the wheels of the cart sometimes sank all the way down to the axle. Our own grandfather began spreading oyster shells on the lane to his house – where Bobby lives now – as soon as it was built in 1913. Eight or 10 times each winter, when there was less field work, he hooked up his mule to the horse-cart to travel the 4 miles to George Island Landing to get a load of oyster shells. Grandpop considered speed next to Godliness. For example, whenever someone was helping him gather corn, he would challenge the helper to a race – who can get to the end of his row first? Grandpop would quickly pull out in front and then taunt the helper by also picking corn in the helper's row – and he would still win the race.

When Ralph Boston took up residence on the adjoining farm, he soon saw Marion going to the Bay for oyster shells and decided to do likewise. Knowing that Marion always rose even before the chickens, he made sure to get on the road before Marion. One day he was elated, thinking that he had beaten Marion. But, as he drew near to the Stockton intersection, lo and behold, there came Marion from the opposite direction, horse-cart full of oyster shells, on his way back home from the Bay.

"Good morning to you, Marion. I see you got an early start."

"Second load, Ralph, second load, and good morning to you."

Grandpop waited too long to check out a nagging health problem. It turned out to be cancer – likely colon or stomach cancer – but too far advanced for surgery to help. Dr. Nock operated on him, but found the cancer had spread throughout his body, and he died within a week or two. Bobby, was allowed to visit him only one time in the hospital, just two days before his death Grandmom allowed Bobby to be the one to announce the birth of 12 puppies to his favorite bird-dog. Grandmom would say years later, "That was the last time anyone saw Marion smile."

"I remember seeing Grandpop stomp on new black walnuts to break the hull off," Bobby said. "Now, 75 years later, as I sit in my lazy-boy picking out black walnuts, as I was doing last evening ... walnuts from the same tree whose walnuts he stomped on, I am comforted by the thought that this humble task still links us across an immense chasm of time. It gives continuity to a life that often seems jumbled, disjointed, and random. Yes, I was alone on the Singapore, which was heading across the Pacific, a crossing that required 17 days of nothing but water and sky, sky and water. But, thanks to the gift

Above: Grandpop Marion with Frank and Kate. Below: Grandmom Annie with her turkeys, c. 1938. (Credit: Frank Jones)

of memory, and the life-gift of someone like Grandpop to reflect on and write about, I felt as though I was accompanied by a host of angels."

AUNT BESSIE, MY DAD'S SISTER

Aunt Bessie, my father's oldest sister, arrived in this world on October, 27, 1900, the first of five children born to Marion and Annie Jones. She left home and hearth on Little Mill Road near Stockton just twice in her life. When starting school, she went to live with her grandparents 8 miles away in Pocomoke so she could easily walk to the nearby elementary school. This allowed her to avoid the two-mile walk, or the horse-cart ride, from the farm to Stockton School, and also avoid missing days due to bad weather. It took Aunt Bessie 14 years to finish 11 years of schooling and earn her high school diploma. She admitted that she had "a terrible time with math," which she finally managed to get through with tutoring after school. Bobby heard her say that once she got a high grade on a Latin quiz, and the teacher said aloud to the class, "I think Bessie sleeps

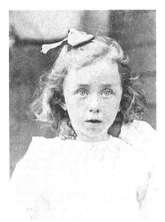 

Bessie Gertrude Jones in 1906 (left) and 1916 (right).

with her Latin book under her pillow."

Aunt Bessie left the farm again to go to nurses training, but got so homesick after a few weeks that she returned home for good. Bessie got a job at Mason's Hardware store in Stockton, but again met her math waterloo. Whenever she had to make change at the cash register, she was frequently reduced to tears and finally renounced the only 9-5 job she would ever hold. When Mason's store closed in 1963, my Uncle Mervin bought the stool that stood at the cash register. It still sits in Bobby's kitchen, reminding us all of Aunt Bessie sitting on it, trying to make change.

Aunt Bessie was a big help to her mother in all the household chores, especially with the younger children. As she got older, she was given the responsibility of taking care of the farm poultry. In early spring Aunt Bessie and Grandmom would buy 250 "biddies" and place them in a brooder house equipped with a coal-burning stove with a circular hood, which the baby chicks would huddle under to stay warm during the night. These biddies became Aunt Bessie's primary source of income, first as "fryers," which she could sell, and still later as layers, whose eggs she exchanged for groceries at Dalt Fleming's store in Stockton. I have a lasting image of her in the barnyard, forming her apron skirt in a pouch, filling it with cracked corn, and scattering the corn on the ground in sweeping motions, calling "Pee-pee, pee-pee," as chickens, turkeys and guineas came running from all directions.

Although Aunt Bessie's assigned chores didn't extend into the livestock of barnyard and pasture, she was given the task of naming the cows and newborn calves. In a little notebook, she recorded the names Hudson, Judy, White Cow, Red Cow, Stump Tail, and others. She also took great interest in the ponies and horses that successively lived on the farm. When I came along on the horse scene, she was in her 50s and somewhat rotund, so I never gave a thought to her being a horsewoman. About a year ago, I came across this picture, probably taken when Aunt Bessie was in her early 20s, and I learned the horse's name was also Bessie.

Bobby and my dad have often told a story that involved Bessie the horse and Bessie the Aunt. Dad's family lived 2 miles from school, a distance he and his siblings often walked as a group. On certain days, if the horse or mule was not needed for farm chores, my dad, Mervin, Evelyn, and Bessie, were allowed to hitch her to the horse-cart and ride as far as the head of Little Mill Road, where they got out, turned the horse and cart around, and said, "Giddup!" In this way, the horse re-turned home on her own, and the Jones children walked the remaining half mile on the paved road.

Bessie with her horse named Bessie, c. 1920.

During one period, around 1920, they were allowed to drive a horse and buggy all the way to school. They stabled the horse at a relative's hostelry, and then drove home again after school. My Uncle Ray DeVries, Aunt Evelyn's hus-band, in his book "The Way It Was," recounts a mishap that unnerved them all:

"There was a famous 'last ride.' One day, as they were returning home, Bes-sie the horse got spooked. She shied at something and bolted, running wild and dragging the buggy at dizzying speed. Mervin and George could not stop her. When they got to the turn-off for Little Mill Road, they did not dare allow her to turn 90 degrees at such a speed. They tried to keep her going straight ahead, to no avail! Bessie turned, but the buggy did not, and all hands landed in the ditch in front of the house, now vanished, that stood on the corner. School papers flew through the air, and books landed everywhere. Thankfully, no one was hurt."

This story was told many times in our childhood – Mervin's and George's laughter always heartier than Aunt Bessie's. – RFJ

When I was 6, my family moved to Stockton, 2 miles from the farm where Bobby had been living with our Jones grandparents and Aunt Bessie, a maiden lady, and Uncle Mervin, a confirmed bachelor. Frequently, Dale and I spent weekends at the farm with Bobby, and it was our Aunt Bessie, who took us to her church every Sunday. Remson Methodist Church was out in the country about 2 miles from the farm.

Starting when I was in first grade and Bobby was in fifth, I sometimes would ride the school bus to the farm with him. Upon entering the farmhouse, we would find Aunt Bessie, standing next to the window, ironing with a flat iron warmed on the wood stove while listening to Stella Dallas on the radio. She would offer us ginger snaps or sugar cookies and a glass of fresh milk, likely from Judy or White Cow, that Bobby had milked before he went to school that morning.

From left: Aunt Bessie, age 11 (1911), 38 (1938), and 54 (1954)

Aunt Bessie always saved her McCall magazines for me so that I could cut out the Betsy McCall paper doll and her outfits. I accumulated quite a collection over the years and wish I could see it one more time. Aunt Bessie also invited me to bring my dolls when I came to the farm so she could make doll clothes using her treadle singer sewing machine. I still have a doll with a dress she made.

When my granddaughter, Caroline, went to college at the University of Georgia, she made friends with a girl who was from Berlin on the Eastern Shore of Maryland. When Caroline was spending a week with her family, I received a phone call. Caroline was excitedly telling me that when her friend's mother was a little girl, she lived on Little Mill Road, just down the road from Aunt Bessie. She said that Aunt Bessie would often pick her up and take her to Sunday School. In fact, she said, she still had a purse that Aunt Bessie had made for her. She gave the purse to Caroline who presented it to me. It is a small world, and we are all connected.

I don't remember Aunt Bessie ever holding me on her lap or even giving me a hug, but I always knew she loved me unconditionally. I know I didn't appreciate her enough when she was with us, but I hope she knew what an important role she had in my life. The harshest criticism or disciplinarian action she ever took was saying, "Do, children, do." That meant to stop whatever mischief we were unleashing, and you can believe that we deserved more than a gentle verbal admonishment. Aunt Bessie died at the young age of 62 and is buried in the Remson Church family plot next to her beloved parents, her brother, and her little sister, not far from where I will be buried when I cross the river.

Remson Methodist Church

5 | My Animals

Trixie

I wish I could tell you where Dad got Trixie or how she became my dog. I don't remember her as a puppy, only as a fully grown dog. She was an excellent hunter and true to her breed as a rat terrier. She teamed up with Spot, Dad's bird dog, and it was entertaining to watch them at work. Being the smaller of the two, Trixie would go under the corn crib to check for rats, and if she heard them, she'd start digging and flinging. Spot would wait, ready to pounce as soon as the rat hit the ground. She grabbed it, gave it a few vigorous shakes, tossed it aside, and waited for the next one. It was a sight to see the rats piled up beside her. You get your kicks where you can when you live on a farm.

Linda with Trixie, 1948.

In the 40s and 50s, not many farmers spayed or neutered their household pets. Over the years, both of our dogs had litters of pups every year; we were always glad when they had them at different times. There were several occasions when both Trixie and Spot had litters at the same time. All went well for a couple of days until one of them discovered there were other puppies in the barnyard and the mother instinct took over. If Trixie's puppies were alone, Spot would pick up each one in her mouth and one at a time carry them all back to her bed, adding them to her litter. When Trixie returned to her empty bed, she followed the scent to Spot's bed and started taking puppies. It didn't matter whose. By that time, they all smelled the same. And back and forth it went. It must have been a pretty confusing time for both of them – fearful of leaving their babies, never knowing how many, if any, pups would be in their bed when they returned. Dale and I intervened many times, helping them sort out the blended litters, putting the black and white spotted puppies with Spot and the black and brown ones with Trixie. Each of the moms were sure that all the puppies were hers. Our pleas to leave the other's pups alone fell on deaf ears, and we were glad when the pups were big enough to take care of themselves and

Linda with Trixie, 1957.

the moms really didn't care where they were.

Somewhere along the way, Dale decided the best way to tease me (and he loved to tease me) was to call Trixie a Russian. By the time I was 9 in 1950, I knew that Russia was our mortal enemy, and I just hated it when Dale called her a Russian. Who wanted a Russian dog? It was the worst thing you could call someone you loved. Well, I guess there are worse things. When I was younger, Dale also told me I was hatched from a buzzard egg that Dad had found in the woods. By the time my children came along, and he told them the story of my humble beginnings, he had embellished it to include his having to keep my egg under the stove, turning it every day to keep it evenly warm, and finally watching me hatch.

Trixie frequently accompanied me when I went horseback riding. That meant she had to trot along with me as I pedaled my bicycle the 2 miles out to the farm on Little Mill Road, then trot along again wherever Sea Star and I went on our ride, and finally one more long trot for the return trip back to Stockton. It was a lot for four little, short legs. As we made our way through the countryside, I confess that it was never far from my mind that a Hollywood movie mogul might spot my little freckled face, riding bareback on my big brown mare with my little black dog trotting alongside, and we would all become famous movie stars.

We frequently took all the old dirt roads through woods and farms, but I knew if I wanted to be discovered, I needed to stay on the main road. The problem that presented was the main road went through downtown Stockton, which was really just a crossroads, but there were sidewalks and stores. It never occurred to me to carry any kind of pooper scooper and plastic bag to clean up after my horse if she left a pile in the street. I simply left it where it fell, but to be honest, I felt bad about it, as I looked around to make sure no one saw. Surely the residents had to know the culprit, but no one ever called me on it. I guess it was a good thing that people didn't expect much of me. Now that I think of it, it was organic manure, so maybe the lady with the beautiful flowers in her garden picked it up and put it to good use.

I kept one puppy from Trixie's last litter, and I named her Pixie (very imaginative – Trixie and Pixie). Before I went away to college, we gave Pixie to the family who lived in the house on the Pocomoke Road at the head of Little Mill

Road. I never saw her after that. When Trixie died, I had a funeral for her, and buried her alongside Spot in the pet cemetery next to the lilac bush in the side yard of the Stockton house.

SEA STAR

When I entered the seventh grade, Bobby left the farm on Little Mill Road to move to Lynchburg to complete his 11th and 12th grades. With a more solid educational foundation, it increased his prospects for going to college, and it presented me with a dream fulfilled. I took over the guardianship of his horse Sea Star. Although she was stabled at the family farm, I rode my bike the 2 miles on weekends and several days a week during the summer months for five years.

Sea Star was not the perfect horse. When I whistled for her out in the pasture the most she would do is look up for a moment and then go back to her grazing. That meant I had to walk all the way to the end of the pasture to catch her. As I got close to her, she threw up her head and trotted to another area and started grazing again, as if there was nothing afoot. I soon caught on to her game, and prepared myself with corn in my hand and her bridle over my shoulder. I stopped halfway from where she was grazing, whistled so she would look up, and then knelt onto the ground, making myself into a ball. This aroused her curiosity, and it wouldn't be long before she approached this odd ball in her pasture. When she started sniffing, I held out my handful of corn for her. As she began to nibble her treat, I slowly slipped the reins over her ears and voila! I caught myself a horse.

At some point, it was decided to breed her, and Bill Hudson, the local horse trader, brought a stallion to the farm. I named him Hero, and he was a perfect horse. He loved to be ridden and came trotting toward me as soon as I made an appearance and whistled for him. For awhile, I had two horses for riding: Hero for me to ride and Sea Star for a

Linda with Sea Star, 1956; painting by Linda's niece Susan Voelker.

friend. When Sea Star became too pregnant to ride and when her foal Stormy was little, I often rode Hero to see my friend Edna Carol who also lived on Little Mill Road. I usually helped her finish dusting all the figurines on her mom's what-not shelves. I decided then that I would never have those dust collectors to clean when I had my own house. Back in the yard, Edna Carol climbed behind me onto Hero and off

Linda (left) and Edna Carol Holland on Hero, 1955.

we'd go, riding double. I was heartbroken when Bill Hudson came to get him a year or two later. When Edna Carol's mother saw us having to ride double again, this time on Sea Star, and realized how much her daughter loved horses, she agreed to buy her an older, safe horse. Prince was a happy horse and got along well with Sea Star, and Edna Carol and I were so happy to not have to ride double.

There were many times when either Edna or I took a tumble as we raced across the countryside. Unlike in the movies where horses waited for their riders, our horses wouldn't wait for us when one of us fell off. Instead, once free of their burden, they made a beeline for their stable. We doubled up for the ride back to the barn where the wayward horse patiently waited to be groomed and turned out to pasture. One time, when we were racing around farm roads, I saw Edna Carol roll off Prince as they galloped around the field. I went in quick pursuit to catch old Prince, but on the next 90-degree turn, off I went too. When we were finally able to stop laughing, we set off on foot for home, but not before picking a watermelon and cracking it open, delighting in the sweetness of life and living in paradise.

That wasn't the last time I fell off Sea Star. On a beautiful summer day in August before I started ninth grade, I was riding with a friend, Janice Hancock. I was bareback on Sea Star, galloping along the grassy shoulder of the Virginia Road on the outskirts of Stockton. Sea Star was a skittish horse, and I had to be super alert to any potential danger. I always joked that she would stop on a dime to examine a chewing gum wrapper on the side of the road. Evidently, I wasn't vigilant this day because something caught her eye before I was aware of it. When Sea Star suddenly stopped and swerved sharply into the paved road, I lost my seating and went down headfirst. I was knocked unconscious when the back of my head hit the road. The fall occurred in front of Janice's cousin's house, and when I didn't get up, Janice called for Becky Sue to help. I was lying in the road, not moving, and they couldn't get me to respond. Even though neither girl had a driver's license, Janice said she felt confident enough to drive me 9 miles to Snow Hill to see a doctor. They gently picked me up and arranged me in the back seat of Becky Sue's father's car. Luckily, as they backed out of the driveway, Becky Sue's dad arrived home. After assessing the situation, he called Dr. LaMar in Snow Hill and arranged to meet him at my house on the other side of Stockton.

Mr. Hancock drove me, still unconscious, the 2 miles to my house and carried me to the daybed in the living room. My parents had gone out for the day to celebrate their 24th wedding anniversary, but Dale was home. Dr. LaMar was able to rouse me to a somewhat conscious state – enough so that I remember him holding up his hand and asking me how many fingers I saw. I remember seeing a blur of fingers, but wanting to please, I guessed at how many each time he asked. As I gave wrong answer after wrong answer, I could hear Dale, off to the side, telling the doctor, "She's faking. She knows how many fingers there are. There's nothing wrong with her. She's faking."

I don't know how I got to the hospital. Perhaps Dr. LaMar drove me there. They were able to track down my parents who arrived at the hospital shortly after we did. I was conscious enough to know my head was hurting during the x-rays, and I remember being told that I had a concussion and a hairline fracture just next to the seam in the back of my head. "Just a slight turn of the head, and you wouldn't be here now," the doctor told me. I was still unable to see clearly, but was told that I would likely get my sight back within a few days. I was put in a room with a little, old lady, the wife of a preacher, so I had lots of prayers said over me for the next couple of days. I regained my eyesight the second day. Although it was blurry at first, it soon cleared up.

My parents decided to keep me out of school for the first half of my ninth-grade year, with a plan to go back after Christmas break. I soon heard that a rumor was started that I had died in the fall, and at 14, I thought that was cool, especially since it wasn't true. We tried to track down the source of the rumor to no avail. My social studies teacher Mr. Dimmick came down to Stockton once a week and brought assignments from all my teachers so I could stay current with my schoolwork. Or, sometimes Louise Littleton, my eighth-grade teacher, or Helen Tull, my seventh-grade teacher, both from Stockton, transported my schoolwork back and forth. My parents bought me a used upright piano, something I had wanted for a long time, hoping it would take my attention away from horseback riding. The preacher brought me a hymn book from church, and Aunt Bessie gave me a piano note chart that I put behind the keyboard. By matching up the notes in the hymnal to the chart and the chart to the keys, I soon learned to play every familiar song in the Methodist hymn book.

I stayed off Sea Star that winter, but when spring summoned me to the woods and countryside, I rode my bike out to the farm and went up in the barn loft and found a couple of old saddles, including a jockey saddle, or maybe it was an English saddle, and the other an army saddle. I put them over a hay bale and tried them out for comfort. It didn't take long to know that the wooden army saddle with a hole in the middle would not make the cut, but the jockey saddle would be more like riding bareback. I lengthened the jockey stirrups to be like a Western saddle, and I was in business. I told my parents about the saddle, promising to use it whenever I rode, and they finally agreed. I had two more years of riding before a cute boy's kisses turned my heart to young love and cars as my transportation.

TRAINING SANDY PAT

One summer in my early teens, I spotted a pretty black and white Chincoteague pony in the pasture next to Edna Carol's house on Little Mill Road. She looked just like Suzie, Bobby's pony that I learned to ride when I was 6. I stopped by the farm to inquire about the pony, and Mr. Outten told me that he had just bought her for his granddaughters, Sandy and Pat.

"She needs some training," he said, "if the youngins' are going to be able to ride her when they come to visit."

I immediately offered my help which he accepted. After all, I had been riding for several years, had read all the Black Stallion and Island Stallion books, plus Misty of Chincoteague, and the Trixie Beldon books. Not to mention, I had seen every Roy Rogers, Gene Autry, and Lone Ranger movie ever made. I must have been 14 at the time and thought I knew everything there was to know about training horses.

I went home and prepared a stall in the old barn on the farm where I lived with my parents and Dale. Looking back, I must have told them what I was doing; I must have gotten permission to board and train someone's pony. I don't remember that conversation. People who knew me in my youth have told me they always saw me as a confident and headstrong lass, which surprises me, because that's definitely not how I saw myself.

The next day after breakfast, I dashed out the door and walked the mile or so back to the Outten farm. Mr. Outten had Sandy Pat (named after his grand-daughters) tied to the rail, ready for her brand-new saddle and bridle. They were bright red with silver buttons, just like the ones in the Sears and Roebuck catalogue that I had longed for – every horse crazy little girl's dream. He told me that she didn't like the saddle, so I walked her the mile back home, later returning on my bike to get the saddle.

When I got back to the barn with her saddle, I put on her bridle, tying the reins to a rail in the barn. I put the saddle and blanket on the sawhorse taken out of my dad's workshop. I spent an hour moving that saddle and blanket from one place to another, sometimes just walking around with one or the other. She jumped, snorted, and threw her head up every time I moved them, her eyes looking wild and frightened. I kept going back to her, rubbing her head and talking in a soft voice and then back to the tack. After an hour or so, I decided to leave the saddle alone for the rest of that day and just worked with the blanket since that didn't making any creaking noises.

By the end of the next hour, she wasn't reacting to the movement of the blanket at all. But, when I first attempted to put it on her back, she pulled back, threw up her head, and moved away from me. I kept talking in a low voice and kept moving the blanket around her until I was finally able to rub it against her and then ease it over her back with little or no reaction. I pulled it over her rump and haunches and continued rubbing her entire back with it. I wanted her to know that it wasn't going to hurt her. That was enough for one day. I staked her in the yard where she could eat grass and relax before I put her in her stall for the night.

All week, I worked with Sandy Pat, putting the blanket and saddle on, taking them off, shaking them as I placed them on the sawhorse over and over until I just wore her down, and she became desensitized. She was finally convinced it wasn't going to hurt her and stopped jumping and jerking her head. I could finally put bridle, blanket, and saddle on her while she calmly waited. Then, I started putting one foot in the stirrup, taking it out, putting it in, taking it out. Next, lifting myself up, I put weight on the stirrup, leaning over her back. She flicked her ears, and moved a little, but didn't act scared. When I was sure she trusted that no harm would come to her, I gently lifted myself in the stirrup and slowly put my leg over her back, lowering my weight in the saddle. No reaction. Good job. I did that for the next hour or so, mounting and dismounting, followed by leading her around the barn and yard.

By the end of the week, I was riding her all over our farm and thought she was ready to return home. Mr. Outten was happy to see me riding her up his lane, praising the good job I had done getting her ready for his granddaughters. From time to time, I saw them riding her as I was going down Little Mill Road and felt great satisfaction in knowing I had a part in her training.

6 | CLOSING OUT THE 40S

How many times have we heard someone say, "I wouldn't want to bring a child into this crazy world the way it is." When someone said that to me recently, I pointed out that through the ages, there are always reasons to think the world is an unhealthy place for children. I suppose the ones of us who take a chance having them also have hope that the world will be better, that human beings can do better. Looking back over my 80-year life, I think it's important to take into account the events and inventions that shaped our culture and our lives, sometimes making the world a crazy place to be and other times making it exciting and interesting.

THE DECADE OF THE 1940S

Having been born at the tail end of "The Silent Generation" (those born 1925 to 1945), I was inadvertently imbued with traits described in a 1952 Time Magazine article. Being born and raised during a war and toward the end of an economic depression, Time Magazine called us "unimaginative, withdrawn, unadventurous, and cautious." I have certainly embodied those traits at different times of my life. Perhaps because I was at the "tail-end of things" and the youngest of six, I was a late bloomer and didn't find my voice until my 30s and 40s, pulled out of my silence by a series of personal events.

WORLD WAR II

The war was definitively the big event of the first half of the 1940s. I came into this world on December 12, 1941, five days after the Japanese bombing of Pearl Harbor. In retaliation, we declared war on Japan on December 8, and just three days later, Germany declared war on the United States. I tumbled into a world filled with fear, anger, and anxiety, already beset with financial distress and concern from the Depression.

Although I was too young to remember the war, I later learned that my mother's brother L.J., a private in the U.S. Army's 90th Infantry Division, was part of the Allied offensive across France and Germany. There was a period at the end of the war when no one in the family had heard from him, and everyone feared the worst. My Aunt June told us the story of that hot August day when a neighbor rushed into the house waving a newspaper with a picture of her beloved husband L.J. sitting on the banks of the Séves River during a brief truce.

According to my cousin, Uncle L.J.'s son Bobby Mc-Gee, the photo was snapped around June 10, 1944 , supposedly by an Associated Press wartime photographer just after the D-Day landings on Utah Beach in Normandy,

Uncle L.J. McGee (left) eating rations shortly after the D-Day landings on Utah Beach in Normandy, France. Both men were privates in the 90th Infantry Division, 1944.

France, and printed in major newspapers across the U.S. It was the first indication in nearly a month that he was still alive.

My brother Bobby recently told me that he remembers being 8 years old, standing near the corn crib at the farm on Little Mill Road when he saw Ruth Ann, age 11, running out of the house waving her arms and shouting, "The war is over! The war is over!" She had heard the joyous news on the radio. They joined hands dancing in circles around and around the corn crib until they fell down, exhausted, and could dance no more.

The Holocaust

Although it didn't happen in our country, our psyches and lives were shaped through knowing about the death camps in Germany, established by the Nazis to murder millions of Jews. Even today, we continue to study the competing myths that Americans either were ignorant of the unspeakable persecution that Jews faced in Europe, or that they looked on with callous indifference. We are still examining the roles that eugenics and racism, as well as xenophobia and antisemitism, played during this crisis and throughout American history. We still struggle with questions that remain essential to our society today: Is America, truly, as it claims to be, a melting pot, a land of immigrants? During the Holocaust, an estimated six million Jews were executed by Hitler's decree; the remaining prisoners were liberated as the Allies conquered Germany.

THE ATOM BOMB

During the war, the U.S. collaborated with the United Kingdom, Canada, and France on the Manhattan Project to build a fission weapon as a deterrent to war. Just two months after Germany surrendered in May 1945, the U.S. successfully tested the first atom bomb at the Trinity site in Alamogordo, New Mexico. Robert Oppenheimer, one of the developers of the bomb, upon witnessing the detonation of the bomb, was heard quoting a line from the Hindu holy scripture *Bagavad Gita,* "Now I am become Death, the destroyer of worlds."

That August, with the war in Europe over, U.S. forces advanced in an island-by-island invasion of Japan. U.S. President Harry Truman made the decision to drop atomic bombs on Hiroshima and Nagasaki in hopes of quickly ending the war. One could easily argue that bringing children into the world was not a good idea at that time.

THE COLD WAR (1947-99)

Japan surrendered after the second city was bombed, but as soon as the war was over, the Cold War began, a 50-year war between the democracies of the Western World led by the U.S. and the communist countries of Eastern Europe led by Russia. During this long period of tension, both sides built up their nuclear arsenals, enough to destroy each other and the world five times over. According to Winston Churchill, it was as if Russia had lowered an "Iron Curtain" across Europe, calling on the U.S. to join with Great Britain to be a beacon for peace and democracy throughout the world, which gave us all hope.

INVENTIONS DURING MY FIRST DECADE

I have often thought that my being born just a day after we declared war on Germany, and only five days after the Japanese attack on Pearl Harbor, must have had an impact on my life. Perhaps more so were the innovations that came as a result of the war. By the time I was 9 years old at the end of the 40s, the first programmable, fully automatic, digital computer called the Z3 was built, filling a 30' x 60' room. Edwin Land invented the Polaroid Land camera that sold for $89.75 and produced finished prints in 60 seconds. Columbia Records introduced the first long-playing phonograph record, holding six times as much music as previous records and helped create the modern recording industry. Bell Laboratories revolutionized the field of electronics with the invention of the transistor, smaller, cheaper, and faster than a vacuum tube. Mobile phones came into existence in 1947, although the first commercially viable phone did not appear on the market until 1983. However, in 1947 the FCC allocated a large number of frequencies so that widespread mobile telephone service would become feasible. Someone could see the way of the future. Also in 1947, Bell Laboratories introduced the idea of cellular communications with police car technology.

During my first decade, the field of medicine saw the development of penicillin, synthetic cortisone, synthetic tooth fillings, and the kidney dialysis machine. I remember my first shot of penicillin for a cold. When I saw the needle and declined to get a shot, Dr. Lamar told me it wouldn't hurt worse than a mosquito bite. As it bit into my tiny buttocks, I yelled, "It hurts worser."

Grand Rapids, Michigan, was the first city to put fluoride in its water supply; Tiffany's, in New York City was the first fully air-conditioned store; the first commercial flights with pressurized cabins were inaugurated; and the Aqua Lung was invented.

Morton Salt showed up on our kitchen tables and Tupperware in our cabinets, and the first electric blanket was manufactured. The microwave oven based on radar technology was first introduced in 1947, but it was 20 years before the kitchen-friendly microwave showed up on our counters. When Mom and Dad got one in the late 60s, my sister Robin and I wouldn't stay in the room while it was on, not trusting the radio waves. The first disposable aerosol cans were developed, the Slinky and Silly Putty were invented, and Elmer's glue and duct tape were making our lives easier.

DANCE AND MUSIC IN THE 40s

As America was pulled into a world war, dancing continued to keep us entertained and happy during a time of national anxiety. The Big Band Era of the 30s with Glenn Miller and Jimmy Dorsey kept dances like the Swing popular into the 40s. Servicemen returned from the war, bringing new styles of dance, including the Jitterbug and Latin dances like the Rhumba, Fox Trot, and Tango. Fred Astaire and Ginger Rogers kept ballroom dancing in the public eye, and tap dancing also became popular.

During the war years, songs such as *Boogie Woogie Bugle Boy*, *I'll Be Home for Christmas*, *I'll Be Seeing You*, *Over There*, and *White Christmas* were popular. Social, cultural, and technological changes during the war years influenced American music, which was ready to march to a different tune. The songs I remember listening to on the radio in the late 40s include Nat King Cole's *Mona Lisa*, Frank Sinatra's *All of Me*, Dean Martin's *Walkin' My Baby Back Home*, Ella Fitzgerald's *Sentimental Journey*, The Ames Brother's *Music, Music, Music*, and Patti Page's *Tennessee Waltz*. I remember hearing Gene Autry when he first sang *Rudolph the Red Nosed Reindeer* the Christmas of 1949.

THE TELEVISION

The television came on the scene in the 1940s. When I was a year old in 1942, only 5,000 sets were in operation, but production of new TVs, radios, and other broadcasting equipment for civilian purposes was suspended during the war years. By 1947, when there were 40 million radios in the U.S., there were only 44,000 television sets. By 1949, the networks stretched from New York to the Mississippi River, and just 2 years later to the West Coast. The shows *Candid Camera*, *The Lone Ranger*, *The Ed Sullivan Show*, *Hopalong Cassidy*, and *Howdy Doody* aired in living rooms across America in the late 40s. Howdy Doody was the first TV show I saw at the home of my friend, Janice Hancock, probably in 1951. The Jones family home in Stockton didn't get a TV until 1954.

The first *Superman* movie, an animated cartoon, debuted in theaters in 1941, along with *Dumbo*, *Fantasia*, and *Bambi*. Other movies became top box office hits, including *Citizen Cane*, *Casablanca*, *The Maltese Falcon*, *The Grapes of Wrath*, and *It's a Wonderful Life*.

We could count on new inventions to give us better ways to communicate, help sick people, and to entertain ourselves. Today we wonder how we ever got along without the inventions we now take for granted.

7 | Teenage Years (1953-59)

Harvest Moon Community Show

One of my mother's best friends in Stockton was Mable Burbage. After graduating from high school, her son Pete moved to New York where he was involved in the theater. In the summer of 1953, before my seventh-grade year, Pete brought a director friend home to visit our little town of 300 residents. Facing the long boring summer, they decided to put together a community show. They put out a call for local Stockton talent and were rewarded with singers and dancers and wanna-be-stars. I think the theme was Harvest Moon, or maybe I remember that because I was in the skit that sang, *Shine on Harvest Moon*. The three Sturgis sisters sang a song, harmonizing beautifully, and Charles Colbourne and Neil Sturgis did a rendition of *Frankie and Johnny*. There were humorous skits, along with piano playing, singing, dancing, and other forms of entertainment.

The star of the show, in my eyes, was my best friend Rita Carol Ward. She wore a pink tutu, pink tights, and pink ballerina slippers, and she twirled and pirouetted and soared in the air throughout her dance routine. Her performance was truly beautiful and motivated me to take dancing lessons. We had rehearsals all that summer, readying ourselves for opening night. Folks from the neighboring towns of Girdletree, Klej Grange, Rabbit Knaw, and, of course, everyone else in Stockton who wasn't in the show, came to one or more of the performances. We had two evening shows and two matinees, just like Broadway. Looking back, it was likely the most community-oriented event ever held in Stockton. I know that back in the early 1900s, hundreds of residents would

Rita Carol (left) and Linda, c. 1953.

gather at Red Hills, a resort on the Chincoteague Bay not far from Stockton, to enjoy the beach and rides at the end of summer, but not to put on a show. As with any community event, it brought us all closer together, and everyone felt sad and the usual let down when it was over.

As much as I admired Rita Carol's ballet dancing, I decided that tap dancing was more my style. So, with a new pair of tap shoes, I presented myself to Rita's dance teacher Lottie Daniels in Pocomoke. I learned a tap routine to *The Sunny Side of the Street*, and I can still remember the first part of it.

The next summer, Rita Carol's mother, Miss Pauline, decided we country bumpkins needed to learn ballroom dancing. Some of us were already in junior high school, and Rita was going to join us that fall. God love Miss Pauline. She was a mother who wanted all of us to be prepared for whatever the future held, and that included dancing. She talked eight children from Stockton into taking ballroom dancing

Stockton and Snow Hill children at ballroom dance class, c. 1953.

lessons with the same dance teacher. We learned how to fox trot, waltz, and cha cha, but the jitterbug was the most popular dance. A few kids joined us from neighboring Snow Hill, and Miss Pauline made sure there were enough boys as dance partners for the girls. At the end of summer, she organized a dance at Winters Quarter Lodge on the Pocomoke River, a fancy but rustic place where we could show off our newly acquired dancing skills. I will always be grateful to Miss Pauline for giving us the gift of dance.

SNOW HILL HIGH SCHOOL

When students completed sixth grade at Stockton Elementary School, we could choose which high school we wanted to attend since we were located halfway between Pocomoke and Snow Hill. Because all my siblings had gone to Snow Hill, that's where my loyalties lay. Half of my classmates chose Pocomoke, so, for the most part, I never saw them again.

I can point to one moment in childhood where the door opened and let the future in. When I was 10 and my brother was 14, Bobby told me that he had met my future husband. He had just spent the weekend with his best friend John Boyer and was introduced to John's 11-year-old cousin Gary Hope. Bobby thought Gary was cute and friendly, with a developing sense of appealing hu-

In Stockton, Md., 1955. Left: Sonny, Ruth Ann, Betty, Bobby, Dale, Linda. Right: George, Ruth.

mor, and very articulate for such a young chap. At that time in my life, if it wasn't a horse or a dog, or a western movie in Pocomoke, it held no interest for me. I couldn't care less about a future husband.

Two years later, when I went into seventh grade at Snow Hill High School, I met the young man ordained to be my future husband. I don't remember any fireworks when I first met Gary, but I do recall that he was soon waiting for me after every class, offering to carry my books, which was an actual thing back in the early 50s. Gary was the smartest boy in the class whereas I was a mediocre student at best. He invited me to my first dance, a sock hop held in the high school gym. His father drove him 9 miles from Snow Hill to Stockton to pick me up, and then collected us at the school when the dance was over to make the return trip to my home. There were several dances and parties during the seventh and eighth grades. For some of those, arrangements were made for my parents to drive me to the event, and his father would drive me home, with Gary and me in the back seat and our observant chaperone keeping a close watch in the rear-view mirror.

At some point, in the eighth grade, I started being annoyed and embarrassed that Gary was always waiting for me after class. I don't remember that we had a conversation about it, or that there was a big break-up, but we stopped going to dances, and he stopped waiting for me after class. However, we remained friends.

BEING A TEENAGER IN THE 50S

As I was finishing ninth grade in the spring of 1956, my parents went into business with my mom's brother L.J. and his wife June. They bought a lot just south of Pocomoke and built a Tastee-Freez franchise. It became so popular that we expanded the window pick-up service to include a restaurant with indoor seating. We were the first "fast-food" restaurant on the lower Eastern Shore, and we introduced pizza and submarine sandwiches to the locals. I worked there on weekends, which provided the experience serving customers I would need to secure a waitressing job in Ocean City the following summer. After my parents sold their share of the Tastee-Freez franchise to Uncle L.J., he renamed it the Pony Ranch. It became a popular hang-out for teenagers in the late 50s, especially after Uncle L.J. offered curbside service.

Like any teenager in the 50s, music and dancing was a favorite pastime – Elvis Presley, Buddy Holly, Fats Domino, The Everly Brothers, and all things rock and roll. I went to sock hops, proms, and parties where the jitterbug was the norm. Since I had taken ballroom dancing classes, I knew how to dance without looking at my feet. Mom had taught me how to do the Charleston, but that was never on the play list in the 50s. In the 10th grade, Gary and I were on the junior-senior prom decorating committee. He had just gotten his driver's license, and he offered to drive me home one night after decorating. I found that I was no longer embarrassed or annoyed to receive his attention and accepted. He invited me to be his date for the prom, and we started going steady that night.

Aside from having a steady boyfriend, one of the highlights of my junior and senior years was meeting Kathy Black. Her family moved to Stockton when her father was stationed at the Chincoteague Naval Base. We became friends the first time we met, while sledding during an infrequent snowstorm. We spent the next two years at her house or mine, and our favorite pastime was memorizing poetry. We loved *Little Orphant Annie*, written by James Whitcomb Riley in 1885, and I continued to recite it throughout my life to my children and grandchildren, and soon to my great-grandsons.

Somewhere in the mid-50s, my family decided that we would draw names for Christmas. Everyone was way past believing in Santa Claus – even I had a job and was making my own money. One year, probably when I was 14 or 15, I was considered mature enough to oversee the name drawing. I prepared the names for everyone to draw at Thanksgiving, since we would all be gathered for the holiday. I have never been able to live this down, but somehow my name was entered twice, and now no one can recall who was left out. I received a record player and my first Elvis Presley album that year. I can't remember the name of the record, which is long gone, but I do remember *Old Shep* was the song that I played over and over.

In 11th grade, I tried out for the cheerleading squad. Because I could do a pretty mean cartwheel and flip and project my voice, I was accepted into the squad, which meant I had to stay after school for practice. I found a ride home with a Stockton neighbor who worked in Snow Hill. After practice, I walked up town to wait for my ride, stopping at the drug store to buy my big treat of the week, a Reese's cup and a Coke.

Gary was the official scorekeeper for the sports teams, which provided an opportunity for us to sit together on the bus to and from away games. We typically went to a movie once a week, either at the Snow Hill or Pocomoke theater, or the Pocomoke drive-in, and sometimes at the Boulevard theater in Salisbury, 20 miles away. In the 50s, we were not allowed to go to the movies on a Sunday, but Gary and I snuck in a few of those as well. I remember going to see *Written on the Wind* in Salisbury on a Sunday afternoon. To celebrate my 16th birthday in 1957, I invited my best friend Ruth Dryden and her boyfriend Tommy Paradee, along with Gary, to my house for dinner. While Mom and Dad were working, Ruth and I prepared friend chicken, mashed potatoes, and a vegetable. My first attempt at entertaining guests for dinner was a success.

Gary and I were inseparable until our senior year in 1958-59 and about to embark on our college journeys. I decided it would be sensible for us to date other people in order to be sure that we were meant to be together. We remained in that state of friendship, dating other people and still dating each other from time to time for the next four years. It was obvious I hadn't thought that through when I learned he invited someone else to the senior prom, and I was left without a date. Dale's best friend, Louis Sims, two years out of high school, stepped up to the plate when I invited him to escort me to the prom. We had a great time laughing and dancing the night away.

Linda and Louie Sims, senior prom, 1959.

GARY'S FAMILY

At some point during our high school dating, I was invited to the Hopes for dinner, which was elegantly served by lamplight on their back porch. Even though I had met Mr. Hope, it was the first time I met Gary's mother. They lived in Snow Hill on East Federal Street at the time and would move out to Pinewood Farm on the Pocomoke River in 1958.

Clifton Hope and Anna Strickland met while students at Washington College in Chestertown, Maryland, and married August 24, 1938. They spent sev-

Gary's parents, Anna and Clifton Hope, with Tony and Ellen, 1966.

eral years in Blacksburg where Clifton taught at Virginia Polytechnic Institute (Virginia Tech). After Gary was born in February 1941, they moved to Snow Hill to be near their parents.

Gary's father, Clifton Hope (June 24, 1917-July 17, 1990) was the son of Dr. James Herbert Hope (October 18, 1882-August 29, 1946) and Eleanor Blades Radcliffe (January 1986-February 16, 1963), both from St. Michaels, Maryland. Clifton was a psychology teacher and guidance counselor at Wicomico High School in Salisbury. He also served as a pastor to several Methodist churches on the Lower Eastern Shore.

Gary's mother, Anna Louise Strickland Hope (February 22, 1917-May 17, 1988), was the daughter of Clarence William Strickland (November 10, 1890-September 22, 1984) of Klej Grange, and Nancy Ellen Jones Strickland (November 26, 1991-September 6, 1988) of Girdletree. Anna was a kindergarten teacher at Snow Hill Elementary School until her retirement. Pursuing her artistic talents, she became a favorite local artist on the lower Eastern Shore.

Clarence's grandfather William George Strickland immigrated from England in 1880 to settle in Klej Grange, an agrarian-industrial, back-to-the-land community, where people tired of urban living could find a more wholesome and rewarding life. Clarence graduated from the University of Maryland with a degree in agriculture. He married Nancy Ellen Jones, a teacher from Girdletree. Clarence served as inspector for Maryland Agriculture College and farmed on a scientific basis. He was also owner and manager of the Snow Hill five-and-ten-cent store on Green Street. The Hopes and Stricklands are buried in the Spring Hill Cemetery in Girdletree.

MY FIRST REAL JOB

In my wildest dreams, I never thought my mother would let me work in Ocean City during the summers. Although only 32 miles from Stockton, it took an hour to drive there back in the 50s. Luckily, my dad knew Ike who owned a little hole-in-the-wall restaurant, just half a block from the boardwalk where Dale worked at Joe's. Bobby worked 15 blocks away at the Beach Plaza, and they both assured Mom that I would be safe and that they would look out for me. My Dad took me to get a work permit because it was the summer before I turned 16. One of the waitresses at Ike's invited me to share her room with two other girls. The regular-sized bedroom was a tight squeeze with two double beds and two girls to a bed, leaving just enough room to walk between the beds. I stayed at Ike's for about a month, and then as soon as a job opened at Joe's, I was hired and moved up the street to the boardwalk, where Dale and I agreed to work on opposite shifts.

Co-workers at Joe's and roommates, from left: Linda, Pat Andrews, Diane Noel, 1958.

The work schedule was grueling – 10 hours a day, seven days a week, and a day off every two weeks when we changed shifts. I was paid $15/week plus tips. The manager of the restaurant, Roy Dayton, owned a small apartment complex a couple of blocks away, and for $15/week, I rented one of his one-bedroom apartments, along with two of my co-workers, Pat Andrews and Diane Noel. We rotated two of us sleeping in the bedroom and one on the pull-out couch in the living room. I got two meals a day at the restaurant, so basically, I was working for tips. Looking back, for a 15-year-old away from home for the first time, I managed very well, making the best of crowded living conditions, working long hours, and not doing anything crazy.

Dale recently asked me how much I saved that first summer at Joe's. The number that sticks in my mind is $300. I do remember that after I started working in Ocean City, I saved enough to buy my own school clothes and supplies.

Dale was making $75 a week at the soda fountain, but didn't receive many tips.

I returned a second summer to work at Joe's, living in the same apartment with the same friends. That summer, my best friend Kathy Black came down for a month and worked and lived with us; my sister Betty also was there for a different month. When we were 16 and 21, Betty and I looked like

Twins: Betty (left) and Linda, 1962.

twins. When we were working on opposite shifts, people who came in to eat breakfast and came back for a late-night snack thought just one person was working 20 hours a day. We didn't disabuse them of that notion, sometimes even encouraging them to feel sorry for us because the tips were better.

At the end of the summer of 1958, I took a waitressing job in the coffee shop at the Beach Plaza Hotel where Bobby had been a waiter in the dining room for several years. My salary increased to $20 a week with the added bonus of free room and board, and the working conditions and tips were much better, so I was moving up in the world. The free room was a huge dorm room in the basement with five or six bunk beds and several single beds, one of which I snagged. I went back to work at the Beach Plaza the next summer after graduation in 1959 and again in the summer of 1960. About halfway through the summer, a single room became available in the back of the garage under the Bo-Con, a condo facility next to the Beach Plaza. It was a windowless private room, just large enough to hold a double mattress almost wall-to-wall on the floor and to stack my clothes in milk cartons along one wall. Having my own private room was worth the inconvenience of going next door for the bathroom and shower and putting up with the gasoline fumes and carbon monoxide, always present in the adjoining garage.

8 | AFTER HIGH SCHOOL (1959-62)

OFF TO COLLEGE

Surely they must have been, but I don't recall my parents being involved at all in my decision to go to college. When Gary won a Maryland Senatorial Scholarship to go to Johns Hopkins University in Baltimore, I decided to go to Towson State Teacher's College, a short four-mile trolley

ride down York Road. During the summer of 1959, my waitressing job at the Beach Plaza in Ocean City enabled me to save enough money to pay for a year of college at Towson. Tuition, room and board, and used books cost $600 a year, equivalent to about $5,000 today. After carefully budgeting my money, I had money left over to buy a pack of cigarettes every week. I also allowed myself one treat a week. Upperclassmen set up an informal snack shop in the dorm where I bought a bologna sandwich and a bag of potato chips for 35 cents. My mother sent me a carton of cigarettes for my 18th birthday, and that was like manna from heaven and probably kept me in smokes for the remainder of the school year.

Once accepted at Towson, I also can't remember my parents offering to drive me to college, or even asking me how I planned to get there. Dale's friend Louie Sims stepped up to the plate again when it was time for me to leave home for college. He came over one morning, and my best friend Kathy Black and I loaded my record player, records, and clothes in his 1957 Buick, which we called the Big Green Ferry Boat. Louie drove me away from Stockton, my home of 12 years.

As we drove across the Chesapeake Bay Bridge, we marveled at how the bridge, finished just seven years earlier, had finally linked the Eastern Shore of Maryland to the Western Shore, bringing progress, development, and more people. Until that time, we had been isolated on a peninsula surrounded by water with the Chesapeake Bay to the west and the Atlantic Ocean to the east.

I didn't realize how isolated we were until I was placed in a speech correction class at Towson State Teacher's College because nobody could understand my Eastern Shore accent. Even though it was an embarrassing turn of events, I have been grateful for it because that's where I learned to enunciate my words and slow down my speech pattern.

Kathy (left) and Linda, 1959 and 2012.

Once we arrived on campus, Louie and Kathy helped me unload and carry my possessions up five flights of stairs to my new home that I would share with roommates Carolyn Compton from Baltimore and Annette McConnell from Leonardtown in Southern Maryland. Since I was the first to arrive, I chose the single bed, leaving the bunk for them. I said goodbye to my friends and went about settling into my new life and surroundings.

I don't remember ever seeing Louie again, but I heard of him through Dale. Kathy and I kept in touch through letters and occasional phone calls. Kathy came to visit me for a week here in Athens a few years ago, and it was as if no time had passed. Still in touch on Facebook, we are best friends forever! Louie and I also connected on Facebook during the Trump administration, and I learned he was an ardent Trump supporter. We had many good arguments and disagreements until Louie died in August 2020.

Here it was, the end of the 50s and the start of the 60s, and I was learning about the world. Although the Civil Rights Movement had been gaining traction during my childhood in Stockton, I was basically unaware that in 1955 Rosa Parks was arrested in Montgomery, Alabama, for refusing to give up her seat on the bus to a white person. Her arrest sparked a 13-month boycott of the city buses by its Black riders and whites supporting the cause, which ended when the bus companies stopped discriminating against Black passengers. I also wasn't aware of the 1954 landmark *Brown v. Board of Education* case and its ramifications. When the Supreme Court ruled that "separate educational facilities" for Black children were "unconstitutional," a nail was driven into the Jim Crow coffin. When I arrived on the fifth floor of my dorm, my roommate pointed out that one of our classmates, a Black girl, had a private room on our floor. I thought that meant we were integrated. I also didn't know until I was doing research for this memoir that the first two Black students to graduate from Towson State Teacher's College graduated in 1959, the year I started there.

Gary and I continued to date during my freshman year at Towson. I often rode the trolley 4 miles down York Road where Gary was waiting for me. We went to several Orioles games, convenient because it was within walking distance. Sometimes we went to parties at his fraternity house or to the movies. I dated other boys too, sometimes a friend of my roommate's boyfriend. I dated one Baltimore boy who took me to his family's house for dinner. After dinner, everybody packed up blankets and pillows and carried them to a nearby park where they planned to spend the night. Row houses, without air-conditioning, were unbearably hot, and the grassy banks around Lake Ashburton were covered in blankets with neighbors sleeping side-by-side. It was a beauty to behold.

I didn't do as well managing my school life as I did my Ocean City life. I didn't know how to study and spent too much time playing bridge. Before I left for college, my sister Betty sat me down at the kitchen table and explained that there was a card game I would need to learn before I went to college. Everyone was playing Bridge, she told me, and I'd want to know how to play. Being from a large family, I had started playing Casino when I was 5 as a way to learn addition. Soon I was playing Canasta, Hearts, and Pitch or High-Low-Jack-and-Game with my siblings and parents. So, being card savvy, it didn't take me long to catch on to the basic rudiments of Bridge, and with a little book she gave me, I got deeper into it than I should have. In fact, I got good at it, and I loved playing. Unfortunately, it would be my downfall because a freshman should spend more time sitting at her desk studying and gaining the required 15 pounds, than in the student center looking for a bridge game. Consequently, I failed a couple of subjects. To advance to my sophomore year, I was required to attend summer school, which put me in a catch-22. I had no money for summer school, and I needed to work in the summer to save money for my sophomore year.

I went back to the Beach Plaza to work the summer of 1960, hoping that somehow things would work out in the new decade. They didn't work out so that I could return to school for my sophomore year. However, a new opportunity opened up for me, and at the end of the summer, I was on my way to live in the Big Apple with my sister Betty.

THE BIG APPLE

Betty came home the Christmas of 1958 when I was a senior in high school. She had finished college the year before and was teaching school in Lynchburg. It was colder than usual that winter, and since she wasn't feeling well, she opted to sleep downstairs where the kerosene stove kept the living room warm, instead of in bed with me where a glass of water could freeze on the nightstand. I didn't think her decision was particularly unusual, but I remarked more than once that she would feel a lot better if she would at least get dressed instead of staying in her bathrobe.

Two days after Christmas, my mother announced that she and Sonny, my oldest brother, and a somewhat recovered Betty decided to drive 1,500 miles down to Houston, Texas, to visit our sister Ruth Ann. I was so involved with my boyfriend at the time that I didn't beg to go with them or even think how peculiar and out of the blue the decision was. Nor did I think anything untoward when, later that day, my Aunt Bessie asked, "What are they going to do about Betty?"

"Oh, nothing," I said. "They have all gone to Texas to see Ruth Ann, so I guess she's feeling better."

Dear Aunt Bessie didn't carry the conversation any further. A week later, Mom and Sonny came back from Texas without Betty, saying she had decided to stay on to help Ruth Ann with her three children, all under the age of four.

Betty ended up staying in Texas for several months, then attended secretarial school in Lynchburg. After completing the program, Betty left for New York in search of a job, and establishing a new life for herself. Betty's college roommate who lived in Fort Washington gave Betty a place to stay while she looked for work. She soon found a secretarial job with an ad agency. In the summer of 1960, having finished my first year of college in questionable standing, I was working in Ocean City when Bobby paid me a visit. He told me that Betty was home from New York and would be coming to Ocean City to visit with me later that day. Further, he said, she was bringing someone for me to meet – her 1½-year-old daughter Ghee.

So, that explained Betty's strange behavior the Christmas of 1958, including sleeping downstairs, living in her bathrobe, the quick trip to Texas, and Aunt Bessie's question "What are they going to do about Betty?" How wrapped up in my own 17-year-old life I had been!

When I met my niece, Ghee, it was love at first sight. I decided in that first visit that I would go to New York as soon as my summer job was over. I wanted to help Betty with Ghee in whatever way I could.

At the end of the summer, Bobby drove me to Betty's Fort Washington apartment where her roommate had just moved out. When I arrived that Friday, Betty told me, "I enrolled you in Speedwriting Secretarial

Betty's daughter Ghee, 1960.

School where you start on Monday. I'll take you as far as Grand Central Station on my way to work and show you how to get the subway to Times Square. You'll get off the subway and find the 42nd Street exit, go up the escalator and look for the address, 55 W. 42nd St."

I was an 18-year-old farm girl, had never been in the big city, had never seen a subway, but I was ready for a new adventure. The closest experience I had was riding the trolley 4 miles from my college to Gary's college, but this travel would be underground. I was so proud at the end of my first day that I not only found my way to the school, but I also found my way back home.

Within a month or two of my arrival, we moved from Fort Washington to a one-bedroom apartment on 72nd Street on Manhattan's east side. It would be another short-term arrangement with a work friend of Betty's until we got on our feet. Maureen and Betty slept in the bedroom with Ghee in her crib, and I slept on the couch in the living room. One of Maureen's friends, Frank

Boyfriend Frank Tozzi and his convertible, 1960.

Tozzi, had a snazzy red convertible, and he took me on my first tour of New York City at night. Like every newcomer to New York, I oohed and aahed at all the tall buildings and lights, lit up like a Christmas tree. Frank also took me to Radio City Music Hall to see the Rockettes and the movie *Spartacus*. I felt like I had really arrived! Frank and I dated the next seven months I lived in New York.

After three months at the Speedwriting Institute, with my new skills of typing 90 words per minute and taking shorthand at 120 words per minute, I soon found a job in the HR department of Franklin Simon-Oppenheim Collins Department Store. I had spent all my savings from my summer job by then and had another two weeks before my first paycheck. Betty had also exhausted her savings moving us to a larger two-bedroom apartment back in Fort Washington near the George Washington Bridge where rents were more affordable. We found a nursery school for Ghee halfway between our work and our apartment. I took her to school in the mornings, and Betty picked her up after work. Aside from living on canned mackerel – we got a deal on a case – and aside from our electricity being turned off because of an unpaid bill, we were settling into a routine of bachelorettes with a child in the city.

When our building superintendent discovered that we were using our windowsill as a refrigerator, he felt sorry for us and ran an extension cord from his apartment in the basement to our first-floor apartment until we could pay the electric bill. Betty started dating Bobby Nelson, a man whose family owned a meat packing plant, so our canned mackerel diet was supplemented on the weekends by an occasional steak or a roast.

We had furniture for Ghee's room and a bed for us, and we soon found a great couch and a chair that someone had left on the street, which we dragged home and put in our living room. We were looking forward to my first pay-check, to having some money so we could soon start buying our favorite foods and other necessities of life.

I was so excited when I got my first paycheck. I cashed it and immediately went out on my lunch hour to buy a new pair of shoes. What a joy to not feel the cold cement through the holes in my shoes. After work, I ran to the subway station, thinking about all the things we could buy with my money. As I stepped onto the subway and the doors closed, someone tapped me on the shoulder and said, "Ma'am, your purse is open."

I looked down with a sinking feeling and saw the catch on my purse had failed to latch, leaving my purse yawning open and my wallet gone! I felt sick. I got off at the next station, caught the next subway back, and retracing my steps, looked all over the platform amidst the throngs of people. I looked in trash cans and on the tracks, all the while knowing I would never see that wallet again. I even told a subway policeman what I was looking for, and he pretty much laughed out loud.

Defeated, I got on the next train, promising myself that I would not cry, as the knot in my stomach tightened, the lump in my throat grew to avocado pit size, and tears welled up in my eyes. As I opened the door to our apartment, Betty greeted me with a big hug, eager to share in our good fortune and new wealth. I immediately broke my promise to myself and burst into tears as I told her how careless I had been and that there was no money. She was very gentle and supportive, telling me not to worry, we could eat canned mackerel for another week until she got her paycheck.

As we were lamenting about all the things that we could have bought, the doorbell rang, and we both went to answer it. Standing in the doorway was an elderly gentleman, bundled in an overcoat, hat, and scarf, who immediately launched into his monologue, as if he had been practicing what he would say.

"I know about you young girls who come from the country up to the big city. You don't know anything about big city ways, and you don't pay atten-tion to what goes on around you. I saw you waiting for the subway and saw your purse fall open and your wallet fall out on the platform. In the crush of the crowd, you didn't notice it, but I did. As you got on the subway, I picked it up and now, here it is, with all your money still in it."

With his lecture finished, he handed me my wallet, along with his card, and after rejecting our hugs during our profuse thanks, he walked away muttering to himself about young country girls in the city. I put his card in my bible and prayed for him for years. So, now we could pay our electric bill, put the mackerel in the back of the cupboard, and I had a new pair of shoes.

While living together, Betty and I combined our clothes and shoes into one closet since we wore the same size. I'm sure I got the better deal since my wardrobe was skimpy compared to my sister's. My biggest purchase in New York was a red coat with mink cuffs and a matching mink hat. I saw the ensemble in a window on my way to and from work, and when I saved enough money, I went into the store and purchased the coat and hat for $125. Until then, I don't think I had ever paid more than $15 for a dress.

For entertainment, Betty and I played a lot of Scrabble and continued playing every time we got together for the rest of our lives. Another good tradition that we started in New York was eating chicken livers and rice for Sunday breakfast, which also continued through our lives. Living in the apartment next to ours was a Chinese family who owned the restaurant half a block from our building. Once their delicious aromas greeted us as we entered our building's lobby, we frequently were inspired to walk down the street to enjoy really good, authentic, and inexpensive Chinese food.

KEY WEST, FLORIDA

I lived in New York for nine months. By May of 1961, it looked like Betty's relationship with her meat packing man might go somewhere; they wanted to have some time to themselves, and I was ready for something new. Five months after turning 20, I quit my job and made plans to go to Florida. This little country girl took a taxi to LaGuardia Airport all by herself, bought a plane ticket, walked out on the tarmac, and climbed the boarding stairs of the first airplane I had ever been on. I flew to Miami and somehow found my way to the bus station where I caught a bus for the final leg of my journey – 130 miles to Key West. I was on my way to visit Kathy Black, my best friend from high school. I loved that bus trip from Miami to Key West, with all the bridges from one key to the next. Even though I took the route again in 1990, it's a road trip that's still on my bucket list. The bridges are higher now, and you don't get the feeling that you are driving right on the water. Kathy and I were thrilled to be back together again after a couple of years apart.

Back in the 40s and 50s, before we knew about melanoma and that the sun was our enemy, I spent a lot of time in the sun. There was no sunscreen to prevent sunburns – only Witch Hazel and Noxzema to ease the pain after it was too late. Those informational brochures you read today in the dermatologist waiting room warn that if you've had five sunburns, your risk for melanoma is doubled. I'm sure I've had thrice that many. I remember after the burn, the blisters, and then the peeling, pulling huge sheets of skin from my body. I have seen pictures of me, as a little girl, wearing a shirt when I was at the beach or on the bay, so I know my parents tried to protect me. As a teenager, I tried to get a tan, starting with 15 minutes in the sun, increasing it to half an hour, but I always ended up red, looking more like a lobster, and then it would fade into freckles. At the end of one summer, when I was waiting tables at the Beach Plaza, a guest thought I had just arrived at the beach.

Beach time in Ocean City, Md., c. 1947. From left: Dale, George, Betty, Ruth, Ruth Ann, with Linda in front.

Surely if I had been there all summer, I would look tan instead of red. After I was married, I had a sunburn so bad that when I stuck a needle in a huge blister, the liquid that came out actually burned my skin. It must have been sun poison, right? I was nearly 40 before I stopped going in the sun.

The worst sunburn I ever had was that May when I was in Key West visiting Kathy. She was dating a military man who arranged a date for me with his best friend. We found a private beach on one of the keys north of Key West, and spent the day having a great time swimming, sunbathing, and having a picnic lunch and dinner on the beach. After I got home and took a shower, I was shocked at how red my body was, and, even worse, I discovered it was painful to move. I walked like a zombie, and it even hurt to move my lips. We had plans to go to Kathy's boyfriend's parents for the evening so I sucked it up and did the best I could. Her boyfriend's father, Ray, was a barber, and a self-proclaimed hypnotist, and I credit him for saving my life that night.

After one look Ray saw my pain. He asked me to lie down on the floor and proceeded to introduce me to my very first guided imagery/hypnosis session. He told me to close my eyes, and starting at my feet, he slowly guided my awareness up my body. He had me focus my attention on each muscle group starting in my feet and ankles, my shins, legs, hips, and arms, then my shoulders and back, and finally my head. In a slow procession, he asked me to tighten the muscles in each area, hold them tight for 10 seconds, relax them, and then move on to the next muscle group. Before he got to my head, I could feel my body gradually relaxing into the floor. Then, he told me to imagine a place where there was a gentle breeze, and suggested that my entire body felt cool, pain-free, and relaxed. I stayed there in that state of relaxation for several minutes. When the session was over, I stood up and moved around, amazed that I felt absolutely no pain, no heat, and I was able to move normally. To top it off, that sunburn never blistered nor peeled.

When I was preparing to give birth to my first child Tony two years later, I wanted to have a natural childbirth and remembered how effective hypnosis had managed the pain, so I decided to adapt the process of self-hypnosis to giving birth. Using the same progression, I was able to relax my muscles, take my mind to a quiet state, separate my mind from my body, so that my body could do the labor it needed to do. My assessment is that self-hypnosis is effective for pain management – it cured a bad sunburn and helped me have natural childbirth for all three of my children.

RUTH ANN AND THE JOHN BIRCH SOCIETY

When my visit with Kathy came to an end, I boarded a bus for a 30-hour ride to Houston, Texas, to visit my sister Ruth Ann and her family. The air was so hot and heavy when I arrived that it was hard to breathe. To make matters worse, when we arrived at their house, I learned that the air-conditioner was out of commission, scheduled to be fixed the next day. How would I make it through the night? Thankfully, it was repaired as scheduled, just in time for me to learn that Ruth Ann and Jerry were members of the newly formed John Birch Society and would be hosting a meeting that same evening in their living room.

Starting with 11 men in 1958, Robert Welch, an unabashed anti-communist, expanded the JBS membership to as many as 100,000 members at its height. Its main activities in the 1960s comprised of monthly meetings during which members watched an anti-communist film, followed by writing postcards or letters to government officials linking specific policies to the "Communist menace."

That protocol was followed at the meeting I attended. After watching a film, we wrote on hundreds of little cards, "Made in a Communist Country." The next day, we took our activism in support of the John Birch Society to the next level by going to local stores and inserting these cards in products that were made in communist countries. We would be doing our part to educate people that by purchasing that particular commodity, they were inadvertently supporting the communist menace.

Before 1961, my exposure to the "Communist menace" was limited to the following events:

I was only 13 in 1954, during the McCarthy Senate Hearings on un-American activities in the movie industry. As long as Roy Rogers, Gene Autry, and Tarzan were still showing up on the big screen every Saturday, my life wasn't affected, but I did know about the hearings. I'm sure I thought if a movie star's activities were un-American, they deserved what they got.

I don't remember any duck-and-cover drills at school in the early 50s and 60s in the event of an atom bomb attack, although I do remember feeling afraid because of the talk about bombs. I remember hearing my dad and Jimmy Lewis, a friend of the family, talking in derogatory terms about Stalin after he died in 1953.

I remember that Khrushchev, during a 1956 meeting at the Polish embassy in Moscow, proclaimed to a room full of western diplomats that Russia would bury Americans.

I moved to New York in 1961, a short time after Khrushchev allegedly pounded his shoe on a desk to protest a speech at the General Assembly Meeting at the UN about people's civil rights being violated. In my mind, the promise to bury us and the shoe banging became conflated. Now, it turns out, there is no evidence of shoe banging, only fist shaking. Even then you couldn't trust what you read in the paper or saw on TV.

At the age of 19, I had never considered participating in any type of activism – anti-communist or any other kind, but what was I to do? I slept fitfully that night not knowing what unintended outcome would result from my participation. The next day, with a can-do attitude on my face, but I admit, fear in my heart, I got in the car with Ruth Ann, and we drove to their local K-Mart. I hid my little stack of cards admonishing consumers for buying communist goods in my pocket, and we purposefully strode into the store. We began to systematically cover the store. We pretended we were shopping while searching for any merchandise made in communist countries, and after finding one, furtively placed our cards securely in the items.

I was relieved when our pockets were empty, and we made it through the store, out to the car, and home without being arrested. I spent the next few days being on edge that my name was certain to be on some list, and I would be identified to suffer some sort of consequence for my actions. As a result of my short John Birch Society indoctrination, I even voted for Barry Goldwater in the 1964 presidential election three years later. It would take 12 years and Jimmy Carter's run for the presidency to help me see the error of my youthful ignorance regarding politics.

During that time with Ruth Ann, we became friends as adults and remained close. At the end of my visit, Ruth Ann, Jerry, and I drove up to Maryland with her four children for a family reunion in Ocean City. We all went to see the new house on Federal Street in Snow Hill that Mom and Dad had just bought. Betty announced that she would marry Bob Nelson, the meat packing man, that spring. Ruth Ann agreed to take Ghee back to Texas with her family while Betty settled into married life. I moved into the new house in Snow Hill, where Bobby would also live. We'd finally get to live under the same roof as brother and sister!

Ruth and George with sons (from left) Dale, Bobby, Sonny, and daughters Ruth Ann, Betty, Linda, in Ocean City, Md., 1961.

LIVING IN SNOW HILL

During my senior year of high school while we were still living in Stockton, my father became very ill with an undiagnosed illness. He was in and out of Salisbury Hospital, and the doctors thought it might be cancer. He had lost a lot of weight, was unable to eat, and was so sick that we were told to prepare for the worst. In the spring of 1959, word of Dad's condition reached Bobby who was traveling in Europe. He

The Lilly Heward House/Jones House, 211 W. Federal Street, Snow Hill, Md., 1961.

came home immediately and arranged to take Dad to Johns Hopkins Hospital in Baltimore. Within a week, the doctors diagnosed Dad with ulcerative colitis, and within another week, with the proper medication and diet, he was able to come home. Bobby stayed with Mom and Dad in Stockton to help with Dad's recovery before he returned to finish his senior year at Washington and Lee University.

After graduation, Bobby got a job teaching French on TV in Salisbury and moved in with Mom and Dad in Stockton. A year or two before his illness, Dad had done quite well selling insurance for Home Beneficial Life Insurance. When he was finally able to go back to work and reestablish an income stream, he and Bobby started looking for a house to buy. Mother was against it from the start, thinking it was foolish to think they could afford a home of their own. Undaunted, they continued their search and were rewarded with 211 W. Federal Street in Snow Hill. They found an estate sale that included a beautiful five-bedroom Victorian house they could buy for $10,000 and all the furnishings for an additional $2,000. It took both Bobby and Dad to convince Mom they could afford the $50 monthly mortgage payment. She finally relented and they closed on the house in May 1961.

I had just ended a year in New York, recently returning from my trip to Key West and Houston. With nothing next on my travel itinerary, I decided to move into the new house with my parents and Bobby. After nearly 30 years of marriage, my mother finally had a beautiful home, complete with antique furniture, on the nicest street in Snow Hill where our family called home for the next 25 years. It would be where we brought our children to see Mom Mom and Pop Pop, and where we'd gather for reunions, weddings, summer vacations, and Christmas and Thanksgiving holiday dinners.

Not too long after I moved into the new house, a friend of my mother's arranged an interview for me with GMAC where I was hired to manage the accounts of people financing automobiles. It was well-paying for the Eastern Shore, and there were benefits. Bobby left the household in September after receiving a Fulbright scholarship to study in France for a year. A year earlier, he had bought a 1960 Valiant, and he agreed to rent it to me for $20 a month while he was gone. I paid my parents $25 a month rent, which was half of their $50 mortgage

Bobby's 1960 Valiant that I rented, 1962.

payment. When Christmas came around that year, I paid one month of their mortgage as a Christmas present for Dad, and I bought Mother a winter coat for $20. Dad continued to do well with Home Beneficial Life Insurance Company, where he won yearly trips to places like Miami, New York, and Las Vegas. Mom never had to worry about whether they could afford the house or not. In fact, she was able to stop working and soon hired someone to come once a week to help with the housework.

That winter, Mom and Dad decided to adopt 2-year-old Ghee. She came to live with us in Snow Hill and was raised by Mom and Dad. Mother always loved the name Robin and decided to use Ghee as her middle name, so she became Robin Ghee Jones.

Ruth and George holding Robin Ghee in front of the Federal Street House, 1962.

PART TWO

LOVE AND MARRIAGE
(1962-80)

Hope family: Tony, Ellen, Linda, Clif, 1968.

1 | THE WEDDING

When I was living in Snow Hill and working for GMAC in Salisbury, I frequently took the bus to Baltimore for weekend visits with Gary, a senior at Johns Hopkins University. It was during one of those trysts, or more likely during Thanksgiving break of 1962, that I got pregnant.

I didn't tell my parents or anyone in my family that I was in the family way. Gary told his parents, who were more supportive than I thought they would be. If they had misgivings, to their credit, they never showed them to me. Of course, they had known me since I was 12, and they welcomed me into their family with open arms. We agreed that we would get married in Snow Hill, or Stockton, when Gary was home for Christmas break. We set the date for December 22, and since we needed a marriage license 48 hours prior to tying the knot, there would be time for Gary to drive from Baltimore to the Snow Hill courthouse to get the required documentation before they closed. However, when he left Baltimore on the Friday we were to get the license, it was snowing heavily and sticking to the ground. It took him twice as long to make the trip across the Bay Bridge, and by the time he arrived in Easton (halfway home), he knew it would be impossible to get to Snow Hill before the courthouse closed at 5 p.m.

He quickly changed plans and did the next best thing. He went to the Talbot County courthouse in Easton and applied for our marriage license there, about 70 miles north of Snow Hill. Gary's father's family had grown up in nearby St. Michaels, and his aunt and uncle and cousins still lived in the area. They were all members of the Royal Oak Methodist Church, which Gary's father and aunt had attended as children. So, we arranged to have our wedding there, with Gary's father, a Methodist minister, officiating. Aunt Eleanor would prepare our wedding reception, and

From left: Betty, Linda, Gary, Dan in Royal Oak, Md., 1962.

Tony would have parents joined in holy matrimony.

The night before my wedding, I was maid-of-honor in my friend Ruth Dryden's wedding in Snow Hill. We had been friends since seventh grade, and I was happy to stand up with her and witness her marriage vows to Wayne Young. They are still happily married today, and I visit them every time I get up to the Shore. To save money, I decided I would wear the same royal blue dress for my own ceremony. It had a full-length over-skirt that made it a little more formal for her wedding. The night before my big day, Mom came into my room and asked, "Is there any-thing you want to ask me?" I presumed

Linda (left) and Ruth Dryden, 1962.

she was talking about what I might expect on my wedding night, but I politely demurred. What a missed opportunity! Now I wish I had asked her to tell me everything she knew.

Ours was a small wedding, and the church was beautifully decorated with greenery and candles for Christmas. My sister Betty came home from New York to stand up with me, and Gary's brother Dan was best man. My parents and Gary's relatives rounded out the witnesses to our marriage. After the ceremony, we gathered at Aunt Eleanor's house on the Miles River for the beautiful reception she prepared for us. All in all, for a shotgun wedding, I think it was well-executed.

After Gary and I spent a couple of honeymoon days in Baltimore, we went back to Snow Hill for Christmas. We spent the first night in my bedroom at my parents' home and were awakened the next morning when 4-year-old Robin threw open the bedroom door with a flourish. She marched into the room, took a good look around, and not seeing what she was searching for, opened the closet and looked under the bed. Finding nothing in either place, she put her hands on her hips, glaring at us still in bed, and demanded, "Well, where are all your children?" She likely felt like I did when Dale and I were unsuccessful in freeing all the little people living in the radio years earlier.

With only six months remaining before Gary's graduation from Johns Hopkins, we decided that I would continue living with my parents and Robin in Snow Hill and working for GMAC to save money. Nearly every weekend, leaving Friday after work, I rode the bus for two hours from Salisbury to Baltimore to see my husband and made the return trip on Sunday. About two months into my marriage, I told my family I was pregnant, which brought shouts of delight from Robin. She rushed over to where I was sitting, pried my lips open, put her mouth next to mine, and shouted into my mouth, "Hello, down there, little baby." During the week, after dinner, Robin accompanied me and "little baby" on walks all over Snow Hill. I answered all her questions about the birds and the bees, or as much as I thought a 4-year old was ready to know. Perhaps I told her too much.

A couple of days a week, I drove Robin to nursery school in Salisbury, and on occasion, Gary's father, a guidance counselor at Wicomico High School, and I would ride together. One day, after we picked Robin up from school, Mr. Hope and I were talking about our vegetable gardens, and wanting to include Robin, he told her how important it was to eat her vegetables so she could grow up strong. Robin quickly replied, "I'm going to eat all my vegetables so that when I grow up, I can be big and strong so I can push a baby out of my vagina, just like Linda."

Gary's parents and I had a standing date every week. They came by the Federal Street house to pick me up, and we drove down to Sinnickson, Virginia to go to Sparrows Restaurant, a little dive across the Chincoteague Bay from Captain's Cove. While we waited for a delicious oyster stew, we ate as many raw oysters as we could, and then when the stew bowls were empty, we finished the meal with a fried oyster sandwich. Those six months in Snow Hill were an idyllic time for me, with few responsibilities, saving money, feeling loved and protected by two families, while I was growing a human being inside me.

I used the time to read everything I could on childbirth. *Childbirth Without Fear* by Grantly Dick Read, published in January 1959, was most influential. The crux of the book is that the human body is designed to give birth; it's only your mind that holds you back. Get rid of the fear and the birthing process is easier. I followed all the exercises he recommended to prepare my body to give birth and also practiced the self-hypnosis/relaxation techniques which were similar to what I had learned in Key West. When I told Mom I had decided to have natural childbirth, she asked me what that meant. I said it was giving birth without medication, to which she replied, "Oh, that's the way I had you and Dale, both at home." It was the first time she told me that I had been born at home, and delivered by my grandmother who held me until the midwife came to cut the cord.

Toward the end of the school year, Gary was offered two jobs, one with Honeywell in Florida and one with Westinghouse in Pittsburgh. He accepted the Westinghouse offer because it paid $500 a year more than the Honeywell job

– $6,500 a year ($60,000 today). Then the day finally came when I drove to Baltimore with Gary's parents to attend his graduation.

After the ceremony, I met Carol Riley, who would become my best friend for many years, and we are still in touch today. She was married to Lance Riley, a classmate of Gary's, who also had accepted a job with Westinghouse. We all would be moving to Pittsburgh. Their daughter Denise was just a year old, and I would become a little mom-in training.

Linda and Gary on graduation day at Johns Hopkins University, 1963.

2 | THE MOVE TO PITTSBURGH

After saying goodbye to Gary's parents, and with our worldly possession loaded into our 1958 Ford, we set off for Western Pennsylvania to begin a new chapter in our life together. After the 240-mile trip, we found a motel on the outskirts of Pittsburgh. To me, that meant it was time to find something to eat and settle in for the night; to Gary, it meant it was time to explore. With a couple more hours of daylight remaining, we drove toward downtown Pittsburgh. The steel mills between us and the Monongahela River were belching fire and smoke and traffic was heavy. After taking a left turn to go over a bridge where the Alleghany, the Ohio, and the Monongahela rivers came together, we entered a dimly lit tunnel. I was certain we would never be able to find our way back to our motel once we emerged from the other side of that tunnel.

Even though I had been to college in Baltimore for a year and spent another year in New York City navigating city streets, trolley cars, and subways to find my way around, I felt completely out of my element with steel mills, rivers, mountains, and tunnels. I started to cry (sobbing, if I'm honest), begging to be taken back to the motel. Perhaps it was the pregnancy hormones. Perhaps it was the sudden awareness that I was responsible for the safety of the little human being hitching a ride in my body. Perhaps it was the realization that I was surrendering control of my life to someone else. Someone other than me would have a voice in my decisions. It is important to note that I was aware at the time that I was not being rational, yet I was unable to still the terror. I can't remember another time when I lost it so completely, like I did that day, especially for something that now seems so minuscule. Poor Gary must have been thinking, "What did I get myself into?" Obviously, we did find our way back to the motel and to food, which transformed me back into my good-natured self. Perhaps it was hormones after all.

After a good night's sleep, we set out the next morning in search of a furnished apartment. It was the first in a long inventory of furnished apartments we occupied during our first year together. Gary's agreement with Westinghouse was to spend a year on the Management Training Program, being transferred to a variety of plants and offices around the country to determine where his skills could best be used, and where he thought he would be a good fit – engineering, sales, management.

Our first home was a one-bedroom, second-floor apartment in a private house in Wilkinsburg, a suburb of Pittsburgh. The apartment, with its entrance into the

First apartment in Wilkinsburg, Pa., 1963.

479 State Street, Sharon, Pa., 1963.

bedroom, had an odd layout; the bedroom was between the kitchen and the living room. We soon reconnected with Lance and Carol, who were living nearby. Carol and I spent most of our days together taking care of their little girl Denise, and when our husbands came home from work, Carol and I had dinner prepared for all of us. After a month in Pittsburgh, our next destination was 75 miles north to Sharon, Pennsylvania, while Lance and Carol went back home to Baltimore. This started a year of monthly upheaval in which I packed up our meager possessions for loading into the car when Gary got home from work on a Friday, followed by the drive to our next destination. Staying in a motel, we had the weekend to find another furnished apartment and settle in so Gary would be ready to report to work on Monday.

In Sharon, we found another second-floor apartment in a large owner-occupied home on tree-shaded State Street. Another odd layout, we entered the eat-in kitchen, then passed through the bedroom to the large living room, with oversized windows overlooking the front yard and street. During our first week in Sharon, we made friends with Butch and Brenda Crouch from Port Arthur, Texas. Butch was also on the Westinghouse Management Training Program, and eventually we all moved to Pittsburgh, where our friendship grew and became an important part of our lives.

By then, I was 7½ months pregnant. Since none of us had been to Niagara Falls, we decided to make the 200-mile trek in a weekend trip. Butch says that our friendship was cemented on the second day when we were looking for a place to eat. Everyone was being very polite, asking, "How about this one?" while Gary passed one restaurant after another. As Gary drove by the 10th restaurant, I finally took control of the situation and said, "Dammit Gary, stop at the next restaurant you see. I'm starving, and I want to eat now." Butch says he never loved anyone more.

Once we were all in Pittsburgh, we visited each other weekly during the next four years. They loved our children like an aunt and uncle. When Gary was transferred to Indianapolis in 1968, Butch and Brenda offered to keep our three children, Tony (4), Ellen (2½), and Clif (1), for a week so we could go house hunting, unencumbered. Butch had even built the children a table

Butch and Brenda Crouch with (from left) Tony, Ellen, Clif, Pittsburgh, Pa., 1968.

with three little chairs to use when we had dinner at their house. Butch and Brenda eventually moved back to their home state of Texas and had a daughter, but sadly their marriage didn't last. Brenda and I stayed in touch, and I spent the night with her and her second husband when I moved from Atlanta to Santa Fe nearly 20 years later.

After I saw Brenda, I started wondering what Butch was up to and I tracked him down in Lake Tahoe, California. I was shocked to find a hippie musician strung out on cocaine. He pulled himself together and came to Santa Fe to visit in 1986. He loved his time in Santa Fe so much that he went back to Tahoe, gathered up all his belongings and moved to the Land of Enchantment. Not long after he arrived, I left for three years, during which time he started working for Bruce McEachern at Babe's restaurant, managing the bar and playing music. When I returned to Santa Fe in 1989, Butch introduced me to Bruce, which leads to another story farther down the road. I have always loved the connections that are made through friends so dear.

Tony Arrives

A week after our trip to Niagara Falls, and a week before leaving for Gary's next assignment, I went into labor on July 27, 1963, a month before my due date. Gary and I spent the day in the hospital playing gin rummy while we waited for Tony to make his grand entrance. The doctor decided to induce labor and within half an hour, I was in the delivery room, refusing any medication, still committed to natural childbirth so I could watch my beautiful baby boy being born. In 1963, most doctors discouraged natural childbirth, preferring the mother to be anesthetized while giving birth. I had met this doctor only once, and he was willing to "see how it went." I had prepared myself like it was my opening night on Broadway. Lights, camera, action – except no camera, and no husband in the delivery room in those days. I used all the relaxation techniques I had learned in my books, especially using self-hypnosis I had learned in Florida. Separating my mind from my body, I allowed my body do what it was designed to do.

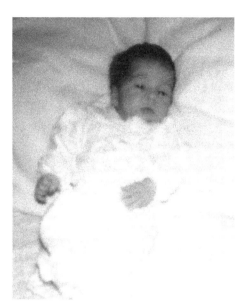

Garrett Anthony (Tony) Hope, Jr., was born July 27, 1963, in Sharon, Pa.

I was able to see Tony's head crown and I could feel him slithering out into the world. As soon as he was born, I expected them to put him on my stomach. As I was reaching for him, without even a good look at him (except seeing a full head of black hair), and without any explanation from the doctor or nurses, a gas mask was clamped onto my face. I didn't know what was happening. As I felt myself sinking into unconsciousness, I began to scream in protest. This wasn't supposed to happen. The scream became a downward spiraling echo as I descended deeper into oblivion. My last conscious thought was, "I am dying, and my punishment for screaming is that I'll have to hear the scream's echo for eternity."

Thankfully, that was not the case. I came out of unconsciousness the same way I went in, but without the scream – faint garbled voices and dim lights, slowly becoming clearer and louder and brighter, until I realized that I was still alive. Yay! They explained that I had not stopped bleeding, and they put me under anesthesia so they could pack my uterus with gauze. "It would have been better if you told me what you were doing and why," I said. Ruth Ann

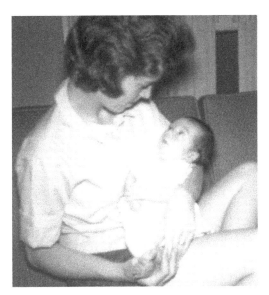

Linda holds her newborn son Tony, 1963.

told me later that continued bleeding after giving birth can be quite dangerous and that was why they acted so quickly. Still ...

While I stayed in the hospital 3-4 days, Gary arranged with his boss for us to stay in Sharon for an extra month. By the time Tony and I came home from the hospital, Gary's mother, truly a blessing, had arrived, ready to help with her first grandchild. My own mother was in Texas taking care of Ruth Ann's children while Ruth Ann was giving birth to Mark, her sixth child born just two days after Tony. That summer, between July 27 and August 28, Mom and Dad had four new grandchildren, bringing their total to 10. Mrs. Hope was such a soothing and gentle presence during the time she was with us, and she gave us the best possible care. When she left a week later, I watched from the living room window as Gary carried her suitcase to the car. After they both got in and drove away, I looked back at baby Tony and thought, "Oh my God, what do I do now?"

Of course, as everyone does, I figured out what to do, especially with the help of diaper service. The major shock was learning to deal with projectile vomiting by an infant. Having been born a month early, Tony didn't have a fully developed digestive system, which manifested when the contents of his stomach were forcefully propelled several feet in a stream. When I witnessed the first explosion, I was shocked by the violent nature and the distance the stream traveled. The doctor assured me that he would outgrow it, and I started feeding him in a raincoat for the duration. One time, after nursing him in bed, I sat him on my lap to burp him, and his projectile spewed all over his dad's bare back, still sleeping next to us. I got a diaper and a cloth and cleaned up Gary's back, and he didn't even wake up.

I had arranged for my sister Betty to come for a week, but I was on my own for the week after Gary's mom left. I was really glad to see my sister when she arrived from New York. Betty volunteered to sleep in the living room next to Tony's bed so she could train him to sleep through the night. Since he was nursing every two hours, her success in getting him back to sleep with just a pacifier was profound. By the time she left, he was waking up for just one feeding in the middle of the night. And, aside from the projectile vomiting (which he grew out of as promised), Tony was a very good and easy baby. I recommend it for your first one.

When we left Sharon in September, even with a baby, we were still able to pack all our possessions in our car. We headed south back to Pittsburgh, found another apartment, our third on the second floor of an owner-occupied house. The odd layout this time required us to enter the apartment through the bedroom, then through the living room and a hallway to get to the kitchen in the back of the house. There was also a small room off the bedroom which we used as Tony's room. The apartment was four doors down from the railroad track, requiring conversations to cease every time a train passed, and then resume when we could

685 Whitney Ave., Wilkinsburg, Pa., 1963.

hear again. We grew accustomed to the quirky layout and didn't think twice about renting it again on other assignments in Pittsburgh. After the second time in Pittsburgh, we were sent to Baltimore, back to Pittsburgh, then to Detroit, and back to Pittsburgh again. Along the way, we purchased a playpen and a crib and picked up a few pieces of baby necessities. For the last couple of moves, we needed a U-Haul to make our monthly treks to the new location.

It was during the time Tony was about six months old that the Beatles set foot on American soil. I remember watching them on the Ed Sullivan show and not being very impressed. I could never understand the "teenage idol" syndrome, even for Elvis back in the 50s. I could do without all the screaming, crying, and fainting. Like everyone else, I eventually succumbed to the magic of the Beatles and was soon singing *I Want to Hold Your Hand* along with them on radio. However, it would be five years, in 1968, before I bought one of their albums, *Yellow Submarine*. By then I was had fallen under their spell.

JFK ASSASSINATION

By November 1963, Butch and Brenda, our friends from Sharon, and Gary and I were all living in the Pittsburgh area. If you ask anyone who was alive on November 22, 1963, they can always tell you where they were and what they were doing. I had luncheon plans with Brenda that day. She had offered to babysit for 4-month-old Tony while I went to a nearby laundromat to attend to Tony's never-ending cloth diapers; we were now without diaper service. Remember, those were the days when we still washed diapers, secured them with large safety pins, and covered them with plastic pants. Even though Pampers had come out two years earlier, I wouldn't use them until 1966 when Clif was born.

I was waiting for my clothes to finish in the dryer when someone came into the laundromat shortly after 12:30 p.m. announcing that President Kennedy had been shot in Dallas, Texas. I gathered the clothes as soon as they were dry and rushed back to Brenda's. By the time I arrived, they announced that Kennedy was dead. Butch had already come home from work so he could get their cars off the street, parking them behind the house. Since they had Texas plates, he was concerned that someone might take out their angst on someone from the state where Kennedy had been killed.

I never did buy into the Warren Commission's lone gunman theory. The idea that Lee Harvey Oswald could hit a moving target, twice, from 90 yards away was simply implausible. To explain the lone gunman theory, we had to buy into their "magic bullet" theory. According to the Commission Report, the second shot actually killed Kennedy. A third shot missed the car altogether, and the "magic bullet" followed an impossible trajectory. According to the autopsy report, the bullet from the sixth-floor book depository struck Kennedy in the back of the head, then changed direction in order to exit through his throat. The bullet then punctured the back of Texas Governor John Connally, exited his chest, changed direction again to go through his right wrist, before burying itself beneath the skin of Connally's left thigh. To top it off, the pristine bullet was found on the gurney that transported Kennedy into the Parkland Hospital. We were asked to believe a lot.

Also, preposterous was the fact that Oswald was shot in the Dallas Police headquarters, surrounded by police and FBI agents. His killer, Jack Ruby, was a paid informant for the FBI. Thirty years after the assassination, I studied the assassination as part of a critical thinking class in college. I wrote a term paper on the events, challenging the accepted, but improbable, theories. Information about the assassination was supposed to have been held for 50 years. Some of it has been released, but a lot is still being withheld. Trump blamed National Security issues; Biden has blamed the COVID-19 pandemic. The only plausible reason I see for still withholding information is that somehow the government has to hide the truth because they were directly involved in the assassination. The Kennedy assassination is when I stopped trusting the government to give complete and true information.

OUR FIRST HOME

In May 1964, after moving seven times during our first year together, Gary was finally assigned a permanent job at a semi-conductor plant on the outskirts of Pittsburgh. We were more than ready to settle down, soon finding a three-bedroom rental on Longview Drive near Irwin, Pennsylvania. We bought three rooms of Danish Modern furniture for $300 and moved into our new home.

211 Longview Dr., Irwin, Pa., 1964.

When Gary heard about the new Mustang automobile that Ford was introducing, he had to have one. The first model Mustang, the Early 1965 Mustang was referred to as the 1964½ and featured a stick shift on the floor, full wheel covers, bucket seats, carpeting, and a padded dash, all for a base retail price of $2,320. I could buy one today for around $40,000. According to Ford, 22,000 orders were taken the day of its debut, and although I don't know for sure, I bet one of them was Gary's. I do know that we got the first one that came to our dealership in Irwin. Ford sold close to 417,000 Mustangs in the first 12 months. We must have traded in our '58 Ford. Our second car was a Volkswagen Beetle. One would think that a young growing family would have had their sights on something more practical.

Sadly, the Mustang was a short-lived vehicle in the Hope parade of automobiles. When I was six months pregnant with Ellen, we were on our way home to Pittsburgh after spending Christmas with our families in Snow Hill. Gary and

Left: Gary and Tony with the 1964½ Mustang, 1964; right: Linda packs the first station wagon, a 1965 Ford Falcon, 1965.

I were in a traffic accident somewhere in West Virginia after someone pulled out in front of us. Tony, free roaming in the back seat, was thrown between the bucket seats in the front and hit his forehead on the gear shift knob. He and I spent the night in the hospital, under observation, while Gary went about getting the car drivable for the rest of the trip home. I am not sure if we had it fixed and then sold it, or if we traded it in "as is." We ended up with a sensible medium size Ford station wagon for me to drive, and Gary drove the green VW bug.

ELLEN ARRIVES

Ellen was born March 26, 1965. We had planned to have our children two years apart, but I must have gotten pregnant as soon as we started trying since just 20 months separated them. When I went into labor, the McConnells, friends who lived two doors down from us, came to get Tony while Gary drove me to the hospital. I was already in the delivery room when the doctor arrived. He had enough time to hang up his hat and coat on the back of the door and delivered Ellen 15 minutes later. It was a spectacularly easy delivery with none of the problems I had with Tony. It was a completely natural childbirth, and I was only in the hospital for three days this time. Gary's parents came for a week to help with Tony and the new baby, after which Betty came again for a week. I always felt so supported by Gary's parents and my family. From the beginning of our marriage, I wrote a letter to Gary's parents every week. I know that somewhere in the barn on their farm there are several boxes full of my letters – news of our travels and stories of all the activities of their grandchildren.

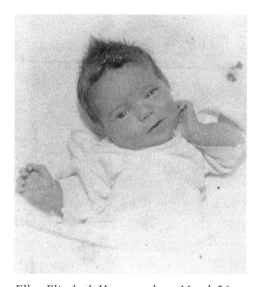

Ellen Elizabeth Hope was born March 26, 1965, in Greensburg, Pa.

After a year in the rental, Gary and I felt like we were ready to invest in a home of our own. We found a two-story, four-bedroom house, in Irwin. With help from Betty for the down

Our first owned house, 590 Semple Dr., Irwin, Pa., 1965.

payment, we bought the house for $16,000 (equivalent to $150,000 in 2023). This house was the first home for Clif, born the next year in 1966. This was a family-friendly neighborhood where I made a lot of friends. None of the women I knew worked, so we were free to pack up our children and go bowling, where they offered day care to watch over the little ones. I got together with another group of moms who played bridge once a week – sometimes at someone's house, sometimes at a park where we took our playpens and jumpy seats. There was always a dummy (the person not playing the bid) who was charged with meeting the needs of the children (sometimes as many as 15), who all got along and had as good a time as we did.

CLIF ARRIVES

The plan was for Gary's parents to come for a visit when the doctor thought Clif's arrival was imminent so that they were both there to help with Tony and Ellen and the new baby. We put that plan in action, but after a week still with no new baby, they offered to take Tony and Ellen home with them, thinking Clif would arrive any day. Three weeks later Clif was born on October 14, 1966.

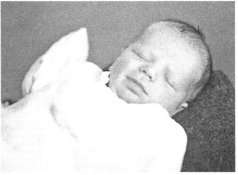

One might think I would enjoy those three weeks with no children, but I missed them very much. As soon as I felt the first contraction, I knew I had to get to the hospital post haste, given the ease with which I had delivered Ellen 17 months earlier. Clif was born, completely natural childbirth, just two hours after I got to the hospital, and I was ready to go home in a day. A week later, the Hopes brought Tony and Ellen home to meet their new brother. After a month with Gary's parents, Ellen was

Above: Clifton Strickland Hope was born on October 14, 1966, in Irwin, Pa..
Below: From left, Ellen, Clif, Tony, 1967.

calling Mrs. Hope "Mommy." If I offered to help her with something, she would say, "No, Mommy do it," as she ran to Mrs. Hope. Tony fell in love with Clif right away and took on the role of big brother. It took Ellen a little longer. One day she told me she thought it would be a good idea if we put that baby in the garbage. Clif was an ideal baby, sleeping through the night fairly early, waking up happy, and everyone fell in love with him. Even Ellen succumbed after the initial shock of not being the baby any longer.

I loved being a stay-at-home mom with three children so close in age. All three were happy children and enjoyed playing together. Having friends made it easy to go shopping or to run errands because I could drop my kids off, always with the expectation that I would return the favor. These were the days when children were bathed in the bathtub every night with clean clothes every day. There was one period of time when I decided I needed to make my mornings easier. After evening baths, I dressed the three children in their play clothes for the next day, instead of their pajamas. They were dressed and ready to meet the new morning. I now feel very blessed that I was able to be home with my children until Clif started kindergarten. I was unaware of the new women's movement taking shape that would expose the patriarchal society we were living under while expanding both women's and men's roles. At the time, I was happy in my role as wife and mom while being financially supported by my husband.

3 | THE MOVE TO INDIANAPOLIS

We were only in our house in Irwin for two years when Westinghouse transferred Gary to Indianapolis in 1967. They not only paid for the move, but paid for the movers to pack us up too. I remember addressing Christmas cards while the packers were wrapping up ashtrays filled with ashes and cigarette butts.

I didn't stop them. I didn't care. I didn't have to do it. During our week-long house-buying trip while the children were with Butch and Brenda, we had found my dream house, a beautiful four-bedroom, white brick Cape Cod in Carmel, just north of Indianapolis. We paid $26,000 (equivalent to $244,500 today) for it, and of all the houses we lived in, I thought this was the prettiest. The children had the two upstairs bedrooms with a shared bath. The master bedroom and office were downstairs. It was the first time we had an actual family room with a fireplace.

The yard was beautiful with shade trees, and I was the one who mowed the lawn every week in the summer. My women friends in the neighborhood said I could only mow the grass during the week while their husbands were at work. They didn't want them getting any ideas. We had wonderful neighbors. The Bond family, with four daughters, lived next door. Thirteen-year-old Marcia was always at our house, playing with the children, and helping with any project I was working on. Two doors down from us lived the "Cookie Lady," who made cookies for the neighborhood children. Every afternoon, the kids would make their way down to her house, knock on her back door, waiting for the cookies she'd bring them – two cookies in each little baggie. We started making homemade ice cream, and once a week, the children took her a quart of ice cream in exchange for her cookies. Tony started kindergarten while we lived in Carmel but would only finish the first half of the school year.

Wherever we lived, one of our favorite past times was exploring the countryside on the weekends. Thankfully, I never had a repeat of the irrational terror that struck me upon my arrival in Pittsburgh five years earlier. The children were good travelers, enjoying the outings as much as we did.

Ellen, Clif, Tony ready for nightly prayers in our Carmel, Ind., Cape Cod, 1968.

Before we moved to Indianapolis, Gary's brother Dan enlisted in the army to become a helicopter pilot. As expected, he was sent off to Vietnam where the situation had become more prevalent on the news every day, and now in our lives as well. Every night when the children said their prayers, they always included Dan: "God bless Mommy and Daddy and God bless Uncle Dan, the helicopter man."

After only a year in my dream house, Gary heard about a business opportunity, selling franchises, and decided to leave the safety of the corporate world to seek his entrepreneurial fortune. I stayed in Indianapolis for six months, selling our house, while he set up his business in Baltimore. With the $2,000 profit from selling the house in my pocket, we said goodbye to our beautiful Cape Cod, and the kids and I joined Gary in Baltimore, where we lived for the next 11 years.

4 | BACK IN MARYLAND

VILLAGE OF PURNELL

In January 1969, we were back in our home state of Maryland. Baltimore was familiar territory – both of us had been to college there, and our good friends Lance and Carol settled in the area. We were less than three hours from our families in Snow Hill, a much shorter distance than the 7-8 hour trips we had made for the last six years.

Gary was trying to make a success of selling franchises, and we both thought we were going to get rich. He rented a nice office in Howard County and leased a Buick Electra so he'd look successful. We started out renting a two-story, three-bedroom townhouse in Village of Purnell, where we lived for the first year. We enrolled Tony in Dickey Hill Elementary so he could finish kindergarten. He also started first grade in the fall, when Ellen started kindergarten there. There was no school bus service, so several of us moms took turns carpooling.

Above: 5004 W. Forest Park Ave., Baltimore, Md., 1968. Below: Clif (3), Ellen (4), Tony (6), 1969.

I set up the dining room as a playroom, and then started a small childcare business since Ellen and Clif were still at home. There was just enough room for us to eat in the tiny kitchen. The money came in handy because, it turned out, we weren't getting rich. Gary's franchise business turned out to be a feast or famine arrangement. When he sold a franchise, that money had to be set aside for the months ahead when no money was coming in. Eventually, we had to turn in his fancy rental car and close his fancy office. When we set up his home office in the third bedroom, Ellen moved in with Tony and Clif in the second bedroom, which was quite crowded with Clif's crib and two twin beds. But it *was* a good set-up for reading bedtime stories. "The Wind in the Willows" was a favorite.

One afternoon, when Clif and a friend were playing on the stairs, Clif fell, hitting his forehead on the wrought-iron

Tony, Clif, Linda, Ellen in Patapsco Park, 1970.

railing. The skin was pressed so tightly to his skull that it wasn't bleeding yet, but we could see his skull. I immediately pressed a damp cloth against it – cover it up, I always said, so you can't see the blood – and we headed for the emergency room. Clif was sitting on my lap in the car, the cloth still held against his forehead. He hadn't uttered a word since his fall, and I thought he might be in shock.

As Gary was speeding to the hospital, Clif finally spoke, in a weak voice saying, "Mom?"

"Yes?" I asked, gently.

Softly and proudly, Clif replied, "I can jump from my crib to Tony's bed."

That's when I knew he'd be all right. While they were stitching the wound on his forehead, I noticed that Clif was being perfectly still except that one foot was slowly rocking back and forth. There was something in that movement, and in his stoic demeanor that suddenly made me feel I was going to pass out. The nurse took one look at me and had me put my head between my knees, and eventually I felt well enough to take my little stitched-up boy home.

WESTOWNE

After a year of renting, Gary talked his Grandfather Strickland into lending us a down payment so we could buy a row house in Westowne, a suburb of nearby Catonsville. The house was the same size as the townhouse we were living in, plus it had a rec room in the basement and a second bathroom. Gary was still trying to get the franchise business up and running, so we turned the dining room into an office for him. Our growing children could now spread out in their lovely knotty pine rec room. Again, we made do with a small table in the tiny eat-in kitchen.

Tony finished the second half of his second grade in his third new school,

Westowne Elementary; Ellen finished the second half of kindergarten; and Clif followed a year later. Since the country was in a period of financial stagnation, the franchise business was slow going. It was necessary for me to start bringing in a salary, and substitute teaching at the elementary school was a good way to start. By working in the school system, I would be on the same vacation and holiday schedule as the children. In 1972, when Clif started first grade, I got a secretarial job in the front office at Lansdowne High School with an enrollment of 2,000 students. It was the 70s, and, over the seven years I worked there, I saw way too many kids strung out on drugs. We called the ambulance to the school at least once a week to take care of a student who had overdosed. I remember seeing one kid's pupils so dilated that I wouldn't have been surprised if they had turned to liquid and run down his face.

209 Westshire Rd., Baltimore, Md., 1970.

The Vietnam War was in full force. Troop involvement had peaked in April 1969, with 543,000 American combat troops stationed in Vietnam and there was no end in sight. Many students, mostly girls, were wearing MIA bracelets as a way to remember American POWs and soldiers missing in action. By 1973 the number of troops unaccounted for was 2,646. The bracelet program kicked off on Veterans Day in 1970, and public response grew so quickly that they soon were receiving 12,000 requests a day. They sold the bracelets for $2.50, a little more than the price of a movie ticket at the time. In all, nearly five million bracelets were distributed, and enough money was raised to produce millions of bumper stickers, buttons, and printed materials to help draw attention to the missing men. Following the Paris Peace Accords of 1973 and the withdrawal of American troops, 591 U.S. POWs returned during Operation Homecoming. The U.S. still sought the return of another 1,600 Americans reported killed in action and bodies not recovered. These missing personnel would become the subject of the Vietnam War POW/MIA issue for years to come. As of July 2019, the Department of Defense listed a remaining 1,587 Americans unaccounted for as a result of the war. It was well after the end of the Vietnam War in 1975 that we began to learn the truth about the war – an unnecessary war. I learned the Vietnamese people call it the War of American Aggression, which was a sobering and believable concept.

In 1973, OPEC placed an oil embargo on the United States because of its support of Israel during the Yom Kippur War. After the sanctions, the price of gasoline increased by 37%, which severely limited the supply. Rationing and long gas lines were common, and the resulting recession forced Gary to abandon his entrepreneurial endeavors. Luckily, he soon got a job working for Nordson, a company that made machines that applied glue to packaging.

We turned his office back into a dining room and bought a piano to put on one wall. Gary's new job led us to meet our new best friends and future business partners, Alec and Marie Iwashenko. The company Alec worked for sold the glue that Gary's machines used, so they frequently worked together to make deals with their customers. Their three children were close in age to ours, and we started spending a lot of time together. We soon decided to go into business together, and GLAMCO, an acronym for Gary, Linda, Alec, and Marie, was born.

RIDGE ROAD RENOVATION

GLAMCO's first project was the purchase and renovation of a fixer-upper on Ridge Road in Oak Forest, one of the nicest neighborhoods in Catonsville. The property had a detached garage, perfect storage for a 50-gallon drum of gasoline. After the hassles of waiting in long lines at gas stations, we wouldn't be waiting any longer. However, the renovation that we thought

1510 Ridge Rd., Catonsville, Md., 1985.

would take 3-6 months to complete ended up taking a year.

While cleaning out the attic, we found a box of old comic books and soon learned that comic books were valuable, according to the price guide we bought. As we started going through the stack to assess our windfall, we were elated when we found one that was worth $1,200. The next few were only $100 or $75, which we tossed aside, until one of us said, "Stop! Wait a minute, these are 10 cent comic books," and we started having more appreciation even for the less expensive ones.

After pulling down plaster and putting up sheetrock in most of the rooms and gutting and putting in new bathrooms, the kitchen was finally the last room to remodel before taking on sanding the floors. The kitchen was a major project to approach when we all were weary with decisions, constant weekend work, and a continuous outpouring of money. However, when Marie and I heard Gary and Alec talking about paneling the walls and installing a dropped ceiling, we were aghast and let them know the kitchen should have drywall installed – not paneling and dropped ceilings. That would look cheap. They listened and agreed, said it sounded like a great idea, and if we wanted it done that way, we were welcomed to take on the job ourselves. Marie and I took one look at each other, quickly lowered our requirements and our expectations, and decided to love whatever our husbands did. We sold the box of comic books for about $3,000, which paid for the kitchen remodel. The floors turned out beautifully, and finally the house was finished and ready to put on the market. Since we did all the work ourselves on the house, I can't say what we spent in sweat labor, and I'm not sure anyone accounted for the expenses on the entire renovation. We all counted it a win.

We bought the house for $30,000 and sold it a year later for $60,000, which was pretty good in a recession. Zillow's estimated price today is $729,000.

NEWBURG AVENUE

Now that Gary and I were both working, and with the sale of the Ridge Road fixer-upper on the horizon, we felt like it was time to find a bigger house for our growing children. It didn't take us long to find our 13-room, three-story Victorian home on an acre of land covered in azaleas, dogwoods, and rhododendrons. It was within a short walking distance to the Catonsville elementary school, as well as the junior and senior high schools. The children could also walk to the library and to their little league baseball and basketball games. In the summer of 1975, Tony turned 12, Ellen was 10, and Clif would soon be 9. Not only was it the perfect place to raise a family, but it was also a lovely house to live out our days.

I fell in love with the century-old Victorian home the moment I stepped from the front porch into the three-story foyer. The wide, majestic stairway gracefully wound up to the second-floor hallway and then up to the third floor. Off the foyer was a room designated for Gary's office and a second room on the other side we used as a music room. All three children and I started taking piano lessons, and it was great to have a separate room to practice our scales and learn the songs for our lessons and recitals. The children each had their own bedroom on the third floor and a playroom for their toys and games. On the second floor, we had a guest room, our bedroom, and a sitting room. Another bedroom on the second floor had been turned into a laundry room that opened to a lovely screened-in porch where the children could sleep on hot summer nights, just like my brothers and I had done at our grandparents' farmhouse on Little Mill Road.

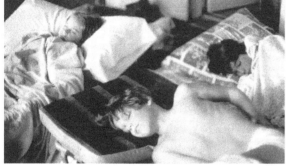

Above: 133 Newburg Ave., Catonsville, Md., 1975.
Below: From left, Ellen, Clif, Tony on the sleeping porch, 1976.

The owner, who had lived in the house for 40 years, told us she had planted the myriad azaleas covering the acre lot. She said the man who lived across the street worked in the experimental lab in the horticulture department at the University of Maryland, and as they developed new species of azaleas, he brought her plantings. She claimed she had planted 4,000 of them, and, as a result, the yard was a wonderland of colors, textures, and petal shapes. I could see garden weddings taking place amid the azaleas. Left unpruned, some were twice as tall as me. When we had overnight guests, I went out in the yard and cut a branch from as many plants as I could until my arms were overflowing, with no two blooms alike. I arranged them in vases for all 13 rooms, which helped to decorate the house – and also solved the problem of pruning.

We moved in our grand mansion with row-house sized furniture. How would we ever fill the rooms? Friends and relatives started offering us furniture they weren't using and eventually we had everything we needed. Our home became a central meeting place for family and friends, and we always had room for everybody. The first year I kept a record, and we had 130 overnight guests, and that wasn't counting the kid's friends who slept over. In the summer, the tall oak trees as old as the house towered over the roof and shaded the dogwood trees dotted throughout the yard. The house was a wonderful place to live in the spring, summer, and fall, but oh, those winters were another story.

The country was just coming out of the oil embargo with high oil prices, and with an oil furnace, the cost of heating the house was expensive. By the end of the first winter, we purchased two air-tight wood burning stoves, including one that kept the living room toasty, with a little heat drifting into the kitchen and music room. The other stove was in Gary's office, where we opened the door at night to allow a meager amount of heat to float up to the vast second and third floors. We also used the old oil furnace to heat the radiators in every room, but with the thermostat in the living room, they stayed lukewarm at best. We loved when company came in the winter because we opened all the doors, turned up the thermostat and made the house comfortable.

Each year, we used about seven cords of wood, all cut and gathered on Gary's family farm near Snow Hill on the Eastern Shore. We made two or three treks a year in an old red panel truck, bought just for this purpose. Gary, his grandfather, and Tony and Clif spent a day cutting and loading, and then we'd all pile in the truck for the 3-hour drive back to Catonsville. When we got back to the house, we all unloaded the wood chunks in the yard where Gary and the boys chopped it into manageable pieces, later stacked on the front porch.

Looking back, I don't even know who that little 35-year-old girl/woman was, who didn't demand that the house be heated like a normal home, or that firewood be bought and delivered for the wood stoves. Just like Scarlett O'Hara said she'd never go hungry again, I finally declared, I'd never go cold again. By the mid- to late 70s, the Women's Liberation Movement emerged in the mainstream as a collective struggle for equality seeking to free women from oppression and male supremacy. I was beginning to see the ways I had subordinated my own ideas and beliefs, and how I agreed with my husband just to keep the peace.

One fall weekend, my work friend Vicki and her husband invited my family to go camping in the Shenandoah Valley. They brought all their own camping gear for our first camping adventure, and we all loved the experience. Snow fell overnight, and when we unzipped our tents in the morning, a winter wonderland lay before us. The kids wanted to go again, and we soon bought two tents – a small one for the children and a larger one for us, and we made our first solo camping trip to Disney World over the Thanksgiving holiday.

We enjoyed setting up our new equipment, cooking dinner on our new camp stove, and going to bed in our new sleeping bags. It started raining during the night, and it wasn't long before all of us realized our tents were leaking. No one had advised us that we had to seal all the seams, and, by morning, we were all soaking wet. Luckily the sun came out, and while everything was drying, we went to a camping store to buy seam sealer. We spent an hour sealing the seams, which made

Linda dons a poncho during the first camping trip in new tents, Kissimmee, Fla., 1976.

us late getting to the Magic Kingdom the first day. As much as we enjoyed camping, we quickly saw the disadvantage of taking down tents in wet weather, packing them in the car, and then drying everything after we got home. Of course, we escalated. We decided to buy a 19-ft trailer, which included a bunk room in the back for the kids, a dining table in the front converted into a bed for Gary and me, and the kitchen and bathroom in the middle. Aside from having to pull it behind the car, it was the best solution for our needs.

It was around this time that Gary purchased a 350 Yamaha motorcycle, and soon moved up to a 500. Alec was talking about buying the 350 so he and Gary could ride together, which motivated me to keep the 350 for myself. I did not want to be left behind while the men had all the fun. Clearly, it was too big for me – my feet couldn't even rest solidly on the road when I came to a stop.

I learned how important that was when I went to get my motorcycle license. As I was making a sharp turn on the course, I was going so slow that I had to stop. As I put my foot down on the slightly sloping roadway, the bike leaned over and because I couldn't hold it up, it kept going until it was lying on the ground. To my credit, I garnered the strength to pick it back up again, which I thought was quite a feat for a 115-pound girl, but the license testing man wasn't that impressed. He failed me. The next time, I borrowed a friend's 125 Yamaha and passed the test with no problems.

One day as I was speeding down a highway on my 350 Yamaha at 60 mph, I suddenly realized the danger I was in and asked, "What am I doing, careening down the highway with nothing separating my body from the road?" I came to my senses, and we traded my bike for a street-legal 125 Yamaha dirt bike. It was just my size and easy for me to handle. When I started selling real estate, I took the back roads on my motorcycle to the office and to meet clients at houses they wanted to see. I never rode on a highway again.

FARM IN WEST VIRGINIA

After the Ridge Road property was sold, we started our second GLAMCO project. Gary and I had been looking for land in West Virginia, thinking it would be a good investment and a great place to camp. When we found a 120-acre farm on the outskirts of Gasaway near Sutton Lake State

Farm near Gasaway, W. Va., 1978.

Park, Alec and Marie offered to go in with us. We planned to sub-divide the bottom land on one side of the road, and the hillside on the other side, paying for the project by selling lots. That would leave us with about 80 acres of hills surrounding the outbuildings and the little house that we'd fix up and use as a vacation house.

We left the trailer out there for a year or more, rather than dragging it 300 miles back and forth over the mountains. We enjoyed exploring nearby Sutton Lake in our canoe and the back roads of West Virginia on our motorcycles. Every time we went out there, in addition to the recreation, we also began fixing up the little house on the property and made progress on sub-dividing the land.

THE BEACH HOUSE

A year into the West Virginia farm project, another more interesting opportunity presented itself before we could get the lots sub-divided and sold. That could wait while we turned our attention from the mountains of West Virginia to the

beaches of North Carolina, an area Alec and Marie had been exploring. They found a lot a half block from the beach in Duck on the northern Outer Banks.

After seeing the lot for ourselves, we agreed it was a perfect location for GLAMCO to build a vacation house. With the guidance of a friend, who had just finished building a round-house on the other side of the island, we ordered a kit. We couldn't wait for it to be delivered so we could begin to build our very own beach house. We spent all our weekends and vacation time that summer working on the project, just like we had done with the Ridge Road fixer-upper. We had a lot of fun working with and hanging out with Alec and

Above: "Mess Around" beach house, 91 Skyline Rd., Southern Shores, NC, 1979. Right: From left, Tony, Linda, Ellen, Clif (front), Outer Banks, NC, 1980.

Marie. Both had high energy, and nothing was too difficult, and they managed to have fun doing everything. We had no sooner finished the house and moved furniture in than we would be faced with new challenges.

Looking back at the four years we lived in our Catonsville mansion, it's amazing how much we accomplished, considering both of us had full-time jobs while raising a family, taking care of and settling into a 13-room house, and entertaining all the company who came to see the big house. The children were in school with all the activities that being a parent entailed, including concerts, plays, and PTA meetings. We remodeled and sold the fixer-upper, bought and started developing a farm in West Virginia, and built a vacation house in the Outer Banks of North Carolina. We still had time to go to the Eastern Shore to visit family for weddings, reunions, and beach time. We took family vacations – camping with the kids at Disney World, going to Busch Gardens, and visiting Gary's brother Dan and his wife Karen in New Orleans. Ellen, Clif, and I took piano lessons, while Tony moved on to taking guitar lessons. The kids all participated in little league games in the summer, and they usually spent a week or two on Uncle Bobby's farm down in Tennessee and another week or two with their grandparents in Snow Hill. Like most families, we were busy, busy, busy.

The Beginning of the End

In 1978, when I decided to change careers and become a real estate agent, I started taking the required classes and tests to get my license. For a while I juggled two jobs while learning the trade, and eventually gave up my secretarial job with the Board of Education. In my first year, I sold seven houses and was just beginning to feel the thrill of success when Gary announced he had been offered a promotion and transfer to the Atlanta area. I was adamantly opposed to the idea and after thoroughly discussing the pros and cons, thought we had made a joint decision that he would turn down the offer. In the fall of 1979, when Gary and I were on our way to the West Virginia farm, we stopped at a 7-11 to get snacks for ourselves and the kids. As I came around the corner of the building, I stopped in my tracks as I heard Gary talking on the phone arranging a trip to Atlanta.

I learned from eavesdropping on that phone call with his boss that Gary had actually accepted the job transfer. The rest of our trip was not fun. I reiterated all my original arguments – Tony was just two years from graduating from high school, and Ellen, a freshman, had just been chosen to be the newscaster on her very own junior high school closed-circuit TV broadcast. Clif was out of elementary school and starting junior high school. Both Ellen and Clif were in their school band, and they all had paper routes. None of us wanted to leave our friends, plus there was my new-found success in real estate. In addition, because of a recent transformative experience, I joined a new spiritual community. I was learning how to recognize how our thoughts and beliefs help to create our reality, and I was not yet prepared to leave an environment of acceptance and empowerment. A move would unnecessarily disrupt all our lives. I dug in my heels and refused to go.

We agreed that the kids and I would stay in Catonsville for the school year while he moved to Atlanta by himself, with a plan that the kids and I would join him after school ended. We bought a three-bedroom house in Snellville, a suburb of Atlanta, for Gary to live in for that year, and then it would become our first rental property after we bought a family home the following summer.

As planned, when the busy school year ended in June 1980, having committed to moving, I went down to Georgia where Gary and I bought a five-bedroom house with a swimming pool out in the country near Alpharetta, north of Atlanta. I went back to Catonsville and listed our lovely Victorian house, the one I thought I would live in for the rest of my life. It sold in a week. I should have asked for more. We purchased it for $60,000 in 1975 and sold it five years later for $120,000.

Three days before the movers were scheduled to arrive, Gary called from Atlanta to tell me he had fallen in love with his "soul mate," and he didn't want me to move with him and the children. When he came home the next day, I spent 24 hours trying to convince him that we should stay together. We were childhood sweethearts, had been married for 17 years, and we always said we would never get a divorce. We had three wonderful children, and *we* were the soul mates – but he would not be moved from his position.

Based on my new belief that "thoughts are creative and I am the thinker," I kept a mantra echoing in my head, "Whatever happens is the perfect thing to happen." I knew deep within that my "higher self" had set this separation in motion. It was exactly what needed to happen for everyone's highest good. Refusing to be a victim, I took responsibility for creating my own reality. In short order, I found myself between trapezes, having let go of one (the security of marriage), yet not yet being able to firmly grasp the other (living life on my own).

SAYING GOODBYE

Gary and I called the children together to tell them that I wouldn't be moving to Georgia with the family, that it was a decision we had come to together. They didn't seem to be shocked, but to tell the truth, looking back, I was not as tuned in to them as the situation warranted. One thing was true, I could never be accused of being a helicopter mom. I had always told them that they didn't come with an instruction manual – that we would all learn from each other as we went along. With this new development, they all seemed so understanding and adaptable.

I took each one aside and talked to them individually, asking something along the lines of, "How are you doing with your dad's and my separation?" At the time, I wasn't thinking of it as my separation from them, although it would

Reunion for George and Ruth's 50th wedding anniversary. From left, Tony, Linda, Ellen, Gary, Clif, 1982.

be nearly a year before I moved to Alpharetta where Ellen, a junior in high school, moved in with me. Tony and Clif, having grown accustomed to the freedoms granted by living with their father, opted to stay with him, but lived nearby.

A thunderstorm was in full force the day I talked to Tony. I stood on the porch waiting for him to come home from delivering papers. I watched as he rode his bike in the driveway and brought it onto the porch. After asking him how he was doing with our decision, he took my hand and led me into the yard, as I shrank from the rain and cringed with each thunderclap.

He turned me away from him and placed his hands firmly on my shoulders, holding me in place. He asked me to lift my chin so the rain would fall on my face and said, "Feel this rain on your face. Listen to the thunder. There is nothing here to be afraid of, or to shrink from. I am out in the weather every day delivering papers, and I am not afraid. I don't want to think of you being out in the world, alone, feeling afraid." Buoyed by his gentle confidence, I could feel my body relaxing, even as the thunder roared around us, the rain washing the tears from my eyes.

Next, I asked Ellen if she felt OK with moving down to Georgia and being the only girl in the house. I knew that she was sad about leaving good friends and an active school life behind. I remember her saying, "I'm glad I'll be going with my brothers."

When I asked 14-year-old Clif how he was sorting out these new changes, he responded, "Mom, I don't want to hurt your feelings or anything, but you and Dad will have to work out your own problems. I have my own life to live. I'm moving to a new town, going to a new school, making new friends. I want to get a job and save up money to buy a car in two years."

I remember feeling hurt that they were already moving forward, but also felt some degree of relief, that none of them had said, "Oh no, we don't want to move to Georgia. We want to stay with you." After all, I had been homeless for just two days, and I had no plan beyond my friend Jim Worsley's generous offer for me to stay at his house in Silver Springs, Maryland. I have often thought that had we not sold the house, the children and I could have stayed in Catonsville and made a go of it. My children and their spouses all say that if we had followed that path, they never would have met and married.

Under the circumstances, I assumed my kids were going to be all right. I taught them to be resourceful and independent, getting up on their own and fixing their own breakfast before going to school. For five years, they had been earning their own money with paper routes and babysitting. They all knew how to cook. Starting in fifth grade, I gave them each the responsibility of fixing dinner one night a week – and not just hot dogs and baked beans, but fried chicken, pot roast, and spaghetti, regular family dinners. They also knew how to do laundry and helped to clean our 13-room house every Saturday morning.

As I was helping my family pack up last-minute items, I suddenly realized that I couldn't be there any longer. It became too painful. I couldn't stay and watch while all their Fisher Price toys and Hot Wheels from the attic disappeared into boxes that I'd never get out for my grandchildren. I couldn't watch Ellen's childhood dresses being packed away – the dresses I planned to use to make quilts for her children. I left them on

Linda leaves Catonsville, Md., 1980.

their own to get ready for the movers to come the next day. I loaded my boxes and suitcases in my car and drove into the next chapter of my life.

It took eight years before I felt the heavy weight and the high cost of that decision and the action that flowed from it. I lived in Atlanta for four years, then Santa Fe for three, and traveled around the world for another year.

After I returned to Atlanta in 1988, I went to the movie *Running on Empty* with friends Don Dugas and Claudia Teagarden. It's the story of a fugitive family, always on the move since the parents' activism inadvertently killed someone. One day the eldest son comes of age and wants to stop running. As the FBI starts closing in on them, the parents quickly arrange for him to stay with a friend to finish high school. Fully knowing that nothing would ever be the same again, the goodbye scene at the end touched my heart so deeply that I began to cry. At first, I just quietly wept until my body could no longer contain all the sadness and hurt and guilt. Then I started sobbing, and it continued until the theater was empty until I, too, was running on empty. Don and Claudia sat with me while I grieved over the path not taken.

5 | SPIRITUAL EVOLUTION

REMSON CHURCH

The year I turned 6, my family moved to the little town of Stockton, 2 miles from the farm where Bobby was living with Grandmom Jones, Aunt Bessie, and Uncle Mervin. My dad often drove Dale and me to the farm to pick up Aunt Bessie and Bobby to go to Remson Methodist Church, where the Jones family had attended for at least five generations. Frequently, Dale and I were already at the farm spending the

Jones family ready for church. From left, Bobby, Aunt Bessie, Linda, George, Dale, Ruth Ann, Grandmom Jones, c. 1949.

weekend with Bobby, and it was our Aunt Bessie, a maiden lady who had never left the homestead, who was the real guardian of our spiritual life. Cleanliness being next to godliness, she made sure our ears were scrubbed, our fingernails were clean, our hair was brushed. It was Aunt Bessie who dressed us in our Sunday best and drove us the 5 miles to the little white church in the middle of corn fields or soybeans, whichever crop was planted that year. My mother, raised in a Baptist household, never went to church with us, claiming she didn't have anything to wear, which we all accepted, since her word was golden.

In its pre-Civil War days, our house of worship was known as Swans Gut Chapel when it sat 2 miles from its current location on another site at the edge of Big Mill Pond. My father's paternal great-grandfather, Samuel Payne (1808-1873) was a member of Swans Gut Chapel, and Samuel's grandson, Paul, remembered helping to move the church building to its present site in 1916. Paul recounted the day they moved the church, and how they rolled the wagon transporting the building part-way up the hill, then all went home with plans to finish the job the next day. When they returned to set the church on its new foundation, the church had rolled back down the hill. Along with its new location, Swans

Gut also got a new name, Remson Church, to honor the preacher who ministered to the congregation.

Two years later, a new sanctuary, nearly twice the size of the original section, with beautiful stained-glass windows was added. The original church, the section with the steeple, was then used for Sunday school classes. To allow sufficient room for the expansion, a few graves disappeared beneath the west end of the sanctuary, but those tombstones were

The Jones School house sits to the left of Remson Church. Painting by Jacques Denier.

moved into the cemetery itself and close to the church wall. Remson cemetery holds the remains of many of my Jones relatives and will be my resting place when I pass from this world. The old Jones school house, attended by my ancestors, was in use from shortly after the Civil War until it closed about 1922. The building, which sat on a contiguous lot, was bought by the church in 1930 and converted to a social hall, which is still in use today.

My father's mother, Annie, told the story that when carpeting was being installed in the new sanctuary, Samuel's daughter, my Great-Grandma Sarah Wise Jones, was sitting on the floor with several other ladies sewing carpet pieces together. In the church, another woman with the same first and middle name, Sarah Wise Landing, was also helping. A third Sarah entered the church and sat down with the other women, saying, "Now, isn't this nice, we have two Sarah Wiseses and one Sarah Foolish."

In addition to the country church we attended, there were two other Methodist churches in the small town of Stockton. Wesley Methodist was in town, and Portersville was on the edge of town, down toward the bay. There was also a Presbyterian Church and an Episcopal Church. It seemed there was something for everyone, except Baptists, in the one-crossroad town of Stockton.

Many small towns like Stockton on the Eastern Shore of Maryland and Virginia have two Methodist churches, a separation leftover from the civil war era. There was one church for northern sympathizers, who thought slavery was evil, and one for southern Methodists who thought slavery was a positive good. The Methodist Church was one of several national churches and institutions that broke apart because it could not withstand the growing tensions surrounding the divisive issue of slavery. Although a slave state, Maryland did not secede from the union, contrary to the desires of many who wanted to take that step. When the Civil War ended, I'm sure families continued in their familiar partisan churches, although by my time, I was not aware of any remnant of partisan sympathizers on either side.

It was only recently that I learned from my brother's memoir that my Grandmother Annie Jones' grandfather Wrixam Payne (1817-1865), upon hearing of the assassination of President Lincoln, arose from his deathbed and proclaimed, "Thank God, somebody finally shot the son-of-a-bitch. I'm glad I lived long enough to see him dead." Wrixam passed from this world two weeks later. So, now we knew where old Wrixam stood on the issues of the day.

My Aunt Bessie, a shy, retiring soul, with a soft, croaky voice, was assigned the yearly task of corralling the 20-25 young Christians at Remson Church to participate in Children's Day recitations. Children's Day observations in the United States predate both Mother's Day (1908) and Father's Day (1910), though a permanent annual single Children's Day observation was not made at the national level. At the Methodist Conference of 1868, the Methodist Episcopal Church recommended that the second Sunday in June be annually observed as Children's Day.

In the 1940s, next to Christmas and Easter, Children's Day was the biggest event in the church's annual calendar. For us kids living in a rural setting, where "nothing ever happens," it was the equivalent of opening night of an off-Broadway play. The church was decorated with flowers as if for a wedding. The children, dressed in their fanciest church clothes, likely bought just for the occasion, were called one by one to walk onto the stage to recite a special poem, chosen especially by my Aunt Bessie for them to memorize. The subject matter was usually sunbeams, joy, lambs, soldiers, Jesus, and God.

On the big day, she called each child's name and the name of their poem, "Linda Jones, A Sunbeam for Jesus." I was then required to take the long walk from the front row in the congregation to the stage, climb the three steep steps, walk to the center of the stage, and face the congregation, every seat filled. I was then required to project my voice to recite what I had learned by heart. I'm sure I was nervous, afraid I would make a mistake, but I soldiered through with a face red from embarrassment.

Remson Church Children's Day; Linda stands on the left back row (No. 1), c. 1949.

Some children mumbled their poems, some shouted theirs, some just froze and forgot everything they had learned. Some started speaking as soon as their foot hit the top step and finished as they were leaving the platform. All the parents murmured and smiled at each other as their children completed their mission. It was likely our first experience in public speaking.

When Bobby was 5 or 6, I am told, and his name was called, he stumbled on the steps on his way to the stage. Something in his movement or cute expression caused the audience to laugh while he was taking his place in the middle of the stage, causing him to balk. Not knowing at such a young age how to appreciate an audience's laughter, he looked out to the faces in the crowd and blurted, "Just for that, I will say nothing!" and he walked off the stage.

Typically, after Sunday School was over, we children were frequently excused from staying for the worship service. One Sunday, after being freed from the confines of the sanctuary, my brothers enrolled me in helping with a project they had been working on in the church parking lot. They had diligently kept a notebook showing the attendance record of the flock. They documented absences and attendance by automobile license plate number, and the resulting grades were recorded and ready for distribution. On this particular day, Dale and Bobby asked me to help pass out report cards to the worshipers. They had written notes on cards, praising good attendance and admonishing truancy, and there were especially harsh comments for those with chronic absences.

"Mrs. Pilchard, we see that you have missed three Sundays in the past two months. Your attendance needs improvement." We placed each "report card" on the windshield of the appropriate car for the owners to find after the service. None of us can remember the fallout from our antics, but we are all certain that we were invited to sit through worship services for the next several weeks. Surely, someone laughed.

About a year after we moved to Stockton, when I was 7, my family took me to see the movie, *The Prince of Peace*, in which I learned that Jesus had been killed. Hung on a cross. Dead. Until then, I must have been most impacted by the Easter teaching that he had arisen from the dead, and all the hymns proclaimed, "He Lives." So, in my young mind, he didn't actually die on the cross, but was still alive, with everlasting life, walking around in another part of the world, like the actors in the movies that I saw.

When I saw on the screen that he had, in reality, been hung on a cross and killed, and he, in fact, had died, I was bereft. I ran out of the theater, crying, angrily questioning, "Why would anyone kill Jesus? This must be a mistake." And, I certainly didn't understand how his death would save me from my sins. I mean, how many sins could a 7-year-old girl have that would have been bad enough for someone to have to die?

WESLEY METHODIST CHURCH

When we were about 11 and 13, Dale and I started going on our own to the Wesley Methodist Church in town. We were probably drawn to sing in the youth choir of 10-12 teenage soldiers for Jesus, and because we could walk to church. We also wanted to join the active Methodist Youth Fellowship (MYF). In my religious education, one of the lessons that appealed to me was that we are "created in the image of God." That sounded pretty good because God was good and great – so, we must be too. But I had questions. If that were true, then how could we also be unworthy to eat the crumbs under the table of Jesus?

As a young girl, the stories of Jesus made a lasting impression on me. In Matthew 18:20, he said, "Where two or more are gathered in my name, whatsoever they shall ask I will give unto them." I took that literally and wondered why people in the church weren't asking and receiving. After hearing the story of Jesus walking on water, and about the healing miracles he performed, I learned from John 14:12 that he said, "All these things that I do, and even greater, shall you also do."

I put all those teachings together and remember running home to tell my mom that if we truly believed, and if others believed with us, that all things were possible, we could even walk on water. She may have nodded and said, "Unh huh." I don't recall that she asked any questions about it.

Our preacher, Reverend Wilson, lived and worked in Delaware during the week, but on weekends came to Stockton with his family to live in the parsonage across the street from the church. He shepherded four congregations – the two in Stockton, our family church in the country, and another one in the neighboring village of Girdletree, 3 miles away. Reverend Wilson used revivals to deliver souls from evil into the arms of Jesus, and, during the summer months, he held them at all four churches. I went to all of them to sing in the choir and to be moved by the spirit.

During one revival meeting at Remson Church, when I was about 13, Reverend Wilson issued an invitation for anyone to come forward to be saved. I had no idea what that meant, but I watched as others went to the altar. Encouraged by my best friend Rita Carol, I stepped into the aisle to go forward to accept Jesus as my personal savior. Because Rita Carol was eight days older than me, and persuaded by the countenance of peace upon her face and her steady confidence from having been saved a few nights before, I trusted her gentle push in the direction of the altar.

After she was saved, we were babysitting together, and when she couldn't explain to me what had happened, she insisted I get down on my knees, and she would do and say everything that had happened to her. Even though she had filled me in, I was surprised by the warmth of Reverend Wilson's hand on my head and then I could feel the warmth spread throughout my body. I remember surrendering to the tears and feeling loved and happy, and maybe, hopefully, even saved, with my ticket

MYF Revival Choir, Wesley Methodist Church; Linda stands on the front row, third from right, c. 1956.

to paradise in my heart, if not in my hand.

As a 13-year-old, having integrated the death of Jesus into my consciousness, I'm sure I believed that the death of Jesus was an atonement for my sins, however few there were. That's what I was taught, so I just accepted it – that's what blind faith is. But it never made sense to me. Try as I might, even now at the age of 81, I am unable to articulate how that can be possible, or why it should be possible? The important thing, I was told, was to have faith, which I must have had because I did believe – back then.

As the revivals drew ever and ever larger crowds, several choir members' mothers (not mine) decided that we could attract a greater number of people to be saved if we had a "Revival Choir." The mothers pulled together the MYF choirs of the pastor's four churches, held bake sales to hire a choir director, and we were in business. I think there were about 50 of us in the choir. Along with singing in our home churches, we were also invited to sing at revivals outside of our district. Once we even went to a church camp in Delaware, doing our part to entice more wayward souls to redemption and salvation.

As a teenager, I was blessed with a progressive Sunday school teacher, Jack Howard, who encouraged us to question everything. And I did.

"If we truly believed, could we actually walk on water?" "How is it possible that by dying, Jesus could save us from our sins?" And "Did we really come into the world, in sin. Even babies?" "Why is it that way?" I only remember my questions, but his answers must have satisfied me because I stayed with the church until I left home at 17 to go to college, where I attended a Methodist church during my freshman year.

Religion wasn't something my group of friends talked about or analyzed. We just lived with our beliefs guiding our way and praying whenever we needed something, like getting a passing grade, or not getting pregnant, or just out of habit. Reverend Wilson left our district, but I still went to my childhood church whenever I went home for a visit. However, I was never as gung-ho as I was in my early teen years, and it would be seven years before I joined another church.

METHODIST CHURCH IN IRWIN, PENNSYLVANIA

Wanting to ensure that my children have a sound religious upbringing, I started taking them to church when they were toddlers. After all, their Hope grandfather was a Methodist minister. We were still living in Pittsburgh in 1967 when the Methodist Church was in the throes of joining with the Evangelical United Brethren to become the United Methodist Church, which they did in April 1968.

After joining our neighborhood church and pledging my tithe, I volunteered to teach the Junior High Sunday School class. I thought I was doing a great job until I used a conversation that I overheard earlier in the sanctuary as a learning moment. The two women seated behind me were complaining about a third woman who kept calling them and asking for transportation to church. They griped about how inconvenient it was to go out of their way to pick her up. They had to get up earlier than usual, and sometimes she called at the last minute, and on and on.

My lesson that day was about "What Can We do to Live as Good Christians." Hopefully, you can see that it seemed fitting, at the time, to use their conversation as a good example of what not to do. You can also see that as a 26-year-old, I was not very political, nor was I very aware of unintended consequences. It turned out that one of my students was the daughter of one of the complaining women, an upstanding member of the church, and subsequently, I was asked not to teach future classes. I stopped going to that church, taking my tithe with me, and it would be another eight years before I joined another church. I didn't give up easily in my quest for the promise of eternal life and salvation.

CATONSVILLE METHODIST CHURCH

The next church I joined during the mid-1970s was in Catonsville, a suburb of Baltimore where Gary and I lived from 1975-1980. It was a beautiful gray stone church with a dynamic minister. Instead of preaching, he told stories from the pulpit in a way that made the Bible more real, complete with marching across the stage, waving his arms, and shouting his commands, and then whispering quiet truths, as his script called for. He held the congregation in his hands. Nobody went to sleep in his church.

TRANSCENDENTAL MEDITATION

It was during this time when the children and I were at the library, that I was drawn to a Transcendental Meditation poster on a bulletin board. I wasn't so sure about the "transcendental" part, but I had been waiting 12 years to hear more about meditation. Here it was, two blocks from my home. You see, when Gary was on the Westinghouse Management Training Program, he was introduced to meditation in one of his orientation seminars. Thinking it would appeal to me, he told me what he had learned, how it allowed the mind to be still and more orderly. Truthfully, I had never realized my mind was not still, or even that it should be, but awareness is the first step in change, of course. There was definitely something in what he said that stayed with me all those years.

The poster announced the transcendental meditation lecture would be held that same evening. I took the kids home, and after dinner, Gary and I went back to the library, excited to learn more about meditation. The promise was that your thoughts would become orderly, you would be calmer, and you would have more energy as a result. What could be more alluring to a 30-something mom with three young children? Gary and I were both intrigued!

We signed up to be initiated into the practice, which included being given a mantra to be repeated silently twice a day for 20 minutes. It wasn't a religious or even a spiritual experience for me, and I didn't give any attention to the guru Maharishi. However, the change in me was so noticeable that even the children reminded me to meditate. I remember once when I came home from work and started corralling them into the car to go shoe shopping, how they stopped me. "Why don't you meditate first, then we'll go," they said.

I became committed to the practice and felt great benefit, especially in being more patient and tranquil. I soon took the children to be initiated with a walking meditation, which some say they still practice in their 50s, when they feel the need to slow down. I began to wonder if meditation might be the key to awakening the 90 percent of our mental capacity that the scientists said we were not using. If we were using only 5-10%, I certainly wanted to access the mother lode and wanted my children to be able to harness that unused potential too. Although this was a generally accepted theory back then, modern brain mapping suggests that all areas of the brain have a function and that they are used nearly all the time, according to Benjamin Radford in *The Ten Percent Myth*.

In the late 70s, I began reading the works of Edgar Cayce and Ram Das, and was quite captivated by the book *The Transparent Self*. The book proposed that we are three "selves" – the self we think we are, the self we show to others, and the self we truly are. The goal was to integrate the three selves into one authentic, transparent self. So began my search to become my true self, now that I knew I had one. I recall having a conversation with my Aunt Stella about my self-discovery journey, saying to her, "I really want to know who lives inside this body," to which she retorted, "Who would ever want to know that!" Well, I did, and I set off on the road to enlightenment.

INTRODUCTION TO REBIRTHING

In the late 70s, my best friend Carol Riley and I were taking a class in Group Dynamics and Leadership, the first class I had taken since I left college after my freshman year 20 years earlier. This class inspired me to return to school and eventually get an MBA when I was 50. Carol called one day and said her boyfriend, a business consultant with a leaning toward New Age, was putting together a Creativity Conference and invited me to attend with her. I agreed, little knowing that it would forever change my life. By then, I was selling real estate, and I wanted to get over my reluctance to cold call potential sellers to try and get their listings.

In addition to many topics of interest, the conference offered seminars on yoga, reflexology, iridology, meditation, and rebirthing. I was intrigued by the brochure on rebirthing and was immediately struck by the statements, "Thoughts are creative," and "You are the thinker." It explained how our birth and childhood experiences can affect the thoughts we have about life and how those thoughts create the life we have. It appeared to fit in with my personal cosmology, so I decided to attend the seminar. I was about to embark on a major continuation of my spiritual evolution.

Bill Decker, the rebirther, gave a brief talk on birth trauma – the use of anesthesia during childbirth, the experience of being expelled from a warm dark comfortable, albeit, tight environment, into a world of loud noises, bright lights, and freezing temperatures. He talked about the decisions we make at the level of pure thought – pre-verbal on an energetic level: "Life hurts, I don't want to be here. Nobody loves me." And he talked about how those thoughts are sent out into the world even before we are swaddled in a blanket and those vibrations can continue throughout our lives.

He explained how the simple act of breathing can take us to the source of those birth decisions, and the decisions that we added because of the way we were treated in our families and at school. Everything he said resonated with me. He then asked if anyone wanted to be rebirthed, and before anyone raised their hand, I was standing next to the comfortable pad Bill had arranged on the floor for the demonstration. I lay down, closed my eyes while the 12 or so attendees were invited to sit on the floor around me and observe the process.

After Bill coached me through a relaxation process, he asked me to begin breathing in a connected pattern, pulling on the inhale and relaxing on the exhale, and to be aware of my breath. As I began to relax even more, my breathing became all that I was, as if my entire body were the breathing mechanism of God. Suddenly, I experienced myself inside the birth canal, soft, wet tissue pressing into me from all sides and a stronger force propelling me, headfirst, forward to freedom.

It was the most exquisite physical experience. I remember thinking, "What is happening here?" But I remember purposefully suspending any thoughts of assessment. I wanted to see what would happen. I was still breathing, and as the pressure on my body became more intense, I felt myself being pushed through the birth canal into the world. As I writhed my way into the world, my body exploded with undulating, pulsating waves of exquisite pleasure, much like the experience of orgasm. It felt like I was my breath, breathing in and breathing out, and as I looked around me at the beautiful faces of the people surrounding me, I was acutely aware that we are, in fact, all one. There are no differences in nationalities, genders, religions. How could we have gotten it so wrong, and even gone so far as to war against each other for our perceived differences?

I was filled with tenderness and yearned to reach out and touch everyone with the love and energy that was circulating through my body. The intense feelings lasted for about 30 minutes, but it would be days before the vibrations subsided. My life changed with that experience. It caused me to question every belief I ever had, and if the belief didn't include the knowledge that we are all one, I tossed it out and chose one that was inclusive. Indeed, it was a strange journey, but not the end of the journey. There would be more adventures. If the experience of birth could be that exquisite, we should take special care to bring each baby into the world in as gentle and loving way as possible.

That rebirthing experience led me to study how to become a rebirther myself, hoping to help someone else see themselves and the world in a more expansive and inclusive way as I had done. I joined a community of rebirthers and bodyworkers and attended workshops and seminars on healing and self-improvement. One of the most impactful programs was The Loving Relationships Training. Even though my husband and I had been childhood sweethearts, it felt like we really didn't know each other at all. He wasn't interested in this self-improvement effort, and, within a year of my "rebirth," we were on the road to divorce. His final departing comment was, "I loved the false image I had of you." So, my assessment about not knowing each other was right on the mark. Obviously, he didn't like my transparent self, and I was learning to love her.

Continuing my search for Truth and for my Self, I also took the EST training during the late 70s. The Erhard Seminars Training, founded by Werner Erhard in 1971, offered a two-weekend (6-day, 60-hour) course. The training emphasized the value of integrity, transformation, personal responsibility, accountability, and possibility. To me, it seemed to be the next logical step in becoming more authentic and present in my relationships. It's when I realized who I was, at the core of my being. Between rebirthing and the EST Training, I'm sure my family thought I was in the clutches of a cult – or two of them. I confess that it took a few years for me to drop the jargon from my vocabulary and to have a conversation with normal people about what I was experiencing.

PART THREE

ON MY OWN BUT NEVER ALONE
(1980-86)

Photo by Joe Sohm

1 | Spiritual Community

Jim and Rebirthing

When Gary and I moved out of our Catonsville house in August 1980, the children went south with him, and I stayed with my new spiritual community to learn to stand in my own center and speak with my own voice. I apprenticed myself to Jim Worsley, a rebirther in Silver Springs, Maryland, organizing his trainings and workshops. I learned the art of sitting with someone, making it safe for them to relax, breathe, and remember the trauma they experienced in their lives – sometimes as they were taking their first breath while making decisions at a pre-verbal level.

Linda with Jim Worsley at a weekend Rebirthing Retreat, 1980.

Babies are comfortably curled in their mother's womb for nine months at a cozy 98 degrees. At birth, they are forced out of their haven into a harsh world 30-35 degrees colder. There are loud noises, lots of activity, and talking. Quite often the doctor cuts the umbilical cord immediately, forcing the baby to take in its first cold, painful breath, which is promptly pushed out. In a sense, the baby's first experience of life is pulling in pain and pushing away life. Frequently, the doctor holds the baby upside down by its ankles, forcing the spine to snap straight after being gently curved in the womb, which is painful enough, and often the doctor spanks the baby to force its first breath. That's some first experience of life. More often than not, mothers are drugged, which consequently drugs the baby. Studies have found that most people had miserable and painful births, their first experience of life, giving rise to such thoughts as "Life is painful." "No one is there for me." "I am going to die." If thoughts are creative, as we believed, some of these pre-verbal thoughts, on an energetic level, that "life is hard" or "everybody is hurting me," are still at work in people's relationships and lives, in general.

As a result of the fear and pain of birth trauma, misinformation from parents and teachers, and churches, trauma stored in the body during abuse, and their profound experiences of love, people create their world based on their thoughts about those events. The act of gently breathing allows one to re-experience their birth and those later encounters to get in touch with the thoughts they had about life and being alive. In some cases, I have seen people have memories about a negative experience from another lifetime. The rebirthing process makes it possible for each of us to sort through which negative thoughts are creating negative outcomes in our lives. I continued being rebirthed so I could examine my negative thoughts and begin turning them around, one by one, to create the life I wanted.

The first thing I did when I left my family in the summer of 1980 was to attend a week-long rebirthing conference in Sun Valley, Idaho, with Jim. He provided the vehicle, I paid for the gas, and we camped along the way. One night we went to see a Willie Nelson movie, Honeysuckle Rose. I had recently heard Willie Nelson's music at a neighbor's party but hadn't really listened to it. The day after we saw the movie, we bought the tape and learned every song. While Jim was writing down the guitar chords, I was writing down the words as we played and sang the songs over and over. Our favorite was On the Road Again.

When we got to Sun Valley, I shared a townhouse with four or five other friends who had flown in from the D.C. area while Jim used my tent to camp out. I had planned this trip before Gary and I parted ways. Of course, I thought I would be flying back to Atlanta when it was over. At the time, I thought it was the most important thing I had done in my life. It was the culmination of all my searching, fulfilling my longing for an expanded spiritual community. It solidified my desire to help others in their healing process.

Back at Jim's in Silver Springs, I was in a place where people could come and just be themselves – even fall apart without judgement. I remember people coming to the house and curling up under a blanket in a corner of the living room, crying for a good part of a day or two. They usually wore out their sorrow or anger by the end of the second day. Sometimes when we found someone in a fetal position, we took them a bottle to nurse. Sometimes we sang them sad songs, other times we simply left them alone. During a rebirthing training, one of the participants shared that her 15-year marriage had just ended, so we sang her every sad country song about lost love while she cried and wailed. Finally, she began to laugh and was able to get through a traumatic experience in record time. I continued to learn more about rebirthing and the spiritual life.

Shortly after Jim and I got back from Sun Valley, we heard that a dear friend had undergone a bad experience following a meditation. His family brought him home from California where he had been studying with a guru. He was left in a state of befuddlement, was unable to eat, and could barely speak. His parents, not knowing what else to do, committed him to a mental health facility, hoping someone could determine what was wrong and give him relief.

To gain insight into what my friend was going through, someone gave me the book, Kundalini: The Evolutionary Energy in Man by Gopi Krishna. Although I had heard of Kundalini yoga, I was relatively casual about the details. The book introduced me to the term "kundalini eruption," an event that happens when energy is released in the body before the mind and body have been properly prepared. The body is overshadowed by sensations of unbearable heat and bleak depression. We thought this might be the case with our friend.

The book explained that, coiled like a snake at the base of the spine, kundalini is the spiritual force that lies dormant in every human being. Once awakened, often through meditation and yoga practices, it rises up the spine and finds expression in the form of spiritual knowledge, mystical vision, psychic powers, and, ultimately, enlightenment. The book is a first-person account of Gopi Krishna, who, at the age of 34, after years of unsupervised meditation, suddenly experienced the awakening of kundalini during his morning practice.

Because I was in a community of healers, I invited Jim, the rebirther, and Jonyl, a bodyworker friend of ours, to come with me to see the patient to determine if there was anything we could do to help to relieve his symptoms. Other than laying on hands, there seemed to be nothing we could do, and his condition seemed hopeless.

When a family member called a few weeks later to tell me that my friend had been transferred to a long-term mental health facility, I immediately made plans to visit him. I hardly recognized him across the activity room, disheveled, sitting in a chair holding a bag of food in his lap. He was shoving a shaking hand in the bag, pulling it out full, and stuffing the food in his mouth, with bits and pieces falling on the front of his shirt and on his lap with each handful. It was shocking. Here was a young man in his early 20s, in the prime of his life, looking like he was 70, mumbling, trembling, eyes darting. His eyes registered no recognition of me as I sat down across from him, our knees touching. I gently removed the bag and took both his hands and held them in mine and looked in his eyes, softly saying his name. He finally locked eyes with me, leaned toward me, and furtively whispered, "You've got to get me out of here." I helped him stand up, and I led him out to the courtyard. As we sat down in the grass, I urged him to lie down so he could feel the earth supporting him. I lay down beside him and took his shaking hand in mine, singing, You Are My Sunshine. Afterward, we lay side-by-side in silence, looking at the blue sky above, feeling the earth grounding us from below. I heard him take a deep breath as his trembling slowly subsided.

When I called the family to report on my visit, I was told the medical team had decided to start electric shock treatments the following week since there had been no progress in his condition. Knowing the history of that type of harsh treatment, I sought another opinion from a woman in Reston who did past life readings. I called and explained what I knew about the patient's condition. She asked for a picture of him and a piece of his clothing, which I took to her. She called me after the reading, telling me that for the first time ever, she agreed that he needed the electric shock treatment – to jolt him back to reality.

My mind and heart were easier after I talked with her. Her written summary about his past lives explained the situation in more detail. It described how his past lives led to this event. The next week, we could hardly believe the results of his first and only shock treatment. He came out of the session seemingly "back to normal." It appeared to have shocked him out of his state of instability, as if he were awakening from a bad dream. Of course, he wasn't completely back to normal that day, but the difference in his awareness and physical steadiness was astounding. Within a few weeks, he gained strength and soon returned to his pre- "kundalini eruption" event and was released to go home.

While I was reading the book, Kundalini, I began to have words for what I experienced during my first rebirthing. Although not as debilitating or as long-lasting as my friend's "kundalini" experience, it was somewhat reminiscent of my own state, following my first rebirthing session just a year earlier when I was still with my family. Thankfully, mine only lasted for two days.

I have said the rebirthing session itself was profound in every wonderful way, but what followed was unnerving and uncomfortable. After the session, my body continued vibrating and was so hot that people could feel the heat emanating from my body from five feet away. I expected it to subside. Instead, I spent the next two days sitting on the concrete floor of the classrooms, sliding along a cinder block wall just to keep my body cool. I couldn't eat, nor could I sleep. On the afternoon of the second day, I finally called attention to my condition. When someone checked my heart rate, it was 150 beats a minute. Luckily, there were people at the conference I was attending who were knowledgeable about healing techniques and applied some of their magic.

My "shaman" lowered the air conditioning in my room to the lowest setting, I removed all my clothes and elevated my feet. I could only drink water by sucking it out of a cloth. I was so cold that I was shaking uncontrollably. Then the shaman who was performing the "magic" pressed his fingers to my left wrist and asked me to recall a time when I felt small and weak. When I indicated I had an image, he moved his fingers to the inside of my elbow. Pressing on that point, he asked me to recall a time when I felt powerful and strong. When I had that image, pressing down on my arm, he drew a line from my wrist back to my inner elbow. Within minutes, as if by magic the vibrations in my body subsided, my body heat returned to normal, and my heart rate was back to 75 beats per minute. I guess it was his version of electric shock treatment, but certainly gentler.

JONYL AND BODYWORK

Shortly after I was rebirthed for the first time, I started attending the Loving Relationships Training, designed to discover and break-through the barriers to having your ideal loving relationship. I soon became an assistant, which provided me with a scholarship to attend the seminars.

The developer of the training was a rebirther, and so were the leaders, many of whom I had met at the conference in Sun Valley. The purpose of the training was to understand how we sabotage our partnerships and to see destructive patterns we develop in our relationships. The first time I saw Jonyl

Jim, Linda, Jonyl; Reston, Va., 1988.

Adams, he was sitting outside the seminar room looking like the saddest man I had ever seen. He had just realized that he might be in a seven-year relationship cycle, and he was afraid he was possibly facing the end of his marriage. I sat down and reminded him that he could make it up any way he wanted.

As we talked, I learned he was the bodyworker for the LRT trainers. You could never say Jonyl was a massage therapist. He was much more than that. He had a way of seeing and feeling where emotional trauma is stored in the body. Creating an environment of trust, a mere touch, or rocking the body could allow his clients to access painful memories and release them. Having no experience with massage or bodywork, I immediately made an appointment for a session. In many ways, I was such a rigid, fearful young woman, and through bodywork, Jonyl opened a doorway that I didn't even know was there. I felt my body in a different way: I discovered my center and learned to stand strong in it. The following week, after I received my first session, Jonyl invited me to go to lunch, so I hopped on the back of his motor scooter, and off we went. What followed was a lifelong friendship, and 40 years later, we still talk to each other once a week. In fact, he was one of my writing partners while I wrote this memoir, and his poetry is epic. One of his poems is at the beginning of this book.

Jonyl became our bodyworker-in-residence at Jim's rebirthing seminars, and sometimes he came over just to hang out. For me, being with Jim and Jonyl was like having loving brothers, the kind who didn't tease me and play tricks on me. We laughed a lot, oh, how we laughed. As Jonyl was leaving after one visit, I started singing to him, *You are a Blessing of the Universe*. I sang it as I walked him to his car and continued, louder, as he backed out of the driveway. He rolled his window down and stuck his head out of the window so he could hear me singing, at the top of my lungs, as he slowly drove down the street, "You are a blessing of the universe, God sent to set us free." Jonyl gave me the nickname, "bliss ninny," because I not only believed all the new concepts I was learning, but I was also practicing them.

After I had been at Jim's for about three months, Jonyl and I were having coffee in the kitchen when Jim came home after being out all night. When I asked where he had been, Jim told us, "I met someone."

Just in the way he said it, and the expression on his face, Jonyl and I could both tell she was an important someone. This one was different.

We asked, "Who is she? Where did you meet her? What does she look like?" Jim answered, "Well, she has two arms and two legs and a head."

Of course, we weren't satisfied with that silly answer, and when he finally admitted to having a picture, we sent him upstairs to fetch it. When he came down with the picture and handed it to us, both Jonyl and I were knocked over by an image of the most beautiful woman we had ever seen. Even in a photograph, light was emanating from her countenance, showing an aura.

Jonyl was the first to speak. "Jim, telling us she has two arms, two legs, and a head, is like telling us your Lamborghini has four wheels, four doors, and a steering wheel."

Beverly was completing her doctorate in clinical psychology when she attended a rebirthing seminar. After seeing profound changes in attendees of the program, she decided to write her PhD dissertation about rebirthing. Subsequently, along with fellow students who served as her case studies, she attended several of Jim's workshops where I got to know her. Jim was definitely smitten, and so were we all. Beverly is still one of my best friends today and another writing partner. I look forward to talking to her every week, and Jonyl and I are certain that she channels her poetry from the ascended masters.

Shortly after Beverly came into our lives, in the spring of 1981, I took off on a three-week road trip

Beverly Rubin (Joyce), 1984.

to California with my friend Carol Riley. This time, I provided the car, and she paid for gas and lodging, funded by her boyfriend who paid for both of us as a gift to her. Carol and I had been like sisters since our husbands graduated from Johns Hopkins in 1963. We had a delightful trip across country, stopping in Houston to visit with Ruth Ann, and in LA to visit with Carol's ex-husband. In LaJolla, we connected with Jonyl who was conducting a body workshop for a rebirther friend who lived there. It always amazes me, when I look back to those pre-tech days before cell phones, how we ever managed to be in the same place at the same time and to find each other.

We had such a great time in La Jolla that when it was time to leave, we all began experiencing separation trauma, even after just four days. So, we decided to kidnap Jonyl and

Above: Linda and friend Carol Riley (Richardson), 1981. Below: Linda and Jonyl Adams, 1981.

take him on the next leg of our journey. Actually, he called his wife, who gave her permission for him to extend his trip. Jonyl, Carol, and I drove north on the Route 1 coastal highway to San Francisco, talking non-stop and laughing in a world that was ours, and in a time that would never end.

When I first saw San Francisco in the afternoon sunlight, cradled in and wrapped around the hills, I immediately fell in love with its colors, its contours, and its beauty. After a few days of sightseeing, visiting friends, and eating sushi, we put Jonyl on a flight back home, and Carol and I started our road trip back to the east coast. When we drove into Lake Tahoe where we planned to spend the night, we saw that John Denver was giving a concert and we were able to get tickets. I had first learned of John Denver's music through one of the students at

Lansdowne High School when I worked there. Having thoroughly enjoyed his show and loving his music, I have always been glad I got to see him perform in person.

Shortly after my return to Silver Springs, changes were in motion. After putting his house on the market, Jim moved in with Beverly in Reston, Virginia, where Jonyl and his wife, also Carol, lived. A friend in the rebirthing community invited me to share her apartment in Reston, of course. I lived with her for a couple of months, and when her boyfriend moved in that summer, Jonyl and Carol invited me to come live with them and their two children. I took care of Anna Laura, their 3-year-old daughter, while Carol worked and Jonyl saw clients. I was so grateful for the shelter and love during that summer.

We frequently got together with Jim and Beverly. We played music and sang songs, we played Scrabble, and we cooked dinners together. Having done a 10-day fast while living in Catonsville, I convinced everyone to do a three-day fast. We didn't take into account that Easter was upon us, and we broke the fast for Easter Sunday dinner – definitely not the recommended way to break a fast, but no permanent damage was done. For several years after that, I did a 10-day fast every year, a three-day fast once a month, and a one-day fast once a week.

Jonyl introduced me to the music of John Prine. For weeks, I kept hearing Jonyl hum and sing songs that he told me were John Prine songs. He'd talk about how great he was while also complaining about having loaned his John Prine tapes to a friend who hadn't returned them. Now he didn't have them, so I couldn't listen to them. One day when we were driving around the Washington beltway, he just wouldn't stop complaining about it or being mad at the person who still had the tapes. Even though I didn't know who John Prine was, I got off at the next exit, went to a store and bought Jonyl two tapes. He was so excited when he opened the bag and gratefully put one of the tapes in the tape player. When I heard the first song, I immediately became a lifelong John Prine fan. Unfortunately, John Prine was one of the first victims of the coronavirus. He died on April 7, 2020.

During that summer, Jonyl went through a bout of depression. He took to his bed for several days and just couldn't understand why I would want to be around him when he was depressed. I told him, "I'd rather be with you when you are depressed than with anyone else who wasn't."

Even in a state of depression, he was a great storyteller, but mostly because he was always willing to take responsibility for his state of consciousness. I also remember lazy days with Jonyl and Jim, floating in a boat on Lake Ann, enjoying each other's company. In addition to childcare, I was seeing my own rebirthing clients, setting up Jonyl's bodywork appointments, and enrolling participants in his Life Purpose Workshop.

Life Purpose Workshop

The purpose of Jonyl's workshop was to discover and breakthrough the barriers to having your body support you in your life purpose. When I asked people what their life purpose was, of course, they didn't have one. Or if they did, they couldn't articulate it. Without having a life purpose myself, I sold them on the possibility of three outcomes from taking the workshop.

Firstly, I told them, you will discover your body in a way that allows you to accept and own it, just the way it is. Secondly, you will have a life purpose. And, thirdly, you will be able to identify the obstacles that get in the way of your fulfilling your purpose. I also had to tell them this, "Further, to accomplish all of the above, you will have to take off your clothes in front of God and everybody." Surprisingly, even with that caveat, people still signed up.

On the first evening of the workshop, our small group nervously assembled in Jonyl's living room; nervous because we all knew it was coming, the point at which we would disrobe. I had told them what to expect, which Jonyl announced again at the beginning of his introductory talk, and then kept saying it was coming. Supposedly, it helped us by drawing out the process, making everyone jittery and anxious on one hand, and wanting to get it over with, on the other.

To extend the angst, Jonyl talked a little about how self-conscious, or unconscious, we were about our bodies, and then he'd say, "Now, in a little while, I will ask you to take off your clothes. But first, let's talk about what it means to have a life purpose," and then he talked about the power of being able to articulate your life purpose.

And then he said, "In a minute, we'll take off our clothes, but before we do, let me tell you about all the things we use to hide our bodies and to make ourselves look good." It seemed endless. During several rounds of teasing the inevitable, all of us vacillated between anxiety and finally just wanting the waiting and anticipation to be over. Eventually, we were all clad in our birthday suits.

Accepting and owning your body was accomplished, it turned out, by standing naked in a circle with your fellow seminar participants. I recall 10 or 12 in the one I attended. If you had been looking at the group from the outside, you would have thought none of us had a body, but only heads. Initially, there was 100% eye contact in that circle, no one's eyes wandering below the noses of their newly naked acquaintances. Oh, we looked longingly, almost desperately, into each other's eyes, perhaps with a furtive glimpse of a mouth here and there, or a glance that strayed and landed on someone's shoulder.

Then, Jonyl gave us permission to look at each other's entire bodies. That created some cognitive dissonance for me, and maybe for others, because I wanted to look at the other bodies, but I also wanted to look at their eyes to see who was looking at my body. I couldn't do both, so I just followed directions and examined the naked bodies before me.

After about 10 minutes, when Jonyl sensed that we were beginning to be bored with looking at naked bodies, he then had each of us say what we didn't like about our bodies. After the first person finished listing their flaws, the task moved on to the next person, and the next, until everyone in the circle had addressed their flaws. If someone forgot a defect they hadn't included, they were encouraged to add it at the end, to make sure everyone had said everything that was objectionable to them about their own bodies.

What didn't we like? *My boobs are too big, mine are too little, mine are too high, mine are too wide, mine are too pointy, mine look like wall-eyed-hard-fried eggs. My nipples are too pointy, mine are too flat. My hips are too wide, mine are too narrow. My butt is too big, mine is too skinny, mine sags. I'm too tall, I'm too short, I have bowed legs, my legs are skinny, I have freckles, I'm too fat, I'm too skinny, my hair is too thin, mine is too curly, my back is too hairy, I have no hair on my chest. My hands are too fat, my fingers are too short, my feet are flat, my toes are ugly.* It went on for a very long time. I don't recall anyone saying anything about wrinkles or gray hair or double chins. I guess we were all young then.

When we grew weary and bored with what we didn't like, we were asked to reveal what we liked about our bodies – and the most amazing thing happened. Suddenly we discovered that some of the things we didn't like about our bodies unexpectedly became the things that we also liked about our bodies – not everything, of course, but many of them. So right there, we began to accept our bodies just as they were, without diverting our attention away from more important aspects of life, like fulfilling our life purpose.

Our homework was to come up with a statement that succinctly declared our life purpose. Jonyl explained that having a well-articulated life purpose had a power that couldn't be refuted. Anyone who heard it immediately grasped the significance and power of it. He described how a mere individual having a single purpose is analogous to plugging a single plug into an outlet. It draws just enough power for that one person to live his or her life – going to school, getting a job, getting married, and only one person is the center of that purpose. If you have a bigger purpose, bigger than yourself, one that is focused on others, it's like plugging into a huge power strip to draw substantially greater power, which gives you more energy to fulfill your purpose. That's why you need a purpose bigger than just yourself.

So, we all went home and worked on articulating our life purposes, ones that were inclusive and expansive. We talked them over with each other, asked questions, narrowed down the wording, and helped each other prepare for the ultimate test for the final class. Standing naked in front of our fellow participants, we had to say our name and articulate our life purpose in a way that everyone was convinced it was true and powerful. If there was any hesitation or some embarrassment or maybe a little nervousness, the "audience" or just one person in the audience could say, "Nope, I didn't get it." And, the presenter would have to say it again, and sometimes again and again, until we all agreed that their life purpose was believable.

One woman, Glory, stood in front of the group, announced her name and her purpose many times, but it didn't sound believable. No one was getting any energy from it. She must have been up there for half an hour when Jonyl suggested she use her given name, Gloria. When she said, "My name is Gloria, and my life purpose is…," it was as though someone new inhabited her body with a life purpose that we could all sign on to. It was beautiful to see.

My first life purpose was "to wake people up to their purpose as peacemakers." I stood in front of my classmates, said my name and stated my life purpose. Everybody got it the first time. Relieved, I sat my little naked self down.

I confess that when I heard Buckminster Fuller's life purpose, I decided to borrow his statement for my own. Bucky Fuller (July 12, 1895-July 1, 1983) was an American architect, systems theorist, writer, designer, inventor, philosopher, and futurist. I had first heard of him when Gary and I were researching round houses and learned about the geodesic dome he invented. Later, I was more interested in his philosophy that we are all in this world together, here on Spaceship Earth, and there are enough resources to go around. Right away, When I read his life purpose, *"To make the world work for 100 percent of humanity in the shortest possible time through spontaneous cooperation without ecological damage or disadvantage to anyone, "*I could see that what he said was more expansive and inclusive than what I was stating, so I embraced his purpose as my own, putting it in my own words. I began saying, "My name is Linda Jenkins, and my purpose is to have a world that works for everyone with no one and nothing left out."

A few years later when I was working in Santa Fe for Larry Wilson, I had the great privilege of working with Bucky's chief engineer, Amy Edmondson. She had graduated from Harvard with a degree in engineering in three years. When Amy heard Bucky give a speech at Harvard, she was so impressed that she wrote to him, asking, "What would someone like me need to do to work with someone like you." He was so impressed with her that he replied, "I have been busy with ever and ever more relevant things…," and invited her for an interview. He hired her at the age of 21 to be his chief engineer. She worked with him for two years until his death in 1983.

As Larry Wilson's assistant, I received a copy of Amy's resume when she was looking for her next job in 1984. When I saw she had worked with Bucky, I ran down to Larry's office, handing him her resume, saying, "We have to hire this woman." I set up an interview, and even though we didn't know what her job would be, Larry hired her. We just knew we wanted her to work with us.

I set her up in an office right next to mine, just over the cubicle. She had just finished writing a book, *A Fuller Explanation*, explaining Bucky's synergetic geometry in lay terms. Having heard Bucky compared to Leonardo Di Vinci, I was excited to have Amy nearby. Many times, during the few months that she was "next door," I called questions over the cubicle wall, "What would Bucky say about extra-terrestrials?" "What would Bucky say about love?" "What would Bucky say about the future of mankind?" Oh, why didn't I write her answers down because after considering what she thought Bucky would say, she answered every question. Even though I had never met him, it felt like Bucky was my friend, sitting in the next office, and I could ask him anything. It was through Jonyl that I had become more acutely aware of Bucky Fuller, and thus could appreciate Amy because of her association with Bucky.

I still treasure my friendship with Jonyl, grateful that we found each other 40 years ago and that we have stayed in touch all these years. Jonyl was a visionary who could see and help people access all the parts of themselves that had remained hidden. I loved working with him and felt like I could explain to others, in lay terms, what he was saying in Jonyl-speak. I have always felt completely safe with him, felt accepted and appreciated, and, best of all, glad that he liked me. He was, and still is, my best guy friend.

2 | Moving to Georgia

By the end of the summer of 1981, after I had been separated from my family for a year, I wanted very much to reunite with my children. They were in Georgia with their father, and I was still in Virginia. Of course, I talked to them on the phone often and had visited them a time or two, but I yearned to be with them. Moving to Atlanta would be a huge step, and I had been waffling back and forth for several weeks, "Should I stay, or should I go?"

After I took the EST Training, I took advantage of the Graduate Training seminars they offered. The promise of EST was to "transform one's ability to experience living so that the situations one had been trying to change or had been putting up with clear up just in the process of life itself."

I decided to put it to the test in real life. One of the exercises was to turn to a stranger, tell them about a problem in your life, and follow whatever advice they gave you. After summarizing my unique situation, my stranger advised, "Go down to Atlanta, and put your family back together."

Accordingly, I began the process of leaving my spiritual tribe and heading off into the unknown, on my own again. But what would I do? Where would I live? How would I start over? How would I earn a living? As I debated about leaving Reston, Jonyl jokingly told me that he had given up his robes in heaven just to come down to the earthly plain so he could prepare me to leave my tribe with which I had become so entwined. His job was over, he told me, I was ready. It was time for me to go.

At the end of my going-away party, someone offered to lead us in a guided visualization. I used my upcoming southern quest as the subject of receiving any guidance that might come my way. Toward the end of the meditation, I heard a voice inside my head, louder than any voice during a normal conversation. It said, "Go integrate spirituality into the corporate world." It is true that I had been dabbling in spiritual disciplines for the previous few years and studying more intensely in the most recent year. However, the corporate world? I had never even considered the corporate world, having worked as a secretary in the secondary educational system and more recently as a real estate agent.

After a year in my spiritual community, I finally felt strong enough and capable to start a new life, to be on my own for the first time in my life. I left Reston with a mandate for the next stage of my journey. I started packing my car with my few worldly possessions and within a few days, I was on my way to Atlanta to put my family back together – and to integrate spirituality into the corporate world without an inkling as to how all that would be accomplished. I had not yet learned about synchronicity and how that would ease any concerns I had. "Trust the process," I said, "Let go and let God."

WILSON LEARNING

The Prince family, friends from Village of Purnell days in Baltimore, had moved to Roswell, just down the road from Alpharetta where my children and Gary were living. I called to see if I could stay with them, and they were happy to oblige. My hosts and I agreed that a month would be a reasonable time for me to find a job and my own place to live. I was grateful for a place to stay with friends while I started my job search in an unfamiliar city. I went to every interview I was offered, even if I knew I didn't want the job because I needed to practice the art of the interview. I was feeling uneasy about being a 40-year-old woman trying to find a job. I thought I was too old and that no one would want to hire me. I don't remember that I even had a resume.

I had been on a couple of these practice interviews, getting the lay of the land, when I saw a job in the classifieds that caught my attention. It didn't exactly say that they were looking for someone to "incorporate spirituality into the workplace," but I recall that it stood out enough for me to draw a bullseye around it. Even though it was after five on a Friday afternoon, I called and left a message, saying I was interested and that I would call back on Monday, which I did. Louise Rogers, the administrative assistant, scheduled an appointment for me with Gary Quinlan, the VP of Sales for Wilson Learning Corporation's (WLC) southern sales division. I eagerly looked forward to the appointment.

When I walked into the office, the first thing that caught my eye was a poster proclaiming their mission statement: "Helping people and organizations become as much as they can be."

"Wow! Here's a star I can hitch my wagon to. I had recently decided that the ultimate purpose of life was to evolve spiritually, to become co-creators with God. Well, that would be 'as much as we can be.' I can ride on these coattails," I thought to myself. Plus, it would all fit into my own life purpose – having a world that works for everyone.

During the interview, I learned that Wilson Learning was an international training and development company that delivered sales, management, and interpersonal skills seminars to Fortune 500 companies all over the world. The company's founder Larry Wilson was a true visionary. He believed it was an organization's responsibility to provide an environment where each employee could grow to their potential. As individual employees grew to their potential, the companies would automatically be swept along to their potential as well. Instead of waiting until retirement for an employee to receive a watch, Wilson Learning presented their employees a Mickey Mouse watch at the end of their first year, as a reminder that work was supposed to be fun.

I was also excited to learn that Larry had invited Marilyn Ferguson to be the keynote speaker at their recently held annual sales meeting at corporate headquarters in Minneapo-

Linda and Louise, 1984.

lis. Marilyn was the author of *The Aquarian Conspiracy*, a book I had recently read. The book brought together all the concepts of the "New Age Movement," describing how a network of advanced thinkers was working together to create a society based on the concept of human potential.

"So, this is how it works," I thought to myself. "You get a directive during a guided visualization to play in the corporate world, and the perfect company presents itself where you can fulfill your assignment." It was also how synchronicity worked. I was offered the job of secretary to the Regional Sales Office in Sandy Springs, just 12 miles south of Alpharetta. It would be my first conscious experience of integrating my spiritual values into the corporate world.

With a salary of $15,000 a year, I started work the following week, replacing Louise as administrative assistant. Her new job at the 1982 World's Fair, training employees in Customer Service and Interpersonal Relationships, would require her presence in Knoxville, Tennessee. Louise kept her apartment in Roswell and returned on weekends and soon became my best friend.

Computers were becoming part of the business world, and I learned to use the Wang computer to communicate with the home office in Minneapolis. As soon as I got my first paycheck, I found a duplex in Alpharetta where my three children were in high school. Ellen moved in with me the same day I moved, and soon Steve, Louise's boyfriend, moved into the other side of the duplex. I was already building a new community again.

My brother Bobby gave me a black kitten as a housewarming present just a few days after Ellen brought another black kitten home from the pet store. Hers was the last cat left in the cage on Christmas Eve, and she didn't want to leave it there by itself. We named my cat Joe; Ellen's cat we named Sam. They were really cute, even the day they got into a loaf of bread on the top of the refrigerator. When Ellen and I came home, bread was all over the house, even upstairs. At some point, after dealing with a second flea infestation, we decided the cats had to go. Ellen took them to a horse farm 4-5 miles out in the country where they could live out their lives as barn cats. About three months later, a bedraggled Sam showed up on our doorstep, requesting entrance, as if he had just finished a bathroom break. We decided if he could find his way through the countryside and cross a busy four-lane highway to our door, how could we send him back to the farm? Sam became a member of the family, and he was a wonderful cat.

MEETING JOE AND CLAUDIA

As soon as I found my job and a place to live, I started going to EST graduate seminars so I could meet people of a like mind. I started rebirthing clients in the evenings and on weekends, and it wasn't long before I was missing my Reston rebirthing and bodywork community. I invited Jim down to give a talk on rebirthing and to lead a weekend rebirthing seminar. That's where I met Joe Teagarden, who would lead me to meet Claudia Mowry, another lifelong friend.

During the Christmas holidays of 1983, Joe and I accepted an invitation to a Christmas party at the home of Letticia and Farrah Allen, founders of the Atlanta School of Massage. I first saw Claudia, one of their students, as she stood in a doorway talking to another guest. We both remember the immediate attraction and connection. We spent the evening getting to know each other and made plans to meet again. Joe, who became part of my new rebirthing community soon told me he was in love with Claudia, and thus she was drawn even more into my orbit.

Through the EST seminars and the Atlanta School of Massage, I was introduced to even more people who became clients for rebirthing and bodywork. As soon as I had enough bodywork clients for Jonyl, I called him with a proposal. I would set up bodywork appointments for him for one week every month. We'd pay for his expenses off the top and split what was left. I set up anywhere from 5-7 clients a day, and we frequently did a bodywork shop – always nude – on the weekends. It became just as normal to sit around naked with new friends as it did to be clothed. Even when we'd break for lunch, preparing and eating our food *au naturel* seemed perfectly ordinary.

Even though we worked 10-12 hours a day, attending to clients, we still had the energy and time for fun. One night after a busy day, Jonyl wanted to go to a sushi restaurant. I'd never had sushi before, but it's been my favorite choice for eating out since then. Beverly and Jim came down a couple of times too, continuing my connection to my northern spiritual tribe and integrating them into my new southern community. On one visit we rented rafts and spent an idyllic afternoon floating down the Chattahoochee River. Another time, we went to Stone Mountain to watch the laser light show.

By the end of the first year, Louise, Steve, and I went together to buy a newly constructed tri-plex in nearby Roswell. Each of us would have a three-bedroom town house joined on the back by a wide deck that overlooked a small lake. It was a great place to have rebirthing trainings and parties, and, of course, I still had my job with Wilson Learning.

A COURSE IN MIRACLES

For three years I worked in the Atlanta sales office, first as administrative assistant and then, as our sales increased, as office manager. At the time, I was studying "A Course in Miracles," a book that my ex-husband gave me before we separated. "When I heard it was about forgiveness, I thought you would be able to use it," he said.

Joe, Louise, and I decided to take the self-study course together, studying a lesson a day for a year. That way, we could support each other any time a disagreement came up, or a problem presented itself. We would just refer to whatever the lesson was for that day and use it to solve our issues. We incorporated the teachings of the course with breathing, affirmations, and bodywork with our everyday life. We were also questioning if the words we spoke were necessary. Taking a lesson from Socrates, before speaking, we would ask ourselves, "Is it true? Is it kind? Is it necessary? If the answer to any of these questions was no, it was wise to be silent. Life was fun and easy. According to the course, our concerns and disputes mostly involved our distorted perceptions, and looking at each situation anew was paramount to inner peace. The course proposed that our natural state of being was love, which sounded true to us. When we weren't feeling love, our goal was to remove the impediments to the awareness of love's presence. It was summed up thusly:

> *Nothing real can be threatened.*
> *Nothing unreal exists.*
> *Herein lies the peace of God.*

One of my favorite lessons in the course was "When I defend myself, I am attacked." I used that one a lot with my boss, Gary Quinlan. Whenever he called me in his office, it was frequently to berate me about one thing or another. I kept that lesson in the forefront of my mind, refusing to defend myself, thereby refusing to be attacked – even when I knew I was innocent, and he was in the wrong.

Once, when he returned after being out of town, he was extra critical. With each issue he complained about, I'd say, "Ok, I'll fix it," or something to that effect.

When he was finally spent, I looked at him and said, "Is there anything else you need to say to be complete with this conversation?"

He stared at me intently, was silent for 15 seconds or so, and then said, "Yes. I need to say one more thing. It's really hard to be an asshole around you."

Bingo! The course worked! And Quinlan – I will call him Quinlan from here on so as not confuse him with my soon-to-be ex-husband, Gary Hope – became my good friend and my mentor in the corporate world, and I became his in the world of spirituality. I was fulfilling my mission of integrating spirituality into the corporate world, but not the mission of putting my marriage back together.

3 | How to Manifest a Relationship

Leading up to the New Year of 2021, while writing this memoir, I asked friends and relatives to share a favorite memory about a past New Year's Eve. My brother Bobby remembered a New Year's Eve in Paris with his partner Jacques shortly after they met. My son Tony immediately remembered bringing in 1986 at the Pecos River Ranch, where I was working when he and Sheryl visited me in New Mexico. After spending the day going through the rope's course at the ranch, we all went to a New Year's Eve party at the ranch that night. I recalled a party to celebrate the incoming 1966 when Gary and I left 9-month-old Ellen and 2½-year-old Tony with a babysitter in order to attend a big hoopla Westinghouse party at a fancy hotel in Pittsburgh. I didn't like the noisemakers or the cigarette smoke, or the drinking, or making small talk with people I didn't know. All I wanted to do was go home to my babies.

One of my most memorable New Year's Eves was the one closing out 1982 and welcoming in 1983. Ellen and I had been living in Alpharetta for a year and a half. For the first six months of 1982, Gary and I made a half-hearted attempt at reviving our 20-year marriage before throwing it on the trash heap of broken vows and outdated dreams. After going on a couple of vacations together with the kids, I decided that it just simply was not going to work. I told him that I wasn't going to do that again – that it wasn't healthy for my body or my mind or my soul. So, we both agreed to call it quits and start divorce proceedings.

Part of my work with the Loving Relationships Training was learning to create supportive relationships. So, in January 1982, I set about creating my new ideal, loving relationship. Each New Year, I usually put together a list of my intentions and goals for the coming year. This time I included the man of my dreams with a list of the qualities that were essential: Someone who had children, loved music, played the guitar, loved his job, was financially secure, spiritual, family-oriented, nice-looking, within 10 years of my age, comfortable with himself. Oh, it was a long and comprehensive list, and at the bottom, I wrote, "This, or something better, will be in my life by the end of 1982." I thought I was being generous by giving the universe a year to make my beloved manifest to me.

During that year, I looked for him everywhere, whenever I went to a party or to a seminar or out to dinner with friends, or when I was in business situations

– not in a desperate way, but more with confident anticipation. I knew he was out there somewhere, making his way toward me. I was certain he was coming into my orbit. There were a trio of wannabes that year. There was Redneck Rick, Bill the Boat Man, and Ray the Pharmacist, but none of them checked off enough boxes on The List.

A new friend, Joy, invited me to a New Year's Eve party with a group of her friends who were folk singers. We started out the evening having dinner at a nice restaurant, and you can be sure I was looking around, checking to see if "he" might be at the next table. "We are seriously getting down to the wire," I said to the Universe, and I was excited to see what she had reserved for me. When I told Joy about my relationship manifestation process, she was all in. That woman was more of a bliss ninny than I was. After dinner, we stopped by a hotel where Ellen and Clif and their friends had rented a room where they could safely drink while bringing in the New Year. We said our hellos, wished them a Happy New Year, and then put in an appearance at Tony and Sheryl's house to wish them and their friends a Happy New Year. Then, on to the home of Joy's friends.

After arriving about 10:00, we were introduced all around. There were about 20 guests. He had to be here, right? I considered each man I met, but didn't see one with my name on him. I maintained my optimism even 15 minutes before midnight. I was standing in the living room, and honest-to-God, the door opened, and a nice-looking couple came in. The hosts greeted them warmly, and I saw the man disappear into the kitchen and several minutes later emerge into the dining room where he stopped to talk with friends. I patiently waited for him to make his way to me. He slowly moved into the living room and came to stand, facing me. He spoke not a word as the countdown to midnight began, but took me in his arms, and tenderly and lovingly kissed me until the New Year was announced with welcoming cheers. We leaned back from the kiss, looking deeply and tenderly into each other's eyes. He spoke, "Hi, my name is Abraham Davidson," and I responded, "Hi, you must be my ideal, loving relationship."

He started laughing right away because he had actually been to one of Sondra Ray's Loving Relationships seminars, so he knew exactly what I was talking about. I wasn't embarrassed at all when I told him the story of how I manifested him, or when he asked to see my list. It turned out that Barbara, the woman he came to the party with, was a friend he had been visiting. Earlier that evening, when she took him to the airport for his flight back to Houston, Texas, they discovered his flight was canceled. It was rescheduled for the following afternoon, which allowed them to come to the party. More synchronicity. It didn't take long for Abe and me to say our goodbyes to the partygoers. We retrieved his suitcase and his guitar – yes, he had a guitar – from his friend's car and dropped Joy off at her apartment, and then I took this lovely man home with me to show him the list that had brought him to me. And, that, my friends, is how you manifest your ideal loving relationship.

We had a lovely time together, although it was barely 12 hours. By the time we got home, it must have been close to 2 a.m., and I took him to the airport 12 hours after that. It felt like we had always known each other. We wrote long love letters to each other, spent hours on the phone talking, and it was the first time I heard the term "geographically undesirable."

A month or two later, Abe came back to Atlanta to help his friend Barbara pack up her house and help her drive to Houston where she was moving. We were able to spend more time together during that visit.

He came back to Atlanta one more time, specifically, to tell me that he and Barbara had fallen in love during their time together packing, driving, and unpacking. I don't remember being heart-broken, just realized that he, after all, was not my ideal, loving relationship. I did end up with a tape of his folk music, though. I found out sometime later that he and Barbara didn't make it either, and he ended up marrying a beautiful African-American woman. According to Facebook, they are still together today.

You can be sure I added "geographically desirable" to The List for the next year. With each passing year, I revised The List, dropping off what had been desirable characteristics but were no longer important. By the time I met Bruce seven years later, The List had devolved from one page to one short sentence – "a single, white, tolerable man." How could I know my true ideal, loving relationship was already making his way into my orbit? I met Tom a year later in 1984, but it would be another 10 years before we recognized each other and knew that we were meant to be together.

4 | The Move to Santa Fe

Interactive Technology Group

When John Wiley & Sons, a book publisher, purchased Wilson Learning in the mid-1980s, it left Larry free to pursue his next ventures. Recognizing Larry as the soul of the organization, Wiley asked what they needed to do to keep him involved. He told them about the two major projects he wanted to develop. Larry had recently purchased a 2,000-acre ranch an hour outside of Santa Fe, New Mexico, that he wanted to develop as a conference center. He wanted to create and deliver outward-bound adventure types of programs for executives of Fortune 500 companies. In addition, inspired by his teenage son Joey's passion for computers and gaming, he was hard at work developing his second vision, adapting his instructor-based seminars to interactive, computer-assisted programs. Larry saw this as the future of learning.

Wiley bought Wilson Learning because they saw the corporate seminars as a complement to their textbooks, and now Larry offered them a glimpse into the future of learning. Wiley agreed to fund Larry's second dream with a million dollars. Using leading edge interactive technology, Larry combined rolling video, computer graphics, touch screens, and holophonic sound (acoustic hologram) with new learning techniques. Because of the ranch's proximity to Santa Fe, Larry obviously wanted to locate his new interactive video company there. He saw Santa Fe as an ideal place to attract a team of young creative people. They named the new company Interactive Technology Group (IT).

Back in Atlanta, when my boss Gary Quinlan was promoted to head up the IT Group, he asked if I had an interest in working with the new start-up and moving to Santa Fe. He knew I had moved to Georgia to be closer to my children, but Ellen was now in college, Clif would be starting in six months, and Tony was working for a funeral home. I had already taken a new step in my career path with the

Linda and Gary Quinlan, Santa Fe, NM, 1984.

company; I was in training to become a seminar leader.

When Quinlan first brought up the idea of Santa Fe, what he actually said to me was, "I'm going to be out there in New Mexico with all kinds of New Age people, and I'm going to need someone to translate for me."

Of course, there was a real job too. At first, he talked about my becoming office manager, but when we learned that Larry had already offered that position to someone else, I was offered and accepted the job of project manager. I would be managing the budgets and timelines for our million-dollar project. This was out of my comfort zone, and I knew I would have a lot to learn. I was reassured by Quinlan's belief in my ability to be a part of the team.

Since both Quinlan and I were leaving the Atlanta Sales Office, and the new VP of sales lived in Charlotte, they decided to move the office there. I turned over my share of the tri-plex to Louise, which she rented out after she and Steve moved to Charlotte. When I told my friends I was moving to Santa Fe, they acted as though we were 10 years old, and I told them I was moving to Disney World. They were so excited for me, exclaiming, "No one ever gets transferred there." I did not yet realize that Santa Fe was the heart of the Land of Enchantment.

AT HOME IN THE LAND OF ENCHANTMENT

In March of 1984, Quinlan and I flew out to Santa Fe on a house-hunting expedition for me, to get the lay of the land, to meet our new co-workers, and to close on his new house. As the plane approached the Albuquerque airport, I looked out the window and surveyed a bleak panorama of desert and green pinon trees in all directions. Gary leaned over to look out the window and said, "Welcome to the moon."

The landscape may have looked like the moon from the air, but on the ground, with an occasional tumbleweed dancing across the highway, it felt like I was riding the range with Roy and Gene. Driving from the Albuquerque airport to Santa Fe, the breathtaking scenery played like an I-MAX film, not just a Saturday matinee on the small screen in the MarVa theater in Pocomoke. The big blue sky with huge fluffy clouds served as a backdrop to The Sandia Mountain, rising 10,000 feet from the foothills to the east. With Albuquerque in our rear-view mirror, the landscape of brown desert and green pinon trees stretched out as far as the eyes could see. Oh my, look how far the eyes could see.

Fifty miles to the west, the entire Jemez Mountain range captured my attention, and looking another 50 miles beyond that, the outline of Taylor Mountain was visible in soft, blue hues. Our destination was 70 miles to the north, where I could see the beautiful and majestic Sangre de Cristo Mountains, rising 10,000 feet, cradling Santa Fe in its gentle foothills.

I was familiar with New Mexico scenery from western movies and Zane Gray novels set in the southwest. I had heard about the Old Santa Fe Trail, first used in 1821 when travelers to the new southwest territories paid $250 for their 15-day journey from Kansas City, Missouri. Settlers, stagecoach lines, and thousands of gold seekers on their way to the California and Colorado gold fields left their mark on the legendary Santa Fe Trail. By 1880, the railroad reached Santa Fe, and the trail faded into history, but the deep ruts left by countless wagons are still visible today. But none of that prepared me for the emotional response I had when I saw the *105 Spruce St., Santa Fe, NM, 1984.* open range and the big blue sky. This was better than anything I had imagined.

As soon as we drove into Santa Fe, I felt completely at home. I loved the architecture, the narrow streets, and the adobe walls. By the end of my first day, everything had already started falling into place. The seller of Quinlan's new house told him about a three-bedroom house that he was renting on Spruce Street. Thinking it was a good option for me, we arranged for me to see it. I hadn't even looked at another property, but when I saw the view of the Sangre De Cristo Mountain from the back patio and the colorful Mexican tiles in the kitchen and bathrooms, I decided right away to sign the lease. I would have room for my

children and friends to visit, and the generous family room with a fireplace could serve as a seminar room if I needed it. With my promotion and transfer, my salary had instantly doubled from $15,00 a year to $30,000, so I could easily afford the $800 a month rent.

WORKING AT IT

The next three years living in Santa Fe, working with Larry Wilson, and meeting the rest of my Western clan was a transformational experience, full of intense excitement, innovative learning, and deep soul fulfillment. With a sense of belonging and supreme happiness, the long hours of work didn't seem like work at all. I felt entirely supported and on purpose in my life, "having a world that works for everyone with no one and nothing left out." I was working for a company whose purpose was to help people and organizations become as much as they can be, and we walked our talk. We all felt we were growing to our potential.

Twenty years later, in 2004, we held an IT reunion in Santa Fe. Every person who had been a part of the IT Group came to sit in our circle for three days, talking about our time together from 1984-87. We all agreed that it was the most impactful work experience of our careers. When we searched for the common denominator, we discovered the most important factor was believing in each other and supporting each other to accomplish our goals and to have fun. We gave credit to Larry who had a vision, believed in us to make his dream a reality. He was a phenomenal role model in manifesting dreams.

Larry initially gathered from around the country 30 talented and creative writers, computer graphic artists, program developers, and video production managers and coordinators who Larry felt could help him bring his vision to fruition. I was hired as the project manager to ride herd on these dreamers and visionaries, to establish realistic timelines and keep the project under the $1,000,000 budget John Wiley & Sons had granted us.

The IT office was in a fairly new building, more contemporary than old Santa Fe architecture, with cubicles in the center with walls of varying heights. The executive's offices were on the window side of the building, with walls to the ceiling and actual doors they could close. I met the office manager, the woman with the job I was supposed to have. There were many times over the next three years that I was grateful that I got the job I did. The receptionist was a young and beautiful Hispanic woman. When I met the VP of production, who was of Chippewa descent, we discovered we had both studied "A Course in Miracles." I also learned that the VP of research and development had as well. No wonder Quinlan thought he needed me to translate New Age for him.

I also met Preston, a full-blooded Native American hired to oversee the video equipment, keeping it organized and operational. Larry had a way of hiring people he fell in love with and then figured out a place for them in his company. It usually worked out. Many times, after I started working directly with Larry, I got a call from someone who said, "I met Larry on an airplane, and he told me to call you, and you'd let me know what I'm supposed to do."

Everyone I met at my new workplace was interesting and interested. The first night I went out to dinner in my new town of 60,000 residents, imagine my surprise at seeing people I had already met that day, having dinner in the same restaurant. Any misgivings I had about leaving my friends and family in Atlanta evaporated on that first visit.

Back in Atlanta a few days later, I packed up my belongings, said goodbye to my children again and my friends, loaded my belongings onto Quinlan's moving truck to avoid moving expenses, and headed west. My friend Joy rode shotgun on the 1,400-mile trip, and my cat Sam stayed under the driver's seat until I pulled him out when we stopped in Arlington, Texas, for an overnight with Brenda Crouch from my Pittsburgh days. Joy stayed to help me unpack in Santa Fe and settle into the first home I ever had on my own. Then I put her on a bus to visit her daughter who was at the Air Force Academy in Colorado Springs.

When Preston heard me talking about plans to hook up my stereo equipment after work, he offered to come do it for me. Since I had never hooked it up on my own before, I had been especially careful to color-code all the wires to their connectors before disconnecting the system in Atlanta. I showed Preston the lovely, color-coded stickers I had painstakingly attached to all the connections so he would know how to recouple them. Preston appeared to have no interest in my stickers, nor did he want any direction from me, so I left him alone to do the job.

When I had given what I though was sufficient time to build a new sound system, I came back in the family room and found all the stickers on the floor, the connections in their ports, but the system wasn't working. When I asked if he had followed the colors that paired the connections, he informed me that I hadn't color-coded it correctly. To my credit, it honestly didn't occur to me that he might be color-blind, but I was aggravated enough to raise my voice a few decibels, letting him know how annoyed I was. As I finally heard the tone and volume of my voice directed at this very nice Native American man whose sin was not following directions, I remembered that, after all, he was the very first "Indian" I had ever met. I apologized and together we worked on it until the system was functional. Preston was one of the few people who didn't last at the IT Group.

My life was full of making new friends, learning new skills, and working with a cast of highly creative individuals, most of them in their 20s and 30s. Not counting Larry, who came in once a week, there were only seven of us in our 40s and 50s. It was fascinating to watch these youngsters at work. They could do anything they were asked to do, and they always made me feel like I could too.

Our first interactive program was about understanding the four social styles – driver, expressive, analytical, and amiable. Every day we all gathered in the conference room to figure out how to do something that had never been done before.

Several of us, including Larry's son, Joey, recounted what Larry told us about his vision. As each idea poured forth, it was captured on the blank storyboards set up around the room. A couple of the graphic artists sketched what people were saying, bringing the story to life in pictures. On a flipchart someone else made a list of all the concepts that needed to be covered, while others made notes on how to integrate the different learning styles, computer graphics, animation, and rolling video with live actors. We discussed the characters that would demonstrate those concepts – how many would be needed, what they would look like, and what they wore.

Since we were teaching the "habits" of each social style's communication mode, we decided the main character was the "teacher," a little hobbit-like creature who wore a nun-style habit. And, wouldn't you know, that adorable being just appeared on the storyboard one day as we talked her into existence. We decided to call the program The Versatile Organization because we were teaching people how to adapt to others' social style. It was positively exhilarating to be in that creative environment every day.

A year earlier, in 1983, the Hewlett Packard Company manufactured the HP-150 computer equipped with a touchscreen, the ancestor of all modern PCs with a touch interface. We wanted to use touchscreens, in addition to the mouse to click on and drag items around the screen. Using the touch screen and rolling video, we devised a way to demonstrate the difference between an analytical social style (low emote) and an expressive social style (high emote). The analytical person on the screen spoke in a non-emotional way, giving facts without any hand gestures. As the user moved the bar on the screen to the right, the person became more animated, had more facial expressions, talked louder, and used lots of hand gestures. Deciding when to use computer graphics and when to use rolling video, and making it seamless was also a part of the equation.

Once a week or so, Larry called to say he was on his way to the office. He had the first cell phone I had ever seen, so just his calling from a car was pretty novel. As news spread that "our leader" was on his way to the office, the staff's excitement rose to a palpable buzz. His presence was felt in the air even before he arrived. Wiley was right when they identified Larry as "the soul of the organization." After leading him to the conference room, we walked him through the storyboards and flipcharts, sharing all the ideas we had come up with and where we were going. His pleasure at what we had accomplished and seeing his vision coming to life on paper inspired him with new ideas that seemed to just tumble forth. We could do this, or we could do that, and then everyone started feeding off his suggestions, adding their concepts and creativity. The brainstorming sessions were stimulating and the most fun I had ever had in a work environment.

When the meeting was over, and Larry was on his way back to the ranch, we all sat dazed and silent, spent of all our energy, and for a few minutes, we wondered what had just happened. Then someone would ask, "What did he say? What does he want us to do? How does he want us to do that?" Then it would start again, sharing what we had captured of Larry's vision, attempting to put it on paper, and then adapting it to the story, to graphics, and to the screen. I wonder if Larry, pleased with the ideas the session had generated ever thought to himself, "This, or something better."

During these creative processes, I was also learning to use the new project management software, and Lisa, a relatively new Apple computer, which would soon be replaced by the Macintosh. The Lisa cost just under $10,000, and a year later when the first Macintosh was less than $3,000, the entire office went to Macs. I was glad John Wiley was paying the bills, but I was responsible for tracking the expense, and staying under budget for each element of the project.

I admit that I felt like I was in way over my head managing a million-dollar budget, but everyone believed in me, especially Quinlan and Larry, and I soon learned the ins and outs of project and budget management. The problem, it turned out, was that I would get all the information entered in the computer, but the production team never met their deadlines, or their budget constraints, no matter how much I pleaded or threatened. They always had an excuse or a good reason for their excesses. In all the years I managed projects after this one, I preferred using an Excel spreadsheet, which was much easier to manage than any project management software I tried. I soon adopted Larry's planning style: Plan your work. Work your plan. But, remember, plans never work.

As the Versatile Organization began to take shape, I came up with the idea for everyone to meet in the morning to articulate and align our purpose and intentions to create a successful product – one that a company would buy. Around 9 a.m., whoever wanted to be involved, usually about half of us, gathered in a circle in the back of the office and took turns leading whatever ritual the leader of the day felt moved to use. We visualized the project in the center of the circle, turning its future success over to the "Universe," offering it up for the highest good of all, asking for guidance, meditating, praying, chanting. We did this under the auspices of the technology of manifestation that Jesus taught, one of those lessons that impacted me as a child and that I had been toying with to manifest houses and relationships – "Wherever two or more are gathered in my name, whatsoever they shall ask, I will give unto them."

To keep everyone healthy, when a couple of the employees suggested spirulina smoothies for breakfast, we all pitched in for supplies and took turns making and delivering smoothies to everyone's desk each morning. By the end of the first year, we talked management into subsidizing our lunches every day and arranged for local restaurants to cater soups, salads, sandwiches, Mexican food, and beverages. I think we each paid $10 or $15 a week for this fare, and we didn't have to use time and energy to go out in search of food.

It was a wonderful place to work, and everyone felt appreciated. Many of us met at our favorite restaurants for dinner after working late and breakfast on the weekends. We celebrated each other's birthdays with parties, and we even celebrated a wedding or two. We thoroughly enjoyed spending time together, both at work and at play.

During that first summer, management arranged a whitewater river rafting trip down the Rio Grande River, running the rapids through the Taos Boxcar Stretch. Quinlan gave us a day off and covered our expenses. We spent about four hours rafting, ending with a lovely picnic lunch next to the river, and then a van ride back to our cars.

Later that summer, a group of us, maybe three or four carloads, took a weekend trip out to Hopi Land in Arizona. Preston arranged for us to have spaces to pitch tents and roll out our sleeping bags at a few of the homes. I stayed in the home of Thomas Banyacya, an elder who took us out the next day to show us the petroglyphs and tell us their stories. He said that three previous human worlds were destroyed when people became greedy, worshiped technology as a god, fought and hurt each other, and repeatedly forgot the ethical teachings to honor the Earth as the source of life and sustenance. He was adamant that minerals should not be taken out of the earth for weaponry and killing, and that weapons of war should not be taken into space. Banyacya said that someday many nations would come together, and we would realize our wrongdoings and dangerous actions. Then, people would be able to begin creating peace and harmony and clean up our messes without bringing World War III upon ourselves. This is what we all wanted.

On a later trip to Hopi, I met and commissioned a wood carver to make a Kachini doll, which is a symbolic representation of the spirits of animals, ancestors, plants, and trees. Also choosing other figures for him to carve, I paid half up front with an agreement to pay the other half when I picked up the carvings. I left my address, and he would let me know when they were done. Months went by, and I finally received a letter at my office addressed to Linda True Hope. Inside was an explanation that my carver had injured his hand and was unable to carve the figures I ordered. I sent my regrets, saying how sorry I was for his injury. I thanked him for giving me my Indian Name, "True Hope," and told

Hopi Land Excursion: IT Group co-workers and friends in front of petroglyphs, 1984.

him I was gifting him the $200. I never saw him or heard from him again.

The average snowfall in Santa Fe is 26-30 inches a year, but that first winter I lived there, it snowed 100 inches! I know that sounds like a lot, but since it is high desert and arid, the snow melts quickly. After a few snowfalls, there was enough built up in the Santa Fe ski basin to warrant a company-sponsored outing where we spent the afternoon skiing or learning to ski or watching others ski. Quinlan gave us another day off and arranged for several vans to ferry us up and down the mountain.

In many ways, living in Santa Fe was like being in a foreign country. I'm fairly certain that my mother thought I was living in Mexico – just the newer part. Santa Fe had three distinct cultures. The Hispanic and Gringo populations were evenly split at about 30,000 each, with about 4,500 Native Americans living in pueblos near Santa Fe. Of the eight northern New Mexico pueblos, five are in Santa Fe County. Many of the New Mexican Pueblo Indian tribes were established hundreds of years ago, and some, such as the Taos Pueblo, are thought to have been continuously occupied for close to a thousand years. The Native American artisans go every day to the town plaza to lay out their turquoise and silver jewelry under the Palace of the Governors portal to sell to the tourists.

I loved the narrow streets with the strange sounding names that I had to learn to pronounce, names like Acequia Madre, Paseo de Perralta, Camino del Monte Sol, and Cerrillos (remembering to leave the double L silent). Not long after I started working in Santa Fe, the receptionist couldn't stop laughing when I asked her to page our office assistant David Mar-TA-nez on the intercom for me. "MartinEZ," she said, pronouncing it correctly, so I would learn. Even worse was the time I went out for a beer after work with friends, and innocently ordered a "Dos-e-q." We all laughed at that one.

After a couple of weeks in Santa Fe, I realized my vocabulary was lacking in adjectives to describe the sunsets. They were so spectacular and each one so unique that I soon announced on the intercom every day for everyone to come to the balcony on the west side of the office so we could enjoy the sunsets together. Each person had to bring a new adjective so I could build my expressions of appreciation. My co-workers called me the sunset police because I threatened to fine anyone who missed a sunset, but usually 10 or 15 of us showed up to pay homage to the exquisite display of colors and light.

The technical terms at work presented me with more stress that learning a new language triggered. The computer geeks, for their amusement, put together a list of commonly used technical terms in three columns under the headings of nouns, adjectives, and verbs. By choosing a word from each column, we newbies could make a complete sentence that sounded techie even though it made no sense at all. The purpose was to make us sound as though we knew what we were talking about, and it made us all laugh, which was the real point. I wish I still had that clever list.

Along with my responsibilities as project manager, I was asked to organize the yearly sales meeting for my work friends from the Charlotte regional office. Quinlan was bringing 20 of them, including my house partners Steve and Louise, out to New Mexico. He wanted to show off the new interactive project, since they would be selling the Versatile Organization once completed. Even though work was underway on the conference center at the ranch, it wasn't quite ready for guests. Instead, I found the perfect location at Bishop's Lodge on the north side of town where everyone could stay and hold our meetings. We ended the three-day conference with a Mexican-style dinner catered at Quinlan's new home in the desert that showed off our new Santa Fe lifestyle. It was wonderful having my old work family in my new surroundings and seeing Steve and Louise again.

VISITED BY ET

During the 2020 Pandemic, I was making headway writing my memoir. My friends Beverly and Jonyl and I met on Zoom to give each other prompts from which we wrote a story or poem to read the next time we met. One day we chose "reverence" as the prompt for our writing. To center myself on reverence, I started making a list of some of the marvels in life for which I have great reverence. I didn't have an end in mind, but I ended with the following true story that happened to me when I still lived in the Spruce Street house in Santa Fe. After writing down the following marvels for which I have reference, for the writing exercise, I settled on the last two in bold.

Watching a baby being formed in the womb, giving birth
The body and how it works – the brain, the heart, hands, eyes
Animals – horses, cats, elephants, birds
The natural world – trees, mountains, flowers, clouds, the sea
The mind of man and his inventions – architecture, electricity, the computer
Language – words, writing, paper, conversation, wordsmithing
Insight, realization, consciousness
Evocative music, musical instruments
Forgiveness, the love of a parent and child
Synchronicity
Inner guidance – especially when it's loud and undeniable
Telepathic communication

The unknown, infinity
The Universe, the planets, the Pleiades

When I was about 10 years old and spending the night at the family farm, I was lying in bed contemplating infinity. Having recently learned about it in school, I started thinking about how far out in the universe one could go. I tried to realize that it never stopped; it went on and on … forever, and I suddenly felt myself as a tiny speck, lying there in my Aunt Bessie's feather bed.

Fast forward 25 years to the late 70s, when I was living in Catonsville and stayed up alone to watch a movie on TV after everyone else had gone to bed. When the movie was over, a short film, called *The Power of 10* began to play as a filler between movies. The 8-9 minute film depicted the relative scale of the Universe, according to an order of magnitude, based on a factor of 10. Captivated from the beginning, I saw a man sitting in a boat on a lake. The camera began to back away, showing the boat on the lake in a big park; next, as a spot in the middle of a city with countryside all around. The next scene was of the United States, then seeing all of Planet Earth, then out into the universe, past the tilted orbit of the moon, neighboring planets, the sun, 1, 10, 100 light years out, the Milky Way, out of the galaxy, a million, a hundred-million light years out. This film showed exactly how I had felt as a 10-year-old, lying in my bed on the farm, just a minuscule particle in the universe, just like the man in the boat.

But there was more. The camera brought us back from our journey out in the universe back to the man sitting in his boat on the lake and a mosquito was on the man's arm, which we followed as the camera explored the depths of the human body. As the moderator continued through the skin and blood, then to smaller and smaller particles down to quarks, I realized that we were a microcosm of the macrocosm – we must extend as far inward as we extend outward. Maybe we too are infinite. So, yes, I have reverence for infinity, the universe, the body, and the mind that can understand and articulate these concepts.

In the 40 years since I saw *The Power of 10*, we have learned so much more about the universe, yet still leaving so much unknown. One of the greatest pleasures of living in Santa Fe was looking at the sky. With 325 days of sunshine each year, the sky was strikingly blue with big white fluffy clouds. The magnificently colored sunset sky offered its own unique spectacle as the sun touched the top of the Jemez mountains to the west. Then, at night it seemed that every star in the sky was visible. I was so much more aware, and in awe, of the firmament when I lived in Santa Fe. When there were meteor showers, a group of us went out to the ranch and spread our blankets on the mesa to watch the meteor showers. Against a sky full of stars that we felt like we could touch, we watched the meteors streak one after another. It was better than any Fourth of July fireworks.

One night, when I was home alone, I took my papasan chair and my comforter out on the patio to watch my own private Perseid meteor shower. As I alternated between dozing and watching the meteors flash across the sky, my attention was drawn to a cluster of stars – seven of them, more radiant than any others. How could it be that I had never noticed that glowing configuration before? Clearly, it was the most beautiful arrangement of stars in the sky. The next day at work, when I drew a picture of the formation to show my co-workers, I was told I had been looking at the Pleiades, also referred to as "The Seven Sisters." I kept the image of that cluster of stars in my mind all day.

Later that afternoon, I set out for a New Age Fair in town in search of a musician who could provide music for our interactive video project. Walking down the first aisle, I came across local musician Jim Oliver. After listening to his music, I asked for his card, explaining his style of music might be perfect for our project, and to expect a call from our vice president of production. As I turned my head slightly to the left, I saw a gentleman standing next to a table covered in books. Looking down to check them out, imagine my surprise when I saw that one of the books had a picture of the shimmering Pleiades on the cover, the same image I discovered from my patio the night before, one that still lingered in my mind. He told me about the "space brothers," as he called the Pleiadians. As we spoke, he told me that he led a weekly seminar where he taught people how to make contact with them. I thought he was "a little out there," but I bought his book, eager to get home to read it. On a side note, the IT Group ended up hiring Jim Oliver, and I ended up taking the class on how to contact and communicate with the space brothers.

That night, I fell asleep after reading about half of the Pleiades book and was awakened by a bumping sound coming from the living room. Jokingly, I thought to myself, "Oh, it's probably one of those Pleiadeans," but realistically, I settled on Sam, my cat, jumping to the floor after coming in the window I left open for him.

Closing the book, I put it and my reading glasses on the nightstand, and noticed the time was 1:40 a.m. as I turned out the light. I closed my eyes, and instantly appearing before me, standing next to the bed, was a tall form, its body looking like closely clustered stars in the night sky or a lighted circuit board. I must be dreaming, I thought, and opened my eyes. Nothing there. I looked at the clock and saw that it was 1:42, and when I closed my eyes again, my ethereal guest was still standing there, patiently awaiting my return. I opened my eyes again, and just as before, nothing was visible. When I closed them a third time, and my visitor was still there, I decided to leave my eyes closed to see what would happen. This, or something better. Instantly, images and concepts began rapidly processing in my brain; I suddenly realized we were communicating telepathically.

I remember being awed and mesmerized by all that I was shown and told. What was to come was better than I had imagined it would be, and I was told the part I would play. I thought about grabbing the notebook from my nightstand to record the stream of information, yet a part of me was confident that I would remember everything. The love emanating from my light visitor began flooding my body until I was overwhelmed by waves of pleasure vibrating from the top of my head to the tips of my toes. I felt myself as a light body, leaving me with a sense of wonder and reverence. I immediately fell into a deep sleep.

Do I remember any details of what I was shown or told? No more than I have said here. The euphoria lasted for weeks, and during that time, I could hardly wait to get in bed every night, thinking and hoping it would happen again. To my great disappointment, I was not visited again. It's all part of the Unknown that I love so much. When I attended one of the seminars on how to communicate with the extraterrestrials, we were told that most children have had experiences with ETs, but after being teased and ridiculed, they learn not to talk about it.

Ethereal guest; drawing by Susan Voelker.

Over the years, I have heard many stories of experiences that people had when they were youngsters. I personally don't remember any contact, but back in January 1959, when I was 17, my mom and older brother got home late from a trip after all of us at home had gone to bed. When we got up the next morning, all they could talk about was seeing a spaceship in the field at the end of our lane. They made all of us walk down the lane with them so they could show us where they had seen the "craft." We were unable to see any landing markings, burn marks, or other telltale signs, so chalked it up to an illusion they had seen after having driven straight through from Texas. Twenty-four hours on the highway might cause anyone to fall prey to strange visions. Or, perhaps the occupants of the spaceship paid me a visit that I couldn't remember. One of the women in the ET seminar made beautiful stained-glass windows with special crystals that she claimed would attract extraterrestrials. I bought one and have always hung it in a window wherever I'm living, just in case they want to know where to find me.

Easter Sunrise at Christ in The Desert Monastery

In 1986, one of my co-workers, Wendy, introduced me to a friend of hers who had just completed a month-long silence retreat. When I asked what she learned, she said that she discovered the mind keeps repeating the same material over and over, like a continuous loop tape. Impressed that she had lasted for 30 days, I thought being silent would be a boost for my own spiritual jour-

ney, but not for that long. To that end, I started looking for a suitable place for a weekend retreat. Wendy suggested Christ in the Desert Monastery in Georgia O'Keefe country near Abiquiu, about 75 miles north of Santa Fe. I did some research and discovered they had a guest house that might be the perfect place for my retreat. When we learned the monastery would be open to the public for the upcoming Easter Sunrise service, Wendy and I decided to attend and check out their accommodations afterward.

Surrounded by the Chama River Canyon Wilderness, the remote monastery is accessible by a 13-mile dirt road, winding above and alongside the Chama River. We didn't want to chance traveling on an unfamiliar dirt road in the dark, so we drove up the afternoon before Easter. About 5 miles from the monastery, we found a lovely campsite just above the river where we set up our tent. We were the only campers there until about dusk when another car arrived with three women who set up their tent about 50 feet from where we were settling in for the night. Planning to get up about 3 a.m., we were soon lulled to sleep by the night sounds of nature, along with the rapids from the river below.

When Wendy and I talked about the experience afterward, we both thought we were dreaming when we heard the first shouts coming from the direction of the dirt road. It didn't take us long to be fully awake and alert to the fact that someone was clearly in trouble. We unzipped our tent and poked our heads out as the calls for "Help. Help me," got closer and closer. Grabbing our flashlights, we could see the three late arrivals also coming out of their tent.

As we hurried toward the desperate pleas, a young man, dripping wet and covered in blood, came stumbling into the campsite. As we held him in the beam of our flashlights, he breathlessly told us that the pickup truck in which he had been a passenger ran off the dirt road and plummeted 25 feet down the cliff to the river below. As the truck settled on the bottom of the river, the water had risen inside the truck about chest high. He struggled to get the driver out and was able to drag him to the roof of the truck. Since he was barely able to manage the steep incline on his own, and with his energy reserves waning, he made the decision to leave the injured driver there and go for help. He implored us to go to the accident site to make sure the driver was still alive and to help him.

Decisions were made quickly. The three other campers would take the wounded passenger to the monastery to get medical help, while Wendy and I would drive back down the road to look for the truck in hopes the driver was still on the roof of the cab. We said we would find him, make sure he was safe, then go to the nearest pay phone in Abiquiu, about 10 miles away, and call an ambulance.

I didn't know how Wendy and I would be able to climb down the steep cliff, get into the rapids to get him off the truck, to say nothing of then having the strength to carry an injured man back up the cliff to the road – all in the dark. However, I have to admit that the thought of putting a bloody and soaking-wet person in my brand new 1986 Cherokee Jeep quickly crossed my mind. And it just as quickly disappeared, for who knew what we would find in the river.

I drove slowly along the road, not totally trusting that it was actually 1-2 miles as the injured man had estimated. We didn't want to miss it. Wendy and I kept our eyes peeled for a disruption in the bank of dirt beside the road, where the truck would have disturbed the neatly piled soil deposited by a recent road scraper. After what seemed like a very long time, we finally saw evidence of wheels going through the dirt and disappearing over the edge of the cliff.

Surprised that we had actually found the spot, we got out of the car and at first could only hear the roar of the rapids. When I reached in and turned off the engine, we could hear shouting from below, "Help me! Help me!" but we could see nothing except the blackness of night. We yelled back, but were persuaded that he would not be able to hear us over the thundering water. We walked to the edge of the steep cliff, looking for a way down, but our flashlights revealed nothing that we could hold onto, just loose rocks and gravel. Moving the car so the headlights were aimed toward the river only lit the bank across the river, not the river itself. However, we thought we might be giving the driver hope that someone was there trying to help. After weighing our options, Wendy and I concluded that the only path open was to go for help. We yelled at the top of our lungs, over and over, that we were going for help, but we only heard his screams in response, "Don't leave me. Please don't leave me."

The hardest thing I have ever done was to get in my car and drive away from the scene of that accident, hearing the man's cries reverberating in my head. In all that turmoil and horror, I somehow had the foresight to set my odometer to zero so we would know exactly where he was. We sped back down the dirt road toward civilization, praying over and over "Oh, God, oh God, oh God. Forgive me for leaving him."

When we got on the straight part of the road, I saw, in the distance, the beams of car headlight coming toward us. As we got closer, I pulled my car across the road, checked the reading on the odometer, and got out, wildly waving my arms. As the car pulled to a stop, I ran over and saw two men and two women inside. I quickly explained the predicament, gave them the exact odometer reading, saying, "Go exactly this distance. Exactly! You'll see where the tires went off the road and over the cliff, and hopefully, with four of you, you can get down to the river to help him. We're going to Abiquiu to call an ambulance and will lead them back to the site."

Back in the car, we continued racing on our mission, finally arriving at the paved road. We drove into Abiquiu, found a pay phone, and contacted the police, who said they would send an ambulance. We told them we would wait at the intersection of the dirt road to Christ in the Desert Monastery. It felt like we waited for an hour, but I'm sure it was less time than that.

Checking the odometer again, Wendy and I started leading the ambulance to the accident site. We kept reassuring each other that the people in the car we had flagged down had been able to find the accident scene and were giving assistance to the poor man stranded on top of his truck. As we neared the area, we could see their car, and another one as well, pulled off to the side. We soon discovered that some of the monks from the monastery had come to lend a hand after they heard the plight of the driver.

Also unbeknownst to Wendy and me, our fellow campers decided that only one person was needed to drive the injured man to the monastery, which left the other two free to walk from the campsite to the accident site, in case we missed it. It turned out that they arrived within minutes of the car that we had met on the road. And, shortly after that, the monks arrived! The people in the car that we had stopped were seasoned campers and had ropes to lower themselves and supplies to the river. By the time we arrived, they were able to get the driver, who was soaking wet and shivering, off the roof of the truck and to the riverbank where someone else had started a campfire. They removed his wet clothes and put him in a sleeping bag to prevent hypothermia. It didn't take long for the EMT's to lower a gurney down the cliff, stabilize the driver, and bring him up to the ambulance. Then they drove to the monastery to pick up the injured passenger who had come screaming into our peaceful campsite.

Back at our tent, Wendy and I tried to go back to sleep, but I think the adrenalin was coursing so strongly through our bodies that we were unable to relax. We did get up at 3 a.m. to go to the monastery for the 4 a.m. sunrise service. One of the monks mentioned the accident and the night's activities. We didn't stay to check out their guest room to use for a retreat. After leaving the service, Wendy and I stopped at the accident site and could see the roof of the cab just clearing the water. We didn't know how either man could have survived a plunge that far down, and thought how lucky they were that the truck landed upright.

On our way back to Santa Fe, Wendy and I stopped at the hospital in Espanola and asked for the two men who had been brought in by ambulance after driving their truck off a cliff into the Chama River. We found them in the same room, both heavily bandaged. After introductions were exchanged, they expressed their gratitude for our help, and we apologized for leaving the driver in the water when we went for help. We learned that the passenger had been hitching a ride to the Monastery where he was going to study to become a monk. The driver, after picking him up and learning his story, had offered to drive him all the way to his destination, even though it was miles out of his way.

I never did go back to the monastery for my silence retreat. Six years later, however, on the occasion of my 50th birthday, I spent a week in silence at the Vedanta Center in Olema, California, about an hour north of San Francisco. If being silent wasn't enough, I also fasted for the first three days, and afterwards, prepared and ate my meals in silence, although there were other people there who were eating and talking. I sat for hours in meditation, alone, and with others who were also on retreat, after which I took long walking meditations around the grounds and sometimes in the woods. I think it was on the fifth day that I yelled out loud to my mind, "Don't you ever stop?" I finally realized that Wendy's friend, the one who had spent a month in silence, was right. The mind is, indeed, a continuous-loop tape.

5 | Life with Leslie

Five months into my new life in Santa Fe, I arrived at the office, and much to my delight, our new project coordinator Leslie Larsen had arrived from Lincoln, Nebraska. Now that our project was ready for the next step, she was hired to coordinate the video production, the rolling video piece of the program that would seamlessly blend with the computer graphics and animation. We hit it off immediately.

Leslie and Linda at the ranch, 1984. Photo by Jill Fineberg.

I invited her to brunch at my house on the weekend. When she arrived, we dragged my futon mattress and several pillows onto the patio so we could lounge comfortably. When I went in the house to prepare our meal, she asked if she could help. I insisted she relax and enjoy the mountain view. Leslie claims, to this day, that my next action was the impetus that caused our friendship to be cemented forever.

Here's the way Leslie tells the story. "I could hear Linda in the kitchen preparing our food. I hear utensils clinking against each other, but when she came out of the house, I wasn't expecting a tray containing three containers of Hagan Daz ice cream and two iced tea spoons . She placed the tray in the middle of the futon and invited me to sample as much as I wanted from all three flavors – chocolate, butter pecan, and coffee. To keep our hands from getting cold, she had thoughtfully wrapped each carton with a folded paper towel, held in place by a rubber band. We each had our own spoon to dip into whichever flavor our taste buds called for. Never before, or since, have I been served only ice cream for brunch."

From the beginning of our friendship, I enjoyed Leslie's lightness of being, her easy laughter, and childlike essence. By her example she taught me how to set my inner child free … to come out and play. We appreciated and enjoyed each other's sense of humor and adventuresome spirit. We became best friends, exploring the countryside on weekends, taking day trips, having dinner together after work, and of course, working together every day. By Thanksgiving, she gave up her little casita where she had been living and moved into the Spruce Street house with me.

MANIFESTING HOUSES

When I told Leslie about the method I used to manifest a relationship, we decided to apply the concept to finding the perfect house for us. We created a list of everything we wanted in our special home – views of the mountains, bedrooms on opposite sides of the house, a garden area, spacious rooms for entertaining. The list was a page long, and at the bottom, we wrote, "This or something better will be ours before the end of the year." We both visited our families for Christmas, Leslie returning to Santa Fe a couple of days before me. She called to tell me she found our perfect home – the Rainbow House out in the desert. She said it was a newly constructed, 3,000-square-foot adobe house, and she couldn't wait to show it to me.

Since it was dark and snowing when I drove into Santa Fe, we had to wait until the following day to go see the house. The next morning, we awoke to see the sun shining on six inches of new snow. We jumped in Leslie's four-wheel drive Jeep, drove 2 miles north of Santa Fe, turned left onto Tano Road, and drove another 4 miles out into the desert on a washboard dirt road. We turned into the driveway, and with no other house in sight, I saw the most beautiful house I had ever seen. And the inside was even more spectacular. When we stepped over the threshold and walked into the living room, it was so beautiful that I burst into tears.

The sunken living room with a stone floor was modeled after the Native American kiva – round with a kiva fireplace. Among the Hopi and Pueblo people, kivas were large, circular underground rooms used for spiritual ceremonies. Our living room gave us our very own cathedral. The ceiling was an artistic masterpiece of vigas

The beautiful Rainbow House, Tano Rd., Santa Fe, NM, 1985.

stacked in an octagonal shape, the logs narrowing from larger to smaller to frame a square skylight in the center. As you stepped down into the living room, one window outlined the whole of Los Alamos, 25 miles across the desert to the west. At night, the lights of the city twinkled in the distance, looking like a living painting. Another window displayed the Sangre de Cristo Mountains to the east. Jim McGorty the builder told us that he and his construction team spent 24 hours camping out on the property before they drew up the building plans, just so they could design the placement of the windows to frame specific views. The adobe walls inside the house were soft and curved, as if sculpted by hand. In the open kitchen/dining area, the wall-to-wall windows overlooked our enclosed courtyard, accessed to the outside world by a big wooden gate. The master bedroom faced the mountains to the east, perfect for Leslie who loved the morning sun. I preferred the western wing because of the sunsets and the extra bedroom that provided sufficient space for guests. The showers had instant hot water and were so large they didn't require shower curtains. We even had radiant heating in the floors so our feet would never be cold.

The only downside was that the house was on the market, but we were not deterred. We knew that houses sometimes stayed on the market for months; some for years. And, since we were living in the moment and loved the house so much, we agreed to decorate it with Leslie's beautiful Santa Fe furniture, in storage, to stage the house and make it available for any potential buyers to see. We each paid $500 a month rent, a deal by any standard since I was already paying $800 for the Spruce Street house. This Rainbow House was definitely "something better" than we had imagined.

Leslie and I loved sharing our beautiful setting and hosted many gatherings and parties. We started a women's group that frequently met on our roof where we sometimes saw a storm building over Los Alamos in the Jemez mountains and watched as it crossed the desert. As it approached the house, we climbed down and ran inside while it passed over and disappeared over the Sangre de Cristo Mountains to the east. Leslie and I still have regrets about not pooling our money and buying the house, but we knew that life was uncertain. As it turned out, within two years, I would be on a trip around the world, and Leslie and her boyfriend would be building a house in Abiquiu.

We had a year in the Rainbow House before it was sold. We had already started working on the list for our next house, though how anything could be better than what we were leaving, we didn't know. We got a phone call from a neighbor, Mrs. Smith, who had put her house on the market months earlier. It was empty, she said, and cold looking, and it just wasn't selling. She heard how beautifully we decorated the Rainbow House and said that if we could do the same with her house, she would let us live there rent-free. *That* was the "something better."

Without missing a beat or a day of work, we moved from one beautiful house to the next. The Smith House had a similar set up as the Rainbow House. This time Leslie's beautiful master bedroom overlooked Los Alamos to the west while I occupied a full two-bedroom apartment at the other end of the house. Aside from free rent, the "something better" also included a hot tub on the patio, a solarium, and a separate guest house.

While living in the Smith House, Leslie and I offered Peter Russell, a friend and the author of "The Global Brain," the guest house to use as a writer's retreat while he wrote his next book. He spent a week compiling an outline of everything he wanted to address in "The White Hole in Time." When he was finished, I invited 20 friends to the house to listen to him lecture from his outline while I audio taped his presentation. There were two talks, each about two hours long. Wendy agreed to transcribe them, and when she was finished, Peter had a manuscript that just needed to be edited. It was rewarding to have a role in the publication of Peter's new book.

We were able to enjoy the Smith House for only six lovely months before it sold. Word got around, and we were immediately offered our second rent-free house, this one in town. After living in the desert for a year and a half,

Smith House and living room, with Leslie at desk, Santa Fe, NM, 1986.

Linda and friend Peter Russell, 1986.

we welcomed the change to city life. We appreciated being close to grocery stores, movie theaters, restaurants, and work. And not driving that washboard road twice a day was a bonus. When I was young, moving was easy. Now, just thinking of moving five times in three years sounds like a nightmare, but Leslie and I had lots of energy and good friends who pitched in so that everything was packed and moved in a day. By the end of a weekend, our new homes looked like we had been living in them for years.

While Leslie and I lived in-town, we started hearing about Harmonic Convergence, a global event that would occur at sacred sites worldwide. We began dreaming about traveling around the world, but where would we go? Just for fun, we got out Leslie's world atlas and took turns, closing our eyes, opening the book, and randomly placing a finger on the map. Then we looked to see where the fates would take us. I had blindly chosen Egypt, Bali, Thailand, and Australia. Dear readers, I kid you not, within a year, I would spend five months traveling around the world, going to all those locations plus a few more. So, I didn't just manifest relationships and houses, but trips too.

Leslie and I have maintained our friendship for nearly 40 years, talking frequently by phone, taking trips together. We both still consider those years together in Santa Fe as a magical time in our lives. We lived together in peace and harmony, we worked for a progressive, exciting company, we had great house karma, and many of the friends we made are lifetime friends. New Mexico truly was the Land of Enchantment.

We lived in our in-town house about six months before it sold. This time, Leslie and her boyfriend decided to move in together, while I was taking over the lease of a friend who was leaving Santa Fe. Leslie had already moved out, and I had lined up friends with two pick-up trucks to help move me to my new home on a Friday afternoon. We had barely started loading – just deciding what to load first – when my boss called asking if I could go back to the office to take care of a problem at work. Not knowing how long it would take, I asked everyone if they could come back the next day, and off I went.

It was dark by the time I got back home, and as I turned the key in the lock and opened the door, I was met with a distinctive hollow sound. My cat Sam greeted me at the door, his plaintive meow echoing through an empty house. And not just empty, but cleaned as well. The kitchen was pristine, the counters sparkled, the floors were mopped. Even the fireplace was swept and clean. With tears of gratitude running down my face, I put Sam in the car to drive to my new residence where another surprise greeted me. All the lights were on in the house, two of my friends still inside, enjoying a glass of wine, having just finished unpacking my entire kitchen and my bedroom. All my furniture was in place, candles were burning, and my bed was made and turned down, as if waiting for a queen. I couldn't thank my ladies-in-waiting enough as they offered me a glass of wine, and I wept grateful tears.

In early 1987, shortly after I moved into my new abode, my friend Jim Berenholtz gave me the details about Harmonic Convergence. He explained that groups of people would be going to Sacred Sites all over the world and meditating for peace for three days in August 1987. He said Harmonic Convergence was the brainchild of art historian and author Jose Arguelles, whose vision was for a critical mass of humanity to activate the ley lines that are believed to link sacred sites around the world. The theory was that when a certain critical number achieves the same awareness, this new consciousness could be communicated from mind to mind. People joined in prayer at these sites would raise the vibration of the planet, ushering in peace and harmony. I invited Jim to give a talk at my house and invited interested friends. It was then that I decided to be in Egypt for the event.

LESLIE AND LINDA'S TRAVELS

Leslie and I made several trips to Minneapolis to Wilson Learning's central office where we had access to their video production facilities. We were asked to produce a Versatile Organization "trailer" as a tool our salespeople could show to their clients. I was so impressed watching Leslie at her craft. She knew how to set up the studio, color coordinate actor's clothing with the set,

Leslie and Linda ready for a horseback ride, with Quinlan looking on, Santa Fe, NM, 1985.

find all the needed props, and direct the actors. While I observed and assisted, I enjoyed learning new skills in production.

On one of those trips, I met Molly, Larry's wife, when I lost my glasses. The building was quite large and spread out and housed about 300 employees, and on that particular day, around 100 clients were in the building for a sales meeting. How would I ever find a pair of glasses? Hoping someone had turned them in, I went to the receptionist who suggested I find Molly to ask if she had seen them. I really didn't want to bother her, but she overheard the end of our conversation as she approached the desk.

"Ask me what?" When I told her my plight, she said without pause, "I saw them in Larry's office on a corner table."

I told her I was amazed that she knew where they were, with everything that was happening. She laughed and said, "You know, I didn't mind your asking me. What I mind is that I know where they are! I keep all that stuff in my head."

Molly and I would become close friends after she and Larry moved to the Santa Fe ranch within the year. Molly was one of the "ladies-in-waiting" who supervised my last move and settled me into the new house while I worked. It would also be Molly who accompanied me on my around-the-world trip two years later.

In addition to business trips to Minneapolis, Leslie and I also took fun trips to Los Angeles. One summer, we were invited to a women's all-day gathering hosted by Marilyn Ferguson. Thirty or so women authors, artists, therapists, actors— some of whom I had already met through my work at the ranch—were all involved in some way in the "New Age Movement." We gathered in a beautiful home situated in a private setting in the hills of LA. The grounds were lovely, and it was a beautiful day.

When we arrived, we congregated in a circle in the great room, and while Marilyn passed around Ecstasy, the women spoke of the work they did in the world. One woman, an officer with the LA Police Department, talked to us about what power looks like. Someone else who worked in the movie industry talked about how film was being used in positive ways to educate the masses. A sex therapist regaled us with stories of her work as a sex surrogate for couples with intimacy and sexual problems. I thought it was an interesting as well as a generous choice of professions. We learned that her services were in high demand with successful results. We spent the afternoon like playing puppies, first in one group and then tumbling into another. The conversations were stimulating and enlightening. I was lovingly welcomed into every circle I wandered into, everyone eager to hear my contribution. I felt like there was nowhere else on earth that I would rather be.

By evening, when the ecstasy had lost its glow, the men joined us for a meal, after which they brought out ketamine. Earlier that day, someone had told us that ketamine, discovered in 1962, was approved for use in the United States in 1970. It was extensively used for surgical anesthesia in the Vietnam War. Classified as a dissociative drug, when injected it gives one the experience of pure consciousness. That is, the body "disappears," we were told. In the past, ketamine was used for surgery in hospitals until people started relating their spiritual experiences. God forbid that someone have a spiritual experience outside of church. Consequently, hospitals stopped using ketamine for humans, and it started being used exclusively for animals. After all, animals couldn't talk about the spiritual experiences they were having.

There was a doctor present, so everyone felt safe since the doctor would give the injections. When Leslie and I heard, "injection," we took one look at each other and knew we were on the same page. Since neither of us wanted to be injected, no matter how enlightened it might make us, we offered to be the "Keepers of the Space" for the evening; our job was to make sure everyone was safe and supported in having a good experience. While injections were administered, Leslie situated herself on one side of the room, and I on the other. Some folks lay down immediately, some sat in a circle, and others remained standing,

Linda and Leslie in L.A., 1986.

walking around. They said they wanted to stay upright and conscious as long as they could, to see if they could remain lucid while experiencing pure consciousness.

As people chose their places, Leslie and I looked at each other across the room, both sets of eyes as wide as saucers. Her group, sitting in the circle, began to bounce up and down, urging others to get on board, "The spaceship is taking off." On my side of the room, where people were lying down, I heard deep breaths of release and relaxation. I could hear soft murmurings like, "Ah, now I remember," and "Ah, this is what it's like." Their expressions were blissful, and any comments were positive. The people who decided to stand were soon sitting or lying down. Leslie's group of space travelers, evidently having arrived at their destination, stood up, and like moths drawn to a flame, encircled a candle that was sitting on a table. Leslie was successful in keeping them from burning down the house. Whenever Leslie and I talk about this experience, we remain grateful that we had the good sense to not take ketamine that day, but it was an interesting sight to watch others.

The next day, on our way back to the airport in the rented car, I convinced Leslie to make a detour to stop at the sex toy shop that our surrogate sex therapist had told us about the day before. I convinced her to come into the store with me, neither of us having ever been in a sex toy shop. Leslie kept her eyes cast downward, unable to look directly at the products, or the people selling them. On the other hand, I put on a good show of not being embarrassed, giving the impression that I knew what I was looking for. Leslie, eyes still averted, kept edging toward the door. After examining the merchandise and seeing how various items performed, I ended up with an amply sized dildo with several settings and movements, along with a small discreet device that could fit easily into a purse. I was hoping to talk Leslie into accepting that one as a gift. As the salesperson was packing the boxes in a bag, Leslie quickly dashed out the door, and I soon followed.

We found the rental car return at the airport, got our luggage out of the trunk, and ran to catch the waiting bus to Departures. Checking my belongings, I suddenly realized I had left the bag with the sex toys in the car. I made a quick return trip to the rental car area and luckily found the bag just where I had left it. I was relieved that I didn't have to explain what I was looking for to the workers who cleaned the cars. On the bus back to the airport, I hastily and furtively transferred the toys from their boxes to a plastic bag. Free of their boxed enclosures, there was space for them in my suitcase. I checked my bag, got my boarding pass, and ran to meet Leslie at the gate.

To save time when we arrived in Albuquerque, I left to get the car to bring it around to baggage claim while Leslie waited for our luggage. When I went inside, I saw her with her back to the carousel, with those big eyes again desperately looking for me to come save her. As my suitcase made its approach around the final turn of the carousel where we were standing, I began to make out a steady hum, a buzzing, as it were, and I could make out the imprint of my recent purchase, as it made its slow sweeps, back and forth, under the soft cloth of my suitcase.

Each time the suitcase had made its way around the carousel, Leslie had turned her back on it, pretending she couldn't hear or see anything, as if she had no connection to it. Seeing the "big sweep" the first time had been enough. I quickly picked up the suitcase and started to open it so I could shut the damn thing off, but Leslie stopped me with a cold, hard stare, daring me to expose it in front of our fellow travelers. Getting her message, I picked up the bag with the vibrator against my leg, obscured from view. Walking out of the airport, Leslie five feet ahead, I could hear and feel the hum of the vibrator as it squirmed and arched itself against my leg. In the privacy of the car, and only then, would she allow me to open the suitcase and finally turn off the Big Bopper, as Leslie named it. When offered the Little Bopper as a gift, she refused, saying it was just too scary. She and I trot out this story anytime we need a good hearty, knee-slapping, doubled-over, finishing-each-other's-sentences laugh.

JAMEZ HOT SPRINGS

One of our favorite spots to visit was the beautiful Jamez Hot Springs, 70 miles from Santa Fe. Whenever we had out-of-town guests, we usually took them to the springs. We didn't think anything about driving an hour and a half to get there, even if we were starting out at 9 p.m. If we got the urge to go, we went. After driving through Los Alamos and passing the Valles Caldera, we parked the car on a small pull-off next to the road. We hiked another half hour up the side of a mountain, crossing a creek on a log that had thoughtfully fallen across the water before reaching the springs.

We often hiked that trail at night to enjoy the beautiful New Mexico night sky while relaxing in the 104-degree mineral water. One night we decided to take a newcomer to Santa Fe to visit the springs and only noticed her western boots when we got to the log bridge. Being a good sport, she took them off and crossed on stocking feet, a true feat in the dark of night. The drive and the hike were well worth the effort when we arrived at the springs. Enjoying the beautiful New Mexico night sky while relaxing in the 104-degree mineral water was priceless.

Chaco Canyon

One weekend Leslie and I drove the 185 miles from Santa Fe to Chaco Canyon where we could hike into the area to see the ruins and petroglyphs. Chaco Canyon was the center of a pre-Columbian civilization in the San Juan Basin of the American Southwest from the ninth to the 12th century. The Anasazi began constructing huge stone building complexes in Chaco Canyon around 850 A.D. The ancient center of a culture was linked by a network of roads and over 70 settlements many miles away. From the air you can still see the impression of those roads. Today, Hopi, Navajo, and other Pueblo Native Americans trace their spiritual and cultural history to Chaco.

We spent the day hiking, visiting the great rooms and the kiva ceremonial rooms, and listening to the silence. One of our therapist friends had told me a story about taking a group of women to Chaco to sit in a round ceremonial room. As they sat in their circle, our friend prayed aloud, "Dear Ancestors, we come to you today with great reverence for all mankind. We appeal to the Grandmother Council to give us guidance on how to create harmonious relationships with the men we live with." After a long silence, she said there was an incredulous voice in her head, "You live with them?"

Built and occupied between 828 and 1126 AD, Pueblo Bonito is the largest of dozens of great houses in Chaco Canyon. Reaching as high as four stories (some with balconies), it included 600-800 rooms, three great kivas (round multi-purpose rooms), and 32 smaller ceremonial kivas. Archaeologists agree that by the end of the 13th century Pueblo Bonito was completely vacated and the Chaco system collapsed. The leading theory for why the Chaco Canyon was abandoned is drought. For hundreds of years, the Chaco Canyon supported their farming life, but it is believed that the climate changed, giving rise to a 50-year-long drought starting in 1130. It is still dry today.

Pueblo Bonito (Spanish for beautiful town). Photo by James C. Wilson.

6 | Working with Larry

Inner Guidance

I was getting more involved working in the production aspect of our video project and enjoying the process of learning new skills. I was considering pursuing that direction instead of continuing with project management when Quinlan asked me if I wanted to be Larry's executive assistant. Since Larry and his wife Molly had moved from Minneapolis that fall and were now living full time at the ranch, he needed an assistant close by, and his secretary didn't want to move to Santa Fe. Quinlan and Larry talked it over and both thought I would be a good fit.

It didn't seem like a hard decision, pursuing a career in production or being a secretary – again. However, there is something enticing about being close to the source of power, and Larry's energy and futuristic vision was seductive. I kept going back and forth, deciding one way and then the other, until Quinlan finally told me I had to give him a decision the next day.

To give my options equal consideration, I decided to get a visualization session with the man whose seminars I had been attending about contacting the Space Brothers. When I arrived, he asked me to lie down, instructed me to stay silent and follow his directions. First, he asked me to choose my surroundings – my favorite place – and waited an appropriate period of time before continuing.

I was trying to decide between the beach, or a mountain, or maybe a quiet lake, when he moved on, asking me to choose my totem animal to walk with me. I was no closer to deciding whether it would be a lion – no, an elephant, but I love horses…it should be a horse…or a dog…or just a plain cat – when he gently led me to a stream. After telling me that my spirit guide was approaching, he asked me to describe my guide.

So, here I was sitting on the beach, next to a small stream at the foot of a mountain. I was surrounded by a horse, an elephant, a dog, and a lion when I saw a beautiful woman. No, it was a man in a flowing robe. No, it had to be an androgynous spirit guide. Before I could narrow it down, they all joined my menagerie and my visualization guide said, "Now, ask your spirit guide the question you came to get answered."

So, I gave up trying to choose and asked all of them, silently, as concisely as

I could, "Should I continue to work in production, or should I work with Larry Wilson?" The words were hardly formed when I heard the answer, in a clear and booming voice inside my head, "Work with Larry Wilson!" There would be no more questioning. I opened my eyes, sat up, and said, "Thank you, I got what I came for." I went in to see Quinlan the next morning and said, "I'll work with Larry," and never looked back. Best decision I ever made. Thank you, Spirit Guides.

Jill and Kia

Before I left Atlanta, a woman who came to one of my group rebirthing sessions, suggested I call her good friend Jill Fineberg when I got to Santa Fe. When I called Jill a few weeks after my arrival, we connected right away. With her sparkling brown eyes and quick sense of humor, she was one of the most creative women I had ever met – a photographer, a

Jill Fineberg (left) and Kia Woods, 1985.

writer, and a public relations promoter. It sounded like she could do anything. We had a lovely first meeting and saw each other for dinner a few times that year.

After I started working with Larry, it didn't take me long to see there was more work than one person could possibly handle. In addition to his two new start-ups, the Pecos River Conference Center at the ranch and the Interactive Technology Group in Santa Fe, he also was an international speaker. About 100 engagements a year at $10,000 a pop required managing a million-dollar business. I called Jill and offered her the job as my assistant.

Jill helped me initiate the process to identify the elements that were needed to get Larry organized. That way his mind would be free to do the important work his visions held. More than that, she cared about his physical and mental state. Once when Jill saw that Larry was stressed out, she went out and bought him a mountain bike that he could ride around the ranch. She and I worked together until Larry decided to hire her to promote the ranch, creating the public relations print material and photographing corporate events, which was more in her area of expertise. My assessment when I first met her was right. Jill could do anything. But now I needed to hire someone to replace her.

That's when Kia entered the picture. I remember her coming to my office for the interview; I asked her one of the questions I always asked prospective employees.

"Tell me, why do you want to work for Larry?"

She looked at me somewhat curiously. "Uh oh," I thought, "She hasn't even thought about it."

Then, she said, "Oh, I'm sure working with him will be great, but I really want to work with you."

Did I ask her more questions? Surely, I did, but with her perfect answer, I made the second-best decision of my life and hired her. Ours was a grand partnership that has lasted a lifetime. In addition to her officiating at Tom's and my wedding ceremony 14 years later, she was also my writing partner for this memoir 35 years later. I cannot image a world without her love and support.

Kia was able to develop systems that brought organization to the myriad tasks facing us every day to take care of Larry and his businesses. Nothing was ever too complicated, and Kia made my work life so easy.

Based on Jill's recommendations, Kia and I made a list of all the projects and goals Larry was interested in developing. He was blown away when we showed him the list outlining the 100 projects he either was pursuing or wanted to pursue. He began to see how scattered his mind must be, trying to hold all that together. We explained that no one could be expected to accomplish anything when they have that many projects pulling them in 100 different directions. We worked with Larry to narrow the list down to 10 current projects and prioritized the rest. "When you complete something on the short list," we told him, "we'll add another project from the prioritized list."

A high volume of phone calls and mail communications consumed a lot of our time and energy. We took care of most of them on our own, but there were many issues that required Larry's personal input before we could take ac-

Larry Wilson, Linda, and paperwork, 1986.

tion. Meeting with Larry was sporadic. Some days I would have to drive to the ranch to meet with him, on others he'd stop by the office on his way to or from the airport. Sometimes we'd have a five-minute phone call. We even met in my car. Several times, I boarded his King Air plane on the dirt runway on the mesa at the ranch just to get half an hour with him on his way to the Albuquerque airport.

Although his mail and phone calls were divided into priorities A, B, and C, we usually only got through the A priorities. It wasn't long, before all the Cs dropped off our agenda, and eventually even the B priorities took a hit. Then, the A priorities devolved into A1, A2, and A3, and you can guess what happened to the A2 and A3 stacks. He was an amazingly busy man, and it took two of us to support his work. As Kia and I became more knowledgeable about his business needs, he trusted us to handle the A2 and A3 priorities. Most days I went home with a stack of mail and spent an hour organizing for the next day. Everything was divided into priority piles, with a separate pile for Kia, one for me, and a page full of my own to-

Larry with his left brain and right arm, 1986. Photo by Jill Fineberg.

do list, including a prioritized list of everything for which we needed guidance. Since many of Larry's and my meetings were rushed phone calls when I could only cover two or three items, I had to be on top of everything.

Kia took care of all the correspondence, thank you, Kia. She wrote the most beautiful and heartfelt letters, covering up my own inadequacies as a letter writer. Even the people she said "No" to, the recipient felt heard and honored. Larry had expressed that he wanted anyone we talked to, or corresponded with, to have the same experience they would have had if they were communicating directly with him. Kia, by her example, has always called on me to be the best of myself. It's like having a guru who already loves you more than you know how to love yourself. I have learned a lot from her through the years of our close friendship. I treasure each and every moment we have had together.

Booking Larry's speeches and meetings and arranging his travel was another responsibility that fell on my shoulders. When he left on a trip, he always carried an itinerary that had flight schedules, hotel information, who would meet him with a sign, and phone numbers of contacts. A few times, when he couldn't find his itinerary, he called me late at night, wanting to know where he was and where he was supposed to go next. I always kept a copy of his itinerary with me so he would never be stranded. Larry and I also had a wonderful partnership and a great friendship. When he started introducing me as his right arm and left brain, I felt entirely respected and appreciated.

Meanwhile, back at the ranch – we used that phrase often – work was going full speed ahead on the Pecos River Conference Center. Construction was nearing completion on sleeping accommodations for 100 clients, plus a swimming pool, dining room, commercial kitchen, classrooms, and a ropes course. Larry was busy developing executive programs to incorporate a zip line, a climbing wall, a ropes course, and a "pamper" pole. These outward-bound adventure-types of programs would help participants recognize they can accomplish the impossible, especially when they have the backing and support of their team members.

Amy Edmondson soon moved from the IT offices to the conference center and started helping with team programs at the ranch. We were always on the lookout for experiences that would help corporate leaders increase productivity and creativity while optimizing the potential of their employees. When Amy told us about Bucky Fuller's World Game, we all agreed it would be a perfect offering for our clients.

The World Game

Bucky had created a "game" that tallied the resources around the world, and, when overlaid onto a map, an accurate distribution of world resources was simulated. It made it easy to see the gross inequalities on a global level. With a new understanding, we could begin to rein in our conspicuous consumption and greed. Bucky's goal, as he always said, was to "make the world work for 100% of humanity, in the shortest possible time, through spontaneous cooperation, without ecological offense or the disadvantage of anyone." This game would increase awareness on many levels.

Bucky designed his world map onto the surface of a polyhedron, which could then be unfolded and flattened to form a two-dimensional map. It allowed for precise proportional integrity in comparison to other mapping methods. The result is a highly accurate map with very little misrepresentation rather than the standard, highly distorted "world maps." When the map finally arrived at the ranch, we were eager to get it out and spread it on the floor in the large auditorium so we could learn how to optimize the presentation to clients.

We set up bleachers so the spectators could see the entirety of the world map and the activities that would take place on it. Our first audience was a combination of clients who were already at the ranch, ranch employees, my co-workers from IT, me, and other invited guests. The participants, who demonstrated the distribution of resources, were divided by country in proportion to the

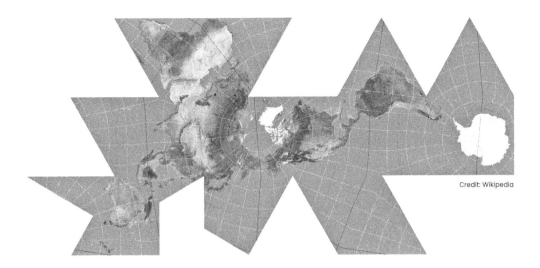

Credit: Wikipedia

population. They were identified by their colored t-shirts with the names of the countries as they took their places on the map. Some third-world countries were so crowded that the inhabitants had to hold on to each other to stay within the boundaries of their assigned country. In the U.S. and other developed countries, citizens had plenty of room to spread out and could roam wherever they wanted.

Runners were assigned ahead of time to bring resources to the countries on the map. Loaves of bread were brought and distributed according to statistics on availability of food. Africa and India had only a few loaves to share among their population, not even enough for everyone to have one loaf. It took the runners the same amount of time to bring loaves of bread to the United States as it took for them to deliver to the rest of the world. The eight or 10 people in the U.S. had loaves falling out of their arms into piles on the floor at their feet.

Next, dolls representing birth rate were brought to the people in each country, another uneven distribution. The U.S. received only two or three dolls, while undeveloped countries received many more because of their higher birth rates. Then the runners came back and took babies away from third-world countries, to represent the infant mortality rate. We in the U.S. kept our babies.

Then flashlights were distributed to represent the level of energy of each country. The auditorium lights were lowered for this part so the audience would be impacted by the disparity throughout the world. Citizens in India and China might be holding four or five flashlights, but in the developed countries, especially the U.S., there were too many flashlights to hold in our arms. We had to set them upright on the floor around us, making us the brightest spotlight on earth.

As the game progressed, the audience and the participants became more subdued and sober; as awareness grew, it was no longer a game. Books were distributed to the countries to reveal the level of education around the world, most going to first-world countries. There were other resources that were ad-dressed, but the last, most impactful demonstration was nuclear weaponry, showing each country's capability to destroy each other and the entire world. Large 10-gallon buckets of metal pellets were delivered to all the countries that possessed nuclear weapons. The countries without weapons just stood staring at the effect of the armed countries. We were all instructed to begin slowly and steadily pouring the pellets onto the floor. The thundering of the pellets hitting the floor was deafening even in the large auditorium. Israel, China, France, and India soon ran out of pellets, diminishing the roar slightly, but the Soviet Union and the U.S. continued, emptying bucket after bucket of pellets until finally the Soviet Union was finished, and our country still soldiered on – all by itself, booming in the auditorium – until all buckets were empty, spent of our nuclear power. Nuclear pellets covered the entirety of Bucky's map and the floor around it. Now it was the silence that was deafening.

There was not a sound in the auditorium for several minutes, and then the weeping could no longer be contained. We all wept for the senselessness of our ability to destroy what we had been given, what we had created. We realized that we have enough nuclear weaponry to destroy the world and everyone and everything in it several times over.

Then, with absolutely no prompting, someone from the audience stepped onto the map and began to pick up pellets and put them back in the buckets. Everyone, eyes moist with tears, came off the bleachers onto the floor to join in the silent clean-up. Surely, we said, when everyone sees this game, the veil will be lifted, and together we can begin to create Bucky's vision – and mine – of a world that works for everyone with no one and nothing left out.

A few days after writing this piece about The World Game, I listened to an NPR interview of Fred Kaplan, the author of *The Bomb: Presidents, Generals, and the Secret History of Nuclear War*. He talked about how, in 2021, we still have enough nuclear weaponry to destroy the world five times over. Some even say 50 times over. For a game to be as impactful as The World Game, I thought that greater advancements would have been made. We have made some, but there is still world hunger, people still live without running water and electricity, and even with all the talk about nuclear arms reduction and non-proliferation, it's still not enough. Will we ever be able to lift the veil of ignorance, blindness, and denial?

THE EAGLES REUNION

Working with Larry Wilson gave me the opportunity to meet the most extraor-dinary people, and the Eagles Reunion was one such occasion. I worked with

Barbara Marx Hubbard and Marilyn Ferguson to put together a gathering of visionaries, futurists, and educators. Barbara was one of my early spiritual teachers whose talks I attended in 1981 when I first moved to Georgia. She dedicated her life to sharing humanity's potential and how we all can achieve a better society when we work together. She became known as the "Mother of the New Age Movement" and came up with the idea of "birthing" humanity, which fit with my rebirthing philosophy. She gave me a draft copy of her book, *The Evolutionary Journey: A Personal Guide to a Positive Future,* in which she outlined the steps people could take to consciously evolve. Barbara believed that the human race is spiritually evolving to become co-creators which leads us to our own deeper life purpose. That inspires us to reach out to others in our communities and the world. But first we much activate ourselves. I put into practice everything she wrote in the book and spread the word among my rebirthing clients.

When Barbara and Marilyn were at the ranch at the same time, we came up with the idea of bringing together the people whose work in the world was helping humanity reach their potential. We named the event the Eagles Re-union because eagles are symbols of strength and courage. They are generally solitary birds and soar to great heights, up to 10,000 feet, thereby having the ability to gain an extensive view of the big picture. The people we invited were like the eagles, and we would all flock together to learn about our projects. In that way, we could determine if there were overlaps where some could work together or offer each other energy and support to accomplish their dreams to help mankind. We sent out a cryptic teaser to 100 "new age" leaders about a year before the event was to take place at Larry's ranch. Inside the envelope was an embossed card that held a feather (not an eagle feather, since that's illegal) and this message:

> *The eagles are gathering*
> *Save the date: August 25-27, 1986*

About three months before the date, we sent out formal invitations with logistical information and the agenda. I think by that time everyone had heard through the grapevine the purpose of the Eagles Reunion and were eager to save their spot. We decided on three days for the reunion because of its significance in scripture, mentioned 75 times. The number three signifies wholeness or perfection and points to what is solid, real, and substantial. As a number that indicates completeness, the number three always identifies some important event. Also, the patterns in many of those biblical stories don't tell the whole story in the first two days – the third day is the conclusion. We wanted to honor the spiritual significance of needing three days to manifest a result.

Everyone we invited came. It was the event of the year, and I had the honor of meeting all these amazing people who became immediate friends. They were the visionaries that Barbara said were the midwives who were helping to give birth to a higher consciousness on earth. Over the nearly 40 years since that gathering, many of the participants are still joining forces to further their own and each other's agenda.

Marilyn said they were each holding a piece of the puzzle that could save the planet. Many times, I heard her ask someone, "What do you know that if the whole world knew, you would feel relieved?"

When I asked her if I could use her question to write a book with the answers, she readily agreed. Jill Fineberg designed my letterhead, Hope International, and I sent 100 letters asking the question of visionaries, corporate leaders, and friends. I explained the question assumed that we each held a piece of the puzzle that would save the earth and all of mankind, and if we all cooperated, like Bucky said, we could solve the problems of the world.

Sidenote on the book, *What Do You Know That if the Whole World Knew, You Would Feel Relieved:* I sent out the question in the spring of 1987 before I decided to go to Egypt for Harmonic Convergence. I started receiving a few answers every day as I prepared for my trip. I arranged with Kia to manage my mail with the intention of writing the book when I returned from Egypt. As it turned out, I didn't come back to the country for six months and never got back to the project. I heard from nearly everyone I sent the question to. Sadly, the answers are still sitting in a briefcase in my garage. Maybe I'll get to it after I finish this memoir. Maybe the title should be, *Were You Able to Share Your Piece of the Puzzle and Did It Help.*

TIME FOR PLAY AND MEETING NEW FRIENDS

I felt like my work in Santa Fe was purposeful and rewarding, and it honestly didn't seem like work most of the time. There was always time for play too! There is a reason New Mexico is called The Land of Enchantment, and Santa Fe is the epitome of a town under a magic spell, in the best possible ways.

Synchronicity was an everyday occurrence, as was a wrinkle in time. Otherwise, how could we accomplish such an incredible amount of work and still have time for play and to entertain guests. During the three years I was in Santa Fe, my sons Tony and Clif came once to visit when I lived in the Rainbow House and again with their girlfriends at the Smith House. Ellen came once by herself and once with her future husband Michael. My sisters Betty and Ruth Ann came, separately, and Bobby and Jacques visited. Beverly and Jim came twice, and my friend Carol, from Baltimore, made the trip once. With overflow friends from the ranch who just weren't ready to leave Santa Fe, our house was busy and full.

On weekends, Leslie and I went on local outings: camping and hiking in the Sangre de Cristo mountains, exploring Indian Ruins, and participating in several sweat-lodges. One weekend we drove up to Estes Park, Colorado, to visit her mother and sister where we learned how to create shields and ceremonial face masks. A Santa Fe artist, Armado, lived across the arroyo behind our Rainbow House. When he went out of town, he asked us to take care of his horses in exchange for allowing us to ride them. We went up to the ski basin, sometimes stopping to walk through the Aspen Meadow.

Late one afternoon, after Leslie and I stopped at a deli to pick up fixings for a picnic supper, we drove up to the ski basin in search of a view before the sun set. Racing the sinking sun, we realized we didn't have time to find "the perfect" place. When we came to the first long view of Santa Fe in the valley below us, we pulled over on the shoulder, spread out our blanket on the side of the road, and laid out our picnic, just in time to enjoy the show.

Leslie and I started a women's group that met once a month at our house. It soon evolved into a healing circle. Each month one woman would sit in the center of the circle, and we would focus our attention on that person for whatever they wanted and needed. Later, when everyone was looking for jobs, we helped each other write résumés. Giving our attention to one woman at a time, the women in the circle would talk about her positive attributes, her skills, and her character, while she was taking notes. From that list, she would develop her résumé. Sometimes other people can see our competencies and talents better than we can for ourselves.

Once the ranch was open for business, there were always rope course events and other activities that we were invited to attend. We entertained many overnight guests whom we met at the ranch and at IT. They became friends, and they brought their friends who became new friends. Hugo Zuccarelli, the gentleman who developed holophonic sound, stayed at our house after he presented his product to our team at IT. We were considering using it for the Versatile Organization, but it turned out to be too expensive.

During the holophonic sound demonstration, we took turns sitting in a chair in the conference room. With a blindfold and headphones in place, a tape began to play. An opening door sounded as though it were coming from the door across the room, which was actually still closed. Then I heard little children come in, giggling as they approached and circled my chair. It sounded as if there really were children right next to me. Then I heard the clicking of scissors, as if someone were cutting my hair in the back. Not only could I hear the scissors snipping my hair, but I could feel it on my neck. It was an amazing experience. The system has been used in film soundtracks, television, theme parks, and in popular music, including Pink Floyd's *The Final Cut*.

An interesting story about Hugo was told a few years later when he met with our friend Wendy. She said that he told her about staying at the home of two lesbians who lived out in the desert. After he described the house and more about his stay, Wendy asked, "Are you talking about Linda and Leslie?"

"Yes, that's who they were," he said.

"They aren't lesbians," she retorted. "I know them very well. They are friends of mine!"

He assured her that we were definitely lesbians, and he was so adamant that after she related the story to me, she turned to me and asked, "You aren't, are you?"

There are too many stories and pictures that flood my mind of my time in Santa Fe to tell them all. It was a time that I felt supremely happy and satisfied with my life and with myself. Leslie contributed to that. Kia and Molly and Jill contributed to that. Larry contributed to that. The people I worked with contributed to that. It was the best of times that shortly would be coming to an end.

Waiting for our turn on the zip line: Joey Wilson, Linda, Larry Wilson, Kelly Cook, Leslie Larsen, Michael Levy.

7 | Leaving Santa Fe

Saying Goodbye to Larry

The times, they were a'changing, and I was moving on. Shortly after I decided to go to Egypt for Harmonic Convergence, we learned that the IT Group and Larry's business connection with John Wiley & Sons would be restructured. After full financial support by Wiley during the start-up phase of IT, and the completion and sale of its first produce, The Versatile Organization, it was time for the company to be self-supporting. In addition, Larry's, Kia's, and

Larry and Linda at the ranch, 1987.

my salaries, also paid by John Wiley, would be transferred to the Pecos River Conference Center, which was not yet financially independent and was unable to cover our salaries.

In the meantime, Larry and Molly's marriage unraveled and his new fiancée decided that she would take over my responsibilities of overseeing his million-dollar-a-year speaking engagements and his project list. Kia and I were given three-month severance packages, but before I left, I agreed to hire and train two secretaries for Larry and his fiancée at beginning wages. I found the perfect replacements and spent the next month teaching them everything I knew about Larry Wilson. Each day, I downloaded more of the details that were involved in my work as his right arm and left brain. As the month progressed, I began to feel a new lightness of being as my knowledge and tasks were transferred out of my brain. On the other hand, I could see the new hires sinking under the weight of those new burdens.

I do not remember the specific occasion when Larry and I said our goodbyes face-to-face. I'm sure we both said what we always said when we parted, "I love you and I'll never leave you. Goodbye." For us, that meant that even though I'm gone, you will always be in my heart. I wish the best for you, and you always have my support.

I vividly remember the last day I saw Larry in March 1987. My replacement Barbara and I had gone to the ranch for her to meet with him on her own for the first time. I stood near the door watching as they went over the mail, phone calls, and travel details. I could see she was doing great, and I was free. I didn't have to hold all that information anymore.

Larry's son Hershel walked over to me, took my arm, and said, "I'll walk you to your car now. It's ok for you to go. We'll take good care of him. He's in good hands."

Walking to my car, I appreciated the beauty around me, taking in the adobe buildings, the mesa in the distance, and the lovely blue sky. I got in my car and drove away from Larry and the ranch for the final time.

I had become good friends with Larry's soon-to-be-ex-wife Molly over the two years I worked with him. Since she also was now as free as a bird, she decided she would go to Egypt with me for Harmonic Convergence. I went to her house after I left the ranch, and, as we sat talking about our upcoming trip, we came to the realization that we didn't have to come back after the event in Egypt. I told her about the countries I had blindly selected from Leslie's atlas a few months earlier, when I had randomly put my finger down on Egypt, Bali, Thailand, and Australia. Molly said she would love to go to all those countries and added China and India to the itinerary, a trip five months away.

GETTING IN SHAPE

During the months before I left on my journey, I decided I needed to get in better shape. My goal was to be able to walk 20 miles with my backpack in the event I was stuck somewhere and needed to walk out. I figured it would take me about eight hours to walk 20 miles, depending on the terrain. Every weekend, I planned hiking expeditions with friends. For my first walkabout, Leslie, her boyfriend, and I walked to the top of Tetilla Peak at the edge of La Bajada Mesa outside Santa Fe. It had always captivated my attention whenever I drove to Albuquerque. The 7,203-foot ascent was moderately difficult, and the views were spectacular from the top. After finding some pottery shards, we enjoyed a light picnic lunch while we feasted on the views before heading down.

One weekend, friends and I hiked in the Sangre de Cristo Mountains. We started at an elevation of 10,000 feet in the ski basin, and the hike likely took us up another 1,000 feet. The Santa Fe Ski Basin, a 4-mile loop trail rated as a moderate hike, features a beautiful forest setting. I remember my friends insisted that we run parts of it just to build up strength and stamina. We weren't trying to get anywhere, just enjoying the views and the woods while getting in shape. I hiked some of my favorite places, also giving me a chance to say goodbye: the Bandelier Indian ruins, Puye Cliff Dwellings, Tent Rocks, the Dixon caves, and the Aspen Meadow Vista Trail. So many beautiful places to hike in preparation for my upcoming trip.

Saying Goodbye to Santa Fe

For what I thought would be my last four months in Santa Fe, I put all my belongings in storage, and my cat Sam and I moved into a friend's house while she was out of town. I was enjoying my freedom from work life. I always had Indian tea brewing and a big pot of soup on the stove at noontime for friends who dropped by for lunch. A friend and I decided to use my down time to develop a prayer book devoted to Jewish, Islamic, and Christian prayers. I became interested in how the three religions converged two years earlier when Larry asked Leslie, Patty Stillwell, and me to videotape the "Tent of Meeting," a bringing together of their symbols and stories. Michelle Zackheim, artist extraordinaire, designed a 25 x 40-foot tent where the stories of the three traditions were displayed on the walls. It confirmed my feeling that we are all one and that peace between the people of the three religions is possible.

I also started documenting the responses I was receiving to my book question, *What Do You Know that if the Whole World Knew, You Would Feel Relieved*? When I initially sent out the letter, I said that I would be embarking on a trip to the west coast before my Harmonic Convergence adventure. I received not only answers to my question, but also many invitations to visit when I was in their area.

Encouraged by the invitations I received, I contemplated a three-month road trip out to the California coast rather than wait around for my August departure date. I always loved driving the Route 1 California coastal highway, and it would take me to friends from San Diego to Seattle. I could be back in Santa Fe in July to prepare for the trip. Wendy had been wanting to go to L.A., so we agreed to caravan as far as Sedona where we would visit friends.

But the days went by, and it was easier to stay where I was, in a warm and comfortable with my friends stopping by for lunch and Sam keeping me company. One day when March blew April into town, I opened the door for Sam to go out and I was met with a sharp wind that cut through me like a knife. It felt like a physical assault. It felt personal, and I decided it was time to leave.

On that same day, Wendy showed up at my door announcing that it was time to go. She was ready to leave the next day. Since we were both inspired to get on down the road on the same day, it was settled. I arranged for an accountant friend to manage my bills, and Kia agreed to manage my mail, especially the letters I was receiving in response to my question. Ellen, back in Georgia, wanted to take Sam, especially since he had started out as half her cat when we lived together in Alpharetta. Jill, who was going to Atlanta, agreed to take Sam on the plane with her, and Ellen would meet them at the airport.

Linda and Sam, c. 1984.

The next morning, my car was loaded for a three-month road trip. After I tearfully said goodbye to Sam, leaving him with Jill, Wendy and I headed south on I-25 toward Albuquerque. As I rolled down the highway, I reflected on my three years, almost to the date, in Santa Fe. It had truly been home for me, and I was leaving a place I loved. I was also leaving Sam, and Larry, and all my friends who had become my family. Glancing in my rear-view mirror as Santa Fe receded from view, all I could feel was excitement and gratitude mixed with sadness. Jill gave me a traveling tape she had made especially for me, and as I listened to each song, I cried all the way to Albuquerque, knowing my life would never be the same. Several times I considered turning around and going back, but I kept my sights on Wendy's car leading the way forward and turned my mind to the new adventures that lay ahead.

Santa Fe in Linda's rear-view mirror, 1987. Photo by Leslie Larsen.

PART FOUR

Traveling on the West Coast
and Around the World
(1987)

Linda and Molly in Bali, Indonesia, 1987.

1 | West Coast Trip

Sedona, Jerome, Joshua Tree

I followed Wendy's car down the highway to Albuquerque, took a right, and headed west through New Mexico. Before crossing into Arizona, we stopped in Gallop to visit the Missionaries of Charity, founded recently by Mother Teresa because of her work with the poorest of the poor. We paid tribute to her good works before driving to Cottonwood, Arizona, where we spent a few days with my accountant's sister, who welcomed us with open arms. It was like that back in the 80s – my sister is welcome, and friends of my sister are welcome to my home.

From Cottonwood, we drove up to Sedona for a day. Since I would be taking part in Harmonic Convergence at the Egyptian Pyramids, I was on the lookout for other sacred sites as I traveled. The Sedona area was a hotbed of sacred sites, boasting seven vortexes. According to those who believe, vortexes are created from spiraling spiritual energy in locations where the energy can help facilitate prayer, meditation, and healing. We were able to visit three of the seven such sites around Sedona where nothing magical happened that I could tell, but the views were spectacular. And those red rocks! I later learned that 5,000 people gathered at the seven vortexes in and around Sedona for Harmonic Convergence.

We also visited Jerome, the largest ghost town in Arizona, once known as the "Wickedest Town in the West." In the early 1900s, Jerome grew from a copper mining camp with 10 tents into a bustling community with 10,000 residents. During its heyday, 800 million dollars in copper were removed from the local mines, but it came to an end when the demand for copper decreased after WWII. The mines were closed in 1953, leaving only 50-100 residents who started promoting Jerome as a historic ghost town. Since that time, sustained by tourists, the population today has increased to about 500 people, mostly artists, craftspeople, musicians, writers, hermits, and old hippies.

After leaving Jerome, we went to visit friends of Wendy's in a remote valley near Prescott, about 25 miles away. Wendy had written to tell them we would drop by to see them when we were in the area, without giving any dates or times, and they had no phone. When we arrived, we found a group of about

15 people gathered in a circle in a field (did they have flowers in their hair?), performing a ritual to assist one of their friends who had passed to the other side. Because the man had committed suicide, they wanted to make sure he was able to go on to his next assignment. It all seemed so normal, welcoming friends and strangers into their circle while helping to send their friend on to his next mission. As I said before, it was the 80s.

Speaking of mission, this is where I was introduced to the soundtrack from the movie, *The Mission*. I was so moved by the music that as soon as we got back to civilization, we went to the movie, and I bought a tape of the soundtrack. It became one of my favorites during my road trip, and the movie was also impactful, and one I often recommend.

Once Sedona had finished sprinkling its bliss ninny dust on us, it was time to head west – Wendy to L.A., where I would rendezvous with her later, and I went to Joshua Tree, a seven-hour drive. According to a story from the Mormon settlers, they named the trees they saw "Joshua" trees when they were crossing the Mojave Desert in the mid-19th century. They felt the trees were guiding them, much like the story of Joshua, with his hands outstretched, guiding the Israelites in their conquest of Canaan. Feeling safe with all the Joshua's around, I found a campsite, set up my tent and soon went to sleep. After touring the park the next morning, I soon set my sights on San Diego where friends awaited. I found a campground outside San Diego, and, with no agenda, I set up my tent early. When it started getting dark, I could hear nearby campers being rowdy. I started making up stories in my head about the dangers of a woman camping alone, so I called a friend in San Diego who came out to spend the night and ease my fears. The next day I went on to San Diego and stayed for several days, but I was eager to get to Los Angeles where more friends awaited.

LOS ANGELES

By the time I left San Diego, I had been on the road two weeks. In L.A., I first stopped in Venice to stay with Ruth Strassberg, Marilyn's executive assistant. Having never been to Venice, I enjoyed the seaside resort with the rollerbladers in bikinis on the 2½-mile boardwalk and volleyball players on the beach. It was a place that I wanted to visit again.

I left Venice to meet up with Wendy, who invited me to stay with her at the Hollywood home of her cousin Donovan, the singer. You will remember him, from the late 60s, for having written and sung the song, *Lelana*, in that soft echoey-kind of voice he had. He was out of the country, but somehow, through him, we were invited to a party of movers and shakers in the movie business – Beverly Hills, that is, swimming pools, movie stars. We thought we were living high on the hog, as Jed Clampett would say.

From there, we went to another party at the home of Robert Chartoff, one of the producers of the movie *Rocky,* where we met a group of Mother Mary devotees pitching a movie proposal to Chartoff. Their story of Mary was likely the Sufi version of her life – that her birth also was a virgin birth and that she was raised in a temple that operated as a mystical school, administered by her parents. It was said that Mary could manifest food in her hands for herself and for others, like her son did with the loaves and fishes. In addition to her having been chosen to be the vessel that carried the baby Jesus, the Sufis considered her sacred in her own right, therefore deserving of recognition. They promised that any devotee of Mary would die a gentle death. Everything that I heard enticed me to honor Mary, as they did.

After a week in L.A., I left Wendy and headed up the coast to San Francisco, stopping in San Luis Obispo to stay with Eagle friends there. I went in search of the church with the black Jesus in the stained-glass window, the one I went to with Jonyl and Carol when we were there five years earlier. After examining it more closely, I would now say Jesus was depicted more realistically as a Jewish man from the Middle East.

J.J. Ebaugh and several other people came down for one night while I was there. I had first met J.J. at the Eagles Reunion and again at the Women's Gathering in L.A. She was engaged to Ted Turner and had a place in Big Sur, 100 miles north. It was like a mini-Eagles Reunion. After my trip around the world, she would hire me to work with her at Turner Broadcasting. The networking from the Eagles Reunion would be churning out connections for many years.

SAN FRANCISCO

My stay in San Francisco lasted several weeks. Jim Channon and Joan Steffey, both fellow Eagles, offered me their lovely home in Mill Valley while they were out of town. I enjoyed the avocado tree in their garden that yielded fruit for my lunch every day. I drove into the city several times to get the required documents and vaccinations I needed for my upcoming trip. I already had a passport but had to get a visa and an international driver's license. I spread out all the immunization shots over a couple of weeks. The typhoid shot was the worst. After I got home, I started feeling bad, and then worse, and then went to bed. As I lay on the bed, I could feel the serum as it traveled through my blood to all parts of my body. I could imagine how horrible it must have been to have the disease. It was the sickest I had ever been. Thousands of people still die every year from it.

After Jim and Joan came back from their trip, I stayed on to visit with them for a few days. They invited their astronaut friend Rusty Schweickart for dinner one night, and I was definitely star struck. I kept thinking, "This man has walked in space." I was fascinated as I listened to him relate a story of his Apollo 9 spacewalk while testing the spacesuit and portable life support system that would later be used by the 12 astronauts who walked on the moon. Just as he started his spacewalk, a colleague's movie camera jammed, and for five minutes Rusty was left alone on the Lunar Module porch, free to take in the vastness of space and ponder the big questions of existence. During that brief period, he felt he underwent a metaphysical experience, as he observed the earth below. He explored the philosophical and evolutionary implications of humanity's first steps into the cosmos, likening it to the birth of a baby. This time it was a cosmic birth. He emphasized that the astronauts were "the only people who have seen the Earth with our own eyes as a single place for all life."

When he came back home, he set about trying to inspire others with that experience. Astronauts typically reported feeling overwhelmed and awed by the fragility and unity of life on Spaceship Earth. They all came back to earth understanding the "bigger picture," feeling a cognitive shift in awareness that we are all connected.

Jim was a U.S. Army Lieutenant before becoming a business consultant and "new age futurologist." Inspired by Stewart Brand's Whole Earth Catalog 10 years earlier, Jim had written the First Earth Battalion *Operations Manual*, a popular book pointing the way toward a transformation in the U.S. military. He was a proponent of swords to plowshares, the concept that military weaponry and technologies could be converted for peaceful applications.

During dinner, Rusty and Jim came up with a story they convinced me to tell as I traveled around the world, just to see if it got any traction. The story was that I had inside information about secret meetings that were being held by world leaders discussing total disarmament and creating peace on the planet. I snuck that story into many conversations during my travels, but I don't think it ever got enough traction to make its way back to Jim or Rusty.

Aside from getting my immunization shots, I mostly hung out with Eagles friends, ate sushi, and went to Muir Woods. I spent some time with Barbara Marx Hubbard and the people in her organization, the Foundation for Conscious Evolution. She invited me to an afternoon soirée hosted by her sister Patricia Ellsberg and her husband Daniel, who was the whistleblower behind the release of the Pentagon Papers in 1971. They were giving a presentation to inform people of their work on nuclear disarmament and to end wars on the planet.

The papers revealed that Harry Truman financially supported France's war efforts in Vietnam, contributing as much as 80% of their costs. When Dwight Eisenhower became president, he was fearful that if Vietnam fell to the communist, neighboring countries would follow, and contributed $2 billion to the cause between 1955 and 1960. The Papers also revealed that Lyndon Johnson distorted the truth about the Gulf of Tonkin in order to intensify bombing. The naval patrols which were allegedly attacked in the Gulf of Tonkin incident were deliberate provocations by the United States in the hope of inciting a major response from the North Vietnamese.

Barbara also invited me to go with her to spend a weekend in Arkansas with Ken Carey, author of *Starseed Transmission*. Ken and his family lived on a large farm without electricity, plumbing, radio, television, newspapers, and magazines. They began selling homesites and were in the process of establishing a community there. They had already built a guest house where Barbara and I stayed.

I was drawn to learn more about Starseeds, especially to see if I might be one of them. Ken channeled an entity called Raphael who said that Starseeds were incarnated Star People who came from other dimensions or planets to assist in raising the consciousness of humanity and assist in the planet's evolution. We spent a lot of time meditating that week, but I did not hear a call that needed to be answered.

Joe Sohm, another fellow Eagle, was an up-and-coming photographer who had traveled extensively in the United States, taking photographs that represented Democracy in America. From his collection of photographs, he put together multimedia slide shows, coupled with inspirational music, and projected them onto giant screens for events. His presentations, *Voices of America* and *Voices of Tomorrow*, accompanied by the National Symphony Orchestra, have been featured at the Kennedy Center, airing on NBC TV, and for MTV's 1993 *Presidential Inaugural Coverage*. You could say I knew him way back when.

A year earlier, in 1986, I had accompanied Joe on one of those "shooting" trips along the coast of California and always welcomed every stop to take another photograph. On this trip, he found me at Jim and Joan's in San Francisco and invited me to go with him to photograph the 50th anniversary of the opening of the Golden Gate Bridge on May 24, 1987. We went as members of the press, and I offered to help carry his equipment. "It will be fun," he said. "And, the views will be fantastic."

When we arrived at the break of dawn, the Golden Gate Bridge was already closed to motorized traffic for the occasion. Since it had not yet been opened to pedestrian traffic, we were practically the only people on the bridge. We leisurely strolled to the center of the bridge where a flatbed trailer had been set up for the 20 or so members of the press who would be photographing and reporting on the event. With our press passes visible, we climbed onto the platform to enjoy the beautiful view of the bay and the hills of San Francisco while waiting for the party to begin.

The event planners estimated about 80,000 participants, and off in the distance we saw groups approaching from each end of the bridge, one from Marin County and the other from San Francisco. Some were pushing babies in strollers, others were riding bicycles, and most were on foot, everyone enjoying this rare opportunity to cross the bridge with no traffic to celebrate its golden anniversary. The two festive groups were fun to watch as they met in front of our platform, greeting each other, laughing, and waving. And the people kept coming, and more people came, and then more people came.

Standing above the crowd, we were in a position to see that there was going to be a problem. There were too many people, and, eventually, as the groups from the east and the west met, a gridlock formed that became so tightly packed that any forward movement was impossible. Going back was also impossible because more people were queued up all the way to the bridge entrance where even more were waiting to start their walk across the bridge.

The planners had not anticipated a human gridlock because they had not anticipated the 800,000 people – 10 times the expected number – who showed up to walk across the bridge that day. But there they were, eyeball-to-eyeball, shoulder-to-shoulder, stuck on the 1.7- mile length of the bridge. It was packed so tight that people began to throw strollers and bicycles over the sides of the bridge because they needed the extra space. I was so grateful to be on the platform, above the fray, and not stuck in that mass of humanity. Generally, to everyone's credit, they were calm and polite and patient.

We tried inviting a few mothers with babies and old people on our platform,

Left: Linda at the 50th anniversary of San Francisco's Golden Gate Bridge opening, 1987.
Right: Gridlock on the Golden Gate Bridge, May 24, 1987.

but they couldn't even move a few feet through the throng of people. When the gridlock finally became obvious to the officials, the bridge was closed. The half-million people who were still waiting to cross the bridge were dispersed to make room for the people on the bridge to move back the way they came. It took three hours for the crowds in the center of the bridge to begin to move, and we could finally leave. We later learned that the unprecedented weight of 300,000 people caused the middle of the bridge to sag 7 feet. *The San Francisco Chronicle* referred to the event as "the largest clusterfuck in Bay Area history where no one actually died."

After I left Jim and Joan's, I settled comfortably into the apartment of another Eagle friend, near Walnut Creek, north of San Francisco. Claudia lived nearby, having moved to Oakland about the same time I moved to Santa Fe. We hadn't seen each other in two years, and like it is with good friends, it was as if we had seen each other the day before. We spent our time catching up, playing Scrabble, hiking in the hills, going to Fisherman's Wharf, eating as much sushi as we could, and just hanging out.

I had been having intermittent trouble with my car since I left Santa Fe. Even though it was only 2 years old, sometimes it would not start. In Santa Fe, I remember going Christmas shopping and locking the car with the motor running so I wouldn't have to worry about starting it. Every time I took it to the dealer, they "fixed it," but a month later, I'd have the same problem. I had taken it to several recommended garages along the way but was unable to find anyone who could figure out what was wrong. San Francisco was no different. I didn't know how I would get up the nerve to leave the Bay Area, not because I had fun and interesting friends to play with and not just because of the car problem, but mostly because for the rest of my trip, I knew I would be on my own.

THE EAGLE AND THE SERPENT

A few days before I headed north from San Francisco, I was in an art gallery/ studio and observed a very nice-looking man coming through the doorway carrying a large object hidden by a protective wrapping. I watched as he put the bundle on the counter and uncovered his artwork to reveal a beautifully detailed wood carving of an eagle. I was enchanted, having recently been involved with the Eagles Reunion. I introduced myself; his name was Tom D'Onofrio, a wood carver, obviously, and I admired his work. We chatted for five or 10 minutes before saying our farewells.

The next day, when I was in Sausalito having lunch with another Eagle friend, I told him about the carving I had seen. We were trying to come up with a way to integrate eagle carvings into the next Eagles Reunion. That reminded him that he needed to pick up a piece of art being framed nearby. As we entered the gallery, a gentleman standing at the counter turned toward us, and there was Tom D'Onofrio again, this time with a box of dolphin carvings he was showing to the shop owner. We visited for a longer time at this meeting. He not only carved dolphins and eagles, but his favorite work was carving sea serpents. He told me he lived in Bolinas; I told him I was on a year's journey looking for sacred sites around the world.

After introducing him to my friend and talking awhile longer, Tom invited me to come to Bolinas when I was ready to leave San Francisco. He gave me specific directions: Take the Coastal Highway and look for the Mountain View Road sign on the right; exactly 2.4 miles after the sign, turn left. He stopped to emphasize there are no signs to Bolinas that designate where to turn off the Coastal Highway. He said the 1,000 or so Bolinas residents didn't want anyone who didn't live there to come and ruin it, so they kept taking down the signs as soon as the county had them installed.

Several days later, I began the last half of my road trip, with six weeks to go before I wanted to be back in Santa Fe. I set out for Bolinas, 60 miles west of Walnut Creek and just above Stinson Beach. I drove until I found the Mountain View Road sign, then proceeded 2.4 miles farther, and took a left on the road with no sign.

I have to admit it was a little spooky, but I hadn't watched any *48 Hours* or *Dateline* episodes at that time, so I was a very trusting soul. I found Tom's rustic wood cabin, surrounded by a grassy yard with numerous outbuildings, including his studio. He had turned one of the sheds on his property into a cozy and comfortable guest room with an en suite, which is where I would spend the next two nights. Tom's girlfriend arrived later in the day, and, after supper, we stayed up talking into the wee hours.

Having learned that I was a horsewoman, the next day Tom and I walked to the neighboring farm owned by Kevin Kelly. While Tom was catching our horses, I visited with Kevin in his studio next to the barn. He was surrounded by his collection of photographs of Earth taken from space. Having selected 150 of them, accompanied by quotes from astronauts and cosmonauts, he was in the process of assembling and editing a coffee table book, *The Home Planet*. The preface was written by Rusty Schweickart, the astronaut I had just met. The pictures were extraordinary. I would call Kevin a year later to negotiate using his photographs for the *Planet Live* TV show I was working on at Turner Broadcasting. So much synchronicity in my life.

Tom and I soon set off on our two trusty steeds, headed for the ocean. It was the first time I had ever ridden on the beach, so I was excited. But getting there! After galloping across an open, grassy field, we began to approach a tree line that revealed a trail that followed a gully down to the beach, 50 or more feet below. I was told the incline was steep and rocky and was instructed to give my horse free rein to choose her own way. My job was to stay on, which I did, because she was a sure-footed and steady girl and knew her way down. I felt like the woman from Snowy River.

What a surprise when we came out on the beach! I was expecting a sandy beach but instead, it was a driftwood beach, nearly solid wood, hence the name Wood Beach. We picked our way around the driftwood until we found an area where we could build a little barricade to protect us against the wind while we had our picnic lunch. While we were looking out at the ocean, he told me the story of when he had witnessed his first sea serpent.

Ten years earlier, he and a friend were discussing the rosewood table Tom had been working on for more than a year and was having difficulty finishing. He promised his clients that he would incorporate a dragon's head, but he couldn't quite picture what the head of the creature would look like. He said he had the feet and the tabletop done, but had been unable to get the detail of the head of a mythical creature. He had used up so much wood that he was afraid if he screwed up again that the table would be ruined.

Tom said he had been feeling emotionally, physically, and spiritually drained, so he got on his horse and rode down to the beach where his friend had set up a day camp and teepee right where we were having our picnic. It was a balmy summer afternoon, nine years earlier, on a day when the ocean was more like a lake. As he dismounted, he spotted something out of the corner of his eye. He turned and saw a dark figure swimming though the surf. It was a big and dark creature, about 40 feet long. He and his friend watched as it came out of the water, and he could see it was a sea serpent with a head like a dragon. It dove down into the water only to rear its head again, clear enough for both men to see, and for Tom to remember, and then it disappeared.

I kept gazing out to sea, half expecting the sea creature to show up for me. Tom said he worked around the clock for four days, finally finishing the head on the table that he was making for Paul Kantner and Grace Slick of the Jefferson Airplane, who were living in Bolinas at the time. Later in the year, Tom and the Rose Dragon Table were featured on the September 1977 cover of *National Geographic* magazine.

Two days later, I said goodbye to the carver of sea serpents and dolphins and eagles. Before I left, Tom called his friends 15 miles up the coast in Point Reyes and introduced us. They invited me to come visit. "Fifteen miles," I thought. "At this rate, it will take me more than six weeks to get back to Santa Fe."

It didn't take long to drive up the coast from Bolinas and to find the couple in Point Reyes. They lived off the grid on a private piece of property, but what captivated my attention was the red gypsy wagon sitting in the field. When I was a child, my mother used to threaten us children with tales of wild gypsies coming through the towns and countryside in their wagons, looking for children to steal. I kept looking for them, but never saw anything that looked remotely like a gypsy wagon – until now. The couple told me they took it out several times a year for Renaissance Fairs and other relevant events, and they offered it to me as my sleeping quarters for a couple of nights.

NORTHERN CALIFORNIA, OREGON, WASHINGTON

I spent the next month meandering up the coastal highway, staying in small motels along the way. Sometimes, if I liked a town, like Bodega Bay, where Alfred Hitchcock's, *The Birds*, was filmed, I would spend two nights. During the previous three years, I had traveled up and down the California coast between San Diego and San Francisco several times, but this was the first time I had been north of the Bay Area and the first time I made the trip alone.

I had heard this stretch of the Sonoma County coast is the most stunning stretch of coastline in the world, and it didn't disappoint. I was entranced by the display of wildflowers, the ocean, and the sky. Every beach beckoned, and I stopped at as many as I could, even if just to pull over and gaze out at the sea, or sometimes I would scramble down the cliff-side trails to the beach. I always looked for little hole-in-the wall restaurants where all the locals ate, and I pretended to myself that I, too, was a local.

Somewhere, along the way, maybe it was Eureka, I wandered into a bookstore and asked the salesclerk what her two favorite books were. She recommended *The Singing Creek Where the Willows Grow* by Benjamin Hoff and *Handling Sin* by Michael Moore. I bought both, and for the rest of the trip, I was never alone. After the first reading, I knew I would have to pace myself so I would have these new friends with me for the rest of my trip. Yes, I read them both at the same time because I found the characters in both books so delightful and vivid. They all found their way into a cozy corner of my consciousness, and it felt like they were in the car traveling with me.

The Singing Creek tells the true story of Opal Whitley, a 6-year-old prodigy who, through a diary, related her adventures in nature. With her as a guide, I developed a keener awareness and appreciation of the natural world around me. The characters in *Handling Sin* were a raucous and rowdy bunch, carrying on in the back seat, making lewd comments, and laughing about our progress, or lack thereof.

When I arrived in Portland, I decided to stay a few extra days. I felt the need to be still in this beautiful city. I called my sister Robin who agreed to fly out from Virginia to join me when I got to Seattle. When I met her flight the following week, it was great to have a change of pace, to be talking to an actual, living person, so I didn't have to keep up both sides of the conversation. We rode ferries, went up to Victoria, laughed a lot, and played along the coast.

After Robin left, I called another Eagle friend who had offered me his cabin at a campground north of Seattle. Still feeling the need for quiet and stillness, I stayed put at the cabin for several days. Back when I was in San Francisco, Jim and Joan insisted that I call a friend of theirs, Tom Robbins, who lived north of Seattle. They both thought we would fall madly in love and claimed that we looked alike. We had the same eyes, they said.

I had read several of Tom's books, *Still Life with Woodpeckers, Jitterbug Perfume,* and *Even Cowgirls get the Blues*, and when we met for dinner, he told me about the book he was working on, which I still have not read. He was very nice, but also reserved. I was shocked to find out he wrote all of his books on yellow pads – no computer! I couldn't see the likeness that Joan and Jim talked about, and we didn't fall madly in love.

And now, it was time to head back to Santa Fe where Molly and I could start mapping out our trip to develop an itinerary. I had planned to take a week to get back, but in my eagerness, it took only three days. I loved the beautiful green rolling hills in Eastern Washington state. I stopped at a roadside stand to buy a bag of freshly picked cherries, which I ate, spitting the seeds out the window as I made my way south.

Trip Planning in Santa Fe

While I was frolicking on the west coast, Molly found "golden" round-the-world airline tickets that we could use for the entire trip, for a year, as long as we kept going in the same direction. The tickets also allowed two or three backtracks so we decided to buy them. I liked the idea that we would circumnavigate the earth, always heading east until we got back home again. I recently found a note in my trip folder that said "airline ticket $2,900," but I am skeptical that we paid that much. My three-month severance package was a good start on my trip fund. I also had rental income on a house I still owned in Atlanta that would hopefully keep me from dipping into my savings.

Molly and I went shopping, and bought a couple of travel books, one of which was *Lonely Planet on a Shoestring.* In addition to day packs, we also bought bigger backpacks that could convert to suitcases, in case we wanted to stay in someplace fancy that frowned on backpackers. We put together a loose itinerary without nailing down exact dates. We would spend two weeks in Egypt, a week in Israel, and a week in Thailand. We also wanted to go to China, India,

Bali, and Australia, but wanted to stay flexible above all.

I turned my Jeep over to Leslie to sell for me, and I packed everything that I thought I would need for a year in my backpack and my day pack. The first leg of my eastward journey was from Albuquerque to Atlanta, where I stayed with Ellen and Michael who were living in Athens with my cat Sam. The next morning when they saw how heavy my packs were, we unpacked everything to consider the necessity of each item. As experienced campers, I trusted that they knew what was necessary and what wasn't better than I did.

"You can take this and this, but not these five things. This will be good, but not those three things."

When they were finished, both packs were much lighter and possible for me to carry. After a few days, Ellen and I left to drive to Virginia with Tony to attend a nephew's wedding and a family reunion. From there, my children put me on an airplane to New York, where I would meet Molly to begin our adventure.

2 | EGYPT

HARMONIC CONVERGENCE

When Jim Berenholtz told me about Harmonic Convergence in early 1987, I immediately bought into Jose Arguelles' concept, which had grown from taking elements from the pre-Columbian Mayan calendar, combined with the I Ching and components of shamanism. The idea was that for three days in August, if enough people took advantage of the energy that would be flowing into the planet, we could set up the conditions to create peace on earth. Jose called for 144,000 self-selected "sun dancers" to ground the new frequencies and to catalyze a positive vision of our common destiny into being. Jose saw it as a way that the values of service and compassion for the higher good would be re-established in the hearts of humankind once again.

According to ancient belief, when a certain critical number achieves the same awareness, this new consciousness can be communicated from mind to mind. Although the exact number may vary, there is a point at which, if only one more person tunes in to that new awareness, a field is strengthened so that this awareness is picked up by almost everyone. Once a critical mass is reached, there is no turning back. I learned about critical mass when I heard about when large numbers of people practiced Transcendental Meditation in a city, the crime rate decreased.

To understand the idea of critical mass, I use the story about the Hundredth Monkey phenomenon. Scientists studying monkeys on a chain of Japanese islands, fed them sweet potatoes that they dumped on the beach. The monkeys carefully cleaned the sand off the potatoes before eating them until one day, they observed a young female monkey taking her sweet potato down to the water and washing the sand off before eating it. As soon as she taught her mother, the other monkeys observing the process also began to wash theirs.

On a particular day, let's say it was the day the hundredth monkey began washing its sweet potato, then all the monkeys on that island began doing the same thing. And even more astonishing, the scientists observed monkeys on other islands in the chain also washing their sweet potatoes. Jose's vision was to have a critical mass of people on planet earth who were meditating and praying for peace so that everyone would begin to share the same goal, prevent global catastrophe, and usher in peace on earth.

Far-fetched to many, I'm sure, Harmonic Convergence made perfect sense to me. Jim explained in more detail that based on the ancient Mayan calendar and on a relatively rare alignment of the planets, portals would open for healing energy to flow into the earth on August 16-18, 1987, facilitating the arrival of a new era. Jim described how we could help the process by locating at sacred sites around the world, consciously connecting these energy centers through the ley lines, while meditating and visualizing world peace.

I knew immediately that the Great Pyramid in Egypt was the sacred site where I wanted to be. But why? Perhaps my Extraterrestrial Visitor had put a bug in my ear during our telepathic communication session three years earlier, or maybe Egypt had been on my radar since I randomly chose it as one of the countries to visit. Yet I also picked Australia, Bali, and Nepal. Why not one of them for Harmonic Convergence? If we were to gather at sacred sites around the world and pray for peace for three days, and if Mother Earth herself is sacred, wouldn't any place on earth serve the purpose? But Egypt it was.

I soon learned that Jim was arranging to join a group whose guide was making all the travel arrangements for hotels, ground transportation, and cruise ships. It made sense for me to follow his lead. This is how thoughts are creative. I spoke the words, "I'm going to Egypt for Harmonic Convergence," and sent out a vibration that attracted energy of a similar quality, and everything started to fall in place. My job came to an end, with a three-month severance package that would pay for my trip, and I had travel companions with a guide and all arrangements made. It's another example of synchronicity.

Molly was the "something better" when she decided to go on the trip with me. I was delighted to have the company of a good friend, especially one as well traveled as Molly. And now with our around-the-world Golden airline tickets that allowed us as many destinations as we wanted for a year, we broadened our itinerary. After Egypt, we would continue on to Thailand, Nepal, Hong Kong, Bali, and Australia in search of sacred sites along the way.

After my nephew's wedding, I said goodbye to my family, and flew to New York to meet Molly for a red-eye flight to Egypt. On the same flight were some of our fellow Harmonic "Convergers" from the United States joining our quest for peace. Settling into our seats for our 13-hour flight, we arranged ourselves, facing each other, with our legs and feet on each other's laps, so we could get some sleep. Oh, to be young again.

PURIFICATION ON THE NILE

When we arrived in Egypt, about 30 of us were met by our host guides who herded us onto a bus. After a short ride, we were taken to our train headed to Aswan, where we would board a small cruise ship for a 10-day purification journey up the Nile River to Cairo where the pyramids awaited. It was the first time I had "slept" on a train. I was aware, with the jostling and stopping and starting all night, that yes, indeed, I was on a train – and sleep was not happening.

Cruise ship on the Nile River, 1987.

The next morning, already travel-worn, the exhausted American contingency met another 50 travelers from all over the world who, like us, had been drawn to Egypt for Harmonic Convergence. They joined us on the journey up the Nile River, following the same path of initiation that the Egyptian priests and priestesses took starting in 1250 BC. We visited temples at 10 stops along the way, each one relating to an energy center in the body. We took part in rituals and ceremonies at each temple, thus preparing us for the three days of meditation and prayer at the pyramid.

The cruise ship was small, accom-modating just 100 passengers. Molly and I found our sleeping compartment to be very clean, compact, and comfortable. At dinner we learned that aside from the 80 of us New Agers on a mission for peace, another 10 passengers were on a family trip. I have often wondered what they thought of us. What they thought we were doing. How many times over the years have they told their stories and laughed over the antics they witnessed? Of course, every day, my group was up on the top deck doing sunrise and sunset rituals, chanting, praying, burning incense, uniting our hearts with others, our arms stretched overhead, our hands reaching out to the heavens – so earnest and purposeful in our commitment to bring about peace and harmony to the world.

Before I left Santa Fe, I had a lot of dental work done, but continued to have a problem with a sporadic toothache. I had it looked at again when I was in Athens, Georgia where everything seemed to be fine. Although I didn't look forward to traveling with a toothache, I reasoned that I could find a dentist on my trip if it continued to give me trouble. Once aboard the cruise ship, I met a doctor from Belgium who told me that he had recently studied the connections between the teeth and specific points on the body and how acupressure could reduce inflammation that could heal a toothache. I submitted to his treatment only to find it was more like acu-ripping-the-meat-off-my-thigh from the hip to the knee. Over and over, he dug his thumb into my thigh and pressing down to the bone, he slid his thumb down to my knee while I breathed into the intense pain. Truly, it was one of the most painful forms of healing to which I have subjected myself. But Hallelujah! After a couple of sessions, I was healed – no more toothache for the rest of the trip.

I did, however, manage to have minor digestive issues like everyone in our group, except for one man. When we asked how he managed to stay well, he showed us his dowser and how he held it, like a pendulum, over any food before he put it in his mouth, asking if that food was safe. If the dowser swung front to back, he felt the food was safe to eat, but if it swung side to side, that was a big "NO," and he would put the food aside. It is believed that the motion of the pendulum is an amplified reaction of your body to the question you ask, similar to the principles of kinesiology, or muscle testing. Honestly, he was the only person on our trip who never got sick, so when I got back home, I got a dowser and have used it for 35 years. I was, and still am, a believer that the body doesn't lie. You just have to learn how to listen to it.

Many Egyptian men who wanted to live in America thought an American wife would be their easiest ticket to a better life. Since they set their sights on every woman who disembarked the ship, all of the women in our group were propositioned at least once every time we went ashore. One young man, perhaps 25 or so, approached me one day and told me I could "have it good and hard, on the ground," if I wanted it. Clearly, they needed to work on their moves. I politely declined. Molly and I had a lot of good laughs about his failed attempt to seduce me, and perhaps, my missed opportunity for a "grounded" experience.

I found most of the people in the villages, along the banks of the Nile, to be friendly and pleasant. The women washed their clothes, bathed their children, and got their drinking water in the river while the water buffalo gathered to drink alongside them. The poverty and lack of sanitation would be appalling if they didn't look so happy. The culture is male-dominated to an extreme. In 1987, girls still could not choose their own husbands, and some were systematically forced around the age of five to have an operation to remove the clitoris. No pleasure for the females.

THE GREAT PYRAMID

Our cruise ended in Cairo the day before Harmonic Convergence was to begin. We found that our ensemble had swelled to 500 peace-seeking souls from around the world. Huge Bedouin tents, complete with oriental rugs, were set up in the desert next to the Great Pyramid for the three-day event. At sunrise on the appointed day, August 16, Jose Arguelles' call was answered – from Mt. Shasta in California and Central Park in New York to Machu Picchu in Peru, from Stonehenge in England to the people in their neighborhood parks and backyards all over the world. And there I was at the Great Pyramid in Egypt. Thousands of us from all over the world were joining together to focus on changing the global perspective of humanity from one of conflict to one of cooperation and peace to bring about harmony on Planet Earth. I was doing my part to have a world that works for everyone.

Since we would be spending two nights in the tents, we stayed at a hotel the first night. We began the next day with a processional from our hotel to the Bedouin tents in the desert near the Pyramids. Everyone was dressed in white or multicolored, flowing garments

Above: Great Pyramid, Egypt. Below: Bedouin tent set up in the desert, 1987.

for the celebration. Some were riding camels, others horses and donkeys, and the rest of us were walking, holding colorful banners and flags, which were snapping in the wind. Along the way the Egyptian people cheered and joined our parade.

For three days, we alternated meditating and dancing with sleeping in sacred circles, our heads toward the center of the circle. The prayers, chanting, and movement never ceased for three days, and it was happening all over the planet. In the desert, we built a mandala that represented the earth while visualizing our connection to the other sacred sites around the world. We sent and received healing energy through the ley lines that joined us, and to everything in between. We heard later that Jose Arguelles, from a campsite near Boulder, Colorado, blew a conch shell 144 times.

After the three-day event was over, we read several American newspaper accounts and learned that Harmonic Convergence made national TV. Even Johnny Carson had his audience "Om" in honor of the event. Many versions mentioned the importance of "holding hands and humming." The news media in

Egypt covered the event generously and enthusiastically – we were all pleased.

So was the occasion a "moronic convergence...sort of a national fruit loops day," as spoofed in the *"Doonesbury"* comic strip? Was it a myth, or was the Harmonic Convergence an impactful event? The only certainty was that Jose's idea resonated with a generation of seekers riding the New Age wave of the 1980s. Early in the decade, actress Shirley MacLaine's assertions about reincarnation had helped stir mass curiosity about alternative spirituality, but Arguelles' galactic event brought it to a peak. According to Melton and Lewis in their 1992 book *Perspectives on the New Age*, the first synchronized global peace meditation attracted "more public attention than any New Age event before or since."

Can we say that it made a difference? Some scholars have described major energy changes as a result of the September 1987 event, citing measurable increases in the energy of our planet Earth. According to Gregg Braden's book, *Awakening to Zero Point: The Collective Initiation*, after resonating at a frequency of 8 hertz per second for thousands of years, the frequency of the Earth "appears to be rising to a fundamental vibration of 13 cycles per second, the mathematical proportions based on the Golden Mean, also called the harmonics of the universe."

I really don't know about all that or about the reported great upsurge in positive emotional and mental energies after Harmonic Convergence. What I do know is the Cold War soon began to thaw, and two years later, in November 1989, the Berlin Wall fell. Also beginning in 1989, the Soviet Union began its slow collapse, and the Soviet flag flew over the Kremlin in Moscow for the last time in December 1991. The Cold War was over, along with the end of the communist dictatorship in Eastern Europe. We did that. Myth or illusion?

HIGHLIGHTS IN EGYPT

1. Beautiful sunsets on the Nile and in the desert.
2. Taking a real bath after 10 days on the Nile.
3. Feeling well again after being sick.
4. The processional from the hotel to the Bedouin tents where the Harmonic Convergence events took place.
5. Galloping a black Arabian stallion across the desert at sunset with the pyramids in the background (fulfilling my Black Stallion girlhood dream).
6. Sleeping in a Bedouin tent – complete with concentric circles, Persian rugs, and fleas.
7. A group of us holding hands and chanting in the Kings Chambers in

the Great Pyramid.

8. Building a mandala in the desert that represented the earth, including many sacred sites. Activating the ley lines by connecting with those sites at the same time the participants were connecting with us.

9. Buying goods in the marketplace and learning to haggle over prices.

10. Having an attendant give me two rationed pieces of toilet paper as I went into the bathroom.

3 | Israel

Mt. Sinai

While we were at the pyramids, Jim Berenholtz and a group of fellow travelers decided they wanted to go to Israel and invited Molly and me to go with them. About 15 of us rented a tiny, uncomfortable bus, and left bright and early the morning of August 20. It was a dreadfully long trip – 475 miles, but broken up with an overnight stay at the

Welcoming the sun on Mt. Sinai, 1987.

foot of Mt. Sinai. Although there were lovely rooms at the base of the mountain, 10 of us opted to hike two hours so we could sleep on top of one of the most sacred sites in the world.

We started our hike about 6 p.m., and when we arrived at the top, we were surprised to find hundreds of people already there, many of them bedded down for the night and some were sound asleep. As crowded as it was, we were able to find sufficient space for us to lie down for the night, but it was also tight enough that we all had to face the same direction, sleeping like spoons. When one spoon turned during the night, all the other spoons had to turn too.

Sleeping fitfully, as we all did, we were thankful to see the sun finally begin to lighten the sky and to hear the rustling of our hundred bedfellows. Everyone was arising to welcome the sunrise over Mt. Sinai with more prayers, chanting, and rituals where Moses purportedly received the Ten Commandments.

On the way down Mt. Sinai, as I was going at my own pace and looking at the ground where I was walking, I became aware that the path I was descending was not the one I had ascended the night before. I looked around me and suddenly realized that I had become separated from my group. I could see a few strangers far ahead of me, down the mountainside, so I wasn't overly concerned. It did occur to me that I might be going down the back side of the mountain and would have to find my way around to the opposite side when I got to the bottom. I wondered what the circumference at the base was and how far I would have to walk, yet I wasn't concerned enough to go back up to see if I could find where I had lost my way.

The white chapel on Mt. Sinai, 1987.

As I continued on my own path, I came upon a small, beautiful white chapel tucked into the side of the mountain, which I accepted as an omen that I was going in the right direction. It felt as though I had been given a gift and wished I had time to explore the chapel and surroundings. Instead, I decided the uncertainty about getting back to my fellow travelers was more pressing, so I continued on my way. As luck would have it, I came off the mountain within view of the hotel where we were staying, so I hadn't strayed off the beaten path as far as I had feared. I still carry the picture of that lovely church and its setting embossed on the celluloid of my brain.

To break up the remainder of our trip, we stopped on the northwestern shores of the Dead Sea near Khirbet Qumran to tour the area where the Dead Sea Scrolls were found in caves back in the 40s and 50s. Afterward, we went to a spa on the Dead Sea where we took mud baths, smearing black mud all over our bodies and letting it dry in the sun. Then we went down to the sea and floated the mud away. The water is so salty that you need to be careful not to get it in your eyes, and lying on your back in the water, your body stays afloat with no effort. While floating, we arranged ourselves in a circle, heads toward the center, holding hands, humming again, and laughing.

JERUSALEM

After we arrived at our hotel in Jerusalem, we freshened up, and five of us went out to find dinner in Old Jerusalem. This smaller group consisted of Jim Berenholtz, Marsha (who had been with Jim in Africa), Geoff (who had been with Jim at Machu Picchu), and Molly and me (who had been with Jim in Santa Fe). We were walking down a side street when a young man who had heard us talking about finding a restaurant poked his head out of a doorway to ask if he could help. As we were explaining our mission, and he was trying to understand, a half dozen other heads poked out around him in the doorway, followed by bodies of all sizes tumbling into the street. Among them was their father who invited us all in for mint tea and fresh grapes that he picked from his arbor while we sat there.

Although none of them were English-speaking, we were still able to communicate back and forth for an hour or more. The old grandfather, who was sleeping on a pallet on the floor of the terrace when we arrived, awoke after half an hour. From his bed, he welcomed us to his home, and we felt *very* welcomed by all of them. They directed us to a neighborhood restaurant nearby where we enjoyed a lovely dinner.

We spent the next two days exploring the city of David where Jerusalem sprang up 3,000 years ago. We went to one sacred site after another, including the Garden of Gethsemane where Jesus prayed just before he was betrayed by Judas in the Old City. We followed the stations of the cross along Via Dolorosa Street marking each spot where Jesus fell or was met with compassion as he carried the cross through the city on his way to be crucified.

Just outside the city walls, we saw what many believe to be the tomb of Jesus. We stood on Mount of Olives, where Jesus is reported to have ascended into heaven. We visited the Wailing Wall, now called the Western Wall, and joined our prayers for peace with the fervently praying worshipers. Later we went to Bethlehem where an ornate church has

Said to be the Tomb of Jesus, 1987.

been built over the stable where Jesus is said to have been born.

There was just too much to see, so the five of us decided we would stay longer in Israel. We easily found a two-bedroom furnished apartment with a peaceful courtyard in the Jewish Quarter of Old Jerusalem. We had to promise the owner that the girls would stay separate from the boys, and we couldn't sing or play music from sundown Friday to sundown Saturday. It was ideal having an apartment of our own, especially being able to cook our own food. We went to the market and bought breakfast foods and fresh ingredients for soup. Lentil soup never tasted so heavenly.

Touring the Northern Country

When Marsha left the group after a couple of days, Jim, Geoff, Molly, and I decided to rent a car so we could explore the northern country. As soon as we got to the Mediterranean Sea outside Tel Aviv, we donned bathing suits and headed into the water. It was beautiful to see from a distance, but not as clear as I imagined it would be. Later, when we saw a nuclear power plant a little farther up the coast, we were glad we hadn't stayed in the water very long. We stopped at villages along the way, ate at seaside restaurants, and stayed in no-frill-but-adequate lodging quarters.

Our first night out, we stopped at a community headed by Rabbi Schlomo. Jim had met him in Taos at the Lama Foundation, and Geoff knew him from New York. The community used to be a kubbitz and recently had changed to a more independent type of organization. The rabbi invited us to stay for a concert, and given the late hour when it was over, he invited us to spend the night. It was a relief not to be hotel-shopping in the middle of the night. We explored Hebron, Jericho, Nazareth, the areas around the Sea of Galilee, and Megiddo, where Armageddon is supposed to take place. It was strangely magical being in all the places whose names are so familiar from my early Christian upbringing. It gave geography and history a new dimension.

Both Egypt and Israel were full of soldiers, nonchalantly strolling around with machine guns slung over their shoulders. In Israel, they were even more casual. We were talking to a couple of them and easily convinced them to let us use their knives, guns, and ammunition vests as props for our photographs. I could hardly believe it when they even offered to help us dress up Marsha and Molly for the photo shoot.

I took on the responsibility of doing most of the driving in Israel; Jim read the map and rode shotgun. One day, as I was driving down the road, I saw a couple of soldiers with guns up ahead. Thinking it was some sort of checkpoint, I slowed down and stopped. The next thing I knew, the soldiers opened the door and jumped in the back seat with Molly and Geoff – with their rifles. We learned they thought we were stopping to give them a ride to the next town, so we told them, "OK, but no weapons in the car." After storing them in the trunk, we enjoyed their company until we dropped them off at their destination. That's how casual the

Linda (left) and Molly flanked by Israeli soldiers, Marsha, in front, 1987.

military is.

On the last day of our five-day driving tour, we all agreed we didn't want to miss Masada, an ancient fortification that occupies the entire top of an isolated 18-acre mesa that towers 1,400 feet above the Dead Sea. Masada is renowned for the palaces and fortifications of Herod the Great, king of Judaea under the Romans, and, also much later, for the resistance of rebel zealots to the Roman siege in 72-73 AD.

Masada fortification.

We were mostly interested because the siege ended in the mass suicide of the 960 Sicarii rebels who refused to surrender to the Roman legion, and we wanted to pay homage to those souls. The Masada garrison was the last remnant of Jewish rule in Palestine. It took an army of 15,000 Roman soldiers almost two years to subdue the fortress, occupied by less than 1,000 people, including women and children. The Romans built a sloping ramp of earth and stones on the side of the mesa to bring their soldiers within reach of the stronghold. When the zealots knew they were doomed to be captured and enslaved, they decided to take their own lives. When the conquerors arrived on top of Masada, they found 960 dead bodies. Only two women and five children, who had hidden in a water conduit, survived to tell the tale. Masada is now part of a national park and is one of Israel's most popular tourist attractions, attracting around a million visitors a year.

Masada was only an hour from Tel Aviv where Molly and I were flying from the next day. We arrived at Masada late in the day and were disappointed to find the gates closed and no one in sight who might let us in. Led by Jim, we started walking the fence line until we found an opening that we could slip through to gain access to this sacred site. Although it was dusk, there was enough light to see our way around. When we found a suitable place, we stood together and prayed for those souls who were here in ancient times, and we gave tribute to those who had chosen death over enslavement.

The next morning, Jim and Geoff dropped Molly and me at the Tel Aviv airport for our flight back to Cairo, and then on to Thailand. As our suitcases were being examined at the airport, we were questioned as to why we had been in Israel. Even though we claimed to be tourists, it quickly became obvious that the authorities were suspicious of our activities. When they started asking us where we had been and where we had stayed, it didn't help that neither of us could answer. I could give them the names of the familiar towns and sites we had seen, but the names of all the other towns escaped me. Jim was in charge of the map. I just drove where he told me to go.

Even though we had honest faces, I could see that our lack of knowledge of where we had been and the absence of receipts for hotel rooms or meals raised a red flag. Jim and Geoff had paid for our food and lodging because they owed us money for the apartment we paid for in Israel. Even worse, we had no receipt for the rental car because Jim and Geoff were still using it. The authorities especially didn't like the fact that we came to their country from Egypt on a bus and were flying back to Egypt on an airplane. So, with their distrust on high alert, they decided to separate us and search our belongings by emptying our backpacks and purses, so carefully and efficiently packed.

Meanwhile, the plane was sitting on the tarmac during the hour it took to search our luggage and body search us. When they were satisfied that we had no weapons or spy materials and that we posed no threat, we were finally released. It took us only two minutes to dump all our belonging back in our backpacks, a task that normally took half an hour. We were escorted at a trotting pace through the airport to catch the bus that took us to our plane.

As soon as the officials left us, and we were safely on the bus, both Molly and I broke into complete hysterical laughter, some of it from relief, some from fear, and some from knowing we'd have a good story to tell. When we finally were allowed to board the flight to Cairo, our fellow passengers booed us for making them wait so long. We, however, were delighted to be on our way to our stop-over in Cairo to catch a flight to our next destination: Bangkok, Thailand.

4 | THAILAND

The flight to Cairo took less than an hour. Once we arrived, we were shuttled from one lounge to another until finally we were next to our gate in an "in transit" waiting area, which meant we couldn't leave. When I tried to call my mom while waiting for our flight, I was told I needed Egyptian money, which I could get in the main part of the airport. Sensing leaving the "in transit" waiting area could be a dangerous mission on my own, I invited Molly to accompany me.

We asked three different men in authority if we could cross the security lines to get money exchanged and were told, "No problem." Now we know that "No problem" is the universal answer to any request that someone in authority isn't sure about. We went through the line, got my money exchanged, waited in line to get back to the "in transit" lounge, and then were told we would need a special form. We finally found a representative from our airline, someone who took pity on us and personally escorted us back to our gate. It was so strange having to ask permission of so many people to get money for a phone call.

BANGKOK

A 10-hour, red-eye flight brought us into Bangkok in the wee hours. Luckily there was no drama and no questions, and it was easy to get our luggage. We caught a taxi to a nearby hotel and fell into bed exhausted. We slept most of the day, feeling disoriented and drugged whenever we woke up. We briefly went out in the streets to find nourishment and were happy to go right back to the hotel and to sleep through the night. We didn't wake up until 10 a.m. – the longest sleep in a long time for both of us.

With 24 hours of rest, we were finally ready to see what Bangkok had to offer – a city of five million, today the population is double that. Our first order of business was to find lodging, so I consulted our *Southeast Asia on a Shoestring* guidebook. We looked at a couple of guest houses with a fan and a shared bath for $4 to $8 a night, but we decided to splurge on the beautiful, air-conditioned Royal Hotel room with a private bath for $20 a night. It was so luxurious that we decided we were not yet ready to explore the city, but rather stayed put for the rest of our second day, taking long baths, ordering room service, and getting our Thai legs.

One of the most memorable experiences in Bangkok was the amount of traffic – 6-8 lanes of cars going both ways through the city and vehicles weaving from one lane to the next to make turns across oncoming traffic. Worse were the pedestrians mixed into the traffic melee, crossing all those lanes, dodging all the different modes of transportation, without getting knocked down. The most common and cheapest mode of

The Reclining Buddha, Bangkok, Thailand, 1987.

transportation was the tuk-tuk – a motorcycle with a rickshaw-type carrier in the back for 2-3 passengers. There were also bicycle-pulled rickshaws, motor scooters, motorcycles, taxis, and trucks. It was not uncommon to see a motor scooter with a child standing on the floor in front of his father who was driving, with the mother on the back holding one or two children, and several bags of groceries.

There are over 40,000 temples across Thailand with at least 400 in Bangkok. Thailand is a very religious country, with about 92% Buddhists. We couldn't miss seeing The Grand Palace where the king of Thailand lived for over 100 years until the early 20th century. Still in use for royal ceremonies and state functions, the architecture of the palace and the Thai art are stunning. Just a ten-minute walk away was Wat Pho, the largest temple in Thailand where The Reclining Buddha lies. The 15-foot tall, 150-foot-long statue, made of plaster bricks and gilded in gold, features the Buddha in a reclining position, the pose depicted at the time of his death when he entered Nirvana.

Markets in Bangkok were a sight to behold. The largest market in Thailand, the Weekend Food Market, boasted 5,000 stalls – compared to 15,000 today – offering everything from Thai-style food to plants, clothes, books, and even pets. Before we left Bangkok, we went to the floating markets on the canals, where people lived on their boats and in shacks on the banks. It was the monsoon season, but we were told it had been the driest monsoon season in some time, and it was hot. After a few days in the city seeing the sights, we decided where we wanted to go next, and boarded an overnight train heading north to Chiang Mai, 420 miles away.

CHIANG MAI AND CHIANG RAI

We had been told not to miss the night market in Chiang Mai. On the first night, we went just to get our bearings and were amazed by the extent and the varieties of products for sale – souvenirs, gifts, local Thai handicrafts and produce, with offerings of anything you could want to eat, and many you wouldn't eat. We went back the next night to make some purchases, being drained of energy both times. Just the immensity, the activity, the humanity of it all was overwhelming. When I was in Chiang Mai in 1987, the population was a little less than 70,000; today it's over half a million.

We hired a tuk-tuk with a driver to take us all over the countryside around Chiang Mai. In addition to temples, there were many villages each specializing in the production of specific products like umbrellas, silk, cotton, lacquerware, and silverware. We went to an orchid farm, and then to a place to watch elephants pulling trees out of the jungle, and their handlers bathing them in the river near a beautiful waterfall. Within a couple of days, we were ready to leave the hustle and bustle of Chiang Mai and the commercial countryside and proceed to the northernmost province in Thailand. The next stop on our itinerary, Chiang Rai, was about four hours north by bus.

According to our travel guide book, we were headed for a delightful-sounding hostel run by Lum Luck, the director for hostels in all of Thailand, and we were not disappointed. The room was spotless, with a private bath, wood floor, high ceilings, four big windows overlooking a river that meandered around the building, and a big porch with comfortable chairs – all for $5 a night. It also came with several geckos, lizard-like reptiles that eat insects. Long before the Geico commercials, I had become partial to the cute little reptiles.

THE HILL TRIBES

Our host, Lum Luck, offered to take us on a couple of day trips to visit the hill tribes of Northern Thailand where they lived in villages on Thai government-provided land. These ethnic minority groups migrated several hundred years ago from Southeast Asia – China, Tibet, Nepal, Vietnam, Laos, and Myanmar (Burma) – and settled in the highlands and hilly areas.

With a total population numbering in the millions, seven distinct tribes each speak their own unique languages, and have their own customs and culture. Although they have lived in the region for generations, most don't hold citizenship. Traditionally, the hill tribes are subsistence farmers who grow rice, coffee, strawberries, and other crops. Their major source of income used to be growing opium until it was outlawed in the 1960s. The government helped the hill tribes switch from opium cultivation to growing cash crops, however, they still grew opium for their own use. Now tourism is also a source of income for them as well.

The first tribe we visited was the Karen hill tribe who crossed over into Thailand from Myanmar/Burma and Laos in the 18th century. We rode in Luck's pick-up for an hour and a half, the final 15 miles on a dirt road. Then we set off on foot for another 2-3 miles into the hills.

We arrived at a village where everyone lived in bamboo and grass huts with dirt floors. There was no electricity, no running water, and no furniture. We could see the women and children bathing or playing in the river that ran near their village. It was primitive yet picturesque with the brown huts, some people in native costumes, and the mostly naked bathers, set against rice fields, banana trees, and green rolling country under a cloudy Thai sky.

Luck asked us if we wanted to smoke some opium. When we agreed, he arranged for us to go to a hut where we found an old woman lying on the floor next to a couple of woven mats, on which we were asked to sit. Looking a little done-in, our hostess had just a few teeth, which were black. Luck told us later that she was 37 years old. It took her a few minutes to ascertain that we were present, whereupon she lit a pipe and reached it over to me. I took a short hit, not knowing how strong it was. I didn't intend to get wasted, but just wanted to see what a little opium buzz would feel like. I took a couple more hits, and truthfully didn't feel any effect at all, for which I was grateful. I really didn't want to have to spend the night there, nor did I want to be stumbling in a stupor the 3 miles back to the truck.

After we hiked back to the truck, Luck took us to another village where we boarded an elephant and rode for an hour to get to another hill tribe village. Molly and I had been wanting to ride an elephant since we had seen the ones working in the jungle. The novelty wore off after about five minutes when I realized my body was in danger of being slowly wobbled to pieces. I'm sure it's less jerky sitting on the elephant's neck, as I recently had dreamed. Sitting on that platform and rolling around on the top of his back was a rough ride. I suggested we might be more comfortable lying on the floor of the platform, keeping a lower center of gravity. It was fun that we rode an elephant, but now I know better.

Nowadays, conscious people would never take part in elephant-riding, complicit in extreme animal cruelty and pushing the majestic Asian elephant to extinction. Elephants belong in the wild, and I humbly apologize to the elephants that I rode during my trip. As penance, in 2012 I marched to free elephants from circuses. Forty years after I rode my first elephant and six years after I marched, Barnum & Bailey finally stopped the practice of using elephants in their shows in 2018. Progress is slow in a capitalistic state.

At the second village, the women gathered around and dressed me in their traditional dress. I'm sure they wanted me to buy their handiwork, but I just couldn't justify purchasing something I would never use. Above all, I didn't want to carry it with me for the rest of the trip. Luck then took us to a beautiful waterfall where we jumped in and refreshed ourselves. The roar of the waterfall was deafening – we couldn't even hear ourselves talk. Although we backed ourselves through the pounding water to the back of the waterfall as far as we could go, we could never get entirely behind the cascading water.

The next day, Luck took us to another village not so far off the beaten track. The teak forests had been decimated from the hillsides, clear-cut like the redwood forests in California. After having lunch at a little restaurant on the Mekong River, we drove to the Golden Triangle where the borders of Thailand, Burma, and Laos all came together. It was here that Luck told us that the people in that part of the world call the Vietnam War the War of American Aggression. The entire time I was in Thailand, I kept thinking about our American soldiers who fought and died in that area of the world – in a war that we should never have been in.

It had been a physically and emotionally exhausting day. When we returned to the hostel, Luck sent a woman to our room to give me a $4 massage for two hours. I felt so guilty that I gave her $6. I still felt guilty. I should have given her $8. She was so grateful for $6 that she kept taking my hands and bowing over them.

Luck was a wonderful tour guide. He spoke beautiful English, asked a million questions about life in America, including about disease, salaries, living conditions, Reagan, authors, singers. He also answered many questions for us and schooled us in customs and proprieties in Thailand. Never touch a child's head – it's considered sacred. Don't prop your feet up so the soles of your feet are facing another person – negative energy comes through the feet, and you don't want to send that to another person. He first mentioned that when we started to prop our feet on the dashboard of his pickup.

When we stopped at a scenic spot to rest and enjoy the scenery, we met a German couple traveling by motorcycle. Luck started questioning them about life in Germany. He suggested to them that he thought East and West Germany would someday come together as one. The German couple said, "Impossible! No way!" I asked Luck if he thought Burma and Thailand could ever let bygones be bygones and he said, "Never!"

I realized more deeply how our nationalistic pride can keep us miles apart. We're still fighting battles that our ancestors started. No one could see a good reason for countries, other than their own, to continue their conflicts. It's easier to see solutions for the other side. "They should be able to settle their differences."

On this trip, I realized more and more that communication is a lesson in patience. When I started to feel impatient, I remembered to take another breath and plunge in again. As I was getting braver, I was willing to take more risks, and I may have driven a few people away. I was trying to explain to our waitress that I wanted the lid left on the water bottle. I showed her other lids, pointing to the one on the toothpick holder and the saltshaker, but she just turned away and wouldn't look at me. I think she was embarrassed for me. That communication was a failure because I didn't get the lid.

I had the most successful communication when looking for Molly and asked a man at the P.O. if he had seen my friend with blond hair – she definitely stood out – and he stuck with me until he understood. He had seen her and was able to communicate back to me where he had last seen her. I always made a point to speak at a normal volume and speed. I finally figured out to accent different syllables in the same way and tempo they speak so that they would better understand. Instead of saying vegetables the way I would normally, I would say veg-e-ta'ble, and they got it more quickly!

GENERAL OBSERVATIONS OF THAILAND

1. Everyone in Thailand seemed to love Americans.
2. It was wonderful being with Luck for two days. He was fond of country music and played Dan Fogelberg's *The Higher You Climb*. We discussed the philosophical meaning of the words, "The higher you climb, the farther you see, the farther you see, the less that you know, the less that you know, the more that you learn, the more that you learn, the higher you climb."
3. I was amazed at the crowded conditions and the pollution, most of which seemed to come from the vehicles that have no emissions controls. I had to put a bandana over my mouth to breathe when I was in the streets, whether walking or riding in a bus or a tuk-tuk. People stared at me like I was a bandit.
4. There are wonderful places to eat everywhere – on every street, in front of every store, down every alley, all along the waterfront, along the train tracks. Food is a commodity. Some of the more out-of-the-ordinary items on the menu in Thailand that we turned down included:
   • Tomyam Thai Soup with serpent head. And, when they offered Boiled Serpent head with soy sauce, I thought the soy sauce would make it too salty.

- Piquant Salad Entrails Beek (I didn't even try this once).
- Thai Style Uterus Salad (I was told not to eat salads anyway). They also had fried uterus, but I just wasn't hungry that day.
- Then there was boiled pig, fried or braised shark fins, several varieties of goose feet – stewed or steamed (with or without red gravy). Mostly, I managed to get by with eggs, rice or noodles, chicken, shrimp, coconut soup.
- One day, I got brave and ordered yam chicken, without knowing what it was. I got a pickled chicken feet salad. This left me wondering what Nepal and Tibet would have in store for our culinary education.

MY HEALTH

1. Almost a year before I left on my trip, I injured my right knee in a way that caused that knee to give way with no warning. I had plenty of misgivings about setting out on such a physically demanding trip, but in actuality, it presented no problem at all. After climbing Mt. Sinai without issue, I felt more confident about my knee.
2. My first week in Egypt, I started having swollen glands, a sore throat, and a cough – not constantly, but enough to be an issue. In Bangkok, I went to a pharmacist, and seemed to have gotten on top of that problem.
3. Stomach disorders seemed to flare up every so often, maybe when we changed countries. It's sort of a way of life, at least with traveling.

5 | NEPAL

KATHMANDU

Next on our itinerary was Nepal, where we planned to spend three weeks. We arrived on September 17, 1987, a month after Harmonic Convergence in Egypt. Since then, Molly and I had spent 10 days in Israel and two weeks in Thailand.

In the Bangkok airport, while waiting for our flight to depart, we met a lovely couple, Sarah and James, both Northern California elementary school teachers who were on a year's sabbatical traveling in third-world countries. They were exploring places and opportunities where they might best be able to contribute their skills. Since they had been to Nepal five years earlier, they gave us a lot of helpful information. We agreed to share a cab to their lodging since our flight would arrive in Kathmandu around 10 p.m., a late start in a new country. After going through customs and exchanging money, we learned that an associate had met Sarah and James, so we were on our own.

Molly and I found ourselves standing on the curb, promptly surrounded by at least 15 taxi drivers, each offering to drive us to the best hotel, guest house, or lodging. They were all pitching us at the same time, and we soon gave the nod to one young man who didn't seem as desperate, appeared trustworthy and reliable, and he agreed to take us to the hotel we wanted, rather than favoring the one where he knew he had a commission waiting. He also agreed to the fare we were told was reasonable.

When we waved to our young taxi guy that we were ready to go to the Blue Diamond, he picked up our luggage, gesturing for us to follow him to his taxi. It turned out he was the driver's pitchman/shotgun. The other drivers were so upset with their loss of income, they began following us, yelling, and making threatening gestures. One actually started a fist fight with Shotgun as he put our luggage in the trunk of his cab. More chaos and confusion ensued, and between punches, Shotgun encouraged us to quickly climb into the back seat. Very reluctantly, at that point, we tumbled into the taxi and, calmly terrified, waited for the fist fight to subside. Ultimately, an airport policeman jumped into the fray and rescued Shotgun by pulling him into the front passenger seat with him. Now, with the law on our side, we turned our attention to our driver who may have been 15, tops.

As the taxi lurched forward, leaving the throng of unhappy drivers, still shaking their fists in the air, Molly and I looked at each other with question marks pouring out of our eyes, as wide as they could possibly get. As the drivers moved aside and faded from view, so too did our imagined headline, "Two American Women Start Airport Riot." Such was our inauspicious introduction to Kathmandu.

We drove out of the airport complex, dropped off the policeman, and were left alone with our prepubescent driver and his pitch man. For a moment, thinking the madness was behind us, we soon suspected that our brakes must not be operational as we careened through dimly lit streets on our bizarre drive to the city. The streets were torn up, full of debris and cows, the national animal of Nepal. Although cows are considered sacred, to be revered and protected, our driver didn't slow down for them, dodging potholes and the cows lying in the middle of the streets or aimlessly meandering in the road. The buildings and houses looked like they had been recently bombed. We had not yet begun to see the humor in this evening's odd set of activities, although it was starting to dawn on us that in the lives of these young men, this might be just another ordinary day.

As we hurtled at full speed onto the narrowest one-lane bridge a car has ever crossed, the headlights of a larger car came into view, moving at a rapid pace toward us. Neither driver slowed down until they both slammed on their brakes at the last minute. In the middle of the bridge, our adolescent taxi driver inched forward, laying on his horn, playing chicken close up. The other driver, also laying on his horn, would not acquiesce.

Who can tell how these things are decided, but our driver finally surrendered. As he started his retreat, we could hear *Jingle Bells* playing, activated when the taxi was put in reverse. Because the bridge was so narrow, and because the other car with horn still blaring just an inch from our front bumper, our nervous driver ran into the side of the bridge. The headlines start forming again.

Both taxi children jumped out of our cab to examine the damage while the other car's driver continued his unrelenting horn blaring. They were finally able to free the taxi from the bridge, allowing the other car to continue, and then we could take our turn.

For the remainder of the ride, Molly and I sat in silence, holding hands as we caught glimpses of more unpaved roads, shells of buildings, debris along the roadside, cows in the road – no lights, no city, no people. We were certain we were on our way to be robbed, ravished, and left for dead.

We finally arrived at The Blue Diamond, which, sadly, also looked like a bombed-out building. Our taxi children waited for us while the proprietor led

up an outside concrete stairway, which was hanging by exposed cables, like a
jack hammer had run amuck. In the darkened hallway, we passed under a bare
25-watt light bulb to open the door to our room. Turning on the dim light, we
saw several, fairly large, reddish-brown bugs scurrying across the beds and the
floor. They were likely roaches, but we didn't stay long enough to identify them.

We quickly shut the door, declined the room, and retreated to our waiting
taxi children who took us to *their* choice, similar to the Blue Diamond, but no
bugs. They had waited as if they knew how it would all turn out, and we were
glad they would get a commission after all they had been through. As we were
dropping off to sleep, Molly and I wondered aloud what time the first flight left
the next morning.

The bed that I slept on that first night in Nepal – the first of many since we
didn't get a flight out the next morning – was as hard as the floor. Most beds we
slept on in Nepal were merely platforms with an inch-thick pad, or sometimes
just a cloth draped over the top. All the beds had pillows, to be sure, but they
were the size and consistency of a punching bag. Before I left the states, my
15-year-old niece Sarah Elizabeth gave me a small travelling pillow with little
yellow ducks on it. It was to be my greatest comfort during the entire trip! My
security pillow made it less uncomfortable to sit for hours on hard bus seats, and
to prop my head against a train window to sleep. When I put it on one of those
hard beds, it made it feel a tiny bit like home.

The next morning, in the light of day, we were prepared to give Nepal a
second chance. Our situation momentarily appeared somewhat improved, but,
in reality, we decided it was only familiar. What we had seen of Kathmandu,
so far, looked like a construction project started 50 years ago, still unfinished.
With map in hand backpacks in tow, we went in search of "something better,"
especially as far as lodging was concerned.

After walking through deserted streets, devoid of any beauty, we finally
made our way into the Thamal District, where the markets were teeming with
people. They were like markets we had seen in Egypt and Thailand. Merchants
beckoning us, sometimes bodily pulling us into their shops, to buy shirts,
carpets, "something beautiful, good price, very nice, special for you." Occasionally, someone would sneak up behind us and furtively whisper, "Change
money, hashish, very nice, good price," as if it were one word. Continuing our
stroll through the city, we also discovered beautiful areas of Kathmandu, with
spectacular wood carvings on Hindu and Buddhist buildings and temples.

Not forgetting our most important goal of finding a more suitable place to
stay, we headed to the Kathmandu Guest House, a favorite for budget travelers
from around the world, according to our guidebook. Along the way, we ran into
Sarah and James, who joined us. The Guest House was spotless with a lovely

courtyard and a luscious green lawn, fruit trees, beautiful flowers, and shrubs. We were impressed, but unfortunately, there were no vacancies, so we reserved a room for the following day. We moved to the hotel where Sarah and James were staying, a small, very pleasant place run by a friendly, helpful family. The following morning, we returned to the Guest House to register and stayed put for several days, until we departed for our jungle safari.

We spent the next few days touring Kathmandu by bicycle. I never thought I would have the nerve to mount a bicycle with only my wits and a bell to negotiate Kathmandu traffic, which is harrowing at its best. The roads looked worse in the light of day, like demolition work had been abandoned, with piles of rubble waiting to be hauled away. Or, in some cases, there were piles of paving material (stones and gravel) waiting for someone to show up to begin repairs or construction on a new road. There I was, dodging potholes, rubble, pedestrians, goats, motorcycles, taxis, and trucks, and, of course, the sacred cows who lie down in the middle of a busy street. Becoming very nonchalant on two wheels, I weaved and merged and slammed on breaks while gaily, and sometimes belligerently, ringing my bell, along with all the other drivers who were ringing their bells and blowing their horns. It was a cacophony of humanity. The exhaust from the vehicles taxed my respiratory system, evidently not healed as I had hoped, and I sought help in a local pharmacy, recommended by our hosts. Even though it looked like a dispensary from the wild, wild, west, I took the advice of the clerk and made my purchase – no prescription required.

We visited various temples and were most interested in Pashupatinath, the oldest, and most visited temple in Nepal. Part of the complex includes the largest crematorium in Kathmandu with elevated platforms on the bank of the Bagmati River. Bodies wrapped in orange cloth are brought daily to the edge of the water and washed by the family while children played nearby. Then the body is rewrapped and placed on stacks of wood laid out on the platform where the cremation takes place. After 3-4 hours when these open cremations are complete, the ashes

Pashupatinath crematorium in Kathmandu, Nepal, features elevated platforms on the bank of the Bagmati River.

are swept into the sacred Bagmati River, which eventually leads to the Ganges River in India. Thanks to the use of camphor and other substances, there is an absence of the stench that normally accompanies dead and burning bodies. Although death is present in every area of Pashupatinath, it is an amazingly serene and peaceful place because in Nepal, death is not considered the final destination, but a journey into rebirth.

Sadhus are also part of the temple experience. These holy men, having given up on all forms of materialism to follow a path of spiritual discipline and achieve spiritual liberation, live in Hindu temples, or sometimes in caves or in forests. Dressed in bright orange with unshaved beards and dreadlocks, Sadhus can be seen strolling around the temples, living on the generosity of others. I was told that Sadhus in Nepal are known to smoke hashish in order to gain a higher level of consciousness.

We also went to the Monkey Temple, so named because it is believed that the monkeys who live there are the descendants of ones who were there during the time of the Buddhist deity Manjushri, which symbolizes the embodiment of transcendent wisdom. It is believed that he came to the area on a pilgrimage and spent time on the small hilltop where the temple is now. It's one of the highest points in Kathmandu and offers expansive views across the city. The site consists of a large central stupa, a dome-shaped Buddhist shrine, surrounded by other shrines, temples, and small shops that specialize in paintings, singing bowls, and a variety of other religious artifacts for sale.

This was the first time I learned about prayer wheels, cylindrical containers mounted on a spindle, offering a shortcut to daily prayers. Traditionally, "Om Mani Padme Hum," a Buddhist mantra meaning "the way to become enlightened," is written on the outside of the wheel, with many thousands of written mantras or prayers wrapped around a "life tree" in the core of the cylinder. According to the Tibetan Buddhist tradition, merely spinning these wheels has the same effect as verbally reciting the prayers that are sealed inside. Rows of prayer wheels are part of every temple, and visitors are invited to spin the prayer wheels, adding their own verbal prayers and spiritual blessing as they pass by.

Getting to the temple involved a steep climb up 365 stairs, where the monkeys loitered and approached visitors somewhat aggressively. James told us when he went there, he was sitting on a bench enjoying the sacredness and peace, when a money jumped on the bench beside him, locked eyes with him, then put one hand on his shoulder and held out his other hand for James to put something in it. Forewarned, I didn't let one get close enough for a confrontation.

We also had time to read, write post cards, update our journals, and enjoy the most delectable food Kathmandu had to offer. Because there is an international blend of tourists, every conceivable cuisine is offered. I tended to stick to the

Nepalese, Tibetan, and Indian fares. We went on an outing to a small village on the outskirts of Kathmandu to look for gifts to purchase. While we were looking at the figurines, antiques, statues, and wooden crafts, we met an English gentleman who was an importer/exporter from Hong Kong. He spent an hour with us, showing us how to identify authentic products and helped us select a few items. When we told him Hong Kong was on our itinerary, he gave us his card and invited us to call him.

Although Tibet wasn't one of my randomly selected countries to visit, Molly and I added it to our itinerary, so we began gathering information about traveling there. We decided that the Potala Palace in Lhasa was the sacred site we most wanted to visit. It had been the residence of the Dalai Lama, the former Tibetan spiritual leader, before the Chinese took over his country in 1959. There were two ways to get there: A 600-mile bus trip across the Himalayans broken by two four-hour treks midway to circumvent two washouts where the roads had collapsed on the mountainside. That option would take five days, averaging 10 miles an hour, and cost $250. We were warned that it was somewhat danger- ous due to the possibility of altitude sickness.

The second option was a flight that took 90 minutes and cost $28. As much as we wanted the bus trip experience, not to mention the stories we would have, we yielded to my still weakened respiratory condition, along with the ridiculously lower price, and purchased airline tickets. We felt like we were giving up an adventure of a lifetime, but our good senses prevailed. We made reservations for Saturday, October 10, three weeks away. And, from Lhasa, we would make plans to take the back door into China. It sounded both exciting and adventurous.

CHITWAN NATIONAL PARK

Since Molly wanted to see Bengal tigers in the wild, and I wanted to go to a jungle, we purchased a jungle safari package for the Chitwan National Park, where the leopards, rhinos, and Bengal tigers are protected due to their dwindling numbers. Because Chitwan is only 150 miles from Kathmandu, we couldn't understand why a taxi should take 7-8 hours to get there. It took 10-11 hours by bus, so we decided on the mode of transportation that would get us there quicker. Leaving our big backpacks under lock and key at the Guest House, we threw our day packs over our shoulders and set off one morning at 7:30 a.m.

The drive to Chitwan was tortuous, even with our excellent driver. The roads, for the most part, were unpaved due to the severe winter weather that resulted in wash outs and holes the size of a large dog. There were lots of trucks and buses slowly inching their way up steep inclines, belching thick exhaust fumes in our faces as we hugged their tailpipes, trying to pass. Nepal had no emission control. Of course, there were the usual pedestrians, water buffalos, and bicycles to weave around, as well. Our driver spoke very little English so was unable to keep us informed whenever he stopped the car in a village. He frequently got out of his taxi, milled around with the locals, or sometimes even disappeared for 10-15 minutes, then returned to us, ready to resume our journey. We learned at one stop that he visited a friend in the hospital. Now we knew why the trip could take 7-8 hours. It was likely the only way he got to visit with friends and relatives.

We passed through stunningly beautiful landscape, amidst towering mountains with terraced rice paddies, like stairsteps for Yeti. We drove through three winding valleys where we could see houses perched on the mountainsides, or nestled between two hills, with miles of footpaths between the homes and the villages. We saw people in the distance, walking along those pathways, and others gathering at natural springs beside the road, taking baths, washing clothes, drawing water to take home, and visiting with each other. People were everywhere!

After six long hours, we arrived at the edge of Chitwan. Thinking we had made good time, I was glad our journey was over although I didn't see a Land Rover waiting, as promised in our package. However, we did see an ox cart alongside the road with two oxen lying beside it. I thought our taxi driver was stopping to visit the man with the oxen, but he soon gestured for us to get out while he put our day packs in the back of the cart. Two German men, Ernie and Ury, joined us shortly, and instead of waiting in the shade, the four of us were instructed to get in the ox cart. So, there we were, four adult human beings, straining to sit upright in an oxless cart while the tongue was still on the ground, tilting the cart forward. With urgings from the owner of the oxen, they reluctantly rose to their feet and obediently backed up to the cart, one on each side of the tongue. Shifting our weight to help change the height of the tongue, they hooked the cart to the oxen. We said goodbye to our taxi driver and set off for what we thought was surely the last leg of our trip.

Do you know how slowly oxen walk? We thought if we rocked our bodies, we might lighten their burden and urge them to pick up their pace, but we rode on and on toward no end that we could see. We crossed small rivers, large mud holes, and passed villages where naked children ran out shouting "Bye-bye, Bye-bye." We passed out crayons and paper we had brought along for just this purpose. Finally, way off in the distance, we agreed that we all could see a small form slowing coming into view. Perhaps the promised Land Rover? As we drew nearer, and the form became distinguishable, I knew that it was not the Land Rover – unless that was the elephant's name.

Climbing onto the elephant's back without a mounting stand was the most entertaining part of the ride. In Thailand, we had a mounting platform to gain access. In Nepal, the elephant, lying on his stomach, stretches his back legs behind him while the driver's helper loops the elephant's tail around to make a stirrup. The passenger steps onto the elephant's leg, puts a foot into the tail stirrup and heaves herself up high enough to grab the side of a tiny platform on the elephant's back. She then pulls herself the rest of the way up onto the platform, which is like an upside-down table with the four legs sticking up.

I was the first one up and could see Molly below following instructions, leaping from leg to tail to back and gaining purchase on the platform. Seeing Ernie and Ury already queued up to climb aboard, I began to feel uneasy about how we all would be able to fit. We were each asked to straddle a leg of the table with our legs hanging over the edges. With our backs to each other, one person in each corner, there was even enough space to stack our backpacks behind us, giving us a backrest. We talked and laughed as we slowly made our way to the lodge – another hour away. So, eight hours in all, as promised.

Our accommodations were native huts with thatched roofs and no electricity. Hot water was available only from 4-7 p.m. The meals were western-cuisine style yak burgers which were just ok. Early the next day we mounted the elephant again and were taken on safari where we saw several one-horned rhinos in the wild. The elephant drivers closed in on one while it was lying in a mud bath. We watched as it clamored to its feet, stood there at a dazed attention not sure which way to run, snorted, chose a direction, and trotted off. We saw no tigers or leopards, as we were told the grass was too high. This particular lodge did not bait animals just so the tourist could see them, which was OK with me. That would hardly be better than seeing them in a zoo.

That afternoon, we were scheduled for a couple of guided walks through the jungle, but I declined the second after issues with the first. On my first hike, I was attacked by leeches – no one else, just me. Luckily, I happened to be looking down at my feet to see where I was stepping when I caught a glimpse of a small black slithering thing disappear into my sock. It was like something out of the X-Files. I immediately sat down and took off my shoes and socks and saw that several leeches had snuck through my sock when I wasn't looking and were already attached to my ankles and shins, happily feeding on my blood. I was instructed to find the mouth of the leech located at the thinner and smaller end of the body. I put my fingers on my skin near its mouth, and slid my fingernail, little by little, to the mouth, and then pushed it to the side. This method pushes off the mouth of the leech rather than pulling it, which leaves a red round mark. I pulled off eight leeches altogether. It was absolutely disgusting at first, but soon I was efficiently sliding them off and casting them aside, one after the other, as if I did this every day. My, aren't we humans adaptable, normalizing the unimaginable? Now you know why I didn't go on subsequent walks in the jungle.

POKHARA

On our way to the Chitwan Jungle, Molly and I decided to go to Pokhara after the jungle safari since we were already halfway there. Pokhara is a beautiful village at the foot of the Annapurana Range and a starting point for a popular trek. We thought it might be the closest we would get to an actual trek. While we were hugging the tailpipes on the way to Chitwan, we were so thankful for not choosing the bus, with people hanging out the windows, goats, chickens, and luggage tied on top, and occasional passengers sitting on top too. I remember Molly saying she really wouldn't mind riding a bus, but she certainly wasn't going to ride one with goats and chickens inside.

After two days in the jungle, we were taken back to the main road, this time by the Land Rover, which was being repaired when we arrived. Hence the earlier elephant transportation. The same taxi driver picked us up and took us to the junction to catch the bus for Pokhara. We could have paid him an extra $50 to drive us there, but in the interest of saving money, we opted to take the bus – under Molly's "no goats or chickens" stipulation.

Having studied the map, we knew we weren't at the right junction because we were in the wrong town. We figured the driver just wanted to get rid of us sooner so he could visit more of his friends and family. With our trust in him waning, and a bus already waiting, we soon found ourselves standing at the open doorway of a bus that was overflowing with Nepalese – but no goats or chickens tied on top. We were told it was the bus to Pokhara The motor was racing, the driver impatiently wanting to stay ahead of all the slow-moving vehicles he had passed since the last town.

Molly asked, "Is this the express bus?"

"Molly," I said, "There are no express buses. Just get on. It will get us there."

Three people squeezed together on each wooden seat, at least half of them smoking. The aisles were full of people straddling bags, boxes, and luggage. Molly and I found a space for our backpacks between our feet, standing with our feet twisted in unusual contortions to accommodate the granted space. After a few passengers disembarked, I was able to maneuver myself to a sitting position on top of my day pack without breaking either of my ankles. Molly decided to continue standing.

After bouncing along for many miles and several stops, the couple sitting next to us got off so we could finally have two-thirds of a wooden seat. While

I was getting out my little duck pillow to sit on, I told Molly this definitely was not an express bus. As we rocked to the sway of the bus, we soon became mesmerized by the drone of the engine and the conversations of our fellow passengers, none of which we could understand. Our eyes were shut against the assault of the cigarette smoke, and the exhaust fumes coming in the open windows. Suddenly we both sat bolt upright staring at each other. "Chickens!" we exclaimed in unison, as the clucking and cackling began to reach us from the back of the bus. Perhaps they had been sleeping until the frequent stopping and the fumes awakened them; perhaps they snuck on while we were dozing. Molly was already committed, so she bravely swallowed her stipulation, and thankfully we stayed on the bus.

Going to the bathroom when traveling in Nepal by bus was an interesting experience. When the driver announced we were stopping for a bathroom break, Molly and I disembarked like everyone else, but there was no building in sight. We soon saw the men going to one side of the road and the women headed toward the opposite side. With everyone's back to the bus, we stood and squatted, averted our eyes, attended to our business, and then got back on the bus. Luckily both Molly and I were wearing skirts that day and we negotiated the awkward situation with as much discretion and grace as we could. From then on, we always wore skirts if we were traveling by bus.

We made it to Pokhara in about five hours and soon found a peaceful guest house on Pokhara Lake with a view of the surrounding hills, backdropped by a spectacular vista of Annapurna Peaks. We spent three nights relaxing in this beautiful setting. We ran into Leslie, a Canadian woman we met at the Guest House in  Kathmandu, and Molly arranged to go on a day hike in the mountains with her and her friends the next day. I decided to stay put, reading *Seven Years in Tibet* in preparation for our upcoming trip. I was also feeling low energy, still nursing that nagging respiratory condition, which hadn't improved by breathing in all the exhaust fumes Nepal was offering. It was wonderful to finally have an entire day to myself.

On our last day, Molly and I rented bicycles to ride around Pokhara Lake and found our way to the Tibetan Refugee Camp to watch the carpet-making process. When the Chinese took over Tibet after years of guerrilla warfare with

Tibetan rebels in 1959, an estimated 12,000 refugees fled to Nepal, where, in 1987, they had been living in limbo in refugee camps for 28 years. The Chinese soldiers surrounded the palace in Lhasa and started closing in, hoping to capture the Dalai Lama. Only 23 at the time, the Dalai Lama was persuaded to disguise himself as a soldier to avoid being captured or killed. He was thus able to slip through the crowds to flee the country of his birth that he would never see again.

Accompanied by an entourage of soldiers and cabinet members, the Dalai Lama set out on foot to cross the Himalayas – destination, India. The journey was a dangerous one, traveling only at night to avoid being captured by Chinese soldiers. For two weeks after his escape, people around the world didn't know if the spiritual and political leader of Tibet was still alive or if he had been killed. The Dalai Lama finally reached safety in northern India, where he has lived for 60 years leading his people from afar. Back in Tibet, reprisals for the uprising resulted in the death of 87,000 Tibetans, according to the Chinese. Tibetan exiles think the number was closer to 430,000. We talked to several men and women who expressed a desire to go back to their home country and to restore their spiritual and political leader.

Dashain in Kathmandu

Molly and I took a chartered bus back to Kathmandu, only an 8-hour trip – so it must have been an express bus. On the road, we saw loaded public buses, even more full than before with people and their livestock, hanging out the windows and tied on the roofs. They all were also headed to Kathmandu for Dashain, their biggest festival of the year. The celebration lasts 15 days and is like our Thanksgiving and Christmas rolled into one. In preparation for the event, the city swept the streets, decorated the temples, and prepared lavish feasts. Both Hindus and Buddhists celebrate Dashain, a festival of love and homecoming that centers on good winning over evil and love transcending pain and suffering. The event ends with the optimistic notion that the next year will be a smooth, happy, and prosperous one.

While all government offices, schools, and businesses remain closed during the festival period, the Nepalese people go to their temples with an animal to sacrifice. During Dashain, hundreds of thousands of animals all over Nepal are sacrificed to help mankind free themselves of their sins and grant them their wishes. We heard that the sacrificial line at one of the Kathmandu temples was four hours long one day. We chose not to witness the sacrifices, but we did see vehicles with splashes of blood on the front as a way of blessing the vehicle.

Since banks were closed when we got to Kathmandu, we started looking for someone to exchange money on the black market – illegal, but easily available, and not as good a rate as the bank. A money changer soon spotted us and came to our aid. After being led down an alley and up a back stairway, we found ourselves in a carpet shop. We decided it was most likely our source's relative who would try to get us to purchase merchandise before exchanging our money. Initially, neither of us had any intention of buying Tibetan rugs, but since we had watched the rug-making process in Pokhara, and, these were beautiful rugs, we each bought three and had them shipped home by air cargo. Best of all, we got a better rate on exchanging our money. By the time the rugs arrived in Santa Fe more than six months later, both Molly and I were unsure if they were the actual rugs we purchased, but we both have enjoyed them for all these years.

The Kathmandu Guest House was full when we returned to the city, so we found James and Sarah again and moved back to their rental house. They were preparing for an extended trek in the Langtang Valley, dominated by Mount Langtang Lirung, just under 24,000 feet.

"Instead of waiting in Kathmandu for your trip to Tibet," they insisted, "why not come trekking with us? You could hike in for three days with us, and then back for three days on your own. This way, at least you'll have a taste of trekking."

They painted an absolutely beautiful picture of the snow-capped mountains, pine forests, swift mountain streams, lush meadows, and the picturesque villages, all of this a several-days walk from the nearest transportation and modern conveniences. I was especially intrigued when James told us about the residents having to porter materials to the villages for everything they needed. He told us about the huge swings they built for the children and the stone they hauled in to lay for their streets. We enthusiastically agreed and set about putting together the absolute fewest necessities for a six-day trek.

TREKKING NOT TREKKING

James, who also leads river-rafting trips and mountain-climbing expeditions back in the States, whenever he's not in the classroom, was our designated leader. Molly and I thought that we could always hire a Sherpa to carry our load if we were unable to keep up, but we found that would not be necessary.

We hired a taxi to drive us the eight hours to the end of the paved road that leads into the Langtang Valley, followed by a 20-mile unpaved road to the next village. Transportation was iffy in normal circumstances and doubtful with the Dashain Festival in progress, so we were lucky to find a driver. We started early Friday morning. Since Molly was sick most of Thursday night, I was ready to cancel, but she assured us she would be OK. Molly sat quietly holding her stomach while the taxi lurched along on a road, somewhat better than the one to Chitwan. Since Molly was not yet ready for hiking, James decided we should stay one night in the village at the end of the paved road. We heard that a bus might come the next day to take passengers down the unpaved road to the next village, which would save us a day of hiking and get us farther up the mountain.

James, Sarah, Linda, Molly on pre-trekking trip, 1987.

We were shown the village's only three available dwellings for guests. One had six beds in a room with a dirt floor. Another was the downstairs of a bar/store arrangement with a doorway facing the most blaring, discordant music we had ever heard. And the third was the second story of a barn, which we chose.

It was a barn in every sense of the word, though deprived of animals. The walls were unpainted, the ceiling was the underside of the roof, and the floor looked like it had never been swept. The room was 7 feet wide and long enough to hold six single platform beds, with only 6 inches separating the beds. Through a small open window at each end of the room we heard the nearby rushing river. It was so much nicer than the other two choices, and we hoped no one else would come so we could have it to ourselves. It was perfect for four people.

We stood on the stairs when I asked about the bathroom. The innkeeper – and I use that term loosely – swept his arm in a gesture to include the entire valley and said, "Is everywhere."

Molly slept the rest of that day and night, and by morning she was feeling chipper and ready to hit the trail. But, alas, Sarah felt poorly, and by mid-morning, we knew there would be no trail blazing that day. By noon on Saturday, James, Molly, and I had brought some semblance of order to our "barn nest." We swept the floors, made our pallets as comfortable as possible, and set up a bucket for an indoor toilet in an adjoining storage room so Sarah wouldn't have to run down the stairs and outside every 15 minutes.

The "iffy" bus never came. It was, after all Dashain celebrations, but "maybe tomorrow." Late Saturday, while we were dozing and reading in our newly cleaned loft, we heard what sounded like a large vehicle coming into town. We walked down to the village center and met seven or eight members of a Polish mountain-climbing excursion and their Sherpas. They were spending the night in the dwelling with the dirt floor. When we told them where we were going, they invited us to ride the bus with them to the end of the 20-mile-long dirt road. That would help make up the day we had lost with Sarah's illness.

When we hurried back to tell Sarah the good news, she promised she was on the mend and would feel well enough tomorrow to ride the bus, to go at least that far. We boarded the bus on Sunday and disembarked at the last village accessible by transportation. Arriving around noon, we found a lovely, clean room on the second floor of a small store/house. It was furnished with the typical hard beds and big pillows, which became less important when we saw the views from windows that overlooked the breathtaking snow caps of the Langtang range.

We agreed that Sarah needed another day to recuperate while we enjoyed this last semblance of civilization. We even had a clean Nepalese-style toilet – a hole in the floor with porcelain foot holders. It was accessed by going down the outside stairs in the front, then down rock stairs on the side of the building, and finally across the back yard of our building. Not very convenient if you have the "runs," but we were grateful.

Monday morning, with two of our six trekking days gone, we were awakened by groans from across the room – not Sarah, but James, this time. With our leader now sick, we spent Monday in our new location, contemplating our lack of progress on the third day of our trekking expedition. Molly and I discussed starting the trek the next morning on our own. We would only be able to trek a day in and a day out since we needed to be back in time to prepare for our trip to Lhasa. At least we could say we went trekking in Nepal.

Tuesday morning came, and, after a short conference, we decided not to go after all. There was no need for Sherpas. I was still on the verge of bronchitis, never totally well since Egypt. I would feel better for a week or two, then feel bad for several days, and so on. I decided if I wanted to be in really good condition for Tibet and China, I'd better not push it.

First, we had to deal with the "iffy" transportation back to Kathmandu. Molly and I waited all that day for a bus, and toward evening, the most crowded bus we had seen to date came lumbering into town. The joke in Nepal is, "How many Nepalese can you get on a bus?" The answer, "All of them." The rumor was that this bus was going to leave at 8:00 the next morning, so we bought tickets with assigned seats.

After saying goodbye to Sarah and James, we boarded the bus and started rolling out of town shortly after 8 a.m. So far, so good. The bus stopped rolling 100 yards down the road to get a permit checked which took 15 minutes. We drove another mile only to stop for an official to board the bus to check everyone's passports and trekking permits. Another hour passed. We started again, went another 2 miles farther, stopped, and waited 45 minutes for three military people whose tours of duty had ended to get on the bus. Finally, by 10 a.m., we were really on our way. We never understood why they didn't check all the permits and passports in the village as we boarded the bus, or why they didn't have the military people board the bus in town. Now we had just enough time to make the three-hour trip to make the connection with our 1 p.m. bus for Kathmandu. "Maybe," we were told, "they would hold the bus." Maybe?

After way too many stops, picking up every Nepalese standing beside the road, we careened into town and saw three buses, loaded and ready to pull out of town. We discovered there were at least 30 trekkers in our bus who needed to catch the bus to Kathmandu. We fell over each other getting off the bus and running to the ticket window, only to be greeted with, "Finished! No more tickets!"

Pondering what to do, several of us started down the street in search of a taxi to rent, but no taxi could be found. We did see an empty bus, ran up to it and asked the driver where he was going. He said, "to Kathmandu," and within three minutes, every seat was filled. Of course, it wasn't leaving for an hour, but we weren't about to give up our positions, three riders to each hard seat.

We had the good fortune of sharing our seat with Michael Connelly, an Englishman living in Kathmandu. He was working with the British Council as an English advisor for the educational system. During the journey, he invited us to stay in his home, which we accepted for two wonderful nights. It felt so civilized to be in a home with glass paned windows, curtains swaying gently with the breeze, classical music playing on the stereo, an English garden, a maid to wash our clothes, and, wonder of all wonders, soft beds and real pillows!

In between the preparations for leave-taking and last-minute buying and some more sightseeing, I took long baths, cooked my own food, took Molly out to dinner to celebrate her birthday, listened to music, and enjoyed being in Michael's home. He was a very gracious host and made us feel very comfortable. He seemed to be glad for the company since his family was back in England.

TIBET NOT TIBET

When we went to pick up our tickets for Nepal Thursday morning, we were told that all flights had been canceled. The border between Nepal and Tibet was closed to tourists because of the protests and riots between Tibetan monks and the Chinese military. We were deeply disappointed, but quickly revised our plans and arranged to fly to Hong Kong instead. From there we could get into China by the front door, and maybe into Tibet too, if a peaceful resolution had been achieved by then.

Our Royal Nepal airplane from Kathmandu to Hong Kong was a brand-new B-757 on its maiden flight. I sat next to a gentleman who told me the plane was bought from Canada. He was on his way home to Vancouver, having lived in Kathmandu for two years, training the Nepalese in maintenance procedures for the plane. I wished I had asked him why they divided smoking and non-smoking on the aircraft with smokers on the left, non-smokers on the right. It didn't make any sense at all.

As we flew toward Hong Kong, I saw Mt. Everest's towering peaks disappear into the clouds to the north. It was awe-inspiring to see from the airplane, but I had no desire to climb it. I was sorry that we had not been able to trek at least a few days and see the remote villages in Nepal. I would have to be content with one primitive story – coping with the leeches in the jungle. Now, on to Hong Kong, Bali, and Australia.

NEPAL HIGHLIGHTS

1. Sunsets in the Himalayas.
2. The Nepalese greeting, "Namaste," said with hands folded as if in prayer, and a slight bow, meaning "The God in me recognizes the God in you."
3. Showing binoculars to children who were eager to look across the valley at villages two day's walk away.
4. Talking with Tibetan refuges for two hours in Pokhara.
5. Taking a bath in the river with all my clothes on.
6. Riding my bicycle three times around a round-about before I could negotiate my way through traffic and out of it.
7. Watching nightly as hundreds of huge bats flew out of a tree, flying over Kathmandu on their way to dinner.
8. The sounds of morning: dogs barking, roosters crowing, people laughing and calling out to one another.
9. Buses, crowded with chickens and goats and throngs of people.
10. The smiles, the children's faces.
11. The temples, the Sadhus.
12. Listening to Sarah and James sing.
13. Meeting other travelers and hearing their stories.
14. Having time to read.
15. Shopping for carpets and gifts.
16. The food.
17. The carvings and artwork.
18. Watching men cut each other's hair in a village square.

6 | HONG KONG

We approached the Hong Kong airport, flying low over the water just slightly above the lighted high-rise buildings. I was mesmerized by the full effect of the skyline. The vista, especially at night, is the most dazzling I have ever seen. It was so beautiful that I wept. I had a similar feeling the first time I saw San Francisco

from a distance, with all the hills covered in white buildings and the city as a backdrop. Both cities, each in their own ways, are a feast for the eyes. Molly and I were glad to be back in civilization. Shortly after landing, we found a helpful electronic bulletin board where we located a private apartment with bedrooms to rent, and a phone within arm's reach to call a taxi.

We rented a room in a two-bedroom apartment owned by a couple with a 10-year plan to leave Hong Kong in 1997 when the British handed Hong Kong back to China. A lot of people we met had similar plans. The 99-year lease brokered in June 1898 by Queen Victoria would come to an end in 1997. The residents of Hong Kong, having fared well under British rule for nearly a hundred years, had no idea of their fate under the Chinese. Having seen what had happened to Tibet, they were dreading the possibilities, none good that they could see. Like many people in Hong Kong, our young landlords and their teenage son were doing everything to save as much money as they could so they could immigrate to Indonesia or another country before China's takeover.

To realize their 10-year plan, they installed a three-tiered bunk bed in an alcove in their kitchen where the couple and their teenage son slept and lived. They rented out the two bedrooms, each with two double beds, and turned their living room into another bedroom, curtained-off for privacy. Molly and I each paid double for one of the bedrooms so we would each have our own bed and not have to share the room with two strangers. The rate of $25/person was based on two people to a bed.

Our hostess, originally from Bali, fixed us tea every morning with a healthy measure of sweetened condensed milk. Although too sweet for me at first, I soon became quite fond of it. When she learned that I was going to Bali, she started teaching me the typical phrases: *Selamat pagi* (good morning) or *Selamat malam* (good night). When we left Hong Kong, she gave me a note of introduction and the address of her brother who lived on the northern coast of Bali.

Hong Kong includes 426 square miles of territory in the South China Sea. With a population of 5.5 million in 1987 and with 7.5 million today, it remains one of the most densely populated parts of the world. From our first day in the streets, I was impressed by how clean and orderly everything was – the streets, the stores, the people. The city was crowded, and even though people moved along at a fast pace, there was no pushing or shoving. Everyone was polite, mindful of their own space, and gave sufficient room for others to move.

Of course, we enjoyed the delicious cuisine, better than anything so far on our trip. We learned from fellow travelers that Hong Kong was the best place to find good deals on merchandise at street markets, wholesale malls, and factory outlets. One day we went to a wholesale mall and bought inexpensive jeans, Chinese silk robes, and other gifts for our families. As we were walking back to our apartment with our purchases, I noticed that I kept lagging behind Molly, feeling like I had to run to keep up with her. I realized that my continuing weakened respiratory condition was affecting my stamina and hoped that here in Hong Kong I could find someone who could help.

When we called the import-export man we met in Kathmandu a couple of weeks earlier, he seemed delighted to hear from us and invited us to dinner on our second night in the city. When we arrived at his high-end, high-rise apartment, we were surprised to find 8-10 other guests. We were utterly speechless at his apartment's view overlooking Hong Kong and the harbor. With floor-to-ceiling, wall-to-wall windows, the views were as stunning looking out, as they had been from the plane when we were flying in.

As we engaged our host in conversations about our trip to China, he had lots of good advice since he was a frequent traveler there for his business. Eventually, he took a long, hard look at me, and said, "You, my dear, have no business going to China. It is the worse place in the world to be if you are sick." I must have looked even worse than I felt. He gave me the name of his doctor who put me on antibiotics. Molly and I discussed our situation and agreed that I would fly to Bali, next on our itinerary after China, and she would join me in two weeks after a quick jaunt inside China. She decided to forgo Tibet this trip. I felt a little sad that I wouldn't be going, but my body was singing and dancing with the idea of having two whole weeks to myself on the beach in Bali, instead of traipsing all over China, trying to keep up with Molly.

Since Molly was already a world traveler when we started our trip, I had depended on her to get the lay of the land when we entered a new country. From the time we got off the airplane, she always seemed to know where she was going, and could quickly process the signs in their strange languages and her surroundings. She could quickly calculate the exchange rate as she walked along, while I was still counting on my fingers and trying to remember what the new money was called. She knew how to find a place to stay and how to get transportation to it. How would I ever manage without her? We made our separate reservations to leave Hong Kong on the same day, with the agreement that I would meet her flight at the airport in Denpasar, Bali, in two-weeks. For the first time in two months, after we said our goodbyes at the airport, we went our separate ways.

7 | Bali

Isettled into my seat for the five-hour flight to Bali, my consolation prize – no Great Wall of China, no Forbidden City, no Yangtze River tour. Bali was one of the locations I had randomly chosen in Leslie's world atlas, back in Santa Fe nine months earlier. Feeling much better after starting an antibiotic in Hong Kong, I was now confident that I could tame the infection in my respiratory system. Although I was beginning to look forward to a restorative fortnight of solitude, I also felt some trepidations.

I opened my trusted guidebook, *Southeast Asia on a Shoestring*, to familiarize myself with my destination, including how to get around, places to stay, and the Balinese people. Bali, an island in Indonesia, is not to be confused with the mystical island, Bali Hai, in the movie, *South Pacific*. It also is not Makana Mountain, also known as Bali Hai, on Kauai's north shore in Hawaii, where the last sunset in the United States takes place each evening.

Bali is renowned for highly developed arts, including traditional and modern dance, sculpture, painting, leather, metalworking, and music. Though the population of Indonesia is primarily Muslim, 80% of the Bali people are Hindus; there are temples everywhere. One of the many delights is watching the beautiful Balinese girls walk in a procession with their offerings of bright fruits, flowers, and rice cakes piled high and balanced on their heads. These women spend a large part of each day creating and placing these ritualistic offerings called canang saris, where you least expect them – perched atop walls, on statues, in planters, on stair steps, or at the foot of a temple.

If you don't notice their visual beauty, you might catch their wafting aromas of fragrant tropical petals or wisps of incense. Early every morning, the Balinese sweep away the previous day's wilted floral offerings fallen to the streets in time for that afternoon's fresh creations and prayers, a daily reminder of the impermanence of our world. The slightly darker purpose of the canang saris is to appease and disperse any lingering demon spirits lingering around one's home or on a nearby street corner.

Denpasar

My residence in Denpasar was a home-stay easily accessible from the airport. It was close to the beach and to the hotel where Molly and I arranged to have our mail sent. We always hoped for letters, a highlight when far from home – two months so far.

After settling into my room, I asked my host to arrange a massage, someone who would come to my room. When I answered the door the following day, I was surprised to find a gentleman wearing sunglasses and holding a cane with a tip, indicating he was blind. After confirming that he was indeed blind, he said that he had found massage to be the best way for someone with his handicap to stay employed. It would be a massage by braille. I disrobed and settled myself on the table he brought, and he proceeded to give me an excellent massage.

The next day, on my way to the hotel for breakfast and to check for mail, I walked two blocks over to the ocean and found lovely trees shading the beach, one of the many gentle offerings of Bali. I bought a sarong from one of the girls selling them on the beach and spread it out on the sand, just to enjoy the experience of being in Bali, sitting in the shade on the beach and looking out at the Indian Ocean.

After my quiet reverie, I continued to the hotel where I picked up my mail and had breakfast of many new fruits unlike anything I had ever seen or tasted. Mangosteen with its white inner flesh was the prize; Rambutan is a 'hairy' bright red fruit that, when opened, reveals a soft, cloudy white flesh, sweet and succulent; and Pomelo, a large citrus fruit, is a cross between an orange and a grapefruit. I went back the next day to enjoy another breakfast.

LAVINA BEACH

By the end of the second day in crowded Denpasar, I was ready for the quiet and less touristy north side of Bali. I chose Lavina Beach, given its proximity to the town where the brother of my Hong Kong host lived. I took a taxi, more like a van, for the two-hour, 50-mile ride. In my guidebook I found a room on the beach at the Kalibukbuk Beach Inn. For a mere $9 a night, my room was on the second floor

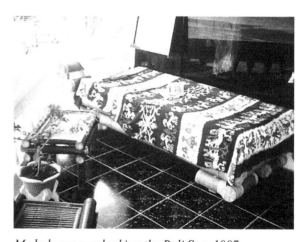

My balcony overlooking the Bali Sea, 1987.

overlooking the Bali Sea. After registering at their open-air restaurant less than 100 feet from my new home, I was then led up the curved stairway to my very own private balcony. This was no consolation prize. This was the crown jewel in the pot of gold. I had done alright for myself, without Molly.

The next morning, with the help of an employee, Nyoman Winatha, I moved one of the single beds in my room onto the balcony to create my little piece of Balinese heaven. Every day, I went to the restaurant for breakfast, lunch, and dinner. I spent time at water's edge, but most of the time I was on my balcony, reading, writing, listening to music, and healing my respiratory system. Late every afternoon, from my perch on the balcony, I watched as the local women come down to the mouth of the river that emptied into the Bali Sea where they bathed themselves and their children. One day, I arranged to go snorkeling, something I had never done. There were three or four of us on a small boat that went out to the coral reef right in front of our home-stay.

I soon became friends with Nyoman, the young man who had helped me move my bed. I bought a dictionary for us so we could communicate. He offered to borrow a friend's motor scooter to take me to several local places of interest, and to help me find the brother of my Hong Kong hostess. We enjoyed a short visit with him after delivering the note from his sister.

When Nyoman asked me if I would like to visit his own family, of course, I said yes. Nyoman, who was the same age as my son Tony, told me he was unable to go to college because his father was diagnosed with lung cancer and unable to work. His two older brothers had gone to college and were now teachers, but there was no money for him to go.

Nyoman lived with his extended family in the Anturan Villages in Singaraja, Bali, their compound surrounded by a stone wall. To gain access, we zig-zagged through gateways built in the wall. He pointed out that, in Bali, whenever possible the main entrance gate is placed facing the sunset side of the compound to discourage malevolent spirits from trying to enter. To further confuse their attempts to get in, several 45-degree turns are built into the entry design. Evidently, the spirits, not being able to go in a straight line, become discouraged, turn around, and go away.

Housed within the wall was a cluster of buildings, much like condos, surrounding a courtyard. While we sat on a small porch in front of Nyoman's house with his family, several neighbors came out to see the American tourist. His father went inside and brought back a large brown envelop that held his lung x-rays. Since we didn't speak each other's language, I wasn't sure why he wanted me to see them, but I got the impression that because I was American, he thought I might be able to explain them to him, or maybe to be able to read them to offer a different diagnosis.

An odd but interesting aspect regarding the naming of Balinese children is that there are only four names, the same for both boys and girls, and they follow a certain order. For example, the eldest boy is always Wayan. Next is Made, followed by Nyoman, and the fourth is Ketut. If the family should have a fifth child, they just start over. The girls' names are in the same order but are proceeded by Ni. I guess when it was dinner time, mothers just called out those four names and all the children knew it was time to go home.

Nyoman took me to a store where local women shopped so I could buy a nice sarong, not like the ordinary ones the girls sold on the beach. We also went to a temple next to a beautiful waterfall and a swimming hole frequented by locals. It was a wonderful day. We had fun using the dictionary trying to communicate ideas and ask questions. I learned that his salary was $9 a month, the same amount I was paying for my room each day. He said there were very few jobs in Bali, and that he would never be able to marry and have a family, like his brothers had. When I left, I gave him $27, three month's salary, and have always wished I had given him more. Even now, 35 years later, every time I see $9 as the price of anything, I think of Nyoman and wonder where he is now and what he is doing. He was such a kind and gentle soul.

THE END OF SMOKING

Looking to change things up, one evening, I walked down the road to a new open-air restaurant for dinner where I met some Aussies who were in the process of starting a cottage industry for the women in that area. They were a rowdy and fun lot, and they smoked Kool cigarettes, which played an important part in my life. I had started smoking early, in 1958 when I was 17, and continued until I got pregnant with Tony when I was 21. To my credit, I always stopped smoking whenever I was pregnant and nursing but would take it up again the day the babies were weaned. Also, to my credit, this was before the Surgeon General's warning. Who knew? When the warnings were articulated in 1971 and written in plain English on every cigarette package, I stopped cold turkey for nine years.

However, when Gary and I split up, and I went to live at Jim Worsley's, it was oh-so-easy to pick it up again with affirmations and breath work to protect me. I smoked for four years, until I was transferred to Santa Fe in 1984 when I decided to be a non-smoker again. But then, I had not counted on Leslie and her clove cigarettes. Oh, how cosmopolitan we were.

Clove cigarettes turned out to be horrible and not cosmopolitan at all, so we soon switched to American Spirit cigarettes, rolling our own – no chemicals, just good old-fashioned American-grown tobacco. Who did we think we were kidding? When I developed a cough, I quit for two weeks, tried it again in case the cough was a fluke, but sure enough, bad cough again. So, I quit again about two years before my around-the-world trip.

Now, here I was in Bali, having after dinner drinks when someone offered me a cigarette. I accepted, even though I never cared for mentholated cigarettes, saying to myself, "It's an occasion." I smoked a few more during the evening. On my walk back to my home-stay, I started to regret those cigarettes. I started feeling nauseous and headachy, and it got worse throughout the night. The upside to the story is that it got so bad that there was no way I would ever want a cigarette again. Those Kools were the very last cigarettes I ever smoked. Just writing about that night gives me that queasy feeling.

REUNITED WITH MOLLY

It was with great sadness that I gave up my Balinese paradise. I packed my bags, said goodbye to Nyoman, and headed to the airport to meet Molly. After her two-week tour of China, she was ready to sit on a beach and be still for a couple of days. That gave us some time to plan our remaining time in Bali. Molly wanted to rent a car and drive wherever we wanted to go, while I wanted to rent a car with a driver so he could drive us wherever we wanted to go. My argument was that it was easy to miss the special places that only the locals know about if you are finding your own way around. Her argument was that she was tired of depending on someone else to tell her where to go and what to see. It was the first and only quasi argument we had. She was insistent. I finally yielded with the condition that I would drive. You would think the winner would drive, but I wanted that control.

It soon became apparent that the width of the roads must have been deter-mined by someone measuring just the width of two vehicles – no extra space in between or on the sides, and, of course, no shoulder. It made meeting cars an interesting game. As I approached an oncoming car, I learned to turn the wheel slightly to the left just enough for the body of my car to lean away from the vehicle, but not enough to run off the road, and then correct once the car was past.

I remember meeting a vehicle on what should have been a one-lane bridge. I could almost feel the car scraping the side of the bridge and turned to Molly, asking, "Did I come too close?" To Molly's credit, she never complained once about my driving in Bali or when I drove in Israel or later in Australia.

The interesting aspect about driving in Israel was that it was OK to pass a car with another car in the oncoming lane. Both cars would move to the shoulder on their side, allowing space for the passing car in the middle. That could never work in Bali. Oddly, we didn't see any wrecks because of these driving hazards. I assumed there would be many pedestrian fatalities in these undeveloped countries because there are so many who use the roads on foot, but we never saw or heard about it.

We stopped at several beach towns and found inexpensive places to stay. Molly recently reminded me of one where we each got our own room since we paid only 25 cents each. We adapted to cold water bathing, soaping ourselves down before rinsing off quickly under a cold shower. Today we know that cold showers are healthy; they increase circulation, close your pores, and are better for your complexion. The weather was so temperate, it didn't take long to adjust to having no hot water.

I had to remember to keep my mouth closed tight while showering since their water is not treated. I drank only bottled water on our entire trip, which unfortunately contributes to the plastic problem in third-world countries. We didn't even think about it back then. The population of Indonesia generates almost 10% of the world's total plastic waste. This number is huge when you consider the relatively small size of the country. As part of a national initiative, Bali, with 16 million tourists each year, has pledged to reduce plastics by 70% by 2025 and go plastic pollution free by 2040.

We chose Mount Batur as our sacred site in Bali. We had read that Bali was home to two active volcanoes. One of the most devastating and recent eruptions was Mount Agung in 1963. After sleeping for 120 years, 1,700 people were killed in the eruption, several villages were destroyed, and 86,000 people lost their homes.

We decided to climb the second active volcano, Mount Batur, which offers one of the best viewpoints of Lake Bali and all of Bali. When we parked the car at the foot of the mountain, we found a guide to lead us 5,600 feet to the top, a two-and-half hour moderate hike over a mixture of rocky and sandy terrain. Before I left New Mexico, I selected special stones to take with me on my trip. I exchanged them with resident stones at sacred sites as I traveled. Molly and I found a site next to a steaming vent near the top of Mount Batur, to perform the stone swapping ritual.

Today, I am somewhat conflicted that I did that, all those stones having to adapt to a new country and a new culture. And where are the stones I brought back with

Molly and Linda conducting a sacred ceremony on Mt. Batur, 1987.

me? I'm afraid I wasn't a responsible and respectful stone distributor. And what will archaeologists say a thousand years from now when they find those stones in the wrong countries?

When we were ready for our descent, our guide directed us to the back side of the mountain, taking only an hour instead of two, he said. It was a loose lava field, and the only way down was to slide, almost like skiing on your feet. Once we started, there was no stopping, and I knew we would end up on the opposite side of the mountain from the car.

When we were finally out of the lava field, we came to the house of our guide's cousin who presented us with lukewarm Cokes for sale. I'm sure getting business for his cousin was our guide's motivation for bringing us down the backside of Mount Batur. We were thirsty for sure, but warm Cokes do not quench. When we got to the main road, we were able to flag down a truck, serving as a bus, and caught a ride back to our vehicle.

UBUD

Having spent most of our time so far along the coast, we set out next to the central part of Bali, to Ubud, which was promoted as the arts and cultural center of Bali. Surrounded by lush rain forest, Ubud is situated in the highlands among spectacular rice terraces and steep ravines in the foothills of the Gianyar Regency. Ubud's population was about 30,000 in 1987, with more than a million foreign tourists each year. In 2020, the population had grown to 112,000, and the tourist population had tripled to more than three million each year.

The area surrounding the town is made up of small farms, rice paddies, agro-forestry plantations, and tourist accommodations. My most vivid memory of Ubud is one of the frogs. They start singing at nightfall and gain in volume as the night wears on. I was certain I would never be able to fall asleep to the cacophony of amphibian voices, singing the songs of their people. The ribbits, resounding through the air, was all encompassing and eventually I finally fell asleep. I was awakened in the middle of the night by the deafening silence. Their concert was over. Next time, ear plugs.

We also attended a cultural dance performance, went to the Monkey Forest, and of course visited a few of the 20,000 temples in Bali.

We were sad to leave this gentle country with kind people, but we were also excited to embark on the last leg of our around-the-world journey, before completing our circumnavigation of the planet. The next morning, we headed back to Denpasar, returned the rental car, and boarded our flight to Australia.

8 | AUSTRALIA

MONKEY MIA

Molly and I left Bali in our rear-view mirror and continued traveling east on our golden around-the-world airline tickets. After a five-hour flight, we arrived in Australia, Molly's final destination on our sacred site trip. I would make one more stop in Hawaii to visit friends. We wanted to swim with the dolphins, so we flew into Perth on the west coast where we spent our first night. It was wonderful to be in an English-speaking country with treated hot water and flushing toilets. The next day, after renting a car, we drove nine hours north to Monkey Mia, where the red desert meets the sea and where tourists can become acquainted with wild dolphins.

When we got there, the park rangers told us the dolphins had already come and gone for the day. We waded in anyway and were excited to see them returning. However, it looked to me like they were coming in at top speed, and since we didn't have any food, I was afraid they would become too aggressive. I quickly retreated to the beach to watch from a distance, while Molly, wanting a first-hand experience, stayed in the water. She didn't get the reception she was expecting – a dolphin nibble but no damage. I told Molly later that I had heard that dolphins bite to express their love.

In Australia, there were many interesting rock formations and trees different from ones in the U.S. We drove inland and "surfed"

Linda at the Big Wave Rock, 1987.

on a rock that looked like a big wave. Driving through the landscape in the U.S., you might see deer running across the road, whereas in Australia, you see kangaroos. And since they boinged, they appeared right in front of the car out of nowhere, and then quickly boinged out of sight. We did see some roadkill where they didn't boing in time to escape.

Linda with Rodney the Roo, 1987.

We stayed at a park where visitors were allowed to interact with the kangaroos. When we got up the next morning, we visited with Rodney the Roo and were allowed to pet and feed him. We also got to hold koala bears. They feel very cuddly when they wrap their arms and legs around you, although we were told they really don't like to be held even if they seem to be holding on to you. Not wanting to insert myself into the life of a reluctant koala, I was quick to put mine back in the tree. On our way back to Perth, we stopped to eat at a pub, where both Molly and I agreed that we felt very out of place. The mentality of the men seemed to be a cross between the wild, wild west and the 1950s before women's liberation. While watching the news, I was struck by how backward and ignorant their politicians seemed. I was reminded of that when Trump became president here in the U.S., and it seemed that we, too, had gone back in time.

From Perth, we flew to Sydney where we were invited to stay with David and Helen Proud. David was one of the VPs of Wilson Learning, managing the Australian branch of the company. He took us out on his boat for a day so we could enjoy and appreciate Sydney and the Opera House from the water. After sightseeing in Sydney and enjoying David and Helen's hospitality for a few days, we headed north to Brisbane to meet up with one of our fellow travelers on the Harmonic Convergence trip.

MT. BEERWAH

When Molly and I were in Egypt, we made friends with Ian who invited us to stay with him in Brisbane. We took a train from Sydney and arrived at Ian's in time for our Thanksgiving. We tried to find a turkey so we could show Ian and his friends how Americans celebrated Thanksgiving, but there was no turkey to be found in all of Brisbane. We satisfied ourselves with chicken, and everyone seemed to go along with a substitute turkey and all the trimmings.

On our second day in Brisbane, Ian took us on a strenuous hike up Mt. Beerwah, altitude about 1800 feet. After an hour or two of scrambling over a rocky trail, we ended at a rockface wall that should have taken 15-20 minutes of climbing to reach the top. Ian, who had climbed Mt. Beerwah many times, was leading, followed by Molly. I was bringing up the rear. Molly and I had been traveling for three months and had climbed several mountains, so I'm sure Ian thought of us as seasoned hikers and climbers. I always thought of myself as more athletic than Molly, but she surprised me that day by scrambling up the rock face like a mountain goat and conquering the summit. Piece of cake, I thought, as we progressed. If Molly can do it, so can I. At that moment, I wasn't taking Molly's longer arms and legs into account.

I made out fine for the first three-fourths of the rockface. None of my previous mountains had a rock face, but I was remembering the instruction I received years ago from my friend Jonyl on my very first rock-climbing experience. While driving up the California coast in 1980, we had stopped the car to enjoy the view when he invited me to climb a large boulder nearby. He said, "You have to plan strategic placement of your hands and feet: Make sure you know where your hands and feet go before you make your next move."

I was proceeding nicely until, all of a sudden, I realized, with a sinking feeling, there was no handhold for my next move. I hadn't been paying attention. Oh, there was a handhold, but I couldn't get a firm enough grip on it without stretching beyond my comfort zone. I searched for other possibilities without success, and thought, what now?

Ian and Molly had already reached the summit. I heard them enjoying the views while they waited for me to make an appearance. But I was frozen, clinging to the rockface, willing my body to merge with the mountain. "Be one with the mountain." I remember thinking, "OK, I'll just rest here for a minute, and gather my wits about me. If Molly made it to the top, so can I."

Then my knees started to tremble, betraying my self-talk. Any instruction that I gave my body went unheeded. I simply could not move, except for the trembling. I started to get angry with Ian for taking a couple of novices on a rock-climbing trail as steep and dangerous as this one, and with no ropes. And following that line of thought, I realized that Molly didn't appear to be a novice, and I fully saw the benefit of having an extra inch or two in the legs and arms. She had climbed like a pro with nary a pause.

I began to speculate just how long I would be able to cling to the rockface before my arms and legs gave out completely. How would I fall when that happened? Would I just let go, lean back and free-fall to the bottom of Mt. Beerwah? I considered the thud my body would make as it landed, and then the 100 or so feet of bouncing and tumbling that would be involved before my body came to rest. Or, I might not lean back at all, but just let go and slide down the side of the mountain, trying to grab hold of something on my way down. Neither appealed as a viable option.

Even with thoughts of my death lurking in my consciousness, I tried to stay calm by breathing and reassuring myself that soon I'd find the courage to reach, and my body would surely begin to respond to my commands. At the same time, I realized it was becoming an urgent situation. I needed to find that courage sooner, rather than later, or I would not be involved in the decision-making process at all. Muscle failure and gravity would decide for me. I communicated my dilemma to Ian and Molly, and, from time to time, I heard them calling down with words of encouragement, "We have confidence in you. Come on. You can do it."

The moment was finally at hand. I reasoned that I had two choices, either one of which could end in my death. Falling would be a certain death, and reaching? Maybe I had a 50/50 chance of survival. I could stay there until my strength gave way, and falling, I would surely die, or I could reach for that meager handhold, trusting that I could use it for leverage to reach the summit. Over and over, I considered my options, but in the end, there was really only one choice, especially given the strong life urge I had. And I didn't want to mess up Ian and Molly's day or end my around-the-world-trip at the bottom of a sacred site.

Once more, I gave the command, "Stretch out and reach for the handhold," and surprisingly, as though someone had turned on a switch, my body obeyed. I grabbed it and found it to be more generous than I previously thought. It held, and I was able to move my foot to the next foothold, reach for the next handhold, and finally crab my way to the top of Mt. Beer-

Linda and Molly after conquering Mt. Beerwah, Australia, 1987.

wah to many cheers and shouts of, "You made it. We knew you could do it." I was alive. "I did it," I thought. When I wondered aloud how we were going to get down. Ian quickly solved that problem by showing us an easy descent path.

From Brisbane, Molly and I traveled to Koranda and found a small apartment on the beach for a couple of nights. We went on a tour boat to snorkel around the Great Barrier Reef where my inability to swim came back to haunt me. Even with flippers, I was unable to make headway, so dear Molly, the consummate friend, took my hand, and pulled me out to the reef where I could float on the surface and enjoy the colorful display of sea life below.

ULURU

We went next to Ayers Rock, the most sacred of all the sites in the country. Uluru, as it is called by the Aboriginals, is one of the most impor-tant indigenous sites in Australia and is listed as a UNESCO World Heritage Site.  At an altitude of 1,141 feet, it is the most recognizable landmark in the country. The area around the formation is home to an abundance of springs, waterholes, rock caves, and ancient paintings. Archaeological findings east and west of the rock indicate that the area was settled more than 10,000 years ago.

Due to time constraints, Molly and I decided to make the strenuous two-hour, steep climb to the top of Uluru rather than the four-hour hike around the perimeter. Back in 1964, a chain was installed to help people make the climb, for which we were grateful. I stopped many times to catch my breath on the way up, and oh, what beautiful views in all directions from the top. The descent was as challenging as the ascent. I clung to the chain and simulated a Charlie Chaplin stance and side-stepped most of the way down. Since the 1930s, thousands of footsteps have eroded the red surface of Ayers Rock, but, in 2017, the Aborigines were finally successful in banning climbing by tourists and locals. After October 26, 2019, there have been no more footsteps on Uluru.

We headed back to Sydney where we visited with Helen and David a few more days before Molly left for Minnesota and I left for Hawaii. I would visit my Santa Fe friends, Wendy and Michael, who were now living on Maui.

9 | Hawaii

Wendy and I worked together at the IT Group in Santa Fe. Wendy was with me when we helped rescue two men whose truck went off the mountain road before Easter Sunrise service. Wendy also led me out of Santa Fe back in April on my way to the west coast. While I was traveling around the world, Wendy and Michael moved to Maui, got married,

Friends Wendy, Michael, Linda, Maui, 1987.

and made their home in what felt like a tree house. It was so relaxing just being with familiar friends after eight months of travel. I felt as at home with them as I felt with myself.

One of the highlights of my stay with them in Kahului was taking the Road to Hana to visit a mutual friend and fellow Eagle John Romaine. The 52-mile drive averages 25 mph due to the 620 mostly hairpin curves and 59 bridges, 46 of which are one-lane bridges. Also known as the "Divorce Highway," the road can take a toll on one's nerves, and it has caused quite a few arguments among some couples. Traversing along the edge of many sheer cliffs, it is the longest rain-forest highway in the U.S. The waterfalls and black sand beaches and huge waves along the way are spectacular.

We were on our way to have Christmas dinner at John's and had promised to bring a cooked turkey. However, when we got ready to cook the bird, the oven was too small to accommodate it. After calling John with our dilemma, he arranged for a pilot friend to meet us at the airport to pick up the turkey and fly it to Hana where John would cook it. Having never cooked one before, we gave him instructions over the phone, to be ready by the time we arrived later that afternoon. The Road to Hana can take 2-4 hours, depending on traffic and the weather. It ended up taking us a little over two hours, and there was no divorce. John had done a wonderful job cooking the turkey, and Christmas dinner was delicious.

John's Balinese house was a work of art, a cross between a ship and a flying saucer. Tucked in a hillside, it overlooked the bay, so I felt like I was on the bridge of a ship when I stood on the deck that surrounds the front and sides of the house. John fell in love with the architecture when he visited Bali a few years earlier. He purchased the house in Bali, oversaw the building of his house there, then had it dismantled piece by piece, numbered, and shipped to Maui. In his little Toyota pick-up truck, he made many trips, back and forth on the Road to Hana, to the docks to pick up all the pieces of his house, and then reconstructed it on his lot in Hana. After his third or fourth trip, he called the Toyota PR/Advertising people and told them what he was doing with his little truck, and they came to Maui with a crew and filmed his trips using the footage for a TV ad.

John also had a wonderful cave on his property. Accessed by walking down a path to the beach, it was a wonderful place to meditate and chant. John invited us to spend the night so we would not have to tackle the road at night. I was given the loft overlooking the bay. Feeling like a queen, I wrapped myself in a cloud blanket and felt blessed to be surrounded by such beauty and love.

The next day, John took us to a black sand beach, and we ran into his friend Kris Kristofferson. Ok, I admit I was a little star-struck, but when he and John started talking about making a movie of Tom Robbins' book, *Still Life with Woodpecker*, I thought it might be something I would like to work on. It was the time in my life when anything was possible, and it felt like the most natural thing to be sitting on a Maui beach talking to Kris Kristofferson about making a movie. John left for the mainland the next day to meet with Tom Robbins to talk about movie rights. Later that week, John picked me up at the L.A. airport since he was still in the states. Unfortunately, movie rights to the book were tied up, so there would be no movie making for me.

It was late at night when John drove me down Rodeo Drive. The empty but brightly-lit streets and all the flashy consumer goods in the windows made me a little sick to my stomach. In the countries I traveled, there could be hordes of people in the dimly-lit streets, the shop owners sitting on chairs in front of their darkened stores. The owners turned the lights on only if someone wanted to go inside to shop or make a purchase. I have to say that it was more of a culture shock coming back to the U.S. than it was when I arrived in the third-world countries five months previously.

I cannot remember where I stayed in L.A., or how long, or who took me back to the airport. It's just a wonder how the mind works – or doesn't. I do remember arriving at the Albuquerque airport feeling a sense of accomplishment: eight countries in five months, a complete circumnavigation of the earth, approximately 45,000 miles from Albuquerque, always traveling east to return to Albuquerque. I was forevermore a global citizen. Jill, Leslie, and Molly were waiting at the gate with a sign with my name, Linda Hope – just as Kia and I used to have a sign waiting for Larry whenever he traveled. I was showered with confetti and hugs, and it felt wonderful to be surrounded by these loving friends welcoming me home.

During one of the few days I spent in Santa Fe, when Leslie and I were on errands, I happened to see a 1983 blue Toyota Cressida with a for-sale sign in the window. We waved the driver to the side of the road, and I made a deal to buy the car on the spot. We took it to my trusty Santa Fe car mechanic for an inspection. After he reported it sound, we went to the bank, signed the papers, and, two days later, I was on my way to Atlanta in my new car.

PART FIVE

MAKING MY WAY HOME
(1988-98)

Tony, Clif, Linda, Ellen at Uncle Bobby's, Gainesboro, Tenn., 1990.

1 | RETURN TO ATLANTA (1988-89)

This was my second time settling in Atlanta, but it would not be the last. After four years away from my family, I wanted and needed to be close to my children again. Clif, 22, had just graduated from Georgia Tech with an engineering degree and was working for an insurance company. Ellen, 24, had married Michael Flynn in 1986, had graduated from the University of Georgia in 1987, and was now teaching kindergarten north of Atlanta. Tony, 25, now worked for UPS.

While I was living in Santa Fe, I had tried to get all of them to move out

Joy Rollins and Linda, 1993.

there with me to no avail, so I would have to make the move to be with them. I arranged to stay with my friend, Joy Rollins, who had a two-bedroom apartment just a couple of miles from downtown Atlanta. Joy was the friend who accompanied me on my move to Santa Fe four years earlier.

TURNER BROADCASTING AND PLANET LIVE

My first order of business was to find a job, one that would make a contribution and be on purpose in my life (having a world that works for everyone with no one and nothing left out). I set my sights on Turner Broadcasting. I met Ted Turner's girlfriend J.J. Ebaugh on several occasions while I was still working with Larry Wilson in Santa Fe and at several gatherings in California. As another fellow Eagle, she was happy to hear from me when I called, and we were excited to see how we might work together. We agreed to meet for lunch.

It didn't take her long to tell me that Ted wanted her to travel more with him, which would require her to hire someone to assist in managing all the proposals that came through her office, trying to get Ted's attention. We agreed that I would read and sort through the project ideas and present the ones I thought would be feasible to J.J.

At the time, Ted was giving her an allowance of $2,000 a month to spend however she chose. He still paid her credit card bills, travel expenses, and any other luxuries, so the $2,000 was pocket change for her. She worked it out with him that she would pay me $1,000 from her allowance if he would agree to pay me $2,500 a month, plus benefits, from his Turner Plantation account.

I stayed on at Joy's apartment, both of us enjoying our renewed friendship and easy living arrangement. I was able to visit with my children on weekends, and even Tom (now my husband) came once for a visit when he had business in Atlanta. I soon got in touch with Claudia, recently separated from Joe Teagarden. She was on her own again which left her free to become my best friend.

When we weren't working, she was either at Joy's and my apartment, or I was at hers. We got together every week to watch the TV series, *Lonesome Dove*, went to the comedy club in midtown every weekend, and often went out for breakfasts and dinners. Our favorite snack was caviar and creamed cheese on crackers when we were playing Scrabble or watching TV. We were living high on the hog. Once, we went to an Avatar training program and were in danger of being thrown out for laughing hysterically when the facilitator introduced herself by saying, "I am an Avatar."

I settled into my job at Turner Broadcasting and my life in Atlanta as though I had never been gone. J.J. had met Barbara Marx Hubbard and Hazel Henderson at the Eagle's Reunion when I was working with Larry Wilson, and it wasn't long before we invited them to Atlanta. Continuing with the networking theme, we wanted to discuss how we might work together to elevate the level of consciousness in the world.

All of us held the belief that TV could be better used for educational purposes. To that end, we came up with the idea of a TV series highlighting the people and organizations who were helping to turn around environmental degradation. J.J.'s job was to talk Ted into accepting the series into TBS programming at a time when it was difficult to get funding for environmental-type programs. Usually they had to be bundled with other more popular shows. Ted agreed to include the series in scheduling but insisted that we get our own advertising. We had our work cut out for us. Our working title was *Planet Live*, changed a few months later to *Earth Beat*. We finally settled on *Network Earth* because Ted believed that, in the future, there would be a TV network devoted entirely to environmental issues.

Shortly after starting work at Turner Broadcasting, J.J. asked me to attend a conference at the Windstar Conference Center in Colorado. The Windstar Foundation was an environmental education and humanitarian organization founded by John Denver and Thomas Crum in 1976. We thought some of their programs would tie in nicely with our new endeavor. J.J. planned to go, but Ted wanted her at his Montana ranch with him, and pointed out that she had hired me so she would have more time to spend with him.

We flew in Ted's private plane, and they dropped me off in Snowmass, where I found my own way to Windstar, staying in the room J.J. had arranged for herself. I saw John Denver on stage at a concert in Tahoe back in 1981, and this time, I got to see him up close, talking to someone about wanting to be the first civilian in space. I also attended a presentation, *Fear Forward*, given by his wife, Cassandra. What I have remembered her saying these past 30 plus years is what her grandmother always told her: "Whatever it is you fear the most, do that first."

The keynote speaker was Mikhail Gorbachev, who gave a talk on Glasnost and Perestroika. Having lived through the Cold War since 1947, we had hated the Russians for more than 40 years, and now we all were experiencing a breakthrough to a relationship of peace. During the standing ovation after his speech, 30 or 40 children came into the auditorium from all directions, singing *Last Night I had The Strangest Dream*, and surrounded him on the stage. There wasn't a dry eye in the house, and there were even a few sobs as we all sang along.

> *Last night I had the strangest dream I'd ever dreamed before.*
> *I dreamed the world had all agreed to put an end to war.*
> *I dreamed I saw a mighty room. The room was filled with men.*
> *And the papers they were signing said they'd never fight again.*
> *And when the papers all were signed and a million copies made.*
> *They all joined hands and bowed their heads and grateful prayers were prayed.*
> *The people in the streets below were dancing round and round.*
> *And guns and swords and uniforms were scattered on the ground.*
> *Last night I had the strangest dream I'd ever dreamed before.*
> *I dreamed the world had all agreed to put an end to war.*
>
> *Written by Ed McCurdy*

The promise of increased transparency and openness in the USSR was in alignment with the world peace theme of Harmonic Convergence just a year earlier, and here it was, in full view. Out of the mouths of babes, the children said it all.

Ted Turner was the first person I personally knew who owned more than three properties. He had six! In the late 80s, his main residence was an apartment on the top floor of CNN Center, an easy elevator ride commute to his office. He also had a private lake property an hour north of Atlanta, which he and J.J. generously offered to me to use when they weren't there. I took them up on that offer whenever I had friends and family visiting from out of town. They also had a love nest in Big Sur, perched on a cliff overlooking the Pacific Ocean. I heard that he gave that to J.J. when he married Jane Fonda.

They vacationed at his Montana ranch near Bozeman, at his southern plantation near Lamont, Florida, and his beach house on St. Phillip's Island. Accessible only by boat, St. Phillips Island is a 4,680-acre barrier island on the South Carolina coast between Hilton Head and Edisto Beach.

One weekend, I was invited along with Carolyn Kleefeld, a poet friend of theirs from Big Sur, to accompany them to Ted's island retreat. Carolyn was staying at the lake house, and Ted's head of security, a man he had known since childhood, was supposed to pick her up and meet us at the airport for the flight to Beaufort, South Carolina. They were late, Ted

Linda and J.J. with Ted at his island retreat, 1988.

was furious, and J.J. and I knew it. Everyone within earshot knew it. When they were half an hour late, he called his office and told his secretary to get in touch with his head of security and to tell him he was fired. I felt terrible for the guy because I knew he had a family, and nobody wants to get fired on a Friday afternoon. When they arrived, Ted raked his employee over the coals and reiterated that he was fired, causing more embarrassment for everyone. Mouth of the South was a good nickname for Ted. Eventually, we boarded the airplane, taking our uncomfortable feelings with us.

Our flight was met by Jimmy Brown, Ted's personal cook, along with Ted's dog. Jimmy was a wonderful man and a great cook who had been with Ted's family since Ted was a teenager. Whenever Ted buys a property, he builds a house for Jimmy, designed to make both their lives easier and happier. Accompanied by Ted's dog, Jimmy travels by SUV to Ted's vacation destinations, meets him at the airport, and prepares all the meals for Ted and his guests.

When he met us in Beaufort, Jimmy had purchased all the food and supplies we would need for the weekend and drove us to the ferry. The boat trip took about half an hour, after which a three-mile drive along a shaded roadway brought us to the house. The drive took us through a beautiful maritime forest that closely resembled the woodlands where Native Americans had lived and early colonists settled hundreds of years ago. Ted told us he paid $55,000 a year to maintain the island and a five-bedroom house. His family only used it 2-3 times a year.

That first evening after dinner, I got up the nerve to tell Ted that his behavior at the airport was troubling to me.

"How would you like to be in his shoes, going home to your family after being fired on a Friday night?"

"Oh, that," he laughed, "I have fired him a hundred times over the years. He knows I didn't mean it. He'll be back at work on Monday."

It was definitely a different management style than the one I had grown accustomed to with Larry. A highlight of the weekend for me happened the next day at the beach. We got close enough to walk alongside a giant loggerhead turtle making her way back to the ocean after laying her eggs on the beach.

After giving a billion dollars to the United Nations in 1997, Ted, with a net worth of 2.2 billion, is the fourth largest landowner in the United States with two million acres. Always the conservationist, his goal was to create a "conservation land trust" with his children that would ensure that his properties would "remain safeguarded in perpetuity." After owning St. Phillips Island since the late 70s, Ted sold it, at a fraction of its appraised value, to the state of South Carolina to be part of the state's park system. The house can now be rented for $12,000 for five days, or, if you want the entire island to yourself, the price tag will set you back $20,000.

Occasionally, after work, J.J. and I met Ted for dinner at one of the CNN Center restaurants. One evening, we grew tired of waiting for him, so we decided to order. We were just finishing our meals when he finally showed up. He announced that he had been talking to his financial advisor who told Ted that he just made the billionaire mark for the first time. While I was trying to grasp exactly what that meant, the waitress brought the dessert tray. When J.J. and I were trying to decide which ones we wanted, Ted told the waitress to bring us one of everything. I guess that's what being a billionaire meant – you could have one of everything.

Network Earth was starting to gain some traction. J.J. was making presentations to her California friends associated with the movie industry. She started hiring people away from lucrative jobs with the promise of being part of a project that would make a difference in the world. Ted moved our offices out of CNN Center to a building in mid-town, next to I-85/75. Not as glamorous, but we felt that we didn't have someone looking over our shoulders. However, I became increasingly uneasy with the number of salaries we would be responsible for with no budget to pay them. J.J. kept saying it would all work out; I didn't think she was being realistic.

J.J.'s relationship toward me started to change. She became more standoff-ish, not sharing information or including me in decisions. When J.J. brought someone into the project to hold a position that I thought had been intended for me, and she promised to pay them twice what I was making, I decided that our time together had run its course, so we parted ways.

I made plans to go to Santa Fe for a month to explore my next course of action. Leslie's mom, Jane Larsen, offered me her guest house in exchange for looking after her property while she was on a trip. Santa Fe was again offering me a soft place to land, and it was the perfect environment for me to sort out what I wanted to do next. I had a contact in the movie industry that could turn into something, and I had been recommended to former astronaut Edgar Mitchell to work with his organization, The Institute of Noetic Science.

Claudia helped me pack my possessions into my blue Toyota Cressida. I said goodbye to Joy and my kids, and headed west again, back home to Santa Fe. I stopped in Texas to visit Ruth Ann, and she decided to jump in the car with me for the rest of my westward journey. Traveling is always better with your big sister riding shotgun.

2 | BACK IN SANTA FE (1989-90)

It was easy to settle into Jane's beautiful, wooded oasis compound. The guest house I was staying in had been the studio of Will Shuster, who was an integral part of the artist community starting in 1920 when he moved to Santa Fe. Shuster is best known for creating the burning of Zozobra, a tradition that still continues. Originally, building and burning a scarecrow-type effigy of Judas was based on an idea from the Yaqui Village, indigenous people in the valley of the Río Yaqui in the Southwestern United States. The ritual represented burning and ushering out all the community's gloom before beginning the yearly festival. It was my first Zozobra, and the practice seemed ideal for my purposes, burning away the old so I could be free to pursue my future.

I soon got in touch with Butch Crouch, a friend from my early marriage days in Pittsburgh, back in the early 60s. He moved to Santa Fe shortly before I left for my trip around the world and was now working as a bartender at an Italian restaurant owned by Bruce McEachern. Bruce retired from the San Francisco Police Department a year earlier, moved to Santa Fe to be near his mother and sister, and bought Babe's restaurant on Canyon Road to pursue his dream of being a restaurateur.

Bruce McEachern and Linda, celebrating at Babe's restaurant, 1989.

While visiting with Butch at the bar, he introduced me to Bruce, and we hit it off immediately. The idea of leaving Santa Fe evaporated when Bruce and I decided to pursue a relationship. After several months, we looked for a place to live together, and true to Santa Fe's bestowing good house karma, we had the good fortune of finding a house on the market located in the foothills north of Santa Fe. Since it was fully furnished, the owner was looking for someone to live in the house rent-free to keep an eye on the vacant property. Bruce, a retired detective, was perfect for the job. I hadn't even made a list to manifest this house. I couldn't have dreamed of anything so grand, so it was a gift.

The impressive 10,000-square-foot adobe mansion with an indoor swimming pool, hot tub, and steam room was on the market for $2,300,000. On the western end was the original three-bedroom main house and to the east the new addition, including the guest quarters/studio where we lived. It was a magnificent 40' x 40' studio with a kitchen on one side, separated from the bedroom by a banco wall. The living room with a kiva fireplace had a large window overlooking Santa Fe to the south; the Sangre de Cristo Mountains were to the east. I sat on the balcony every evening to watch the murder of crows as they made their way back to the mountains after feasting at the back doors of restaurants all day. I loved hearing their calls to one another as they shared their best

Linda and Bruce were caretakers at the Bill Bush House in Santa Fe, which boasted a light-filled studio that served as their living quarters, 1989.

stories of the day and called out impatiently to the laggards. The house included a guest room for our many guests. A maid came every week to clean the main house, and her husband tended the gardens and grounds.

One day, I got a call from the realtor saying she was bringing Jane Fonda and her entourage to look at the house. I watched from my desk at my end of the house as they all got out of their cars and made their way into the front door of the main house. Within two minutes, the door opened again, and everyone spilled out, got in their cars, and sped away. The realtor told me later that Jane took one look to the left, and one to the right, from the front door, declared, "This will never do." And out they went. That was as close as I ever got to meeting Jane Fonda.

I soon started working in Butch's restaurant, helping to manage and schedule the staff and overseeing the restaurant. We were open from 11 a.m.-2 a.m. or thereabouts, mainly because we also had a very successful bar attached to the restaurant. To keep our sanity, Bruce and I appreciated time off, together and apart. To that end, I set up a schedule so that I was managing by myself one day a week, Bruce was managing by himself one day a week, and Butch managed one day a week so Bruce and I could have a day off together.

3 | Travels with Bruce (1990-91)

One Sunday morning, a year into the restaurant business, I was mopping the floor in the men's bathroom and asked my-self, "You're 47 years old. What in the hell are you doing with your life? How are you fulfilling your life purpose?" Bruce and I discussed our situation, and he admitted that it had been a while since he had gotten any pleasure out of owning and managing a

Bruce and Linda in Key West, Fla., 1990.

restaurant, and definitely none from the bar. Neither of us liked catering to people who started drinking at 11 a.m. and kept at it until the bar closed. It was not what he thought it would be. We decided that it would be fun to travel, maybe get an RV and travel around the country.

Within two months, Bruce sold the restaurant and gave his old clunker car to a friend. In the spring of 1990, we gave up our beautiful mansion, packed up what we thought we would need for a year, and put our "stuff" in my storage space. We set off in my blue Cressida in April with a tent and camping gear in the trunk. It was the same tent Gary and I bought for our trip to Disney World back in 1978, several lifetimes ago.

Having already looked for an RV in Albuquerque, we planned to stop along the way to shop for just the right one. We didn't want a house on wheels, but rather a small camper, no longer than 20 feet. That way we could park it in a city parking spot, have the freedom to travel back roads, and we'd be closer to the ground, closer to nature. Having a small vehicle would encourage us to get outside more often. That's what we wanted after two years of being cooped up in the restaurant and bar.

We stopped in Phoenix to check out the dealerships, without success, so we headed north to see the National Parks – Monument Valley, Bryce Canyon, Zion, and Canyonlands. Alternately, we camped and stayed in motels along the way and leisurely made our way to San Francisco where Bruce's family lived.

We stayed in the Bay Area for a month, using his ex-wife's get-away apartment in Marin County as our base. From there, we scoured the area looking for our RV, and still couldn't find just what we wanted. It gave us time to visit Bruce's family and friends and to plan a general itinerary for our first month on the road. From San Francisco, we planned to wind our way up the Pacific Coast Highway, with stops in the Redwood Forest, Mt. Shasta, Crater Lake, and Mt. St. Helens.

Leaving San Francisco in mid-June, we took a month to cover Northern California and Oregon, which kept us moving to a new campsite every day. Tent camping was time consuming, and it soon became wearisome to set up the tent every afternoon and pack up everything the next morning. We mostly ate in restaurants, not wanting to take the time to shop for groceries, set up the camp stove, cook, and then clean-up. We continued looking for our home on wheels but were unsuccessful. We also visited with friends and relatives along the way, giving us a break from sleeping on the ground.

By mid-July, while we were staying with friends David and Herschel Kaplan in Seattle, we finally found the Grey Goose, the RV that was perfect for us. It was a 19-foot 1987 Ford Explorer with only 7,000 miles, and it was completely self-contained. I left the Cressida with my friends to sell, and, when we set out on July 22, three months after leaving Santa Fe, we felt like we were finally on our way. Victoria, Vancouver, and Banff were in our sights. After that, our plans were less specific and more relaxed.

We weaved back and forth between Canada and the northern states. We loved the Rockies, especially the Banff and Lake Louise areas. We made stops at Calgary, Toronto, Montreal – our favorite, and Quebec City. We spent time in Montana and especially enjoyed Glacial National Park. We went to a round-up and barbecue in Wyoming and saw the majestic Grand Tetons. In Idaho, we meandered along the Snake River, and in Sun Valley we went to the largest non-motorized parade in America. We spent fall touring New England and then on to New York City where we spent two weeks. I was surprised to find NYC so clean and friendly. Having lived there for a year in the early 60s, I dreaded going back, but I also wanted to visit my many friends there. The plight of the homeless is blatant and sets the mind spinning in quest of possible solutions for that flaw in our society. Sadly, it still spins. Due to a trend, starting in the 60s and 70s, to move psychiatric care from federally funded mental institutions to locally funded community care, many psychiatric hospitals were closed and the patients left to fend for themselves. There seems to be no will of the people or the politicians to make a change.

While Bruce lingered in Greenwich Village to attend some acting classes, fulfilling a 1950s beatnik fantasy, I spent two weeks in Salisbury with Mom

Bruce and Linda with the Grey Goose, 1990.

and Dad. They had sold the beautiful house in Snow Hill and moved to an apartment while I was traveling. They spoiled me with old family favorites – crab imperial, king fish, turnip greens, butter bean soup, sweet potato biscuits, clams, and oysters. I was in culinary heaven again. Betty joined us for a week, which gave us time to take Mom and Dad to Atlantic City, Mom's favorite haunt. I left them to go to Baltimore to visit my dear friend Carol Riley, where Bruce picked up the trip again. We set out for the Blue Ridge Mountains and visited friends Beverly and Jim Worsley in Virginia for several days. Then we went on to Tennessee, where we met my children at Bobby's for Thanksgiving. We planned to spend the winter in Florida, spring in New Mexico, and head back to San Francisco by the summer. All in all, it was a lovely trip. Along with living with Leslie Larsen, working with Larry Wilson, and my around-the-world odyssey, our trip across America was one of the highlights of my life.

What surprised me the most about the trip, aside from two people being able to live together 24/7 in such close quarters and not kill each other, was that there was no place, in the entire country, where Indians had not lived, yet we see them almost nowhere today. We wiped out an entire civilization and took their ancestral land, believing that we deserved it more than they did.

4 | LIFE IN CALIFORNIA (1991-92)

When we got back to California, after a year of touring the country, Bruce and I decided to move into the farmhouse on his 20-acre farm north of San Francisco, located between Petaluma and Santa Rosa. Beautiful Barb, my friend who handled my finances while I was traveling around the world and one of the "ladies in waiting" who

Bruce's Petaluma farmhouse on right, with barn in center of photo behind trees, 1990.

moved me into my last house in Santa Fe, was moving to Seattle and offered to bring my worldly possessions. She loaded my furniture and boxes from storage, along with my piano from Molly's, and brought them to me on her truck. That piano had made several moves, and I was glad to have it again.

Much to my disappointment, Bruce sold the RV, but got almost what he had paid for it – $23,000. I hoped we could continue taking shorter trips. Although Bruce was ready to stop traveling, I knew he would need to keep moving. He always had to have a project going, and it wasn't long before he decided to renovate the old chicken house/barn into a house. He spent the next year designing and building a home that was beautiful. It was two levels with an open concept living room/dining area/kitchen on the lower level, and the upper level boasted a bedroom with one wall of barn siding. The bedroom was large enough to include a spacious sitting area/study. There was also a loft, accessed by a ladder, for guests. Bruce soon rented out the farmhouse where we were living, and we moved into the remodeled chicken house/barn.

During this time, Claudia, who was still living in Berkley, and I spent a lot of time together. When I was still in Santa Fe, someone gave me a book on yoga, which I took with me on my trip across America. There wasn't much room to practice inside the RV, but I read, studied, and tried it out. Bruce left me at a campground outside Sun Valley, Idaho, while he went back to San Francisco to attend to business. Since I was by myself, I used that week to start my yoga practice. When I returned to the Bay Area, I immediately called Claudia and we signed up for a hot yoga class in San Francisco, the same kind that my yoga book taught. The book promised that if you did exactly what was prescribed every day, you would have a different body at the end of three months. I took on that challenge, spending an hour a day practicing yoga, and, as promised, it was the best shape my body had been in since I was a young girl on a horse.

About the time we moved into the remodeled barn, Bruce started taking an acting class, and I began thinking about finishing my college education, having completed only my freshman year. When he learned about a study-abroad program in France, Bruce decided to take advantage of the opportunity. He had always dreamed of studying in France, and this seemed to be the perfect time to check this off his bucket list. I decided it would be the perfect time to enroll in Santa Rosa Junior College with the goal of earning an associate's degree.

Above: Open concept living, dining, kitchen, 1991. Center: The cat came with the house. Below: Linda studying with a redwood tree serving as a backdrop outside the window, 1991.

BACK IN SCHOOL

I had not anticipated that in order to get an associate's degree, I was required to take a math class, one that required a firm grasp of algebra. I really couldn't claim even a loose grasp since my last algebra class was 30 years earlier in 10th grade. Math had always been my least favorite subject; I could never say I felt confident in my understanding. However, I *was* confident that I didn't want to spend a semester taking an Algebra 101 class I had already taken. I met with the professor, explained my situation, and he advised me to take it again anyway. He further offered that I would likely fail his advanced class without it. Despite his warnings, I enrolled in his class anyway.

When I got a D on the first test, I knew I had made a terrible mistake and called my good friend Kia in New York

Santa Rosa study group, plus Claudia, 1991.

and told her my plight. She and I had worked closely together when we were in Santa Fe, and she knew me fairly well.

"Linda, I know you," Kia said, "and I know that you will develop a strategy to learn the math you need, to not just complete this class, but to do well."

Kia to the rescue again. So, I took her advice. My strategy was to find some younger students who had a good understanding of algebra and who were willing to join a 50-year-old woman in a study group. Since they knew algebra and I knew how to learn, we became good study partners as well as friends. I felt somewhat confident after taking the mid-term exam, but a little nervous when the professor passed out our graded papers. Holding one test paper aloft, he announced that no one had ever turned in a perfect mid-term in his class before, and he said he had gone over this particular paper with a fine-toothed comb, looking for the error that he knew had to be there. I started glancing around the room to see who the lucky person might be, wanting to see their face when he announced their name. Then I heard him say my name, "Linda Hope." I was absolutely floored and so proud of myself when he placed the test with a 100 on my desk. Not only an A, but a perfect A. I finished the class with an A, the first I had ever gotten in math. Because of that success, I was only mildly disappointed when the school announced they decided to add a second math class for students to qualify for an associate's degree. I eagerly signed up and got an A in that one too.

MASTERPATH

Before Bruce left for France and before school started for me, we visited his mom in Santa Fe. While there, Don Dugas invited another friend and me for a walk in the Aspen Meadow. As usual, it didn't take us long to move to the topic of spirituality. I admitted that a few weeks earlier, during an intense experience of feeling alone in the universe and dissatisfied with my progress toward enlightenment, I had called out for a teacher who could take me to a higher level of consciousness. I had been studying Yogananda's works through the Self-Realization Fellowship and I wasn't as far along on the path as I knew was possible. Don began to tell us about the MasterPath, a new spiritual path he had recently undertaken. He called it the path of light and sound, and spoke of the teacher, Sri Gary Olsen, an American Sat Guru whose purpose in life is to lead readied souls back to their heavenly home. The more Don shared, the more I wanted to learn. Feeling as though I had come to the end of the road in my current spiritual endeavors to raise my consciousness on my own, I considered this might just be the teacher I was seeking.

Intrigued with everything I heard, I agreed to go to an evening seminar where I was even more impressed. Sri Gary related that the "MasterPath's objective is to re-establish the divine link between the mortal human and the immortal Creator. He defined the three essential requirements needed to achieve the heights of spiritual consciousness through the attainments of Self and God Realization – a True Teaching, a True Master, and the True Spiritual Current of Light and Sound. The same path followed by past saints and masters, "it is the scientific method of entering and realizing the Kingdom of Heaven while still living on Earth in the human body." By embracing this path, my life purpose would change focus from the outer world of duality to the inner world in order to recognize my soul and liberate it from the body/mind consciousness. I admit that it was a relief to shift my attention from the macrocosm to the microcosm. It is said that when the student is ready, the teacher will show up. I signed up for a course of study with the MasterPath.

While Bruce was in France, he left me in charge of the farm's two rental houses and several other rental properties he owned in the Bay Area. In my new endeavors, there was nothing I loved more than spreading out my schoolbooks and my MasterPath books and learning what they had to offer. I was in heaven, feeling on purpose and fulfilled again in my life. I was learning that we lived in the lower world, a world of duality, and my goal was to remember the Inner Master in every moment in order to rise to a higher level of consciousness. I looked forward to the daily spiritual exercises – "praying" without ceasing. I practiced putting my attention on my third eye where the soul and mind are knotted together and where the Inner Master resides. I was learning to discriminate between the mind and soul, and I turned over anything that was a worry to me to the Inner Master.

A year later, when Bruce returned from France, we decided that our relationship had run its course, so I moved in with a friend, Annie Cooke, from school. We were in a critical thinking class together, and we met with other classmates once or twice a week for dinner to discuss the reasoning skills we were learning.

When the professor heard about our meetings, he frequently joined us for dinner and participated in our interesting discussions. Annie and I were the "older" students but felt totally accepted in the group. Annie's beautiful home in the Santa Rosa hills was the tranquil setting I needed to finish out my school year. Again, I was surrounded by beauty and friends who loved and supported me.

While choosing my classes for the next semester, Ellen called on November 22, 1992, to tell me that my first grandchild, Eric Daniel Flynn, had arrived. As soon as he was born, I was drawn to be near him, wanting to be a hands-on Grandmom. Although I hadn't finished my associate's degree, I figured the credits I had from Santa Rosa, added to the ones I had earned along the way, plus the ones from my freshman year at Towson State would be equivalent to an associate's degree. So, I packed up my belongings once more and headed east, back to Atlanta to be near my children and new grandson. When I stopped in Santa Fe to visit my friends, Molly introduced me to Beth Davis, a new friend of hers who had a home in Atlanta, as well as one in Santa Fe. We hit it off and agreed to get together after I got settled.

5 | RETURNING TO ATLANTA AGAIN (1992-99)

THE MESCON GROUP

Before Eric was a month old, I was back in the Atlanta area, living with my son Clif in nearby Winder. This would be the first time he and I lived under the same roof since our family split up 10 years earlier. As soon as I bought another Cressida, I found a job as a project manager with the Mescon Group, a consulting firm in Midtown Atlanta.

I called Molly's friend, Beth Davis, who invited me to dinner. We stayed up until the wee hours talking non-stop. I ended up spending the rest of the night in her guest room. We got along so well that Beth invited me to share her beautiful home in Buckhead, just 10 minutes from work. I have always been grateful for the

Above: Mescon Group co-workers, 1992.
Below: Claudia, Linda, Beth, 1992.

people in my life who have made my life easy and fun. Beth was one of those people.

For only $500 a month, phone and utilities included, I had the basement apartment which may sound dark and dreary, but it was just the opposite. With 12-foot ceilings, two bedrooms and two bathrooms, it was beautifully furnished, and I had access to the exercise room. My living room had a stacked stone fireplace and marble floors around the carpeting. The living room opened to a sunroom/dining room with wall-to-wall, floor-to-ceiling windows that overlooked a magical lake and a goldfish pond. The apartment was absolutely stunning. Because my kitchen was small, whenever we had company, we always used her upstairs chef's kitchen.

Beth gave me a beautiful place to live while I started over one more time. She and I became good friends and still call each other at least once a year on our birthdays. Within a few months, the Mescon Group moved to downtown Atlanta, to one of the new high-rise buildings with fabulous views from our offices on the 16th floor of One Peachtree Center.

An MBA

During my last job search, I became more keenly aware that without that sheepskin, I couldn't even get interviews for the higher-level jobs I knew I could perform. I also didn't want to lose momentum toward getting my college degree, so I asked one of my business associates – the perfect one, it turned out – for advice.

"I am 50 years old, I still have to work to support myself. I'm not getting any younger. What advice can you give me on how I can fast-track a college degree?" I asked him.

It just so happened that he was an adjunct professor in a new Executive MBA program for working professionals at Kennesaw State College. He explained that they were accepting older, experienced students who might not have a college degree. So, I submitted the required dossier, outlining how my educational and work experience could relate to a bachelor's degree, took the GMAT, and was surprised when I was accepted into Kennesaw's 18-month executive MBA program.

My sister Betty loaned me half of the $18,000 tuition which I paid back after I got my degree. The program was team-based, which was like having another study group. Classes were held every other weekend, which allowed me to continue working. The company agreed that I could work four 10-hour days and have every Friday off. Each month, I used one of my free weekends to drive four hours to Cookeville, Tennessee, to stay with my aging parents who were living with Bobby. It enabled him and Jacques to get away at least one weekend a month. The other non-school weekend, I devoted to family visits and getting to know my grandson.

Since I was in college again and would soon have an MBA, I decided this would be a good time to get my teeth straightened – again. My parents paid $300 for my braces in high school, but over the years, my teeth drifted back to their preferred positions. I was determined to be an executive with straight teeth. The day I was fitted with the metal brackets, I thought I had made the

Left: Linda, George, Ruth, 1992. Center: Clif, Linda holding Eric, Tony, Ellen, 1993;
Right: Linda graduating with an MBA, 1995.

worst mistake of my life – total pain, and I felt like I was in prison, from the inside. This time the cost was $3,000. I also continued to study the MasterPath, with morning contemplations, constantly remembering my goal – self, soul, and God realization – and attending seminars in New Mexico and California.

It was a busy 18 months, juggling work, school, family, and maintaining a connection to my inner world, but I ended up with a master's degree without ever having received an undergraduate degree. As promised, it was the fast track. Now, I would be able to get interviews for just about any job I wanted. I had worked as a high school secretary, real estate agent, property manager, and restaurant manager. I had worked as an executive assistant in the corporate world and as a project manager in consulting, training, and development. I was excited to see where this sheepskin would take me.

Shortly after I got my MBA, the Mescon Group began to restructure and downsize their organization. When they announced that they would need to lay off one of the support staff, I raised my hand, volunteering to be the one. I decided there was no future for me with that organization. I wanted to be free to pursue my future, and I knew that looking for a job was a full-time job.

I set my sights on the Georgia Center for Continuing Education at the University of Georgia in Athens and sent them my resume. I followed-up with the director and the manager of programming and was informed that although they were having a hiring moratorium, Dick Field agreed to meet with me. It turned out that he was from the Eastern Shore of Maryland, growing up in Salisbury, just 25 miles from where I grew up. We talked Ocean City, steamed crabs, and my ex-father-in-law who had been his high school counselor. It is a small, small world, but it would be another three years before I would work at UGA.

The Georgia Academy

Due to the early 1990s' recession, it took a year to find my next job. Beth was selling her Buckhead house, and I moved from my beautiful apartment on the pond back to Winder into Clif's house. He was moving in with Paula, his girlfriend and future wife, so I would have the house to myself. While I continued my job search, I was able to find freelance work, doing contract work for a consulting firm and editing workbooks for the UGA J.W. Fanning Institute for Leadership Development. I also helped my good friend, Patti Wood, set up a home office. We were co-workers at the Mescon Group where she was a trainer and speaker and an expert in Body Language. We bonded at the sushi bar where we went for dinner every Thursday evening to discuss life, work, and spirituality. She had left the company when I did, and I continued managing her speaking engagements.

Above: Linda and Patti Wood, 1994. Below: Grandchildren Eric and Caroline Flynn, 1995. (Photo by Jill Fineberg)

On June 6, 1995, my granddaughter Caroline Elizabeth Flynn was born. I felt very honored when Ellen invited me to be in the labor room during Caroline's birth. It was lovely having a grandson and now a granddaughter. I was living less than half an hour from Ellen's house, so we were able to visit each other for an hour or so without a big production. As Eric and Caroline got a little older, they both came for weekends at Mom Mom's house. Each had their own room upstairs, and I was finally getting what I wanted – to be a hands-on grandmom.

My next job was director of program and training support with the Georgia Academy, a non-profit organization that delivered training programs to social workers. I finally needed my degree to get this interview, and the job requirements seemed designed to incorporate my particular skills in project and systems management, training and development, and, my favorite: staff development. I loved the job, I loved the people I worked with, and I soon fell into a rhythm with the hour commute into Atlanta every morning and afternoon.

I still believed it was the organization's responsibility to create an environment where each person could reach their potential, and this was my first real management position where I could test that concept myself. It was always shocking to me, in all the jobs I held, that upper management typically gave no thought to organiza-tional intelligence; they didn't

Co-workers at the Georgia Academy, 1994.

consider what information would be lost when someone left to pursue other opportunities. I felt it was important to save as much of that knowledge as possible, and my staff and I started developing job descriptions, performance standards, and policy and procedures manuals. It made training new employees easier and faster, and it gave the current employees a sense of pride in their jobs.

I also believed it was my responsibility to provide my staff with the tools to do their jobs. To that end, I asked every week in our meetings, "What do you need that will make your job easier." I always involved them in developing new systems to streamline their workflow and improve productivity. We also cross-trained employees so they could do each other's jobs, and when I left two years later, almost anyone in my division could have done my job.

GEORGIA CENTER FOR CONTINUING EDUCATION

In 1997, I finally got my long-awaited call from Dick Field at the Georgia Cen-ter for Continuing Education on the University of Georgia campus in Athens about a newly created position that was perfect for me. They wanted me to help them develop a new business outreach at the Gwinnett Center, a consortium of three colleges: Georgia State University, UGA, and Peachtree Community College. Located less than half an hour from my home, there were no more hour commutes to downtown Atlanta. I began setting up systems to assess the needs of local companies, and then developed, promoted, and administered those program offerings. I was a one-woman show, except for the teaching part. I always hired instructors for that aspect.

At 58, I finally felt like I had found the job that I would have until I retired. In just 13 years, I would be eligible to receive a 20-year pension because UGA would allow me to buy back seven years from the Baltimore County Board of Education. My greatest fear would not be realized, after all. I would not be penniless in my old age, living in an apartment with a cat and a single marigold in a dry pot on the windowsill.

I continued to study the MasterPath and found peace from the daily contemplations. I traveled to Albuquerque four times a year to attend MasterPath seminars. On one such trip, Claudia and I agreed to meet after the seminar and treat ourselves to a road trip. We spent a week completing the "Circle Tour," which included the National Parks in Utah and Arizona and touched on Colorado and New Mexico. Aside from the Route 1 Coastal Highway in California, this is one of my favorite road trips in the United States. I had first discovered it

Linda at Bryce Canyon, 1997.

when Bruce and I traveled in that area and knew I wanted more time to explore. Before the 2020-2022 COVID-19 pandemic, Leslie and I took the same trip and found that it never gets old. Highlights: Monument Valley, Canyon De Chelly, Bryce Canyon, Canyonlands, Arches, and Zion.

PART SIX

LIFE WITH TOM
(1999-PRESENT)

Tom and Linda, 1999

1 | A Love Story (1984-99)

I never thought I would ever say, "I'm moving to New Jersey," especially with the joy with which I was saying it. You see, I was in love and the heart wants what the heart wants. I was giving up the opportunity to ever have a pension, and at the age of 58, I was also giving up being near my children and my grandchildren. This was a beautiful love story for the ages, and everybody loves a good love story. It was a long time coming and it was most certainly better than anything I could make up.

Linda and Tom in limerence, 1999.

Have people asked you how you met your husband or your wife, or a beloved? I have asked that question a lot, especially while I was waiting for love to come my way. After my divorce, when I was 39, I assumed I would meet someone new, fall in love, and get married again. However, 17 years passed, and although I met lots of wonderful men, none of them was Mr. Right. So, I decided to stop looking, telling a friend, "Someone is going to have to come looking for me. Someone is going to have to ring my doorbell." Well, Tom didn't exactly ring my doorbell, but he did telephone me, so the ringing phone counts, right?

The first time I met Tom, I was on a business trip to Minneapolis in the fall of 1984. While staying at the Hotel Sofitel, I stopped by the registration desk to request a wake-up call when I overheard the gentleman next to me also asking for a wake-up call.

"You know, when you answer your wake-up call, you will be greeted by a woman with a French accent saying, 'Ze croissants are in ze oven," I said to him.

He laughed, we introduced ourselves, and chatted for a few minutes. His name was Tom Jenkins, a Training Manager for DuPont in Wilmington, Del., and was on business in Minneapolis with Wilson Learning, the same company for which I worked. We said goodnight, and we each went our own way.

A few months later, when I was out at the ranch waiting for Larry to finish giving a tour to a guest, I looked up the hill and saw him with someone vaguely familiar. As they approached, Larry began introducing me to Tom Jenkins. We both recalled our chance meeting at the Hotel Sofitel the previous year. We talked for a few minutes and then, again, we each went our own way.

In the summer of 1985, Larry and his wife Molly and I were invited to a weekend party in L.A. at the home of Marilyn Ferguson , the author of *The Aquarian Conspiracy.* Her book described the network of people working to create a "New Age," a different kind of society, based on an expanded concept of human potential. As a result of her work, she drew an ever-widening group of minds, hearts, and resources of the most advanced thinkers from every corner of America. At this party, there were about 50 visionaries, writers, artists, and otherwise gifted people from around the country. And guess who showed up at the gathering for our third "chance" meeting? None other than Tom Jenkins!

Toward evening, Ecstasy was handed out, as was common at Marilyn's parties. It was still legal then, but on the verge of being criminalized. It had been used successfully in couples and family therapy, having the effect of breaking down the defensiveness and lack of trust that prevent honest and compassionate communication. We all thought it should be put in the drinking water throughout the world to give people a sense of how life was meant to be – accepting, expansive, inclusive, and caring. I had taken it a couple of times before and decided not to take it in this setting. Since it was a practice at such gatherings to always have a handful of people present who weren't high, I volunteered to be one of those guardians. This way, I could also keep a protective eye on Larry and Molly.

At one point in the evening, I found them in Marilyn's bedroom, talking and laughing with five or six other people. I saw Tom, alone, lying on the floor in front of the fireplace. I stood over him for a moment, looking down at him until he opened his eyes. And, then gently, I lay down on top of him, our hearts meeting, and I joined my breath with his. We stayed there, breathing together, for about 10 minutes, neither of us speaking, and then I got up and continued on my way. When we talked about that experience years later, we decided that I must have "marked" him then, as if to say, "I'll come back for you later."

A group of us, including Tom, met for breakfast the next morning, and from that time onward, we became good, albeit distant, friends. He lived in Maryland, and I was in New Mexico, but whenever he came to see clients in Albuquerque, we met for lunch or dinner. Whenever I went to visit my family in Maryland, we arranged to meet for breakfast or lunch. Once, he met me at the Baltimore airport and drove me to meet my sister Betty.

"He's in love with you. I can see it in his eyes," Betty said to me after he left.

"Oh, no," I protested. "We're just friends. Men and women have friendships now, and you see kindness in his eyes."

She did not believe my take on what she saw. Tom and I have determined that over the next 10 years, we saw each other about 7 or 8 times, and they were always heartfelt reunions.

We had been out of touch for about five years when I called him to tell him about a consulting project that I thought would be of interested to him. He was dismissive and rude. Undeterred, I told him I was working on my MBA.

"Why would you ever want to do that?" he responded. Tom, who had a PhD in chemistry, appeared to be turned off to the business world, and it was another five years before we spoke again.

On my 56th birthday, two weeks before Christmas in 1997, my phone rang. Tom called to wish me a happy birthday. He was looking through Christmas cards and came across an old one from me and wondered where I was and what I was doing. He called our friend Molly to get my number, learned it was my birthday, and used that as a reason to call. A few weeks later, he called again and told me that he was running for congress. He asked if I would be one of his campaign advisors.

"You ask such good questions," he said.

Over the next nine months, we spoke frequently, and fortunately, in retrospect, he lost the election. We continued to stay in touch.

About a year later, I was planning a trip to DC to attend a continuing education conference, after which I planned to rent a car and drive to visit my family, three hours away. I called Tom and left a message, inviting him to spend a day with me driving around the backroads of the Eastern Shore of Maryland to visit all the haunts of my youth. I also told him I was on a search for the best oyster stew I could find. It was a couple of days before he got back to me to make plans. He later told me that he waited so long because he knew his decision would somehow alter his life.

So, in January of 1999, after Tom picked me up at my brother's, we spent a lovely day meandering. We went to Stockton, where I grew up. We went to the family farm on Little Mill Road, and the renters invited us in the house for a visit. I showed him Red Hills on the Chincoteague Bay, a popular resort in the early 1900s, but now pine trees and sand fleas are the only thing that remain. While I sang him the song, *It Was So Easy Then*, I realized that being with him was just like being with myself.

We went to Chincoteague for lunch and found a decent oyster stew, however, not as good as my dad's. We went to Melbourne Landing where my family used to gather every year for reunions and picnics. He gave me three chaste kisses while I was standing on a railroad tie in the parking lot. Later, when we drove past a field of Canada geese, we stopped the car, and rolled down the windows so we could hear their cacophonous conversations. As we continued down the road, a flock of red-winged blackbirds surprised us as they took flight in front of the car. When we saw a for-sale sign on a farm, I jokingly said, "Why don't we just quit everything we're doing, pool our resources, buy this farm, and live out our days here?" We laughed, and he took me back to my brother's. We each went our own way, one last time.

After we returned to our homes, Tom and I started talking more frequently on the phone, sometimes discussing more personal aspects of our lives. I became aware that I was looking forward to his calls. On one such call, when we were talking about different kinds of relationships, I asked him how he would define our 15-year relationship.

"Let me think about it, and I'll get back to you," he said.

After hanging up, I chided myself, "What have you done? You don't ask someone to name or define something, because when they do, it becomes something different." So, I immediately called him back to retract my question, but there was no answer.

"Well," I said to myself, It's in the hands of the Universe." The next morning, March 9, 1999, approximately 15 years to the date, from when we had first met in Minneapolis, I opened my computer at work, and found this e-mail from Tom:

I studied an advertisement – for what, I do not remember – in the Continental magazine when I went to Mexico. The ad was based on a painting. It showed a standing couple, the woman holding a half pomegranate, and the man holding a pomegranate seed in position for the woman to eat. The essence of the message was that love requires the care, patience, and attention analogous to that need to feed the beloved an entire pomegranate, one seed at a time, without dropping a single one.

A serigraph of "Seeds of Desire" by Yuroz hangs in Linda and Tom's home.

Would you like another seed now, my dear?

"Oh my God," I thought, "a true romantic." And I responded:

Yes, yes, yes!
Yes, to starting the day right
Yes, to the image and the swoon it invoked
Yes, my dear...now

We soon arranged for Tom to come for a visit so we could more closely examine these new feelings we had for each other, to see if they were as strong as we each thought they were. He came for St. Patrick's Day week, and by the end of the first day we knew that we wanted to spend the rest of our lives together. We had to decide how we were going to make this work.

I was living in Winder, Georgia, working for UGA, while Tom was living in Hammonton, New Jersey, working for Patriot Manufacturing. For five months, we took turns, flying back and forth, visiting each other every other weekend. My granddaughter Caroline, four at the time, fell head over heels for Tom the first time they met. On their first visit, when Ellen brought the children over to meet him, Caroline immediately took his hand and led him upstairs. She was so confident that he would be interested in seeing her dolls and animals and where she slept. Of course, he followed wherever she led, and he read her a book while she cuddled in his lap.

Ellen told me later that when they were backing out of the driveway to go home, Car-

Above: Tom meeting Caroline for the first time, 1999. Below: Going-away party at Clif and Paula's, (back row) Tony, Tom, Michael; (front) Sheryl, Eric, Linda, Caroline, Ellen, Clif, Paula, 1999.

oline asked, "Is Mom-Mom going to keep that man?"

Ellen explained that he lived and worked far away, but he would be back to visit. Caroline replied, "Well, I think she should keep that man forever."

So did I! Over the next several months, every time I saw Caroline, she never failed to ask, "When are you and Tom going to get married?" Of course, I put her off one way or another, saying we hadn't decided. By August, love couldn't wait any longer, and I gave up my job, along with my last chance for a pension. We just wanted a normal life, to be able to read a book or watch TV in each other's presence. The limerence was just too much. After a beautiful going-away party at the home of Clif and Paula, we packed up my household in one of those you-pack-we-drive pods, said goodbye to my family, again. Hammonton, where Tom worked, was smack dab in the middle of the Garden State, where we found a comfortable two-bedroom cottage in the country, surrounded by blue-berry fields.

A year later, on Valentine's Day, Tom asked me to marry him, and of course, I said yes. We decided to wait to tell Ellen and the children until they came to visit over spring break. Before Caroline, five, could ask her marriage question when we met them at the airport, I told her that I wanted her to be the first person to know that Tom asked me to marry him and I said, "Yes."

She thought about it for a minute and then asked, "Are you going to have children?"

Slightly taken aback, I told her we really hadn't talked about that, and asked her, "What do you think?"

And she answered very seriously, "That's your decision. It's your body."

2 | NEW JERSEY (1999-2001)

I was enjoying not working, and at the same time, was eager to see what my next job would be. After a month in New Jersey, Tom invited me to have lunch with him and Joe Umosella, the owner of Patriot Manufacturing where Tom worked. When I told him about my work experience, Joe offered me a job managing the order entry staff of seven young women. It turned out

Country cottage, Union Rd., Hammonton NJ, 1999-2001.

that a million dollars' worth of errors a year fell on their shoulders, and he wanted me to remedy the situation.

Hammonton, population 20,000, was 35% Italian, and Patriot's office workforce was likely 50%. In the plant where the windows were manufactured, the workforce was 80% Hispanic. I noticed my Italian co-workers were loud, emotional, and fun to be around. It was also obvious from the start that they were very family oriented, and I enjoyed developing those relationships. From the beginning everyone was suspicious of me – Tom's girlfriend. They liked him all right, but they soon learned I knew nothing about making windows, so they naturally questioned why I was hired as a manager in a window company.

So, I focused on developing relationships, talked about helping them develop their potential, asked them what they really wanted to be doing. I met with my order entry staff as a group every week and asked the question, "What does management need to do to make your job better, easier?" When I met with them individually, I asked them what they thought the problems were, why were there so many errors. And I started making a list of what we needed to correct.

First, I developed a tracking system to reveal where the errors were coming from and why. The women hated it because it looked like I was trying to put the blame on one of them. However, when they started to see that I didn't want them to be blamed for something that wasn't really their fault, they all got on board. It was tough for me being brought into a manufacturing environment, my first foray in that industry. While it was true that I knew nothing about making windows, I did know about needs analysis and process improvement. I had to earn every ounce of respect I would get, not only from my small staff, but everyone in the company.

It didn't take long to reveal that the ordering process was haphazard. Customer service took orders from customers over the phone and gave a page of handwritten notes with the number of windows, window types, and measurements to my order entry staff, which they used to enter the data. Our first step was to develop an order form that included every possible window we made, with every option available. Custom windows had a special place for a drawing and space for all pertinent information. From then on, the order form was in the hands of the customer, and it would be incumbent upon them to give accurate information to customer service, who would be responsible for confirming the information before passing it on to the order entry staff. That, by itself, cut errors by 75%. My staff was no longer blamed for the errors.

The next solution involved moving from individuals to teams. Instead of each staff member having specific customers, we created teams where two or three workers shared customers. That way, more people were familiar with the types of orders and each customers' requirements. If someone had to be out sick or on vacation, those orders were familiar to the staff who entered them.

We also set up a cross-checking system where every order entered by one worker was double checked by another. By springtime, we reduced the number of errors by 95%, and I rewarded them by setting up a schedule where everyone, if they wanted, could work four 10-hour days so they could have a three-day weekend with their families during the summer. I had earned their respect. They loved me, and the company loved me. I have stayed in touch with one of the order-entry staff who is now a customer service manager in another company. She always thanks me for believing in her, even more than she believed in herself.

With our successes in Order Entry, Joe asked me to expand my little department to include Customer Service. They fit right into the team-based structure since they already worked closely with Order Entry staff. An awareness of satisfaction and accomplishment rode on my shoulders as I arrived for work each day. In less than two years, I found ways to save the company a million dollars a year in avoidable errors. I also successfully led the company through a physical move to a newer modern building – not just offices, but the entire manufacturing facility – with a total of $50 million in revenue and 500 employees.

During my first year at Patriot, we learned that talks were underway to sell the company to a conglomerate out of New York. We didn't know what changes were coming, but one day, shortly after the sale, all the women in the office stared in amazement as a half dozen men dressed in well-cut suits and turtlenecks, with great physiques and not a hair out of place, came strutting into the office. We joked that they were a cross between a Chippendale dance troupe and made-men in the mafia – we were in New Jersey, after all. Any day we expected them to present us with a flash mob. We were told these men would serve as sentinels, on the lookout for avenues of theft in the company. This was surprising information to staff because none of us had heard that products were missing or misappropriated.

It was after the buyout that Tom, VP of corporate development, and the security manager began to suspect that our trucks transporting windows to locations up and down the east coast were possibly used to smuggle contraband. He shared his suspicions with me after I told him about the Chippendale-made men. Maybe they had another purpose than what we had been told. It wasn't too long before the security manager was fired, given no cause.

After Tom proposed to me on Valentine's Day 2001, we started talking about when and where to have the wedding. Then we received an e-mail from my brother Bobby, which was also sent to brothers, sisters, cousins, nieces, and nephews, inviting everyone to a July reunion at the family farm that he inherited 20 years previously. The land and house were rented out during those intervening years, while Bobby and his partner, Jacques, were working in Tennessee. When they retired in 2000, they made the move to Stockton and now were ready to host a family reunion at the farm. Tom and I, less than two years into our relationship and newly engaged, started making plans to attend. When we saw all the favorable responses to the reunion invitation, the perfect guest list for our wedding began to take shape. The farm would be an ideal wedding venue. After talking it over with Bobby, he agreed, saying he would be honored to add wedding festivities to the family reunion.

Back at work, we were completing the massive company-wide move. As we were settling into our new environment, it appeared that the move was all worth the efforts everyone made to make it happen. My staff was happy in our new office workspace, a 50 x 50 square-foot open space separated by low office partitions. My staff told me several times how much they appreciated the new team approach to customer service. Each morning as I arrived, I stopped to say good morning to each group on my way to my office, asking if there is anything they needed from me. I loved being able to survey my entire domain from my windowed perch at the back of our workspace. One day, as I opened my to-do list to see what was on my docket for the day, my phone rang.

It was Rhonda Roche, the new VP of personnel inviting me to her office. Since the company had been sold, changes were happening every day, so it was not unusual for me to meet with her. She came to us from M.W. Windows, the manufacturing company that we were merging with, and it was their money that funded the move to our new location.

Rhonda asked me to take a seat, opposite her, at the conference table. With no lead in, she told me that I was being let go and that someone else would take over my position, effective today. When I asked her why, she said that I wasn't a good fit for the new organization.

I expressed my surprise, given my successful record, which I quickly summarized for her, to no avail. In addition, I was aware that she was a fan of Larry Wilson's programs and pressed her, "Explain to me how I'm not a good fit, if I believe, like you, that it's the organization's responsibility to provide an environment where each individual can reach their potential. That's what I've been doing. I thought that I was a perfect fit."

When she refused to answer my question, I admitted to myself that it was going to be useless to try to save my job. At least, I thought, Tom would still have his job and income. As if reading my mind, she told me that the manager of personnel was meeting with Tom, as we talked, and his tenure was ending, as well. I was rendered speechless.

One of the secretaries in personnel escorted me on my "walk of shame" to my office, along the wall rather than through the center of the customer service area. She instructed me to get my purse – just my purse. I could come back after hours, when all the employees were gone, to pick up my personal items. I could see my staff starting to stir in their seats, some standing up, all looking at me as I picked up my purse and exited my office. I heard them asking, "What's happening? What's going on?"

Their voices became louder and more demanding as I purposely led the secretary through them. I was instructed not to speak to anyone, and they were signaled not to speak to me. My head held high, I made eye contact with each person, but I obeyed the directive of not speaking. My escort and I left the barrage of questions and walked into the quiet hallway. I didn't speak to her either as I opened the door and stepped into the sunshine and fresh air. The door closed behind me, my escort no longer at my side. As I walked to my car, I could see Tom waiting for me. Our eyes met, both of us stunned by the realization that we had both been fired, especially after our mutual successes in the company.

Before we had a chance to speak, the door to the building was suddenly flung open, and Tom's and my staff poured out of the building. They evidently decided not to obey management's directive.

"What are they going to do, fire all of us?" they insisted. They were in as much disbelief as we were. "Why you? Anyone but you two? You have done so much for us and the company," they said as they gave us hugs and well wishes.

Several people from management came out and herded the wayward staff back into the building.

With their love and support still echoing around us, Tom and I looked at each other as incredulity began to give way to something that resembled giddiness, a lightness, a sense of freedom, suddenly realizing that we were free to go anywhere we wanted to go, that we could do anything we wanted to do. We would start over.

"Where do you want to go?" I asked.

"How about Athens, Georgia?"

We went home to our cottage in the middle of blueberry fields and started packing. We arranged for another you-pack-we-drive pod, and within a week, by the end of May 2001, we were headed south to our next adventure and finally home, at last.

3 | RETURNING TO GEORGIA ... FOR GOOD (2001)

MOVING TO ATHENS

Before I moved to New Jersey, I was working at UGA's Georgia Center for Continuing Education in Gwinnett County. Since my business frequently took me to meetings at the main center on the University of Georgia campus in Athens, I found it to be a charming college town with big trees shading the downtown streets. The Georgia botanical gardens were there, as well as the Athens music scene, lots of great restaurants, and of course the university. Located 70 miles northeast of Atlanta, Athens had a population of about 115,000, which included 25,000 UGA students. I checked out the real estate and found Athens to be a very affordable and livable community. I felt confident that Tom and I could get jobs at the university, and maybe I could get back on track to earn a pension. We would be relatively close to Tony and Sheryl in Dawsonville, Clif and Paula in Roswell, and Ellen, Michael and the grandchildren in nearby Jefferson. Athens would make the perfect midpoint as a meeting place for my family.

CATCHING UP WITH TONY

Even though the children and I always stayed in touch during the years I was traveling and living away from them, I missed out on a lot of their transition into adulthood. I'm sure that's true with many families. Children leave home after high school, go on to college or work, and make lives of their own. After Tony graduated from high school in 1981, he spent five years working for a funeral home and then tried his hand at real estate. Before marrying his high school sweetheart Sheryl Grey on October 1, 1988, he started driving for UPS. After 15 years

Tony and Sheryl on Oregon Beach, 2005.

of back-breaking work, Tony cast his lot with Sheryl's brother and dad and their company, VideoCraft. About the time Tom and I moved to Athens, Tony and Sheryl moved from Fayetteville to Dawsonville. In 2012, having gained experience as a videographer, Tony joined the syndicated TV show *Small Town Big Deal* as their cameraman. You can go to their archives on their website and see all the wonderful places and events they cover on their TV show.

ELLEN – TEACHER AND MOM EXTRAORDINAIRE

While I was living in Santa Fe in 1985, Ellen brought her boyfriend Michael Flynn out for a visit. A year later, I flew back east for their wedding on July 5, 1986. A year after that, just before I left for my trip around the world, Ellen graduated from the University of Georgia with a degree in early childhood education and started teaching kindergarten at Flowery Branch Elementary School. When she invited me to sit in on one of her classes, I was amazed at how adept she was at getting the little

Eric, Ellen, Michael, Caroline, Holden Beach, NC, 2011.

students to do what she wanted them to do. She was a natural. She and Michael bought a house on the outskirts of Jefferson just in time for their first child, Eric Flynn, born on November 22, 1992. That's when I got the call and decided to move from California back to Georgia, a move I thought would be my last. Caroline joined the family on June 6, 1995.

CATCHING UP WITH CLIF

Clif graduated from Georgia Tech in June 1989, ready to start his life on the fast track. By November, he settled into his first job, bought his first home in Winder, and married his high school sweetheart Tracy Wynn. Unfortunately, the marriage lasted for only two years. Clif put his focus on his career and now holds an

Clif and Paula with dogs, Roswell, Ga., 2015.

executive position for an insurance company. In December 1997, Clif and Paula Smalley married and bought a home in Roswell where they still live. Athens was the perfect place for Tom and me to live, with my three children living within about an hour's drive.

SETTLING IN ATHENS

Even before Tom and I left New Jersey, both Ellen and I had started looking online for places to rent. Surprisingly, she and I both came up with the same little 3-bedroom house available for a three-month sublease. We thought that would give us enough time to find jobs and determine where in Athens we wanted to live permanently. Ellen's in-laws, Connee and Bill Flynn, came over to welcome us to Athens and help us move into our new home. It was a delight to think about being able to spend time with my children and grandchildren again. Both Eric and Caroline, 9 and 6, spent one or two weekends a month with us, and we loved having them with us.

Caroline and Tom had a strong bond since their first meeting and always had the best time together. Their favorite game was following the instructions in the book, *How to Massage Your Cat.* Tom read the directions while they alternated turns being the cat and the masseur. Each massage direction was funnier than the next, pinching each other's lips shut, pulling their ears back until they snapped, tugging on arms, and directing a volley of rapid slaps to each other's back. The laughter was non-stop for the duration of the cat massages.

When the first Harry Potter book came out in 1997, Eric was only 5 years old, but it wasn't long before his mom was reading them to him. By the time he was 9, he was reading them on his own. When he started reading the series a second time, it piqued our interest enough so that Tom and I decided to read the books too. Over the next year, we took turns reading the entire set aloud to each other after we went to bed. That is, until the last book when the listener fell asleep too soon, and the reader kept on reading. We finished that one on our own. When the movies came out, we accompanied Eric and Caroline to the theater, enjoying them as much as the kids did.

Once we settled into our sublet, we also settled into job hunting, which is, by itself, a job. After we submitted our resumes to positions at the University of Georgia, we both were called for interviews. However promising, a moratorium on hiring was implemented soon afterwards. Sadly, UGA would not be our new employer because we couldn't wait. We each had gotten a severance from Patriot Manufacturing, but it would only carry us another couple of months, and we didn't want to dip into our retirement savings. I got in touch with Elaine Cook, an old friend from Turner Broadcasting days who was the communications and public relations director at Athens Regional Medical Center, one of the local hospitals. Since she was well connected in the community, I thought it would be a typical networking meeting. However, when I arrived for the meeting, she announced she already had the perfect job in mind for me.

One of the doctors at the hospital was in the beginning stages of pitching the idea of a holistic medicine venue within the hospital. Similar endeavors were being implemented across the country, but this was the first in Athens. Elaine arranged a meeting for me with Dr. Rich Panico, an internist with the hospital who was championing this new enterprise.

His path to holistic medicine started with internal medicine, then after seeing the connection between body and mind, he switched to psychiatry. When he developed chronic fatigue syndrome and was unable to perform his medical duties, all the doctors he went to said there was nothing they could do to help him. That's when he began to study and use functional medicine, as a way to heal himself. As he began to get better, other doctors in the hospital system started consulting him on their patient's medical conditions that hadn't responded to allopathic medicine. When they started having positive results, they began asking about their wives and their own problems. Consequently, with all the success stories, there were several doctors who were willing to incorporate a holistic practice into the hospital.

Rich and I hit it off during our first meeting and agreed to work together in this new undertaking. Because there was no budget yet to pay me, Elaine had to pull some strings, arranging to hire me in her department to manage special events, and then I could work with Rich's start-up project as an event. It would take her a couple of months to make that happen, and I kept busy while I waited.

MARRIAGE VOWS

During the three months leading up to our wedding on July 28, Tom and I were working with Kia, my Santa Fe friend and co-worker, to create rituals for our marriage ceremony. Kia, who moved to New York City to be closer to her daughters, agreed to officiate and help us plan a beautiful wedding. We

The wedding venue in the backyard of the Jones family farm, Little Mill Rd., Stockton, Md., 2001.

wrote our vows, which we agreed to memorize, necessitating many practice sessions in the weeks leading up to the ceremony. I would not advise anyone to memorize their vows; it was much too stressful – better to speak from the heart, I think. Even though we both went off script, it all worked out and our appropriate promises were duly spoken and recorded.

In addition to wedding planning, job hunting, and visiting with my family, Tom and I were also looking for a house to buy or rent when our 3-month sub-let was over. The agent showed us the house we currently live in, and since neither of us had a job yet, we asked if we could rent it instead of buying it. The owners agreed to take it off the market for a year, and we moved in just two weeks before the wedding. We planned to rent a vacation house in Ocean Pines, Maryland, to share with Ellen and her family the week before the wedding, so we had just a week to move and settle in before getting on the road to Maryland.

A year earlier, when Tom and I were at Bobby's in Tennessee, Tom handed my dad a note that said, "May I have your permission to wed your daughter, Linda." Dad took his time reading it, looked up at Tom, his eyes brimming with tears and a big smile on his face, saying, "Hah! You're the only one that's ever asked. The others just came and took them away." "Hah!" had always been Dad's signature exclamation.

At the time of the wedding, my parents had been living in an assisted living facility in The Woodlands, Texas for a couple of years. Ruth Ann, accompanied them to the reunion and wedding. Dad was returning to the home that his parents built when he was two. He remembers the wheat brushing against the side of the cradle when he was carried in it across the field from the Old House to the Big House. He grew up on Little Mill Road with his two sisters and brother, and when he was 10, he helped his grandfather plant the maple tree under which Tom and I would be married.

With Kia's guidance, Tom and I, wrote a beautiful wedding ceremony and created vows to seal the deal. We incorporated a Native American conch shell blown in the four directions by Kia, the reading of a poem about ancestors kneeling on sacred ground, a gong played at significant moments by my grandson, Eric, and a Quaker blessing ceremony to which our guests contributed.

Dad, 90, was hearing impaired, and we were concerned that he not feel isolated with so many family members around. We set him up in a comfortable chair under the tree with his notepad for people to write on and a laptop for the younger generation to type messages for him. I left him there to go in the house to get dressed for the wedding and lost track of anything that was going on outside.

I started to feel overwhelmed with helping our two flower girls – Tom's and my granddaughters, Rachel and Caroline – get dressed, as well as myself,

George "walkers" Linda down the aisle, 2001.

when my niece's girlfriend came into the room and took over the little girls. She fixed their hair with flowers and decorated their flower baskets. I was never so glad to see someone I had never met. She was a life saver that day.

As the first strains of *Duettino-Sidl'*, the aria duet of *The Marriage of Figaro*, wafted to my ears I walked onto the back porch. I watched the flower girls and ring bearer, my great-nephew Jack Overbeck, walk between the five rows of chairs and down to the altar. I walked down the steps and over to where my dad was sitting by himself in the back row under the maple tree he planted 80 years before. He must have felt a sense of pride and belonging, looking out over his seven children and their spouses, 16 grandchildren, and 17 great-grandchildren. His walker in front of him, ready to go, I tapped Dad on his shoulder and helped him to his feet so he could walk me down the aisle toward the only son-in-law who asked for the hand of any of his daughters. There was a moment of confusion when we got to the altar. We had not planned or practiced this part of the ceremony, and I sensed Dad wanted to do something more, but Clif stepped forward to help him get settled in the empty chair next to Mom in the front row, waiting for Dad's official duties to be over.

While we were planning the wedding, I told Caroline I was thinking about finding some poems or prose and asking guests to read them during the ceremony. She thought it would be better if they wrote their own poems, whereupon she went off to her room and came back to me with this:

> *Love never breaks*
> *Love is special*
> *Life goes on*
> *I hope you live as long as you can*
> *It is nice to have you together*
> *You are nice and*
> *I hope you live in peace*
>
> *Caroline Flynn*
> *July 2001*

During the Quaker blessing ritual of the wedding, when guests were invited to speak to the bride and groom, Caroline indicated she wasn't ready to read or recite her poem in front of 50 or so guests, so I recited it for her. When I was finished, I said I thought it was profound for a 6-year-old to write, to which Tom replied, "Or a 60-year-old."

My cousin Bobby McGee, a professional photographer, took pictures and gave them to us as a gift after the wedding. Tony videotaped our ceremony, which Tom and I have watched many times. Before Caroline's wedding in 2018, we watched all the wedding videos – Ellen and Michael's, Connee and Bill's, and Tom's and mine.

One of the dearest, most poignant moments of our ceremony was when Eric rang the gong. The reverberations were loud and clear enough for my dad to hear, and you can hear him say, "Hah!"

During the blessing ceremony, Tom and I stood up from our seats to greet Mom and Dad as they approached us. Dad took my hand in his right hand and Tom's hand in his left and brought them together, giving my hand to Tom in marriage. That was his blessing. That was what he had wanted to do when he delivered me to Tom at the altar – he wanted to place my hand into the hand of my beloved, fulfilling his duty of giving me away. This would be the last time Dad set foot on the land upon which his ancestors had knelt. Less than a year later, a month before his 91st birthday, my dad passed from this world.

Family in the wedding, 2001. Above: Flowergirls Rachel (left, Tom's granddaughter) and Caroline. Center: Grandson Eric sounded the gong during the ceremony. Below: George places Linda's hand in Tom's to "seal the deal."

Above: The Jones family, including Linda's parents, 6 children, 23 grandchildren and 3 great-grandchildren, 2001. Below: Tom and Linda's joined family, 2001. Photos by Robert McGeee.

4 | 9/11 Changed Everything

Once the wedding festivities were over, we returned to Athens to settle into our new rental house. Tom started to work with an associate from his consulting days, selling an educational product, and I was still waiting for Elaine Cook to work out the details so I could start working with Athens Regional Medical Center (ARMC).

A couple of months after we moved to Athens, we went to Columbia, South Carolina, to spend the weekend with my old friends Louise and Steve. We spent one afternoon hiking through the cypress swamp at the Congaree National Park. We took a lovely 2.5-mile hike through the wetlands, made especially easy by an elevated boardwalk. The day after we got home, I noticed that my feet were hurting, and they kept getting worse every day. I finally went to a podiatrist who said I had plantar fasciitis (heel spurs) and set up an appointment the following week to get cortisone shots.

On Tuesday morning, September 11, I set off for my 9 a.m. podiatrist appointment. I turned on the car radio as I drove down the driveway and heard that a plane had just flown into the North Tower of the World Trade Center. As soon as I got to the doctor's office, I told the staff there what I had heard. They turned on their radio, and by the time I went into the exam room, we all heard a second plane had flown into the South Tower. My head was spinning. What was happening? Was the world going crazy?

When the doctor stabbed the tender inside of my right heel with a needle, I thought I would die from the excruciating pain. There was no way I would give him access to inject the left heel. I limped out to my car and turned on the radio just as a third plane crashed into the Pentagon. My mind just couldn't hold what I was hearing about hijacked planes crashing into buildings.

When I got home, I turned on the TV to hear reports about a fourth plane crashing in a field in Shanksville, Pennsylvania. It's possible target was the White House. I spent the rest of that day sitting in my recliner watching TV, and, like everyone else in the country, tried to grasp what was happening and what consequences would follow. Over and over, they showed the planes crashing into the buildings in New York, and the bright flash of light at the Pentagon, caught by just one camera. Each time they showed the Pentagon, I could not see a plane or an entry point, only the explosion. Why couldn't I see

a plane? And the Pentagon roof over the area where the plane entered the building at 10:37 a.m., the point of impact, was still intact. How could that be? That had to have collapsed. I still was asking, "Why can't I see any of the plane?" To contribute to further confusion, the roof didn't collapse for 45 more minutes.

How could a plane have gone into the building without leaving its footprint where it entered and why didn't the roof collapse?

As I watched the horrible scenes playing over and over, I started to notice a pattern on the second day. Every time they showed the Pentagon with its lone flash of light, the feed immediately went to one of the plane's dramatic explosions as it flew into the World Trade Center. I never saw one Pentagon image that wasn't followed by an actual impact scene in New York, one where I could see a plane actually crash into a building, a flash of light, and an opening where it entered. I felt like I was being manipulated. I was also asking why we had only one view of the Pentagon? Surely, the safest building in the world had more than one camera pointing at it. Where were the videos from other vantage points?

I learned later that there were 85 cameras on the Pentagon, some of which were not working because of the recent construction, and all the other recordings were confiscated by the FBI and have never been released.

The first pictures we saw of the Shanksville crash scene created even more cognitive dissonance – because there was nothing there. We saw a few dozen men in hazmat suits walking around an empty indentation in the earth with wisps of smoke wafting about. No evidence of a plane crash. One news report announced the discovery of a second debris field about 6 miles from this site, and then we didn't hear any more about that. Two debris fields, 6 miles apart? How could that be?

But life goes on, and I went on with my mine. Like most everyone else, I went along with the accepted story of 9/11. I soon went to work at Athens Regional, getting involved in the business of setting up a holistic medical practice with no time to dwell on my questions and doubts. That ended about a year later when Tom and I went out to Santa Fe to visit Leslie. When we arrived at her house for dinner, she refused my help in the kitchen, saying she wanted us to watch a video, and then to let her know what we thought about it. We sat in her living room watching *In Plane Site*, a documentary of the events of 9/11, highlighting the absence of a plane at the Pentagon and in the field in Shanksville. The documentary affirmed that my cognitive dissonance as a result of my observations on September 11 were justified, and confirmed I had a right to expect a better story than the one we were being told.

According to FBI reports, two planes crashed – one into The Pentagon and one into the ground in Shanksville, and both immediately and completely disintegrated. Well, not completely because in Shanksville, they found an intact red bandana and an ID card supposedly belonging to one of the hijackers. And yes, most Americans believed it. But I remained skeptical.

Since that day in Santa Fe, I have spent many hours studying the events of 9/11, reading books, watching documentaries, and listening to panels of experts talk about the impossibilities of what we were told about 9/11. Much like the Kennedy assassination and the Vietnam War when we were given half-truths, no truths, and outright lies, we also were gaslighted about 9/11. I'm not here to convince anyone of anything, but for those interested in learning about the unanswered questions and possible answers, I highly recommend spending five hours to watch the comprehensive documentary *September 11: The New Pearl Harbor* by Massimo Mazzucco. This documentary summarizes 12 years of research and public debate on 9/11. All the most important issues in the debate are presented in full detail, showing both the positions of those who reject the official version, the 9/11 Truth Movement, and the positions of those who support it called "the debunkers." But I know what I saw. And what I didn't.

When I say 9/11 changed everything it was never more evident than when Bush declared "war on terrorism." I knew then that we would be at war forever, all while supporting the military industrial complex. I thought we should approach the 9/11 events as a crime, as we did for the first attack on the World Trade Center in 1993.

Air travel was dramatically changed making it nearly impossible to enjoy traveling. Anti-Muslim violence increased, giving us a new enemy to fear and hate. Surveillance was increased everywhere leading to NSA's unchecked ability to eavesdrop on American phone calls, text messages and emails under the premise of targeting foreign nationals suspected of terrorism. And, finally, we were safer...or were we?

5 | Establishing My Roots

The Mind Body Institute

Rich had already held a couple of community meetings to determine there were sufficient people in Athens interested in a holistic health center. When I started working with Elaine's group, I helped him hold formal focus groups and sent out surveys from which I compiled the results into a feasibility study. As a holistic healing center, our goal was to offer an array of services within three overlapping areas that comple-

ARMC marketing group co-workers, 2001.

mented each other: clinical services, educational programs, and research. We decided to call ourselves the Mind Body Institute, a resource for healing. We were creating a new department within the hospital – from nothing.

Having never worked in the healthcare industry, I worked with Elaine and other department heads to develop a budget in line with the hospital system. I even got to design my own job description as department manager, except we had to call it program manager. Tom jumped in to help us develop a business plan to go along with the feasibility study and the budget which we presented to management for approval. When I wasn't working on Mind Body Institute business, I helped Elaine's group coordinate special events for the hospital: Relay for Life, Christmas holiday activities, and a party for 2,400 employees. Elaine's group was great to work with and we always had a lot of fun.

After Rich, Tom, and I presented our business plan to management, our proposal was accepted, and our new start-up was becoming a reality. We were initially given office space in the Diabetes Center with treatment rooms in the Rehab Center one floor below. After we hired a secretary and a yoga instructor, we started offering our services and programs. As much as we wanted a space outside the hospital campus, we could not turn down the 4,500 square feet of free-rent space in the basement of the Imaging Center.

We designed the area to include a waiting room and front office, six treatment rooms, two medical consulting offices, three administrative offices, and a large activity room to hold yoga and meditation classes and educational programs. We had ample room to offer all the programs and services we had planned. Since the hospital was also covering the cost of decorating, I worked with the interior design coordinator to choose furniture, carpeting, colors, and wall decorations. It was a softly lighted, peaceful environment for people to come for healing.

Since we were a new medical practice, I also had to develop protocols, determine pricing, analyze staffing needs, and develop credentialing requirements. It also fell on me to find and interview office personnel, salaried and contract healthcare providers, and program facilitators. Additionally, I wrote their job descriptions, as well as our policies and procedures manual. We developed a brochure that showcased our clinical services and educational programs. To assist Rich in identifying patient issues, I developed an intake form that covered every possible complaint a patient could have. By the time we moved into our new space, we had two secretaries, two massage therapists, a rolfer (bodyworker who specializes in connective tissue), an acupuncturist, and a yoga instructor, along with Rich, our medical director and healer extraordinaire, and me as the everyday problem solver extraordinaire.

When Rich saw patients, no matter what their complaint, the first order of business was to put them on a detox program. How can anyone expect to get better if they are eating foods containing toxins? Everyone got a copy of *20-Day Rejuvenation Program* by Dr. Jeffery Bland, the founder of the Institute for Functional Medicine. Every patient who followed the 20-day program felt better as a result of giving up sugar, wheat, dairy, pre-packaged foods, and a few other items. In fact, patients felt so much better that they wanted to stay on the diet. Many patients had not felt so good in years. Each month, we held a covered dish supper for our patients who brought new "toxin-free" recipes for everyone to sample. It was truly an honor to be in the presence of healing through natural means.

There were many accomplishments, of which I was proud, but the one that was most gratifying was the Intern Program that we developed in coordination with the UGA Honors Program. Most, but not all our interns, were pre-med students who were interested in pursuing careers in holistic medicine. They were an inspiration. I put them in charge of developing and leading our outreach program, coordinating research programs, and assisting with the yoga and meditation classes. They not only did whatever was asked of them, but offered their own suggestions on what we could do to create an even better healing environment. They were so young and so smart. I am still in touch with two of them on Facebook. One went into holistic medicine and the other went into marketing.

In addition to developing and monitoring our budget, I was also responsible for tracking and reporting our financial progress to management. As we built our programs and services, it became necessary to develop outcome study initiatives so we could show which programs and treatments were the most successful. UGA became our partners in that endeavor, as well, and I turned over gathering the data and writing the reports to my clever interns.

The biggest downfall to the Mind Body Institute was the limit on how many patients Rich could see in a day. First appointments were scheduled for two hours and subsequent appointments for one hour. Compared to a regular doctor who sees 20-30 patients a day, Rich saw five or six. I kept saying we needed another holistic doctor, but aside from the acupuncturist, we never went in that direction.

I was 58 years old when I started with the Mind Body Institute, and I was sure I would work there until retirement. Everyone told me that no one ever gets laid off from the hospital. However, in the fall of 2003, we learned that 70 ARMC employees would be laid off because of reduction in Medicare and Medicaid payments. I got caught up in the last-in-first-out policy and lost the job I thought I would have indefinitely. The only thing to do was update my resume and start looking for my next job.

GOODBYE, DADDY

Shortly after I started working at ARMC, I had a dream about my dad. He was getting in the back seat of a car, leaving without saying goodbye. I ran after the car calling for him to stop so we could say goodbye, but the car continued moving away from me. With the uneasy dream still on my mind, I went to the office.

Later that morning, Ruth Ann called me to say that Dad was in the hospital with dehydration and possible renal failure. Not wanting him to leave without saying goodbye, I immediately made plans to go to Houston the next day. I sat with him in the hospital for five days, feeding him because his hands were too shaky and helping him sit up and walk. He was optimistic and was eager to do whatever was necessary to get better.

When the hospital staff deemed him ready for rehabilitation, he was admitted to the rehab facility located next to The Forum Assisted Living where he and mother were residents. I left for home on the second day of his rehab. Unfortunately, his body was unable to persevere without the intravenous fluids he had been given in the hospital, and on March 23, 2002, Dad died. I was on my way home from the airport when Betty called on my cell phone to tell me of his death. When I got home, I wrote this poem:

Goodbye Daddy, I love you

I dreamed you were driving away
You were leaving without saying goodbye
Overcoming my anger and hurt
I waved goodbye and called, I love you
As your car disappeared from view.
I awoke with a start, and went on with my day
I was not surprised to hear Ruth Ann's voice on the phone,
"He's in the hospital. The doctor doesn't think he'll live."
There was no hesitation. I went to sit by your side.
No leaving without saying goodbye.
As I sat by your bed, I listened to you breathe
It sounded so labored and difficult
When you awoke, I rubbed your feet and your legs
And put lotion on your dry, bald head
I fed you your meals because your hands were too shaky
You looked at them and laughed.
While napping, you saw a floating barge of oysters
"$25-$30 a bushel," you called out.
"Hurry, see if your sister brought her purse."
You were so disappointed when you awoke and realized
You were in Conroe, Texas – not on the Chincoteague Bay.
"What's he using to pull the house," you asked, while napping
"A bulldozer? Who's driving? Go tell him he's going the wrong way.
We're to the Boston's and we'll have to go in the back way
It's wrong. See if he can't turn around."
You thought you were on Little Mill Road where you grew up.
You were eager to sit in the chair by your bed
You were eager to walk farther than the day before
You wanted to get well. You wanted to get strong.
You wanted to go to a seafood restaurant for your 91st birthday celebra-
tion.
You wanted one more molasses cake.
It was time for me to go
Time to leave your side
You were better they said
I kissed your cheeks

I kissed your head
We said goodbye.
I got the call from Betty
When I was on my way home from the airport
I was grateful for the dream
That brought me promptly to your side
No leaving without saying goodbye.

BUYING A HOME

Before I lost my job at the Mind Body Institute, Tom had started teaching chemistry at Athens Technical College, so I knew we would be able to pay the bills, which was a good thing, because a year earlier we had bought the house we were renting. The owners took it off the market when we signed a year's lease, and, as we had agreed, they put it back on the market after a year. We started

415 McDuffie Court, Athens, Ga., home of Tom and Linda, 2001.

the house-hunting process again, and after seeing 25 houses, we could not find anything we liked better than the house we were living in. Prospective buyers came to look at the house from time to time, and one evening, we overheard a young couple and their realtor writing a contract.

As I eavesdropped, I heard they were offering less than the listing price, and they had some contingencies. We called our agent immediately and asked her to write up a full price, no-contingency offer, and present it to the seller that night. She did, we got the house, and we have been living here for 23 years, the longest I have lived anywhere. Tom and I joke that we paid $143,000 for a house just so we wouldn't have to move again. We were paying $800 a month rent and our mortgage payment was $850. After I found my next job, we were able to double up on the payments so we could pay it off before we retired.

Yes, we were seriously thinking about our retirement plan. When we first started talking about marriage, we agreed that our number one priority would be to save money for a secure retirement. Buying a house was part of the plan, but job insecurity was not helping. I think what helped us the most during that time was our ability to remain optimistic, always knowing that everything would work out to our satisfaction. This…or something better.

Never did I think we would live in this house for 20 years. It was convenient being just a couple of miles from Connee and Bill Flynn. It was comforting to know we had each other to count on and it also made it easy for Ellen and Michael and their children. Connee and I started calling ourselves the co-grandmothers and took turns hosting holiday dinners. After Bill died in 2010, Connee and I started going to the beach for a week every summer with Ellen's family. We looked forward to spending time with the children and with each other. Connee and I became good friends.

After we purchased the house, Caroline and Ellen were

Above: Connee and Linda at the beach, 2011.
Below: Feline friends Lulu (left) and Patches.

over visiting when we heard a lot of commotion from under the house. Unbeknownst to us a feral cat had found a way into our crawl space and had two kittens. Tom and Caroline crawled under the house and pulled out two kittens, maybe 5 or 6 weeks old. They put up a big fight, but we were able to set up an enclosure on the back porch where they could look in the window of the back door and see all the fun human activities. In that way, hopefully they would want to become members of our household. In time, after much cuddling and cajoling, Patches and Lulu finally succumbed to domestication leaving us with two wonderful cats for nearly 15 years.

ATHENS-CLARKE COUNTY GOVERNMENT

Within a week of my leaving the Mind Body Institute, I saw a job posting online that described qualifications that I already had, as if I had been in training to do this particular job. If I had made a list of the responsibilities I wanted, that job description would have matched it. I knew that all my skills would be utilized in this job for the local government. By this time in my work history, I had worked in the healthcare industry, manufacturing, non-profit, education, and in the corporate world in consulting and in training and development, so why not add government to the list of industries I had served.

At the age of 62, I was hired as the program coordinator in the Transportation and Public Works Department for the Athens-Clarke County government. It wasn't exactly on my radar for fulfilling my life purpose of having a world that works for everyone, but it was perfect for my spiritual purpose and inner training. Besides, it paid the bills, and if I could last for 10 years, I would get back on track to have a pension.

I worked with managers in five divisions – Traffic Engineering, Streets & Drainage, Stormwater Management, Roadway Construction, and Fleet Management – to help them improve performance. Together, we evaluated their workflow processes and developed systems to analyze and manage man-hour utilization, revenue and expenditures, inventories, and employee training. I was also responsible for developing yearly budgets for each of the divisions, in addition to the budgets for 20-25 roadway and stormwater construction projects. I loved working with these men, and just as I had gained the respect of my co-workers in manufacturing, I was able to do that again working in a government agency.

It didn't take me long to realize that every time someone left our department, their knowledge went with them. That was my cue to start working with each employee to create a task list for their position and procedures for each task. That way, each division would have a policy and procedures manual that also served as a training manual for each position. I was amazed that it had never been done before, but I was glad I could make that contribution. I suppose I could say that I was helping to make the world work, in that regard. It was my legacy with each job I had.

One interesting project that I oversaw was the Sidewalk Program. Whenever someone from the community requested a new sidewalk, I entered the information into our sidewalk database that we used to keep track of existing sidewalks and to prioritize new requests. I went out in the field to gather information based on 25 criteria, such as length, type of roadway, speed limit, how close to schools, population density, etc. We usually had enough money in the budget to construct about 2 miles of sidewalk each year, and about 10 miles were requested, so it was important to select those that needed it the most.

I also oversaw a new initiative – getting Athens designated as a Bicycle Friendly Community. I had to demonstrate which requirements we had already achieved, such as number of miles of bike routes, and identify the hurdles we needed to overcome. Then I had to show the headway we made each year in improving our status to advance in the Bicycle Friendly endeavor.

Another rewarding and creative project was putting together a booklet that showed the yearly accomplishments of our department. Using before, during, and after pictures of construction projects that I had taken during the year, I wrote summaries of the projects to report and demonstrate our activities. All this information was laid out in a 12-15-page magazine that went to the mayor, the county manager's office, and other department heads.

I absolutely loved my work, and I enjoyed the people I worked with, but the person I had the most difficult time with was my boss. I admired his taking a chance and hiring a 62-year-old woman, so kudos for that, but he had a temper he could not, or would not, control. He yelled, not only at his staff, but even at citizens who disagreed with, or didn't understand, one of his policies or decisions. I tried to spiritualize my interactions with him, but he would have tried the patience of Job. The only reason I stuck It out for 10 years was because I wanted that pension. It helped that my office was in a different building, away from him, and I didn't have to see or hear him every day. Since he was rude to everyone, I learned to not take what he said to me personally, but he put that to the test many times. Although he was extremely smart and knowledgeable, he was less than an exemplary manager. It was such a departure from my experiences in other jobs, especially my work with Wilson Learning and Larry Wilson.

During my last year in the job, he berated me and sent me home one day, "Without pay!" he yelled as I walked out of the office, making a bee line for human resources. After I explained to my HR representative what had transpired, she asked me what I thought should happen as a result of his behavior. I considered the action I thought would help him the most to become a better person and a better manager. I recommended that first he be required to go through anger management classes. In addition, I asked that he be required to apologize, in the presence of everyone, to me and to all the employees who heard him yelling at me. To HR's credit, he was required to do all those things. I also was paid for the day he sent me home "without pay," and also for the next day that I took off, just because. He got the last word though as those "in power" often do. He retaliated by moving my office downtown across the hall from his office. I was within earshot of him for a rough six months, giving me an opportunity to shower him with kindness and respect every day. Luckily, I was able to finish the second half of my last year back in my own office.

At the age of 72, when I finally retired, I was happier to get out of his orbit than I was to stop working. It was a relief to know I'd never see or hear him again. Looking back on my interactions with him, I feel sure that I missed an opportunity to grow more in a spiritual sense. I must have forgotten to apply my favorite saying, "Someone always holds the key to our understanding on a higher level" to him. If I were being tested, I'm pretty sure I failed.

Two years after I started working for the county, Tom and I decided to bring my mother to Athens to live out her days with us. She was still living in the assisted living facility near Ruth Ann in Texas when it was determined that she needed a higher level of care and would be transferred to their Alzheimer's unit. Since it would be twice as expensive as assisted living, we knew she would run out of money in less than a year. Tom and I thought we could find a caregiver during the day when we were at work and stretch her money to cover several years of care. I called Ruth Ann, who agreed with our proposed plan. She packed up Mother's possessions and was delighted to accompany her to Athens and pass the caregiver torch to her youngest sister.

6 | A DAUGHTER'S PROMISE

The first time I heard about Alzheimer's disease was in the 1970s, when Ruth Ann and I, in our 30s, visited our parents in Snow Hill. Our 56-year-old mother told us about a TV program she had seen about the disease. As a life-long worrier, she was not too keen on losing her identity, along with her memory. We laughingly said she needn't worry, because if she had Alzheimer's, she wouldn't know it, or if she knew it, she wouldn't remember it.

As we sat around the kitchen table, drinking coffee and smoking cigarettes, Mom fretted about who would take care of her and Daddy when they got old. Ruth Ann and I both chimed in, assuring her that we would take care of her, but the

Ruth Ann (left) and Linda promised to take care of their mother Ruth when she got old, 1972.

boys would have to take care of Dad. We reasoned that he had been a difficult father when we were little, yelling a lot and belittling us whenever he didn't like something we had done, or the way we had done it. We thought Mother would be a piece of cake, compared to him.

When we affirmed our willingness to be her caregivers, she took it a step further by opening her desk next to her place at the kitchen table. She took out a piece of stationery and wrote a contract, "We, Ruth Ann and Linda, do hereby promise to take care of our mother, Ruth McGee Jones, when she gets old." Lines were drawn by each of our names for us to sign, which we did. How could we not? We had promised.

MOM AND DAD MOVE TO TENNESSEE

Twenty years later, in 1992, after Mother had two strokes and Dad had been diagnosed with Parkinson's, Bobby offered them three rooms and two baths in his home in Cookeville, Tennessee. Even though he was raised by our Jones grandparents and Aunt Bessie and Uncle Mervin, and even though he had not signed the "promise," my brother was the first one who stepped forward to give our parents the security of a home with family, where they lived for seven years. None of us thought for a minute that either of them would live that long. Also, none of us counted on the changes that would occur in Mom and Dad as their hormones fluctuated in the aging process. My mom,

Ruth's 80th birthday at Bob's house in Cookeville, Tenn. Standing from left: Bob, Dale, Ruth Ann, Robin, Linda. Seated, George, Ruth, Beth, 1994.

who had always been the buffer between Dad and us children, took on a more dominant and argumentative role, while Dad became docile and grateful, agreeable to anything we suggested for his care.

The first indication that anything was amiss with my mother was when she started telling us about the little red men who rode their bicycles out of her clock, which sat on her bureau across the room from her bed. As they proceeded to ride along the chair railing around her room, she would remark, "Aren't they the cutest little things?" I sometimes would lie on her bed with her and look for the little cyclists, but they did not make an appearance for me.

We thought it might have something to do with her glaucoma, or perhaps she had been dreaming. But, when she told us about the fish she had seen flopping on the floor of her bedroom, we chalked that up to her medications or a dream because she seemed relatively normal in other ways.

Mom and Dad Move to Texas

When Bobby retired in 2000 and felt he had fulfilled his familial responsibility, Ruth Ann agreed to having Mom and Dad move to Texas. She found The Forum, an assisted living facility 10 minutes from her home in The Woodlands. I always admired Ruth Ann for not bringing Mom

Ruth Ann with parents Ruth and George on a lunch date in The Woodlands, Tex., c. 2000.

and Dad into her home, knowing the disruption it would cause for her husband and family. My sister was a great support for our parents. She visited them every day at their apartment, took them to doctor's appointments and shopping, managed their finances, and did their laundry. Even though they were not living in her home, she fulfilled her promise with devotion, love, and good humor. Mom and Dad were always included in all the holiday celebrations and all the birthdays associated with Ruth Ann's having three children and six grandchildren in the same community.

MOM'S DECLINE

Although I called my mom from time to time, after Tom and I got married, I started calling her every week. When I heard Tom call his mom every Sunday, I thought it was a sweet thing to do. During one of my weekly phone calls, Mother interrupted our conversation and started talking baby talk to someone in the room with her. When I asked her who she was talking to, she said. "I don't know who he is, but he is the cutest little thing." We discussed if he might be the grandchild of one of her neighbor's. We ended the conversation with my suggestion that she call someone who could help the child find his family. However, as the year progressed, the cute little boy gained a sister, and the two of them would frequently "be in my mother's care" when I called. Sometimes, she was worried because she didn't know where they were, "I'm afraid they have gone down to the barn and could get hurt." My sister and I decided that she was definitely hallucinating. Maybe it was her medication. Looking back, we just didn't want to admit that it was Alzheimer's.

On the occasion of my marriage to Tom in 2001, Ruth Ann accompanied my parents from Texas to the Eastern Shore of Maryland where they had lived all their lives. Bobby had moved from Tennessee back to the family farm when he retired, and it was there that Tom and I said our vows. And it was there Ruth Ann stayed with Mom and Dad and realized something was muddled in our mother's mind.

One day, Mom was standing at the kitchen window looking across the field at the county road at the end of the lane.

"That's funny," she reflected, "there used to be a river there, where we played when we were kids."

Thinking she was confused, we assured her that this was the house Dad's parents had built in 1913 and where he had grown up. She soon let us know that she knew exactly where she was, and what she was talking about. While it is true that she had once lived in a house on a river when she was a child, it was clear now that she was confusing the past with the present.

While Ruth Ann was helping Mom get ready for Tom's and my wedding ceremony, I overheard her tell my sister that she just didn't understand why Bertie, her sister who died six years previously, would marry such an old man. Later, Mother approached me directly and asked me why I was marrying an old man. I reminded her that my name was Linda, not Bertie.

"Linda?" she said, looking wistfully in the distance, "That's nice. I had a daughter named Linda."

When they returned to The Forum, Ruth Ann reported that Mom started taking pictures off the walls and putting them in

The Jones family, after Linda and Tom's wedding; back row: Linda, Dale, Sonny, Bobby; front row: George, Ruth, Betty, Ruth Ann, Robin, 2001.

suitcases, along with her clothes. One night, she poked my dad with a pen, woke him up and told him she had called Buster, her brother who had been dead for eight years, who was coming to take them home.

The next day, Ruth Ann took her to the doctor who gave the dreaded diagnosis: Alzheimer's. The staff began making arrangements for her to be admitted to a nearby Alzheimer's facility. When Ruth Ann arrived to drive her to her new place, she found Mother saying goodbye to her friends, telling them, "Don't worry. I'll be back. I am going to beat this."

After three months in the new facility, one of the nurses told my sister, "Your mother does not have Alzheimer's. She does not belong here," so back she went to The Forum. For the safety and well-being of my father, Mother was now housed in her own room, doubling the cost of their care. It was determined that she had age-related dementia, not Alzheimer's. As far as Mother was concerned, though, she had beaten Alzheimer's.

When I went through her papers after she died, I found a notebook in which she had written, "Alzheimer's, Alzheimer's, Alzheimer's. This is really scary." This was very touching to me, realizing that she went through that fear alone. My mom had been afraid of the boogieman, gypsies, monsters in the sea, and thunderstorms when we were little, probably since she, herself was little. When there were storms, she woke us from a sound sleep, got us all out of our warm beds, and brought us downstairs with her, huddled together against the thunder and lightning. And, when we went to the beach, she warned us away from the monsters that lived in the ocean.

She told us many stories of her time in the Alzheimer's facility. She told us how she had taken care of the "children," who had followed her to the new facility. In one of her notebooks, I found notes that she had written to them.

Ruth, seated, and her daughters from left: Ruth Ann, Linda, Betty in front of the buffet that stored George's ashes, 2002.

When you get back, stay here and wait for me.
I have gone to lunch.

According to my mother, the staff had "wild sex parties down in the woods," which she thought was disgraceful. Back at The Forum, she was glad to get "the children" away from all that debauchery. I began to dread my weekly calls and any talk of the children because I just didn't know how to respond. My sister always tried to keep her grounded in reality, but that strategy just wasn't working for me since reality seemed to agitate her.

When my dad died in 2002, we children decided to keep his ashes in an urn until Mom died. Then we could put both their ashes in a cremation box for two and bury it in the family plot. We did have a memorial service for him, which Mom attended. Many times afterwards, when Mom expressed her annoyance that Dad hadn't come home yet, Ruth Ann would remind her, "Remember Mom, Dad died last year," to which Mom would indignantly reply, "Well, nobody told me!"

There were other times when those synapses would connect, allowing her to remember that Dad had died. Then she fretted that he had not been buried, and she'd ask, "What are we going to do about George?" We told her that he was happy where he was, his ashes sitting in an urn on Bobby's buffet, in the farmhouse on Little Mill Road where he grew up.

Mother began to accuse the residents and staff at The Forum of moving her room while she was at lunch or dinner. Returning to what she thought was her room, but on a different floor, she would walk into the room of another resident. That naturally upset the resident, and Mother was mad that someone else had been put in her room with their furniture. Staff took her by her arm and showed her that she was on the wrong floor and lead her to her room, a floor below. Even though all her furniture and possessions were there when they arrived a few minutes later, she insisted that staff had just moved everything back, and no amount of reasoning could convince her otherwise.

Many incidents told the story of her losing her grasp on reality, but the morning Mother came down to breakfast with her slip on the outside of her dress, the Forum staff decided that she needed more daily assistance and determined she needed to be in the "Memory Unit." It was twice as expensive, and her already decreasing nest egg would be gone in a year.

MOM MOVES TO GEORGIA

Tom and I had "the talk" and determined the best course of action was to bring Mom to Athens to live out her days with us. Since we both worked, we would hire a companion/ caregiver to stay with her during the day, and we would be "on duty" the rest of the time. That way, her money would last a little longer, and I would be able to fulfill my long-ago promise, in writing, to take care of my mom when she got old.

I called her and invited her to come live with us and she accepted! In a way, it was a little like getting braces when I was in graduate school getting my MBA. If I was going to be miserable, I may as well go all the way. I was 64 and had eight more years to work if I was going to get a pension. I figured if I was going to be working, I may as well take on the care of someone with dementia.

Tom and I moved our king-sized bed into the much smaller guest room across the hall and gave Mom the master bedroom. We bought her a new bedroom suite with a double bed and dresser, and a new sofa. We had a walk-in shower with grab bars installed in her en suite bathroom, and we built a wheelchair ramp off the back porch to give her easy access to the house. My siblings contributed money to help pay for those improvements.

At the airport, Tom and I met Mom who was in a wheelchair and Ruth Ann with a big smile on her face. Ruth Ann stayed for a week to help get her settled in, and I'm sure she sighed the biggest sigh of relief of her life when she got on that airplane to return to Texas. She had fulfilled her promise!

It took a few days for Mother to notice Ruth Ann was gone. When she asked where she was, I told her Ruth Ann had gone back to Texas.

"Well, I wanted to go with her. I need to go home," Mom announced.

"Remember? Tom and I invited you to live with us and share our house," I said.

"Well, nobody told me," she said.

Mother was with us for nearly 2½ years, the most intense yet rewarding years of my life. The best piece of advice that she always gave her children was to "keep things funny." I was tested many times to adhere to that guidance, and even dealing with dementia, I am here to say that it is possible.

One of the first things Tom and I decided was to never ask her if she remembered something and to allow her to be in whatever time-period she was in. Once, when we asked her to name her seven children, she laughed and said, "Children? I'm not but 16." It was no longer necessary to bring her into the present.

Another time, when she did know she had children, I asked her who her favorite child was. She thought and thought, trying to remember, so I suggested, "Was it Linda?"

"No!" she immediately retorted.

I pressed further. "Was it Ruth Ann?"

"Yes, it was Ruth Ann," she said resoundingly.

My brothers and sisters said I deserved that answer, but I say, "I did it for the laugh."

Sitting at the kitchen table, Mom often looked into the backyard where we kept a wood pile covered by a green tarp.

"Look!" she'd say, "Buster is here in his new green Buick. Why isn't he coming in?" "Oh," I'd lie, "he's out there in the garage with Dad, looking at a chair he's refinishing."

Mother had nine brothers and sisters, and although all had passed from this world, they came to visit Mom at our home on McDuffie Drive in Athens, Georgia on a daily basis. She often got mad with Aunt Stella.

"I just don't know why she doesn't come to see Mom more often," she said.

And she seemed to think I was Aunt Bertie some of the time, which pleased me because Bertie was her favorite sister, but it pleased me more when she knew who I was. One day when I was fixing dinner, she looked at me from her place at the kitchen table.

"Linda, would you please bring me a glass of water," she asked. I could not get it to her fast enough. In that moment, she knew who I was.

The McGees (Ruth's mother and siblings): seated from left, Grandmom McGee, Ruth, Hazel; standing from left, Buster, Edwin, Bertie, Freddie, Billy, c. 1962.

It didn't take Mom long to ask about "the children" back in her Texas assisted living home. I explained that their parents had been looking for them and contacted Child Services, who found the children at The Forum, and they were all overjoyed to be reunited.

"They wanted me to thank you for taking good care of them. And this is a really good thing," I said, "because you and I are just too old to be taking care of little children like that."

She agreed, saying that it had been a worry for her, and she was glad they were with their parents. My relief, however, was short lived because a couple of days later, when we were sitting at the table, Mom said to me, "You aren't going to like this, but 'they' want to start up with me again." I knew exactly who she was referring to, so I reluctantly agreed to their joining our household, along with Mother's brothers and sisters, her parents, my dad, and "the black man who shot out her teeth."

My mom had false teeth since I was a child, but after a short hospital stay during her first year with us, she refused to put them back in her mouth. From time to time, she shook her head in disgust, and said, "I don't know why that black man shot my teeth out." When questioned, she offered few details except that he walked up to her on the street one day and shot out her teeth. She would not be dissuaded from this story no matter now implausible.

When Caroline, my 8-year-old granddaughter, was visiting, I overheard Mom relating the story of how she lost her teeth to Caroline. Mom leaned toward her great-granddaughter and whispered, "And, if you ever see him, I want you to kick his ass." Caroline's face fell and her eyes looked at me in bewilderment. Was she really supposed to kick someone's ass?

Having learned from an early age not to lie to my parents, I found lying the only way to keep her mind calm, and I must admit, it ended up providing me with some comic relief. And I didn't just lie. I added details to the lie.

When she asked where Dad or "the children" were, I told her that Dad had taken them with him to Dale and Sandy's to work in their garden, and Sandy had invited them to stay for dinner. Sometimes, I even told her what Sandy was fixing for dinner. She frequently wanted to go see her mother, and I usually had to explain that it was dark or too late, or that a storm was coming up, and it would be better to go another time. She was always relieved when these problems were solved so easily, and I found that my strategy was better than the truth.

My mother fell in love with my husband, Tom, that "old man" I had married a couple of years before. I could not have managed the care of my mother without Saint Tom, as my family called him. He was so kind to her, never impatient, and he flirted outrageously with her, and she gave it right back in kind.

When she heard his car in the garage, she would pat her hair and smooth her clothes, asking, "How do I look? Does my hair look ok?"

Once she asked, "Do you think I have a chance with him?"

I always assured her she looked lovely, or I would fluff up her hair, and say, "Yes ma'am, you have a chance with him."

Tom would walk over to her chair and with a big smile, take her hand, and ask, "How's my girl today?"

She would look up at him and croon, "Well! You're good looking."

Having never seen my mother flirt, it was so cute to see that side of her, and I could easily see why my dad fell for her.

Ruth and Tom "walking out," 2007.

Every evening, Tom took her for a walk around the house, and she acted as though they were "walking out." One evening after I had put her to bed, I retired to the den. Tom came in a little later chuckling, saying, "I think your mom just invited me into her bed."

He heard her talking and went in to check on her. As he was fixing her covers, she lifted them and said, "Do you want to get in here with me?" In defense of her honor, she had also invited me to get in bed with her that same way, as she did when we were children.

Once, when she might have been worried about putting the move on my husband, she told me that there must be two Toms, and I happily agreed. On one occasion, when he and I were sitting at our desks, with her between us playing with her cards, she reached over, put her hand on Tom's shoulder, and said, "George, are you ready to go to bed?" My dad's name was George.

When Mother had a fretful evening, Ruth Ann offered to go in and lie on the extra bed we had in Mom's room. After half an hour, Ruth Ann came in the den, laughing, "You'll never believe what Mom just said in the cutest sing-song voice."

> *Hello, my name is Polly Pepper. I'm here to apply for the job you advertised. I need to make some money because I'm going to Hollywood to become a movie star. And down the street she walked in her little red high heels, clickity-clack, clickity-clack.*

We had never heard our mother say anything remotely like that. After a

Google search, we discovered that starting in 1939, actress Edith Fellows was in a film series, *The Five Little Peppers and How They Grew*, in which she starred as Polly Pepper. Mother's synapses must have connected to the memory of seeing that movie and remembering that monologue.

Mother often couldn't recall a word that she wanted to use, and would say, "I can feel that word right in my mouth." She became very adept at rearranging her sentences to get her point across. For example, she loved something sweet after dinner and one evening, I gave her a Pecan Sandie, a crumbly shortbread. She took the first dry bite, and, after some difficulty swallowing, she held up the cookie to me and said, "If these cookies ever present themselves to you again, just walk away."

When my friend Jill came for a visit from New Mexico, she brought Mom a deck of animal cards. She loved playing with them, favoring them to regular playing cards, which she also liked.

When I came home from work one day, she showed me the zebra card and said, "Isn't that the prettiest thing you have ever seen? I would like to have a zebra, and I want it tall enough so that I can walk beside it with my hand on its back. I bet we could even sell tickets and make money with it."

The next day, I went shopping and found her a stuffed zebra, not as tall as she wanted, but one that she could hold and put on the table. She frequently sat at the table with pictures of her family, her animal cards, her zebra, and her babies that my daughter Ellen made for her.

The best gift for all of us was when Ellen brought her grandmother a soft cloth doll, a girl baby in pink, that she had made. Mom cooed over this baby, holding her, telling her how beautiful she was, feeding her, and talking to her, planning their escape. We could hear her whispering, "Do you want to go in the car with me? I'll take you to see my mother. And we can find an apartment together. Do you want to do that?"

Mother was much happier when she had a "real" baby to hold and to love. The girl baby was soon joined by a boy baby in blue, also made by Ellen. Because he had quite a bit more stuffing than the girl, Mother was always teasing him about needing to lose weight, "You are fat! We will have to put you on a diet," she said jokingly. When these babies became her daily companions, she didn't fret as much about "the children."

After arriving home from work one day, I found her crying at the table, holding the naked boy baby with his clothes on the floor beside her.

"What's wrong?" I asked.

"I don't know what we're going to do," she cried, "Look at him. He doesn't have a tom pete."

"Well," I told her, gently covering his genderless body, "I can get that fixed at the doctor," and immediately she calmed down, knowing I would take care of it.

All of my siblings came to help from time to time so that Tom and I could get away for a few days. My sister Robin came several times, and my three children came to help too. My brother Sonny and his wife Martha came many times, and, once, when Martha was unable to come, my sister Betty came to help Sonny so he wouldn't have to be the caregiver on his own. Dale and Bobby came together for a visit, which lifted Mom's spirits. She was so responsive to them that you would never know she had dementia.

After a trip to the hospital with a broken hip the second year, she continued to deteriorate mentally, but she was able to get on her feet again and take her evening walks with Tom. She would forget she had fallen and broken her hip, frequently saying, "I don't know what's wrong with my hip."

Ruth feeding her zebra at the table, and with her two babies, which brought her the greatest pleasure and comfort, 2007.

At one point, Mother stopped eating and lost about 20 pounds. She was mostly bed-ridden by then and being spoon fed. We felt successful if we coaxed her to eat 3-4 spoonfuls during a meal. It seemed the end was near, so we called hospice.

About this time, my no-nonsense brother Sonny came with his wife. On the second day, he got Mom out of bed, settled her in her wheelchair, and brought her to the table for dinner. When she said she didn't want anything, he said to her, "Do you know that if you don't eat, you'll die?" She looked at him and said, "Well, I don't want to die." And she started eating again. We supposed that she had just forgotten that she needed to eat.

All in all, it was the best of times, and it was the worst of times. We didn't realize how fragile she was when she first came to us, or how disagreeable she could be. When she came to live with us, she was on 17 prescriptions, which prompted Tom and me to put together a spreadsheet with all her medications, their side effects and contraindications. I hated giving them to her, and she hated taking them, and it was too much to ask her caregivers to do. One day, when I gave her a handful, she shook her head and told me to give them to my friends. Once, she told me to give them to her doctor.

Over that first year, after we were able to reduce her prescriptions down to two essential ones, she became much calmer and more reasonable. And I have to admit that she was easier to care for after she was wheelchair bound following a broken hip. I didn't have to worry about her wandering off and hurting herself.

In addition to my daytime job, I also had to interact with her caregivers: one full-timer and two part-timers. I drew up a chart for them to record what and how much she ate, how many times she had been to the bathroom, and what medications they gave her. She woke up a lot at nights fretting, and there were many times I sat singing to her until she went back to sleep, and I still went to work the next day. Friday nights were especially difficult, stopping at the store for groceries, going to the pharmacy for supplies, rushing to get home so the caregiver could leave on time, always knowing the shape of the weekend ahead. On my way home one Friday night, in my weariness and frustration of all I was faced with, I called out, "When is this ever going to end?"

MOM TAKES HER LEAVE

That night, after supper and after getting her in bed, I fell into my bed, exhausted, and woke up about 3 a.m. to go to the bathroom. I tiptoed by Mom's door, peeked in and saw her blanket on the floor. I went in to cover her and discovered that she had died during the night. I didn't need to wait long for my answer. She died on November 17, 2007, three months before her 93rd birthday.

I called the hospice nurse, who came at daybreak to record her time of death. I called the funeral home and arranged for them to come for her later that afternoon. I wanted to have the day with her at home. I washed her hands and face and feet and thought about changing her clothes, especially since she was wearing my favorite turquoise turtleneck sweater, but decided she was too heavy to manage myself, and I was not going to ask Tom to help.

Tony, Ellen, and Clif came over to sit with her while we shared our memories of her. The undertakers came for her body at 4 p.m., and the house was oddly quiet. I picked up her ashes the next week after preparing an altar for her in the living room, where she waited until we held her memorial service in Maryland on April 12, 2008.

Ruth's ashes on her altar await the spring memorial service, 2007.

We put her urn and Dad's together in a walnut box, and Bobby dug their grave in the family plot behind the headstone that had been waiting for them for 15 years. I looked around and saw the graves of my relatives whom I loved: my aunts and uncle, my grandparents, and now my parents. I gazed at the nearby headstone engraved with my name and Tom's, along with my brothers' and their spouses'. After lowering the box holding our parent's ashes into their final resting place, each of us helped to fill in the grave. As I took the shovel and covered the box, I felt good, knowing I had fulfilled a daughter's long-ago promise to take care of her mother in her old age.

Above left: George and Ruth's interment, Remson Methodist Church. Above right: The Jones siblings at Remson Cemetery, (from left) Bobby, Dale, Ruth Ann, Linda, Betty, 2008. Below: The Jones siblings at Remson Methodist Church, (back row) Bobby, Dale, Sonny; (front row) Linda, Ruth Ann, Betty, Robin, 2008. Photograph by Robert McGee.

7 | Becoming the Elders

Ruth Ann Moves to Atlanta

After Ruth Ann's husband died in January 2008, just two months after Mom, she continued alone in the Woodlands, still near three of her children. When we all went back to the Shore for Mom's memorial service in April of 2008, Ruth Ann, Betty, and I found a lovely rental house on the Chincoteague Bay, just 15

Sisters playing Scrabble on the Chincoteague Bay, (from left) Ruth Ann, Betty, Linda, Robin, 2010.

minutes from Bobby's farm on Little Mill Road. For the next five years, we continued to rent the property for a week every spring or fall, sometimes accompanied by Robin; Dale and Bobby would usually join us for a night or two. We always enjoyed our time together, fixing our favorite meals, playing Scrabble, showing slides and pictures, and telling family stories. A week was never enough, so several times we went for two weeks. After I retired, we planned to go for an entire month.

In 2013, Ruth Ann called me, so excited she could hardly get out her news. Her daughter Susan, who worked out of Cincinnati with Delta Airlines, had accepted a transfer to Atlanta, and she and her husband invited Ruth Ann to make the move with them. You can imagine our delight! After 30 years, we would be near each other once again. They bought a house in Fayetteville, just 95 miles south of us. As soon as she settled in, we set up her transportation to Athens, using the Groome Shuttle. Susan took her to the airport to catch the shuttle, and an hour and a half later, I'd pick her up just 15 minutes from my house. She came to visit for a week nearly every month that year, and it was heaven to be together again. When she wasn't visiting, we Skyped every night, a lovely way to end the day. I don't remember a cross word between us, not even a shadow.

Family Reunion 2013

In the summer of 2013, Bobby hosted another Jones Family Reunion on the Shore. Our numbers had increased dramatically since our 2001 reunion, so we decided to use the social hall at Remson Church for most of our activities. However, when the day was over, we all meandered back to the farm on Little Mill Road where we sat in the yard watching the children play while dusk fell, just as our parents, grandparents, and aunts and uncles had watched us in the 1940s.

The descendants of George and Ruth Jones, including children, grandchildren and their spouses, and great-grandchildren, 2013. Photo by Robert McGee.

Bobby's Stay in Athens

Brother Bobby suffered a stroke in November 2013, and Tony went up to Maryland to lend him a hand after his rehab. Tony called me and we decided that Bobby should come down to Athens to stay with Tom and me while he recuperated. I was finishing up my 10-year stint at the county government and was able to take him to physical therapy sessions and doctor appointments. When Ruth Ann came for a week over the Christmas holidays, we realized it was the first Christmas we had slept under the same roof in 60 years. Bobby stayed with us into February 2014 when I finally retired. And, I finally had earned a pension.

Ruth Ann, Bobby, Linda in Athens for Christmas, 2013.

My first thought after retirement was, "Now, my sisters and I can spend a whole month on the Chincoteague Bay." Little did we know that this plan was not to be.

RUTH ANN TAKES HER LEAVE

During one of her visits in mid-October 2014, after a short walk in the neighborhood, Ruth Ann and I were sitting on the back porch, when she told me how much she missed Jerry. We started talking about death and dying, and when and how we thought we would go.

"I'm ready to go anytime. I'm ready to see Jerry and Mom and Dad again," she told me.

Ruth Ann, Linda, Huntington, W.Va., 2011.

Personally, I wasn't sure that's how it would work out, but I certainly wasn't going to cast any doubts on her dreams and expectations.

Two days later, she suffered another stroke. I called an ambulance, and Susan met us at the hospital. At the age of 80, Ruth Ann was ready to fight to recover, like she did 10 years earlier, after her first hemorrhagic stroke. When they transferred her to physical therapy a few days later, we assumed she was getting better and would recover again. Unfortunately, two days later, she suffered another stroke and was soon admitted to hospice.

I spent every day with her, and her daughter Susan was with her every minute for the two weeks it took her mother to pass from this world. On October 27, 2014, Susan was holding Ruth Ann in her arms, and I was standing at the foot of her bed, cradling her feet in my hands when she died. Now, in 2023, I just can't believe she has been gone for nine years. We never got to spend our month together on the bay.

> *A person whom one has loved seems altogether too significant a thing to simply vanish altogether from the world. A person whom one loves is a world, just as one knows oneself to be a world. How can worlds like these simply cease altogether? But if my sister does exist, then what is she, and what makes that thing that she now is identical with the beautiful girl laughing at her little sister on that forgotten day?*
>
> *Rebecca Goldstein*

CAROLINE AND JASON GET MARRIED

After her first year in the dorm at the University of Georgia in Athens, Caroline asked her Grandmother Flynn if she would like a roommate. They had a wonderful three years together while she finished her bachelor's degree in Animal Science. A month after Caroline's graduation in 2017, she married Jason Barnwell, who had just finished his master's degree in Forestry and Natural Resources at UGA.

Caroline, Andrew, Jason, Eli Barnwell, 2023.

Jason's job with Georgia Pacific moved them to Arkansas, Tallahassee, and finally home to Georgia in August 2019. Caroline, newly pregnant, was allowed to work remotely with her company.

Their first son Elijah Scot was born on January 7, 2020, making me a great-grandmother, and Andrew James was born on March 12, 2022. With both children at home full time and Andrew recovering from an unexpected heart surgery, Caroline made the decision to become a stay-at-home parent. Jason now works for Novelis in a hybrid role, enjoying the benefit of spending time with his family at home in the new post-COVID world. Caroline is an active volunteer in her church, at Eli's preschool, and has just completed her first marathon.

ERIC AND COURTNEY TIE THE KNOT

In 2014, Eric graduated from his Uncle Clif's alma mater, Georgia Tech, with a degree in psychology. He spent the next couple of years working with children at the UGA Rock Eagle 4-H Center and in the elementary school system where his mom worked. Eric always had a passion for photography since he got his first camera at four year old. When he started taking pictures of the children's activities, he realized he could turn a hobby into a profession. He decided to go back to school to get his master's degree in photojournalism at The Ohio State University. Eric married

Courtney Lipscomb on August 3, 2019, shortly before classes started. The CO-

VID pandemic required him to take classes remotely for half a semester, but he completed the rest of the program on campus. Eric secured a job as a photo engineer technologist with National Geographic in Washington, D.C. Courtney worked for an independent bookstore in D.C. before she found her dream job at a nearby horse farm where she manages the barn and trains horses.

FOUR FRIENDS ON THE BAY

The three most important aspects of my time on earth have been my spiritual journey, my family, and my friends. I appreciate my early Christian upbringing and the spiritual teachers that showed up in my life as if on cue. I was blessed with a large family and considered my siblings my friends while I was growing up and all through my life, and my children are the ones I kept coming back to after my marriage to their father dissolved. I have

Bobby hosts four friends at his home on Little Mill Road. From left: Kia Woods, Linda, Beverly Joyce, Claudia Terry, and Bobby, 2019.

mentioned friends throughout this book and consider them my extended family. My spiritual path, my family, and my friends have provided me with sustenance throughout my life.

In September 2019, in the "before times" (before the pandemic), I sent an invitation to four of my dearest friends to join me for a week in October on the Chincoteague Bay. They each knew of each other, but had never spent time together. Three of them answered my call and plans were laid to gather at the beautiful house on the Chincoteague Bay. Leslie was the only one who was unable to come, but she and I had recently completed the Circle Tour including the National Parks in Utah and Arizona. Claudia, who lived in the San Francisco Bay Area flew to Atlanta so she could drive with me to Richmond, Virginia, where we met Beverly, who lived in Charlottesville. The three of us drove to the Norfolk airport to meet Kia who was flying in from New York City.

To have three of my favorite people together and watch them get to know each other was a special gift in my life. We went to Assateague Island to walk on the beach (no wild ponies were seen that day); we got up every morning to have coffee on the porch and watch the sunrise over the bay; we played games, read to each other, and practiced yoga together. Brother Bobby invited us to his home where we dined with him, Dale, and Tony on steamed crabs and clam chowder. We were planning to repeat the gathering the following summer, but alas, the pandemic.

8 | PANDEMIC 2020

SOMETHING IS VERY WRONG

I remember seeing those shocking videos from China during the first week of February 2020. I was watching a news report that showed Chinese authorities, clad in Hazmat suits, forcibly dragging residents out of their homes. If they refused to go for testing or quarantine, as some did, they were sealed inside their homes for forced isolation. It was shocking and ominous. What was going on? Something terrifying was happening, and you could see even the Chinese government was scared. The WHO had been reporting on a respiratory flu-like outbreak since January 5. While Trump was being briefed about the global dangers of the virus, he was downplaying it to the public when asked about it by reporters.

On February 1, following the WHO declaration of a global health emergency because of the virus and a State Department warning against travel to China, the Trump administration finally issued a travel ban from China. By then, we had eight confirmed cases in this country. Americans, returning home after being evacuated from Wuhan, where the virus was first detected, were quarantined for up to 14 days at the Air Reserve Base in California. This was the first mandatory quarantine order in the U.S. in 50 years, according to NPR.

We were told that all other travelers from China would be tested when they returned to the country. Incoming flights from China were limited to seven airports – San Francisco, Los Angeles, Seattle, JFK in New York City, Atlanta, Honolulu, and O'Hare Airport in Chicago. I watched as news reporters interviewed passenger after passenger who were disembarking from those flights, declaring that there was no testing, not even temperature-taking. Great, I thought, now the virus is in all those cities, and likely even farther afield. Even so, I was still hopeful that we would contain it. After all, we are the United States of America.

Next, we began to hear of cruise ships being stranded at sea because countries were refusing to allow them to dock because of fears of infection. That was perplexing. On February 4, the U.S. cruise ship Diamond Princess was finally allowed to dock in Japan, and the entire ship was immediately put under a 14-day quarantine. By mid-February, 300 American passengers from that ship were flown back to the states on U.S.-chartered airplanes. Fourteen people were infected with COVID-19, but not separated from the uninfected. They were all placed in quarantine at military bases in California and Texas or at a hospital in Omaha, Nebraska. All of it was out of the realm of normality to my mind. It sounded like the beginning of a Netflix disaster series, or a Stephen King novel. Never in my lifetime had I heard of people being taken off cruise ships and airplanes and put in quarantine. By the last week of February, we began to hear stories of outbreaks in nursing homes. That's when I decided to cancel my hair appointment, my eye doctor appointment, and my dentist appointment. I had been going to Silver Sneakers exercise classes five days a week since my retirement. With this unsettling news, I stopped going to exercise classes, stopped having lunch with friends, and gave up my memoir writing class. Basically, Tom and I became hermits except for grocery shopping.

On March 9, the Grand Princess was the first ship to dock in the United States. After being forced to idle offshore for two weeks, they were finally allowed to dock in Oakland. Adding to the strangeness of this new reality, I found it unusual that it took three days for the passengers to disembark, some being sent to hospitals for treatment, and some put under further quarantine. By this time, there were 600 known cases in the United States, and 26 confirmed deaths from the virus. Two days later, on March 11, the WHO declared the COVID-19 outbreak a pandemic.

While I was venturing out to the grocery store once a week, our president was still downplaying the virus, comparing it to the flu. It was only after Fox News broadcaster, Tucker Carlson, reported on March 18 that this outbreak was serious and couldn't be compared to the flu that Trump finally succumbed to the science, or at least to Tucker Carlson. Yet it took him another two weeks to make a dramatic turnaround when on March 30 he finally issued Stay at Home recommendations. Unfortunately, that only lasted for two weeks. Luckily, governors and mayors, across the country, had already begun to act to minimize the effects in their states and cities.

The library closed for a while and when it opened again, it offered curbside pickup. I started ordering my groceries online and picking them up curbside, a new service. I also ordered for and delivered to my 90-year-old co-grandmother, Ellen's mother-in-law. Since we were told that the virus can live on surfaces, I developed a system for disinfecting grocery items by separating perishables from non-perishables. The non-perishables stayed in the car for 4-5 days, the fruits and vegetables got washed in soapy water, and I used Clorox-wipes to clean everything before putting items in the refrigerator. We now know that groceries offer the lowest chance of getting COVID-19, and after a year I gave up the practice.

By the middle of March, I figured if we could all stay at home for three months, we could wipe this out. We wouldn't give the virus anyone to infect. I even thought I would be able to have our week at the beach in June with my family. I can't tell you how many times I have wished we had the kind of forward-thinking leadership that could get out in front of this outbreak and follow the lead of the countries who were being successful at flattening the curve. Wouldn't it have been a source of achievement if we could had stopped our cases at 30,000? It seems to me that we are a country of contrarians who just want to be right, and we have an overinflated idea of what freedom means.

By the middle of September 2020, with nearly 200,000 dead, there was still no end in sight – and no leadership to guide us through a global pandemic. Trump was determined to act like it wasn't so bad, claiming it would be over soon, masks weren't really necessary, and that we shouldn't shut down as a country. There was no national plan for testing and tracking, nothing to ensure that opening businesses and schools were safe, but we were opening them anyway. Everybody was on their own to try to decide what to do. There were too many who jumped on conspiracy theories and lost sight of what was real.

With the release in September 2020 of Bob Woodward's book *Rage*, we discovered that Trump knew in early February how deadly the virus was, weeks before the first death, yet he consciously decided to downplay the virus so he wouldn't panic his people. His public comments at the time, insisting that the virus was "going to disappear" and "all work out fine," were in stark contrast to what he actually knew. The book, using Trump's own words, revealed a president who betrayed the public trust and the most fundamental responsibilities of his office – "to keep our country safe." But in early February, Trump told Woodward he knew how deadly the virus was, and, in March, admitted he kept that knowledge hidden from the public.

"I wanted to always play it down," Trump told Woodward on March 19, even as he declared a national emergency days earlier. "I still like playing it down, because I don't want to create a panic."

Experts now say that if Trump had acted decisively in early February with a strict shutdown and a consistent message to wear masks, social distance, and wash hands, they believe thousands of American lives could have been saved.

A Year+ into the Pandemic

As of January 2021, still with a long road ahead of us, several vaccines, requiring two shots a month apart were hurriedly developed. They were distributed and injected into people's bodies without knowing how long they would provide immunity. We were told the vaccine reduces the risk of infection by 95%, but we were also told that there is no absolute guarantee of protection for any particular individual. It feels like we are guinea pigs in an experiment, just like the March 2020 Netflix series *Pandemic: How to Prevent an Outbreak.*

By May of 2021, 27% of the population have been fully vaccinated and 43% had at least one shot. New COVID-19 cases in the U.S. declined by 61 percent, compared to the peak level on January 8. In nursing homes, cases were down 96%. Both Tom and I had our two shots which allowed us to finally be able to meet in person with family members, also vaccinated, without masks. We shared hugs for the first time in over a year. Restrictions were lifting in states where COVID-19 was on the decline, and travel to certain countries in Europe resumed. It was starting to feel like we may be able to return to normal by the end of the summer, but then the Delta variant began surging through England. I was able to make a quick trip up to Maryland to see Bobby and Dale before the new variant started running rampant through the United States.

Sadly, by November 2021, only 60% of Americans had been vaccinated. Science determined that the vaccines' protection only lasted six months and everyone was required to get boosters, which got us through another six months. Vaccines were then approved for children.

Because of Trump, there are still many people who don't believe the virus is real and refuse the vaccinations. It's now being called the Virus of the Unvaccinated because they are the ones hospitalized and dying. They just don't understand that until we can get ahead of COVID-19, other variants will continue to rise, each one worse than the last. The Mu variant was identified in 48 states immediately following the Delta variant. There have been recent treatment discoveries so those, along with the vaccine, I'm hoping we won't go into year three of the pandemic.

By September 25, 2022, the authorities were arguing over whether the pandemic was over or not. People were still getting COVID, being hospitalized, and dying from the disease. After the initial two-shot vaccine, two follow-up boosters are recommended. Many people who followed recommended doses still got COVID-19; lots of people got it twice. Now the big worry is Long COVID in which the damage caused by the virus causes symptoms to continue for months, even years. It doesn't just affect people who had severe cases, but also those with mild cases, and others who had COVID but didn't know they had it. Even worse, sometimes the symptoms can disappear only to return at a later date. As of July 2021, Long COVID, also known as post-COVID, conditions, can be considered a disability under the Americans with Disabilities Act.

To make matters even worse, a link between COVID-19 and Alzheimer's was recently reported. Now we can worry about that. Between February 2020 and May 2021, researchers analyzed the health records of over six million adults over the age of 65 who were not previously diagnosed with Alzheimer's. Participants were divided into two main groups – a COVID-19 group and a non-COVID-19 group. The results revealed that those who had been infected with COVID-19 had an increased risk of a new Alzheimer's diagnosis, compared to those who had not been infected with COVID-19. The risk was especially high for adults over 85 years old and for women across all age groups.

Everyone is weary with each new report. Most people are not wearing masks out in public. I have not resumed my exercise classes, but we have started having our memoir writing meetings in-person after being on Zoom for two years. Some of us still wear masks and we arrange our seating so that we are a few feet apart, but not 6 feet. I know some people who have had it two and three times, and I still don't want it even once. I have received the first two initial vaccine shots, followed by two boosters. On September 29, 2022, I submitted to one more "updated" booster that offers little more than hope that it will do some good.

Since September, I have been going maskless to events. COVID-19 still exists, along with "the flu," and now a respiratory virus (RSV) that is affecting young children and old people. The deaths from COVID-19 per day have come down from their high of 4,000 per day in early 2021 to 500 per day, although still not as low as it was a year ago (200 per day). A million people in the U.S. have died from COVID-19 since 2020. Surely "vaccines" have helped. After killing an estimated 6,619,792 worldwide, we have been informed that the coronavirus is now with us – something to deal with along with other viruses. There are still arguments about how it started – with a bat in some remote cave in China or in a lab in Wuhan, China. Fundamental questions remain about when, where and how COVID first infected people. Likely, we will never know.

WELCOMING EMMA

About a year into the Pandemic, Tom and I became weary of the isolation and absence of social contact. I saw a picture of a beautiful cat in our neighborhood newsletter. The cat's owners were looking to rehome her, and Tom and I agreed that adding a cat to our household was a good idea. Emma came to stay with us for a week to make sure we were well suited, and she has been with us since then.

9 | AND THEN THERE WERE TWO

DALE AND BETTY TAKE THEIR LEAVE

My family was shocked when Ruth Ann died in 2014 at the age of 80. Both parents had lived into their 90s, so obviously we all thought we had years before we needed to worry about dying. We got news from my oldest brother's son that Sonny died on June 23, 2021, at the age of 88.

After Ruth Ann died, Betty and I went up to Maryland a few times to stay at the beautiful house on the Chincoteague Bay, but it just wasn't the same without our big sister. We even tried Betty's timeshare in Hilton Head where we invited Dale and Bobby, along with my son Tony, to join us a couple of times. Then the pandemic was upon us, and with Betty confined to a nursing home, we had to forego our trips to the Shore.

Dale's health had been slowly going downhill since his wife Sandy died in 2012. By the time the pandemic was well underway, doctors were unable to diagnose his condition. He started losing a lot of weight, it became difficult for him to walk, and finally he was unable to drive. I think they call that "a failure to thrive." On March 16, 2022, he died peacefully in his sleep. I was able to travel to Maryland for

Above: Betty and Linda at Westminster Canterbury Nursing Home, Lynchburg, Va., 2022. Below: Linda and Dale, family reunion 2013.

his memorial service and to say goodbye by reading about our childhood from this memoir. Unfortunately, Betty's mental state had started to decline, and she was not well enough to make the trip.

In October of 2022, Ellen and I made another visit up to the Shore to celebrate Bobby's 85th birthday and to visit with Tony and Sheryl. They had moved up to Maryland a year earlier to help Uncle Bob age in place and keep him out of a nursing home. On the way back to Georgia, we decided to make a side trip to Lynchburg to visit Betty in the nursing home. While we visited with her for two hours, she confided in me that she just didn't feel like herself.

Two weeks later, she stopped eating and went to bed, sleeping around the clock. It appeared she had given up and was ready to die. I made one final Face-Time call with her, although she was unable to speak. I sang *Carolina Moon* to her and *Oh, You Girls, Girls, Girls*, songs our dad used to sing to us, while she smiled and went back to sleep. She died four days later on November 8. During a 15-month period, half of my siblings took their leave of this planet. Sonny was the first to go in June 2021, then Dale in March 2022, and now dear Betty in November 2022. How is that possible? With Ruth Ann, also gone, now just Bobby and I are the only two who remain of the original six siblings.

Bobby and I remain to carry on the stories of our family. He and I are working on the *McGee Chronicles*, the story of our maternal grandparents and their 10 children. There is a *Jones Chronicle* waiting in the wings.

In 2011, Bobby started a building project, saving two houses, built in the early 1800s: The Boston House, next door to his farm, and the Old House, where my grandparents started their married life and where my parents had taken refuge with their five children during the Depression. Both houses had been abandoned for years, and Bobby wanted to save them. He moved them both to a lot on the far corner of his farm and joined them together. He added a cedar shake roof, wood siding, and double paned windows and installed geothermal heating. Without warning, a stroke in 2013, halted all progress on his project. When Tony and Sheryl decided to move to the Shore, Bobby turned

Marriage of the Boston house (top left) and Old House (top right), with a new addition in between, 2021.

over the project to them in 2020. They added plumbing, bathrooms, kitchen, flooring, gas fireplaces, and a hundred other things that a 175-year-old house needs. They finally got their certificate of occupancy on November 30, 2022, and moved into their new old home. Bobby will continue to live in the "Big House" where he has lived since he was 3 years old. It's the same house my dad grew up in and where I spent many happy days while I was growing up.

REFLECTIONS ON THE LONG JOURNEY HOME

My life, revealed in these pages, has been a long journey of moving from one house to another. Some were homes, and some just houses where I lived while waiting for the next adventure to unfold. At the beginning of writing this memoir when I laid out the chronology of my life, I could hardly believe I moved 50 times during my 81 years. I have often said that time and place define us. Growing up on a farm in the 40s and 50s definitely impacted how I developed as a human being. Looking back, I can see the life lessons I learned and the growth I experienced in each of the places I lived.

We moved to Stockton in 1948, where I lived from first through 12th grades – it's where I came of age. Even now, I think of Stockton as home because it is still a familiar touchstone. It is rich with vivid childhood memories, family ties, school days, horseback riding, trips to Ocean City, crabbing in the bay, making homemade ice

Rowley Farmhouse, Stockton, Md., 1948-1961.

cream, climbing trees, first job, and first boyfriend. It is the home I left to go away to college. The Stockton farmhouse is no longer standing – nothing left to hold the echoes of a happy childhood in the 40s and 50s. Home can be the memories that echo in my heart that I share with you.

During the 17 years between 1963 and 1980, I lived in 10 different houses with my husband and three children. Of those 10, the only one I considered "home" was the three-story, 13-room Victorian house in Catonsville, Maryland. I fell in love with it the moment I walked through the front door. It held all the hope I had for my family's future. It felt like a place where I could grow old. It was where I dreamed I would host graduation parties, wedding receptions, and family reunions; one where I would welcome the families of my children, where my grandchildren would come for sleepovers and picnic lunches on the porch. We lived there for only five years before those hopes and dreams fell apart. It was the last house we all lived in together and the one I left to live life on my own. Home can be memories of your visions of the future.

The next time and place I felt like I was home was in Santa Fe, where I lived in five houses in three years. Within a week of arriving, the land, the sky, the architecture all felt so familiar – like I belonged there. I was on-purpose in my work life; I felt like I was an integral part of the organization and competent in my contributions. The same is true with the friends I made in Santa Fe – they were my tribe and many still are an essential part of my life. I thought I would live there forever. But more long journeys lay ahead. After Santa Fe, I took a trip around the world and consciously practiced being at home wherever I was. I wanted to experience myself as a global citizen, not limited by the boundaries of continents

133 Newburg Avenue, Catonsville, Md., 1975-1980.

The Rainbow House, Santa Fe, NM, 1985.

Jenkins Home, Athens, Ga., 2001-present.

and countries laid out on a map, by pledges of allegiance and anthems we sing. I discovered that home is a state of mind. Home is the present, wherever you are.

A farmhouse in the country, the oldest house on the edge of town, a Cape Cod on a tree-shaded street in the Midwest, apartment buildings, row houses, and condos in the city, adobe houses in the desert, brick houses in the suburbs, even a log cabin in the woods. I lived in them all. I have lived in the home I'm in now for 22 years – longer than I have lived anywhere. This is the home where I welcomed my grandchildren for weekend sleepovers and picnics on the porch.

This is where my family gathered for Thanksgiving and Christmas dinners and for birthday celebrations. Yet, after they all leave and the house is quiet, it still doesn't feel like my idea of what home should feel like. Sometimes, it feels like I'm just visiting and playing a role, so it's really the people who made it a home. Home for me has been my family, my friends, the people with whom I share my life.

My purpose in writing my memoir was twofold. I wanted to leave a legacy for my family so my children and grandchildren could know about my life and who I am. I also wanted the record for myself. When my mother was sinking into dementia, there is nothing she loved more that hearing stories and seeing pictures of her family and her life. I reasoned that if I were besieged with a failing mind in my later years, my children could entertain me by reading this collection of my own stories and showing me the pictures. Perhaps I would even recognize myself.

Writing this memoir, a three-year process of recounting years of life experiences, has brought a deeper understanding of what the journey home means. Sometimes, home comes in the guise of a house, a dream, a place, a person, a memory, or a state of mind. As I contemplated "home," I began to understand that each move, each encounter, each experience that made me feel this state of "home" came from where I was residing inside myself, my spiritual home. When my heart was full, no matter where I was, who I was with, or how long ago it was, I knew I was home. This book is a reflection on the journeys I have taken to reach the final stretch of my life, and on the people who traveled with me. Now, in my 80s, I am ever mindful that the greatest journey home is still ahead of me – the journey into the great unknown.

In Closing (2023)

I once heard that a person's lifetime can be divided into thirds. The first third is used for childhood and education; the second is dedicated to marriage, family, and community service; and the third is for devoting attention and energy to the inner spiritual life. All three of those divisions have overlapped during my life, and now that I am in my 80s, my life purpose has shifted from an outer focus to the little-explored inner world.

Now I find that I am even more drawn to the mystery of what's on the inner … and what's next. What does it really mean that we are "created in the image of God," and the "Kingdom of Heaven is within"? And, "If thine eye be single, the whole body will be filled with light," and "Knock and the door will be opened unto thee"? I'm discovering that they just aren't sayings, but keys to our understanding on a higher level – pointers to the Truth.

We never did discuss spiritual questions in my family – either with my parents or my children. Who am I as a spiritual being? What is my spiritual potential? What must I do to reach my potential? What happens to me when I die? What happens to my consciousness? These are the questions of interest to me now. My spiritual teachings are urging me to look deeper into those mysteries. I never did buy into the belief that God was incomprehensible. Why then are we created in His image? Perhaps we haven't been doing the research in the right places. I am just beginning to see that it's the mechanical mind that can't understand God, but perhaps the soul can. Perhaps it is the soul that can access the other 90% that we humans don't use. But, how do we learn about anything new if we're told it's incomprehensible?

In this book, I have talked about the MasterPath, my spiritual path for the past 30 years. I confess that over the past 10 years, I have become somewhat casual about my spiritual life – exercises, readings, seminars. Several months ago, after a deep philosophical conversation with my daughter-in-law, Sheryl, I decided to re-read one of my Master Path books. It took only a few pages to remember why I chose MasterPath all those years ago. It answered all my questions. Just as suddenly, I was struck by the ease with which I drifted away from it. How could I have forgotten my spiritual goals and wandered from the practices that always brought so much harmony and joy in my life. With my renewed commitment, I am now more confident and at peace about my final journey home. If I decide to write another book, it will be about my spiritual path, what it has meant to me, how I drifted away, and how I found my way back home.

Life has always given me what I needed and often what I wanted, with many wonderful surprises along the way. I will continue to trust the shape of life.

This … or something better.

A CHRONOLOGY OF HOUSES
The Homes of Linda Jones Hope Jenkins
1941-2023

Sep 1941-Dec 1941 – Ranier Farm, Mount Hermon Road, Salisbury, Md..

Jan 1942-Aug 1946 – Log cabin on Corkers Creek, Pocomoke Road, 4 miles west of Snow Hill, Md..

Aug 1946-Dec 1946 – Chicken Coop tenant house on Duncan Farm, Dividing Creek Road, Pocomoke, Md..

Jan 1947-Dec 1947 – Tyndall Farm, Mile Branch Road, Newark, Md.

Jan 1948-Jun 1959 – Rowley Farm, Stockton, Md. (parents stayed until 1961)

Jun 1957-Aug 1957 – Joe's Restaurant, Ocean City, Md.

Jun 1958-Aug 1958 – Joe's Restaurant, Ocean City, Md.

Jun 1959-Aug 1959 – Beach Plaza Hotel, Ocean City, Md.

Sep 1959-Jun 1960 – Towson State College, Towson, Md.

Jun 1960-Aug 1960 – Beach Plaza Hotel, Ocean City, Md.

Sep 1960-Oct 1960 – Laurel Hill Terrace, Fort Washington, New York City, NY (Betty, Linda, Ghee)

Oct 1960-Nov 1960 – 399 E. 72nd Street, Apt #8D, Manhattan, New York City, NY (Maureen, Betty, Linda, Ghee)

Nov 1960-May 1961 – 452 Fort Washington Avenue, Fort Washington, New York City, NY (Betty, Linda, Ghee)

Jun 1961-Jun 1963 – 211 W. Federal Street, Snow Hill, Md. (Mom, Dad, Bobby, Linda, Robin Ghee)

Jun 1963 – Apartment in Wilkinsburg, Pa. (Gary and Linda Hope)

Jul 1963-Aug 1963 – 479 State Street, Sharon, Pa. (Gary, Linda, Tony)

Sep 1963 – 685 Whitney Avenue, Wilkinsburg, Pa. (Gary, Linda, Tony)

Oct 1963 – Apartment in someone's home, Crownsville, Md. (Gary, Linda, Tony)

Nov 1963-Dec 1963 – 685 Whitney Avenue, Wilkinsburg, Pa. (Gary, Linda, Tony)

Jan 1964-Feb 1964 – Apartment house in Detroit, Mich. (Gary, Linda, Tony)

Mar 1964-Apr 1964 – 685 Whitney Avenue, Wilkinsburg, Pa. (Gary, Linda, Tony)

May 1964-Jun 1965 – 211 Longview Drive, Irwin, Pa. (Gary, Linda, Tony, Ellen)

Jul 1965-May 1967 – 590 Semple Drive, Irwin, Pa. (bought 1st house) (Gary, Linda, Tony, Ellen, Clif)

Jun 1967-Jan 1969 – 9609 Maple Drive, Indianapolis, Ind. (bought 2nd house) (Gary, Linda, Tony, Ellen, Clif)

Feb 1969-Jan 1971 – 5004 W. Forest Park Avenue, Village of Purnell town house rental, Baltimore, Md. (Gary, Linda, Tony, Ellen, Clif)

Jan 1971-Jul 1975 – 209 Westshire Road, Baltimore, Md. (bought 3rd house) (Gary, Linda, Tony, Ellen, Clif)

Jul 1975-Aug 1980 – 133 Newburg Avenue, Catonsville, Md. (bought 4th house) (Gary, Linda, Tony, Ellen, Clif)

Aug 1980-Dec 1980 – 10802 Margate Road, Silver Springs, Md. (Jim Worsley)

Jan 1981-Mar 1981 – Reston, Va. (Renee)

Apr 1981-Jul 1981 – Reston, Va. (friends Carol and Jonyl Adams)

Aug 1981-Sep 1981 – Roswell, Ga. (friends Sandy and Larry Prince)

Sep 1981-Sep 1982 – 193 Roswell Street, Alpharetta, Ga. (Ellen Hope)

Sep 1982-Feb 1984 – 1030 Dassow Court, Roswell, Ga. (Ellen Hope)

Mar 1984-Dec, 1984 – 105 Spruce Street, Santa Fe, NM

Dec 1984-Nov 1985 – Rainbow House, Tano Road, Santa Fe, NM (Leslie Larsen)

Dec 1985-Jun 1986 – Smith House, Tano Road, Santa Fe, NM (Leslie Larsen)

Jul 1986-Oct 1986 – Arroyo Tenario and Garcia Street, Santa Fe, NM (Leslie Larsen)

Nov 1986-Feb 1987 – Foothills of Sangre Cristo Mountains, Santa Fe, NM (Joan Ward sublet)

Mar 1987-Apr 1987 – Alameda, Santa Fe, NM (Lisa Larsen house sit)

Apr 1987-Jul 1987 – Traveled California coast, Oregon, Washington, Norfolk, Va. (Micky's wedding)

Aug 1987-Jan 1988 – Traveled to Egypt (Harmonic Convergence Aug 16-17-18), Israel (Aug), Nepal (Aug), Thailand (Sep), Hong Kong (Sep-Oct), Bali (Oct), Australia (Nov), Hawaii (Dec), Santa Fe (Dec), Atlanta (Dec) (traveled with Molly Post through Australia)

Jan 1988-Mar 1989 – 4717 Roswell Road, NE, Apt. S-3, Atlanta, Ga. (Joy Rollins)

Apr 1989-May 1989 – 550½ Camino del Monte Sol, Santa Fe, NM (Jane Larsen's guest house)

Jun 1989-Mar 1990 – Bush House, Brownell-Howland Road, Santa Fe, NM (Bruce McEachern)

Apr 1990-Dec 1990 – Traveled around U.S. in the Grey Goose RV (Bruce McEachern)

Jan 1991-Aug 1991 – 6790 Petersen Road, Petaluma, CA (Bruce McEachern)

Sep 1991-Aug 1992 – Moved into remodeled chicken house/barn (Bruce and alone)

Sep 1992-Dec 1992 – 5040 Boulder Lane, Santa Rosa, CA (Annie Cook)

Dec 1992-Feb 1993 – 139 Crest Point Court, Auburn, Ga. (Clif Hope)

Mar 1993-Jun 1995 – Two Vale Close, Buckhead, Ga. (Beth Davis)

Jul 1995-Jul 1999 –139 Crest Point Court, Auburn, Ga. (Clif and alone)

Aug 1999-Jan 2001 – Apartment in Hammonton, NJ (Tom Jenkins)

Feb 1999-May 2001 – 221 Union Road, Hammonton, NJ (Tom Jenkins)

May 2001-Jul 2001 – 635 Huntington Road, #802, Athens, Ga. sublet (Tom Jenkins)

Jul 2001-present – 415 McDuffie Court, Athens, Ga. (Tom and I bought our 1st house)

I LOVE YOU

I love you
I will always be here with you
I whisper in your heart's ear
I beat within your pulse
Syncopating with Life
I am you
There is no separation
Reverberates on hummingbird wings
On the owl's hoot and the cat's meow
Out to the galaxy
Across the Milky Way
And you thought you were alone
Let your laughter ring out loud
Let this joy tumble through the ground
And water the stars

Beverly R. Joyce © 2021

ACKNOWLEDGMENTS

I am that person who always reads the acknowledgments in a book. Without fail, it interests me to see the many people involved in the production of a book. The same is true for my memoir.

My first thanks go to everyone mentioned in this memoir. I am glad our paths crossed and I am a better person for having known you. Thanks for making my life fun and interesting and for helping me grow. A heartfelt thanks to friends and relatives who welcomed me to their home and gave me shelter and set a place for me at their table. I am grateful for Kathryn Howard who made it safe and normal to talk about extraterrestrial experiences.

Thanks to my parents and siblings who made my life interesting enough to warrant a memoir. I wish I had written it sooner so everyone could have read it before they crossed the river. A special thanks to brother Bob who has always been my champion and who did a first read and edit.

I am forever grateful for Larry Wilson who paved the way for me to grow to my potential. Working with the Wilson Learning family was the gold standard by which I measured future organizational excellence. And, it was Gary Quinlan who offered me the opportunity to move to Santa Fe and take part in the greatest adventure of my life.

Thanks to my travel companions: Molly Post for accompanying me around the world, and Bruce McEachern for buying an RV so we could enjoy the beauty of the United States. To my daughter Ellen, I am forever grateful that you saved all my letters from my around-the-world trip. A special thanks for my photographers: Bobby McGee, Jill Fineberg, Joe Sohm, your photographs are worth thousands of words.

I appreciate my monthly OLLI Memoir Writing Group who listened to my stories each month and made the process of writing a memoir possible – just by being there. Effusive thanks are showered on my writing partners, Jonyl Adams, Beverly Joyce, and Kia Woods who kept telling me my stories were good and worthy of a memoir. You helped me make a little progress every day because sometimes every day for months, you listened to each new story and asked for more. You were, and are, an inspiration.

I give a bowed-down gesture of gratitude to my editor, Tracy Coley, who came strolling into my life at just the right moment. I had finished writing my stories and didn't know what the next step was. You took me under your wing and made the memoir better through your suggestions and skills in editing, design, and layout. You were a pleasure to work with every step of the way.

I am especially grateful for my husband Tom, my first reader of every story, and who reread them all when I showed him the first draft. Thanks for your loving support.

Thanks to my three children, Tony, Ellen, and Clif for being mine. I like to think you chose me. I know I chose you. I likely would never have written a memoir had you not been born. I can only hope to convey how much I have loved being your mom. I wrote this for you – a legacy for my children, grandchildren, great-grandchildren, and future generations who may pick this up a hundred years from now.

Someone even unknown to me may want to sit down with a cup of tea or a glass of wine and cozy up with my book and travel through my life. For family and for friends, old and new, my book is an invitation to share the warmth of our remembered friendship.

Milton Keynes UK
Ingram Content Group UK Ltd.
UKHW050932191223
434651UK00008B/397